"A-List helped me improve my scores with their unique approach and so much A-List for making my goals into a reality! You're the best!"
-Marcelle B.
Accepted into NYU

"A-List prepared me for both the SAT and ACT better than I thought imaginable...I recommend A-list to anybody trying to get a great score."
-Adam G.
Accepted into University of Florida

"I loved my experience with A-List... I couldn't be more appreciative of all the help that A-List has provided for me, and would strongly recommend A-List to any future SAT or ACT takers!"
-Evan S.
Accepted into University of Pennsylvania

"Working with A-List helped me to realize my potential in standardized testing, and gave me the confidence I needed for the college process and the future... A-List taught me skills that have tremendously improved my comprehension, writing and general intelligence. I give A-List an A+!"
-Alex B.
Accepted into Northwestern University

"A-List helped me get into the college of my dreams, and I will thank them forever for that...The vocab cards were very easy to use and helped me get only one word choice problem wrong on the SAT! Thank you for everything, A-List..."
-Daniel R.
Accepted into University of Pennsylvania

"My scores jumped way up after A-List."
-Sam V.
Accepted into Bowdoin College

"I was given the necessary materials in order to raise my SAT/ACT score. I felt confident and prepared walking into the test."
-Lindsay P.
Accepted into Tulane

"I definitely enjoyed my experience with A-List. I found the materials excellent; the vocabulary flash-cards had sentences that had very helpful context clues and even better word groupings. The Book of Knowledge taught me so many things. I was more than satisfied with my final score on both the SAT and ACT exams... I would definitely recommend A-List to anyone."
-Dara B.
Accepted into University of Michigan

A-List

The Book of Knowledge

SAT

5TH EDITION

Cover photo by Sarah Scott-Farber

ISBN   978-0-9891605-4-4

A-List Services LLC

363 7th Avenue, 13th floor

New York, NY 10001

(646) 216-9187

www.alisteducation.com

www.vocabvideos.com

TABLE OF CONTENTS

INTRODUCTION TO THE SAT

elcome to the SAT! This book will show you everything you need to conquer the SAT. We'll run through the content you need, show you tricks and shortcuts specific to SAT-style questions, and warn you about traps and common mistakes. This book is the product of the sum total of A-List's expertise, combining the knowledge gained from countless hours of research into actual SAT questions with the practical experience of successfully increasing thousands of students' scores.

Before we dive into the specific concepts and techniques, let's take a minute to look at the test as a whole and get a good picture of what we're dealing with.

SECTIONS AND FORMAT

The SAT is big. Really big. It contains 10 sections, with some 200 questions plus an essay. It takes 3 hours and 45 minutes—and that's just the actual testing time. Once you add in all the breaks and the time spent getting signed in, finding your room, and filling out all your forms, it can last 6 hours. This will not be fun.

Overview

Here's an overview of what the test looks like:

Sec	Time	Subject	Length	Content	Order
1	25 min	Writing		Essay	Always will be first
2	25 min	Reading	24 Q*	Sentence Completions and Passages	
3	25 min	Math	20 Q	All multiple choice	
4	25 min	Reading	24 Q*	Sentence Completions and Passages	
5	25 min	Math	18 Q	8 multiple choice, 10 Student-Produced Response ("Grid-in")	These sections may be in any order
6	25 min	Writing	35 Q	11 Sentence Improvements 18 Error Identifications 6 Paragraph Improvements	
7	25 min	Equating	18–35 Q	May be Reading, Math, or Writing Does not count towards your score	
8	20 min	Reading	19 Q*	Sentence Completions and Passages	These sections may be in any order
9	20 min	Math	16 Q	All multiple choice	
10	10 min	Writing	14 Q	All Sentence Improvements	Always will be last

* Exact number may vary. See below

Reading

Here's an outline of a typical Reading section:

25 minutes	8 Sentence Completions	Mini passage: 2 Q Mini passage: 2 Q Double passage: 12 Q	24 Questions
25 minutes	5 Sentence Completions	Double mini passage: 4 Q Medium passage: 6 Q Medium passage: 9 Q	24 Questions
20 minutes	6 Sentence Completions	Long passage: 13 Q	19 Questions
70 minutes	**19 Sentence Completions**	**48 Passage Questions**	**67 Questions**

Please note that the way that these questions and passages are split up between sections will vary from test to test. Even the exact number of questions per section may vary (although the total will always be 67). But some things will be constant:

- There will be three reading sections, lasting 25 minutes, 25 minutes, and 20 minutes.

- All questions will be multiple choice.

- There will be 19 **Sentence Completions** split across the three sections. These questions present a sentence with one or two blanks, and you must determine which word or words in the choices belong in the blanks. Sentence Completions always come at the beginning of the section.

- There will be 48 **Passage-Based Questions** split across the three sections. These questions present a short passage on a particular topic followed by questions asking you about what the passage says. Passages may be as short as one paragraph with 2 questions about it. Or they could be as long as a full-page double passage, featuring two essays on the same topic, with 13 questions about it.

- Sentence Completion questions are ordered by difficulty. Passage questions are ordered roughly "chronologically" in order of the parts of the passage they ask about.

For more information about specific question types, jump ahead to the Critical Reading chapters.

Math

You will see three math sections on the SAT:

25 minutes	20 multiple-choice questions
25 minutes	8 multiple-choice questions 10 Student-Produced Response questions ("Grid-ins")
20 minutes	16 multiple-choice questions
70 minutes	**54 Questions**

Some general comments about the format:

- Calculators are allowed on all math sections. You may use Scientific and Graphing calculators. According to College Board guidelines, you may not use: cell phone or smart phone calculators; handheld minicomputers or laptop computers; electronic writing pads or pen-input devices; calculators with typewriter-style keypads (known as "QWERTY"); calculators with paper tape or printers; calculators that talk or make unusual noise; calculators that require an electrical outlet. Calculators that can do your taxes, are larger than a Chevy, possess human emotions, can feel pain, or are armed with any kind of torpedoes and/or death ray are also forbidden.

🖝 Calculators are not allowed on Reading and Writing sections. This should not need an explanation.

🖝 Questions within each section are ordered by difficulty. The first questions are easy, the last questions are hard.

For more information about specific question types, jump ahead to the Math chapters.

Grid-ins

The Student-Produced Response Questions (called "Grid-ins" for short) are the only questions on the SAT that are not multiple-choice (except the Essay, of course). Here, you will be expected to come up with your own answer and fill it into the grid provided (thus the term "Grid-in"). At right, you'll see an example of the space in which you must put your answer.

We don't have any specific techniques or strategies for the Grid-ins other than those we have for all the other math questions. The content and style of these questions will be just like the rest of the section; the math itself is no different. However, they may seem a bit weird to those of you who are unfamiliar with the test. Here are some miscellaneous notes about the Grid-ins:

🖝 As mentioned above, math questions are ordered by difficulty. The Grid-in section will be divided into two parts: first 8 regular questions (numbered 1–8) and then 10 Grid-ins (numbered 9–18). *Each of these parts is ordered by difficulty separately.* So question #8 (the last multiple-choice question) will be hard, while question #9 (the first Grid-in) will be easy.

🖝 Unlike the other multiple-choice questions, you *do not* lose points for a wrong answer on the Grid-ins. A wrong answer will be scored the same as a blank.

🖝 Notice that the Grid has two elements to it: spaces at the top to write in your answer, and bubbles at the bottom to fill in (just like when you fill out your name at the beginning). **You must fill in the bubbles.** The spaces at the top *are not scored by the machine.* They are only there for your benefit so you can easily read your answer and can fill in the bubbles more easily. If you write in the boxes but don't fill in the bubbles, the machine will read it as a blank.[*]

🖝 You can put your answer in any column. It doesn't matter how you position it (to the right or left).

🖝 Notice that there is **no negative symbol** in the grid—there will never be a negative answer on the Grid-ins. If you get a negative answer, you messed up. Try again.

🖝 If your answer is a decimal, you must be as accurate as possible when gridding in your answer. For example, if the right answer is 2/3 (which, as a decimal, is .66666 repeating), .666 would be okay, and .667 would be okay, but .6 or .66 is not okay. Take the decimal as far as space allows. (Of course, you could also just enter 2/3 and avoid the whole issue).

🖝 You do *not* have to reduce to the lowest possible fraction. If the right answer is 2/3, an answer of 4/6 will still give you credit. Of course, if you get a fraction that doesn't fit into four spaces, like 10/15, then you will have to reduce (or convert to a decimal).

Calculators

You get to use them. Congratulations. Some of us weren't allowed to use calculators when we took the SAT.[†] So make sure you have one and make sure you know how to use it.

Calculators can be very helpful when you have big computations to do. Nobody wants to divide two-digit numbers on paper. However, you should know that the SAT is **calculator-optional.** That means there's never going to be a problem where you *must* use a calculator. There's no logarithms, no trigonometry, no matrices, no fourth-root of negative π over seven. Everything on the test *can* be done in your head or with

---

[*] Conversely, that means that you don't *have* to write anything in the boxes at all. You could draw little pictures of ducks in there or write messages to the College Board and no one will ever know.

[†] Some of us are very old.

a paper and pencil. That also means that you don't need a big HAL-9000 supercalculator. Everything you need to do can be done with a cheap-o four-function drug-store calculator that's missing the 7-key.[*]

While there will occasionally be some computations that are just faster with the calculator, don't go leaping towards the calculator every time you have to do math. We don't want to see people jumping to the calculator to do $7 + 5$.[†] The better you are at doing simple math in your head, the faster you will work. This sounds counter-intuitive, but yes, it is faster to do simple math in your head. I promise. Some people have no faith in their abilities and insist on punching everything into their calculators because "the calculator is always right." These people are cowards. And guess what? The calculator may always be right, but there's a chance *you* might make a mistake typing stuff into your calculator. It's been known to happen. Especially if you have trouble doing $7 + 5$ in your head.

Now, since the SAT changed in 2005, there may be some questions on which a graphing calculator *can* help you. These questions are not common, but there are some fancy tools that can sometimes help you—if you know how to use them. So if you are *really* good with a graphing calculator, having one *might* work to your advantage *every once in a while*. But if you don't have one, or if you have one but barely know how to turn it on, don't sweat it. You'll be fine. Just learn $7 + 5$. That's all we ask.

Writing

Here's an outline of the three Writing sections:

25 minutes	1 Essay
25 minutes	11 Sentence Improvements
	18 Error Identifications
	6 Paragraph Improvements
10 minutes	14 Sentence Improvements
60 minutes	**49 Multiple Choice plus 1 Essay**

You will actually get three writing scores on the SAT. You will get separate scores for your essay and your multiple choice. Then the two scores are combined using a complicated formula to get your final Writing score. See "Scoring" below for more information on how that calculation works.

Essay

- The **Essay** will always be the first section of the test. Your Essay will be graded for the strength and development of the argument as well as the clarity and effectiveness of your language.

- You will have two pages and must write your entire essay within the box in the space provided. You must write the essay in pencil.

- The Essay will be read by two graders, each of whom will give it a score from 1 (bad) to 6 (good). If their scores differ by two points or more, the essay will go to a third reader. So your final essay score will be from 2 (two 1's) to 12 (two 6's).[‡]

Multiple Choice

- You will get a separate Multiple Choice component score that combines with your Essay score to get your final score. The Multiple Choice score will be on the same scale as a normal SAT section, but with two digits (20 to 80) instead of three digits (200 to 800). This is the same system they use for the PSAT Writing section.

- There will be 25 **Sentence Improvement Questions**. These present a sentence with a portion of it underlined, generally a long phrase. You are given five choices for how to word the underlined

---

[*] Well, okay, you probably need the 7-key.

[†] It's 12.

[‡] It is possible to get a zero, if your essay is off-topic or written in ink.

phrase, correcting for grammar, usage and style. Choice (A) is always identical to the original underlined portion. Sentence Improvements will be split across two sections.

- There will be 18 **Error Identification Questions**. These present a sentence with four words or short phrases underlined. You must decide which choice contains an error in grammar or usage. If there is no error, pick choice (E).

- There will be 6 **Paragraph Improvement Questions**. This section presents a short two- or three-paragraph essay, followed by questions about grammar, development and organization of the passage in context.

- All questions are about Standard Written American English. That is, the kind of English you'd see in *The New York Times*. If you speak a weird regional dialect where folks do things differently, we don't care.

For more information about the Essay or specific question types, jump ahead to the Writing chapters.

Equating section

Each test will contain one section called the *equating section* that does not count towards your score. The purpose of this section is to calibrate the scoring for that test so that students' scores are standardized fairly. That is, they want to make sure that scores are equivalent no matter when you take the test. The equating section will always be a 25-minute section; it will never be an essay or a shorter section. But it may be in any subject: Reading, Math (multiple choice *or* Grid-in), or Writing.

You will not be able to tell which section is the equating section. It will not "look weird" or have special experimental problems. It will look exactly like any other regular section. **Do not try to guess which section is the equating section.**

You can sometimes narrow it down to two: if your test has two Grid-in sections, then you know one of them must be the equating section. But you won't be able to tell which one is real and which is equating.

You might be able to figure it out after the test is over. On a given test date, all the sections that count will be the same for every student, but different students may get different equating sections. So if your test had a Reading passage about bumblebees, but none of your friends had a passage about bumblebees, then that section must have been your equating section. But again, while you're taking the test, you won't be able to tell; the bumblebee passage will look just like any other passage.

Again: Do not try to guess which section is the equating section. Do every section as if it counts. But take solace in the fact that one of them won't.

Notice that whenever the College Board publishes a test, they remove the equating section. So your practice tests will be one section shorter than the real test will be.

SCORING

So SAT scores are in that weird 200–800 point scale, and it seems like each question is worth a different number of points or something. Why do they do that?

Each time they give the SAT, they use a new test form. But they want the scores to be standard across all students on all dates (thus the phrase "standardized test"). No matter how hard they try, there will always be slight variations in the difficulty level of each test form; this one will be slightly harder or slightly easier than the last one.

So instead of just counting up how many rights and wrongs you got, they convert your performance to a **scaled score**—that weird 200-800 score. Each test has its own scoring table that adjusts for the difficulty of the test. If a particular test form was harder than usual, the scoring table will be more generous, and a given number of right answers will give you a slightly higher score. If a form was easier than usual, the scoring table will be harsher, and the same number of right answers will give you a slightly lower score.

This is all done to ensure that your final SAT score is not affected by the date you happened to take the test. **There is no such thing as "the easy test date".** There are some urban legends floating around about how the May test is easier or the March test is harder. *None of these rumors are true.* Your score is **not** based on the performance of the other students on your test date.

The test is administered and designed by very many very smart people, people with PhD's in statistics, people who understand math in ways you can never imagine. They have anticipated your objections, and they go through great lengths to ensure that all test dates produce equivalent scores.[*]

So how is the test scored?

For each section, you **get one point** for a right answer and you **lose one quarter of a point** for a wrong answer.[†] That gives you your **raw score** for that section. Each test has a scoring table used to convert the raw score to a scaled score. For the Writing section, your multiple-choice raw score and your essay score together determine your scaled score.

As we said, each test has a different scoring table. On one test, a raw score of 26 on the Math might correspond to a final Math score of 500. But perhaps a different test was a little bit harder overall. There, maybe a raw score of 26 gives you a 510 and a raw score of 25 gives you a 500.

---

[*] If you *must* know, here's a massively oversimplified description of how it works:

To set a scoring table, they compare the results of your test to those of an earlier test that already has a scoring table. In order to correct for the difficulty of the test, they match up the percent of students who got a particular raw score. Say on one test the 50th percentile in the Reading was a raw score of 30 but on your test the 50th percentile was a raw score of 33. That means the group as a whole did better on your test, so the scoring table should be harsher. So if that 30 on the old test got a scaled score of 510, then a 33 on your test will get a scaled score of 510.

Now you're thinking: "But what if the kids who took my test just happened to be smart kids? What if there happened to be a lot of Super Nerds taking this test who thought it was easy, but it was really hard for me? Now I'm being penalized with a harsher scoring table!"

That's why they give you the equating section. The same equating section will be reused on multiple test forms, so the equating section you get has already been used on a previous test. They use everyone's performance on the equating section as an "anchor": they only compare the students who got the same score on the equating section, and therefore will be at roughly the same skill level. So your score will not be affected by the relative nerdiness of your peers because you're only compared to other students who are as nerdy as you.

[†] The exception here is the Grid-ins. There, you still get a point for a right, but you don't lose anything for a wrong. More on this in "The Guessing Rule" below.

But the differences between scoring tables are never very drastic. No scoring tables will be different by more than 30 points. Therefore, we can get an approximate sense of how much each question is worth on your actual final score.[*]

	Reading	Math	Writing (MC)	Essay
Each Right Answer	+6.5	+8	+8	+15
Each Wrong Answer	−1.5	−2	−2	
Each Blank	0	0	0	
Difference between Right and Wrong	8	10	10	
"Writing (MC)" column shows the value of each *multiple-choice* question on your *final* Writing score, *not* on your Writing multiple-choice component score.				
"Essay" column shows the value of *one* point on the essay on your *final* Writing Score.				

Some notes on this table:

- ➤ This table shows the value of each question on your final score. So getting one Math question right adds about 8 points to your final, getting one wrong subtracts 2 from your final, and the difference between a right and a wrong is 10 points. That means that if you get a Math question wrong that you should've gotten right, it cost you 10 points: you should've gained 8 but instead you lost 2.

- ➤ Furthermore, this can give you a sense of how your mistakes are actually affecting your score. It can quantify your mistakes. For example:

  - ○ Each *blank* Reading question you convert to a *right* gets you about 6.5 points. So if you work faster and get 5 right that you would've otherwise skipped, that's an additional 30 points on your Reading score.

  - ○ Each *wrong* Math question you convert to a *right* gets you 10 points. If you missed 5 Math questions that you could have easily gotten right if you'd used Plug In, that's an additional $5 \times 10 = 50$ points on your Math score.

  - ○ Each Essay point gets you 15 points on your final score. So if you tighten up your organization and raise your essay from a 7 to a 9, that's an additional 30 points on your final Writing score.

  - ○ Hey look! You just did those three things and increased your overall score 110 points. You are awesome.

- ➤ Questions on Reading sections are worth less than those on Math sections because there are more Reading questions on the test, so each is worth less.

- ➤ Obviously, this is an approximation. This is not an exact exchange rate. You can't get a 506.5 on your Reading section. In reality, getting one more Reading question right might increase your score 10 points. Or it might not increase your score at all. But we're looking at the test *as a whole* here. Adding 5 right Reading questions *on average* increases your score 30 points. Adding 5 right Math questions *on average* increases your score 40 points.

- ➤ While these approximations hold up most of the time, things get a little messed up at the very top of the scale. Because so few students score so highly, once scores get above 700, questions are usually worth more than the values above. For example, on one test form a Math raw score of 52 gets you a 760, but a raw score of 53—just one more right answer—gets you a 790. Again, all these numbers are approximations, and the approximations fail at the extreme endpoints.

---

[*] These figures were calculated using actual scoring tables from actual SATs from 2005−2008.

- Remember also that all SAT scores should be considered **ranges**. There are all sorts of factors that contribute to your test score besides the scoring table. Not every change in your scores constitutes an actual increase or decrease. Even if you do no work, you're not going to get exactly the same score every time out. You'll score 30 points higher or lower just by pure chance. According to the College Board, total scores must differ by 60 points to be considered a "true change". In fact, when you get your actual SAT scores, your score is listed as a range in addition to an absolute number. And you know what? Colleges know that too. Your school isn't going to reject you because of 20 points. So don't sweat the small points.

- On the other hand, *do* sweat the big points. As we saw above, doing a lot of little things better can quickly add up to big score increases. Substantial increases are well within your reach.

The Guessing Rule

Some people take a look at that point value table and think, "Hey, since I lose points for a wrong and get nothing for a blank, it is better to leave a question blank than get it wrong. Therefore I shouldn't guess unless I'm totally sure of my answer. Because I don't want to lose points."

That couldn't be more false.

Look at these point values—these numbers aren't arbitrary. The reason they have this system is to prevent *random* guessing from helping you. Imagine: if they didn't take off points for a wrong, then when you're running out of time you could just fill in (C) for all the questions you haven't done. Since (C) would probably be the right answer on some of them, you would pick up a couple of points. They don't want that to work on the SAT.[*]

Let's take a look at a sample. Let's imagine a monkey is taking the test. His name is Bobo. Somehow he's managed to learn how to fill in bubbles, but that's all he can do. He's just filling in bubbles randomly. Let's say he does this for five math questions. There are five possible choices for each question, so just by chance he'll get one question right and four wrong.

	Questions	Points
Right	1	+8
Wrong	4	$(-2) \times 4 = -8$
Total	**5**	**0**

The four wrong answers counteract the one right answer for a net score of zero. So guessing randomly will give you the same score as leaving everything blank. THEREFORE, *if you can guess better than a monkey, you can do better than blank*. Let's say you eliminate *one* choice on each of those five questions. Now, you're guessing out of four choices instead of five, so you've got a better chance of guessing right. So let's say you get two right and three wrong:

	Questions	Points
Right	2	$(+8) \times 2 = +16$
Wrong	3	$(-2) \times 3 = -6$
Total	**5**	**+10**

Now, **you're ahead overall**. Remember: you're still guessing here. You don't actually know how to do any of these five questions. But by guessing out of fewer choices, you're more likely to guess right, so you'll have a *net score increase*.

---

[*] By the way, this *does* work on the ACT. There, they don't take points off for wrongs, so you can guess randomly to your heart's content. If you're running out of time on the ACT, start bubbling the ones you haven't done yet.

The moral of this story is that **_YOU MUST PUT AN ANSWER DOWN FOR EVERY QUESTION THAT YOU HAVE TIME TO READ OVER AND THINK ABOUT, EVEN IF YOU'RE NOT SURE IF YOU'RE RIGHT._** If you have time to read over and think about a question, you should be able to eliminate *something*—even if it's only one choice. And when you guess from fewer choices, you're more likely to guess right.

Yes, you're still going to guess wrong sometimes. That's why it's called "guessing". Yes, you will lose some points for the questions you guess wrong, but you will get *many more* points for the questions you guess right. So for the test *as a whole*, you'll gain points.

This doesn't mean you should guess *randomly*. Don't fill in (C) for all the questions you haven't gotten up to. And don't guess if you can't eliminate anything. For example, if you have a sentence completion where you don't know *any* of the words in the choices, then anything you guess would be random, so you should skip it. But you know what? That shouldn't happen often. Most of the time, there's *something* you can do to eliminate some choices, even if it's only one choice. And once you eliminate something, you've got to guess from what's left.

This rule holds true for the entire test—Math, Reading, and Writing.[*] Every multiple-choice question on the test uses this scoring system. So for every multiple-choice question that you have time to read over and think about, you must eliminate something and you must put an answer down. You must do this.[†]

THE PSAT

What is it?

The PSAT is practice for the SAT. It's basically a shorter version of the SAT. Most students take it in October of their junior year. Some students may also take it in October of their sophomore year.

Why do I have to take it?

You don't, actually. Some schools may require their students to take the PSAT in their junior year. But for most of you it's optional. It is not a factor in college admissions. Your colleges will not see your PSAT scores. It is purely practice.

It does count for one thing, though: the National Merit Scholarship program. Students scoring around the top 4% of PSAT scores in their state will get a National Merit Letter of Commendation. Students scoring around the top 1% of PSAT scores in their state will qualify as National Merit Semifinalists. These are good things. They will look very good on your college applications and may help you get scholarships. The qualifying scores are different every year and differ from state to state but if you think you're scoring at high levels, you definitely want to do as well as you can on the PSAT.[‡]

Of course, even if you're not scoring in the top 4%, it's still a good idea to take the PSAT. It's good practice in a real-test situation. It gives you an accurate sense of where your score is. It gives you feedback on your strengths and weaknesses. And it's low pressure: if you do poorly, it doesn't matter—colleges never see these scores.

---

[*] There is one exception—the Grid-ins. Obviously, they aren't multiple-choice, so there's nothing to eliminate. Anything you guess will be entirely random. But this is exactly why they don't take points off on the Grid-ins. If you want to guess randomly on the Grid-ins, be our guest; it will neither help nor hurt you. There are 10,000 possible integer answers for a Grid-in question, and that's not even counting fractions and decimals. Good luck.

[†] You must do this.

[‡] For example, in New York State, the qualifying score in the past has generally been around 199 (66 per section) for a Letter of Commendation and around 210 (70 per section) to be a Semifinalist. But again, these numbers will vary from year to year and state to state.

How is it different?

It's shorter

The PSAT only has 5 sections, organized thusly:

1	Critical Reading	25 min	24 Q	SC/Pass
2	Math	25 min	20 Q	MC
3	Critical Reading	25 min	24 Q	SC/Pass
4	Math	25 min	18 Q	MC/GI
5	Writing	30 min	39 Q	20 SI 14 EID 5 PI

- ☞ Sections are always in this order.

- ☞ The 25-minute Reading and Math sections are just like those on the SAT. Instead of two Writing multiple-choice sections, 25 and 10 minutes, there's one 30-minute section.

- ☞ And there's no essay. So that's nice.

- ☞ Note also that unlike on the SAT, section numbering is continuous across the sections within a topic. So the last Math question in section 2 is #20, and the first Math question in section 4 is #21. Questions are still ordered by difficulty within a single section.

Slightly less math

The SAT contains some Algebra II concepts that you are expected to learn during your junior year of high school. Since the PSAT is given at the beginning of junior year, the test makers realize that not everyone has learned these concepts yet and don't include them. So the SAT will have some additional concepts, such as higher-level function problems, more graphing, and some absolute value.

Scoring

SAT and PSAT scores are calibrated to each other. That means you can expect that your PSAT score is roughly the same as what you'd get on the SAT if you took it the same day. Except that for some reason, PSAT scores are given as two-digit numbers instead of three-digit numbers. So a 51 on the PSAT Reading corresponds to a 510 on the SAT Reading.

Many students naturally will do better on the SAT than the PSAT, both because they've learned more and because they've had more practice. The average junior-year PSAT score is usually around 140, while the average SAT score is around 1500.[*] Since average SAT scores are higher than average PSAT scores, the same *percentile* on the two tests will correspond to a higher SAT score and a lower PSAT score. And the same score will have a higher percentile on the PSAT.

As a result of this (and because the number of questions is different) the approximate number of points per question will be different, too:

	Reading	Math	Writing
Right	+1.00	+1.20	+1.10
Wrong	−0.25	−0.30	−0.27
Difference	1.25	1.50	1.37

---

[*] Of course, this does **NOT** mean that you will automatically improve from your PSAT score without doing any work. There is a lot of variation between individuals. Only around 55% of students improve their scores on each individual section from the PSAT to the SAT.

Mathematics

MATH TECHNIQUES

Welcome to SAT Math! I think you'll like it here. Let's take a look around.

SAT math is not exactly the same as the math you do in school. Yes, a lot of your old favorites will show up here (ratios, two-variable equations, the Pythagorean Theorem, and many more!) but the questions are a little bit different. In school, you learn *content*. They teach you something and then test you on it. The SAT is a *reasoning* test. That means it's less about specific rules and methods than about problem solving. For example, in school, they teach you *algebra* and then test you on *how well you use algebra*. On the SAT, they give you a *problem* and ask you to solve it *any way you can*. That could mean algebra or it could mean arithmetic or geometry. On any given problem, there's no one way that's "the right way" to do it. Almost every problem on the SAT can be done several different ways. Now, some ways are faster or safer than others, so our job is to show you *the best way* to do a given problem.

Throughout the next few chapters, we'll be talking about two types of things: content and techniques. *Content* is the literal stuff you need to know (like the Pythagorean Theorem[*]). *Techniques* are methods for doing lots of different kinds of problems (like Plug In). Both are equally important. However, a lot of the content you'll already be familiar with from your adventures in school; it's the techniques that will be new for you, so that's where we should concentrate.

I. GENERAL STRATEGIES

We'll start with two quick and easy things you can do to help organize your time, be more efficient, and cut down on careless mistakes:

1. Circle the Question

2. Show Your Work

Circle the Question

This takes all of two seconds to do but can significantly help you.

- ☞ It can help reduce the number of careless mistakes you make (more about this in the next section).

- ☞ It will help you understand how to do the problem. By focusing on the thing you're trying to find rather than the things they give you, it's easier to think about what you need in order to find it.

Do this on every problem. No exceptions.

Show Your Work

You're probably tired of hearing math teachers to tell you to "Show your work!" Well, too bad.

SHOW YOUR WORK!

We can already hear you complaining:

"Why bother? It's not like you get partial credit for doing it correctly."

True, you don't get partial credit, and there is no single "correct method". But that's not the point at all.

The point is that not writing down your steps is *the single greatest reason* for students' careless mistakes. We are astounded by how often we see students do an entire test worth of math problems without writing a thing on any page. These students are not getting the scores they want.

---

[*] Actually, you don't even need to know that either.

This is not a memory test. You can't possibly keep track of everything in your head, and you should never have more than one step in your head at any moment. By just writing down what you're doing as you do it, you can turn a complex problem into a series of small, basic steps. And you can *significantly* reduce your odds of making a careless mistake, like adding instead of subtracting, or solving for the wrong variable.

Furthermore, showing your work gives you a record of what you've done. This makes it easier to find mistakes when you're checking your work during a test. And it makes it easier to look over your performance when you're reviewing a practice test you just finished. This way, when you want to know why you got #10 wrong, you'll see what you did to get your answer.

"But I don't need to write stuff down. I'm good at math and can do it all in my head."

No, you can't.

"No, really, I can."

No, really, you can't. SAT problems are complicated. You can't hold every step in your head at once. And you know what? You don't have to! If you write stuff down, you don't have to remember everything.

And these questions are designed to fool you. Many students' biggest problem isn't that they don't know enough math—it's that they're missing questions that they already know how to do, because they make careless, stupid mistakes.

"That just slows me down. I don't have time to show my work."

You don't have time to write down numbers? That's ridiculous. What, are you writing with a calligraphy pen? We're not asking you to write out every single step in complete sentences and perfect penmanship. Don't write out annotated Euclidean proofs; just keep track of which variable is which.

Seriously, we're not kidding around. Just write stuff down.

Let's look at a sample problem to see how these rules work:

4. Points *A*, *B*, *C*, and *D* lie on a line in that order. The length of $\overline{AB}$ is 8, and the length of $\overline{CD}$ is 7. Point *C* is the midpoint of segment $\overline{BD}$. What is the length of segment $\overline{AD}$?

    (A) 7
    (B) 14
    (C) 15
    (D) 22
    (E) 23

> SAT math questions are numbered by difficulty within each section. Accordingly, all sample questions throughout this book reflect that numbering. This question, for example, would be #4 on a 20-question section, so it should be relatively simple.

First thing to do: **circle the question.** Not the whole problem, smart guy; just circle the thing that they're asking you to find.

Points *A*, *B*, *C*, and *D* lie on a line in that order. The length of $\overline{AB}$ is 8, and the length of $\overline{CD}$ is 7. Point *C* is the midpoint of segment $\overline{BD}$. What is the length of segment $\overline{AD}$?

Wrong.

Points *A*, *B*, *C*, and *D* lie on a line in that order. The length of $\overline{AB}$ is 8, and the length of $\overline{CD}$ is 7. Point *C* is the midpoint of segment $\overline{BD}$. What is the length of segment $\overline{AD}$?

Right.

Okay, now what?

SAT questions are complicated. There's often a lot going on within a question, so it's easy to take your eye off the ball. Other times there might be so much information that you're not sure what to do with it. If you're not sure how to get started, **ask yourself two questions:**

1. **What do I *want*?** That is, what is the question asking me for?

2. **What do I *know*?** That is, what information does the problem give me?

Then your goal is to **connect these questions**. Look at what you want and work backwards to see what you need in order to get it. Or use what you already know and see what else that tells you.

What you want: The length of $\overline{AD}$.

That's why we circled the question—to find out what we want.

What you know: $AB = 8$, $CD = 7$, C is midpoint of $\overline{BD}$.

Write down what you know. This question is about a line, but no figure is given. So **draw the figure**.

First draw the points in order:

Then label the lengths you're given:

And since C is the midpoint of $\overline{BD}$, $BC = CD$:

$\overline{AD}$ is the whole length, so we have everything we need: $AD = 8 + 7 + 7 = \textbf{22}$.

Our answer is **choice (D)**.

This is an addition to our rule about showing your work: if a geometry problem doesn't already have a picture, **DRAW A PICTURE!** It doesn't have to be perfect; even a rough sketch can help you understand the problem and catch careless mistakes.

Notice that we didn't know where we were going when we started. We just played with the stuff we knew until we got what we needed. The point here is to not be scared. There's always *something* that you know, and something that you can figure out. Just put down what you know and try to connect it to what you want. If you work forward from what you know or backwards from what you want, chances are you can connect them in the middle. Even if you're not sure where you're going, the more you right down, the easier it will be to make a connection.

II. COMMON MISTAKES

The people who make the SAT aren't chumps. They know how high school kids think. More importantly, they know how high school kids mess up. Therefore, when they write the SAT they intentionally include wrong answer choices that kids who make certain common mistakes will choose. However, once you know what these mistakes are and how to avoid them, you will be much less likely to make them.

RTFQ

Take a look at this question:

5. A certain bookstore gets a shipment of 24
    copies of a new book and sells 18 of them.
    What percentage of the books was **not** sold?

    (A) 75%
    (B) 67%
    (C) 50%
    (D) 33%
    (E) 25%

Okay, so 18 over 24 is 0.75, which is 75%. That's choice (A), right?

WRONG! That's the number of books that were *sold*; the question is asking for those that were *not sold*. They even underlined it for you! Pay attention!

We call choice (A) the **RTFQ** choice. "RTFQ" stands for "Read the full question." It's what happens when all your math was correct, but you didn't solve for the thing they were asking for.

RTFQ choices show up *all over* the test. They could show up on question #20 or on question #1. It is a very easy mistake to make. But it's also a very easy mistake to avoid: *just read the question*. Take an extra two seconds to make sure that the number you're choosing is the number they want.

In fact, we've already given you two ways to help cut down on RTFQ mistakes: **Circle the Question** and **Show Your Work**. Both of these things will significantly help you keep track of what you're doing.

A lot of people don't put enough weight on these mistakes on practice tests. "Oh, I *knew* how to do that one," they say. "I just wrote down the wrong answer." What? That's *so much worse!* If you don't know how to do the math, fine. We'll teach you how to do math. But you don't know how to write down what they're asking for? You are throwing away points by missing questions *that you already know how to do*. Remember: the difference between a right and a wrong is 10 points. If you make just three RTFQ mistakes, that's 30 points you've tossed out the window. These things add up.

Here's a harder one. Give it a shot, and make sure you *read every word of the question*.

$$A = \{1, 2, 3\}$$

$$B = \{3, 5, 7\}$$

15. **If *a* is a number selected from set *A* and *b* is a number selected from set *B*, how many different values for *a* + *b* are possible?**

    (A) 5
    (B) 6
    (C) 7
    (D) 8
    (E) 9

Fool's Gold

Take a look at this problem:

20. **Scott drives to Bob's house at a speed of 30 miles per hour and drives back at a speed of 50 miles per hour. If he takes the same route both ways, what was his average speed, in miles per hour, for the whole trip?**

    (A) 35
    (B) 37.5
    (C) 40
    (D) 42.5
    (E) It cannot be determined from the information given

We want the average speed for the trip. His two speeds are 30 and 50. So the average is 30 + 50 divided by two. That's 40. Choice (C).

Wow, that was easy. Hmm. A little *too* easy.

Wait a minute. This is question number 20 out of 20. They order questions by difficulty. That means this is the *hardest* question on the test. There's *no way* that the hardest question on the test can be done by just taking the average of two numbers *that they give me!* That can't possibly be right.

Look at it this way:

1. We know for a fact that SAT math questions are ordered by difficulty.

2. A question's difficulty is determined by looking at the percentage of students who get it right.

3. Most kids probably had the same instinct I did: take the average of the speeds.

4. But I <u>know</u> that most kids got it wrong. *That's why it's number 20.*

5. Therefore, taking the average of 30 and 50 is wrong. If it were right, most kids would get it right. *So it wouldn't be number 20.*

6. Therefore, I can eliminate it.

We call this a ***Fool's Gold*** choice. It's when a hard question has a choice that's so easy and so obvious that it can't possibly be right. We *know* the question must be harder than this. It must be a trap.

So if you see an easy choice on a hard question—***eliminate it***. You know it's a hard question. You know everyone gets it wrong. So the obvious answer *can't* be right.[*] Sometimes we see students who even *recognize* a choice as a Fool's Gold choice, and then pick it anyway because they can't think of any other way of doing the problem. So they wind up choosing the <u>one</u> choice that they *know* is wrong. That's madness. Utter, utter madness.

Let's go back and take another look at that #20 above. We eliminated (C) as Fool's Gold. Hmm. But if that's not right, how else would you do the problem? All it tells us is the two speeds; we don't know the distance traveled or the time it took. So maybe there isn't enough information. That's Choice (E). Right?

Wrong! "Cannot be determined" is a *classic* Fool's Gold choice. Number 20 is not going to be as easy as, "Well, uhh, they don't tell me anything, so I guess I dunno." Don't be a quitter.

> Choice (E), "Cannot be determined", isn't *always* wrong. It's often Fool's Gold on hard questions, but perfectly plausible on easy questions.

So we've eliminated (C) and (E). Worst-case scenario, we can guess from the three remaining choices. Remember, if you can eliminate even one choice, you *must* guess, because you get a lot more points for a right than you lose for a wrong.

So how do we do actually do this? The reason you can't just take the average of 30 and 50 is because those are already rates. In order to find the average speed for a trip, you have to take the rate of the *total* distance over the *total* time. Hmm. If we knew the distance traveled, we could find the time it took, but we don't know either. But the answer can't be (E)—that's too easy. So it probably *doesn't matter* what the distance is. You probably get the same answer no matter what.

So let's make up a value for the distance. Let's say it's **150 miles** from Scott's house to Bob's house. Since $d = rt$, we can use the distance to find the time each leg of Scott's trip took:

To Bob's: $150 = 30t_1$ | From Bob's: $150 = 50t_2$

$5 \text{ hours} = t_1$ | $3 \text{ hours} = t_2$

So Scott's trip took 5 hours one way and 3 hours back for a total of **8 hours**. His total distance traveled is **300 miles** (*twice* 150). So:

$$\text{Average Speed} = \frac{\text{Total Distance}}{\text{Total Time}} = \frac{300}{8} \quad \boxed{= \textbf{37.5 mph}}$$

---

[*] Obviously, Fool's Gold choices only occur on the hardest questions on the test—about the last third of each section. If there's a choice on question #3 that looks really easy, it probably really is that easy.

© A-List Services LLC   – 21 –

That's choice (B)! We're done! Wait, but we only got (B) after using a number we made up. How do we know we won't get a different answer if we chose another number? Well, try it. Make the distance 300 miles and see what you get.[*]

III. TARGET NUMBERS

This is one of the most powerful strategies that we have, so much so that it gets its own section. If you ignore everything else we say, at least pay attention to this.

One of the biggest problems that students have on the test is *timing*. You've got a finite amount of time to do a lot of questions. As a result, most students feel rushed trying to finish the test. Remember that the questions are arranged in order of difficulty—number 1 is easy, number 20 is hard. So kids rush through the early questions and make a lot of careless mistakes: they add instead of subtract, they solve for x instead of y, they misread the question, etc. Then they spend a lot of time on the hard ones and get those wrong too—because they're really hard. So you're getting nailed on both ends of the test. You're missing hard questions because they're hard and easy questions because you're trying to get to the hard ones.

But here's the thing: *the easy questions are worth the same number of points as the hard ones.*

The solution is incredibly simple: ***DON'T DO THE WHOLE TEST***. You don't have to get *every* question in order to get the score that you want. The biggest problem most kids have isn't that they don't know enough math; it's that they're missing questions *that they already know how to do.*

Here's a chart to figure out your target numbers:[†]

Start Score	20 MC	8 MC	10 GI	16 MC	Target Score
650 & up	1–20	1–8	9–18	1–16	**800**
600	1–19	1–7	9–17	1–15	**730**
550	1–17	1–7	9–16	1–14	**670**
500	1–16	1–6	9–16	1–12	**640**
450	1–14	1–6	9–15	1–11	**600**
400	1–12	1–5	9–14	1–9	**570**
350 & below	1–10	1–4	9–13	1–8	**520**

So let's say your incoming score—your Math score before doing any review with us—is 500. According to the chart above, in the 20-question multiple-choice section, you will do questions 1 to 16. In the 18-question section, you will do questions 1 to 6 of the multiple-choice and questions 9 to 16 of the Grid-ins. In the 16-question multiple-choice section, you will do questions 1 to 12. You will do all of these questions and you will do *only* these questions. If you do them successfully, you will score a 640.[‡] *That's a 140-point increase! On just the math section! Wow!* And you get it by doing *less* work.

Okay, so you're doing fewer problems, but how do you know you'll do any better on those problems than you were doing before? Because now you've got *fewer questions* to do *in the same amount of time*, so you

---

[*] You've just seen a sneak preview of Plug In, one of our fundamental Math Techniques. We'll see a lot more of this very soon…

[†] This chart is geared toward the SAT. For the PSAT, there are two differences. First, there's no 16-question section. Second, the numbering of the problems doesn't restart each section. So the 8 multiple-choice will be #21 to #28 and the 10 Grid-ins will be #29-#38. These are cosmetic differences. Stick to your target numbers on the PSAT, too.

[‡] The target scores listed in the chart above are approximate. Each test has its own scoring table, so if you get the exact same number of questions right on two different tests, you may get different scores. In this table, we list the average score you would receive if you get all your target questions right. In the example above, you'd probably get around a 640, but you might score anywhere from 610 to 670, depending on the scoring table.

can spend more time on each question. The more time you spend on a question, the more confident you can be of your answer. Since you get so many more points for a right answer than you lose for a wrong, those careless errors you fix will translate into a higher score.

People tend to think about SAT scores in the wrong context. People tend to think of them like figure skating scores—there's a perfect ten and then points deducted for your flaws.[*] Instead, think of them like basketball scores—you're just trying to get as many points as possible. As such, your *shooting percentage* is much more important than the number of shots you take.

This strategy is amazing. You can get a score increase by literally doing *less* work. You can get a higher score not by learning new things but by nailing all the things you already know how to do. It's miraculous.

Frequently Asked Questions about Target Numbers

1. Why are you making me do this? What, you think I'm too *dumb* to get #20? Jerk.

Let's say this right upfront: *we're not saying you're too dumb to get #20*. We firmly believe that *anyone* could get #20 if given enough time for it. This isn't about skipping questions that are too hard for you. The goal here is simply to *do fewer questions*. That's it. So if we're doing fewer questions, we're not going to skip the easy ones; we're going to skip the hard ones. That's just common sense.

Yes, if you did the whole test, you *might* get number #19. But why worry about #19 when you're still missing #3? We *know* you can get #3. That's the goal here—to nail *all* the easy questions. Why worry about the hard stuff when you're still missing points on the easy stuff? Let's get those down pat before we do anything else.

2. I finished my target numbers, but I've still got some time left. Should I move on to more questions?

NO! If you finish your target numbers and still have time, *go back and check your work*. Again, the point here is to make sure that you're as sharp as can be on the easy questions. If you have time left over, don't keep going, and don't stare blankly at the wall for five minutes. Go back and check your work.

3. I stuck to my target questions, but there were still some hard ones in there, so I left them blank too. Is that okay?

NO. Remember, the goal here isn't to "skip hard questions". We're telling you exactly how many questions you need to do to get a good score increase. That means you have to do *all* the questions within your target numbers. Remember: you must put an answer down for every question that you've had time to read over and think about. You may not leave any blanks.

Yes, there will still be some hard ones in there. They aren't all as easy as #2. But that's why we have four more chapters about Math! You didn't think we'd just stop here, did you? There's a lot more we have to go through, and we're going to show you some great techniques that will help you with those hard questions that are within your target numbers.

4. I'm supposed to stop at #16, but I don't know how to do it. But I think I can do #18. Can I skip #16 and do #18 instead?

NO. The very fact that you're asking this question means you've read and thought about two questions, 16 and 18. That takes time. Again, the point here is timing—we want you to spend time making sure you get the easy questions. We do NOT want you to spend time on trying to figure out which questions to do. That's a big waste. We want your game plan to be set before you go to the test.

Some of you are thinking, "Oh, but I *really* know I can do #18." First of all, no you don't. It may only *look* like you can do #18. It might be more complicated than it seems. There might be a Fool's Gold choice. Who knows?

But you know what we do know? That you *really* know how to do #2. If you've done everything you can on #16 and still can't even eliminate one choice, *GO BACK AND CHECK NUMBER TWO!!!* Do not move

---

[*] Wait, is that how figure skating is scored? I have no idea.

on. Yes, there may be questions beyond your target numbers that you are capable of doing. But the goal of this technique is to *spend more time on the easy questions.* The questions past your target numbers are not there. They do not exist. We would tell you to rip those pages out of the test book if you were allowed to do that.[*]

5. I nailed my target numbers on this practice test. Can I do more on the next one?

First of all, if you nailed all your target numbers, congratulations. You probably have a 100-point increase in your math score. Fantastic. But for the next practice test, keep the same numbers. We want to see you do it again. Once might have been a fluke—maybe you were in the zone that day or just happened to get a lot of question types that you're really good at. If you nail all your target numbers *twice in a row*, then we can start to talk about raising them.

But then again, you might not want to raise them. If you really do nail your target numbers, I think you'll be pleasantly surprised by what that does for your score. You might be happy where you are.

6. I work really slowly and I never finish the test. What should I do?

We were going to tell you not to finish the test anyway. Congratulations! You're one step ahead of us. Are you psychic?

Again, the goal here is to be *accurate* on the questions that you *do*. If you're not quite making it through all of your target numbers, that's okay—as long as you've got a high shooting percentage on the ones you *do* get to. Plus, once we get to work on the nuts and bolts of the math, you should be able to get through those easy problems much faster.

7. Why should I skip any of the Grid-ins? They don't take off points for wrong answers there.

That's true, they don't count off for wrong answers on the Grid-ins. However, this strategy is about *timing*. Grid-ins still take time to do. And you're just as likely to make careless mistakes on Grid-in questions as you are on multiple-choice questions. So don't waste time trying to do hard Grid-ins when you could be cementing your answers on the easy Grid-ins.

8. Do these pants make me look fat?

Of course not. You look great. Now stop thinking about your outfit and pay attention.

9. I have extended/unlimited time for the SAT. Do I still have to do this?

Hmm… are you still making careless mistakes, even with extra time? Then yes. Yes you do.

10. Should I do this on the Reading and Writing as well?

No. The reason we do this for the math is that people make careless errors on early questions, so they're missing questions they know how to do. On the Reading and Writing sections, chances are that carelessness is not the problem, so having more time per question probably won't substantially help you. Additionally, in the Reading section, only the Sentence Completions are ordered by difficulty; the passages are not.

On the other hand, if you are having trouble finishing the Reading or Writing sections, this should make you feel a bit better. You can still get a good score there without answering all the questions.

---

[*] You're not. Please do not rip pages out of your test book.

IV. THE TECHNIQUES

The techniques are *ways of doing problems*. They can be used on just about any type of problem: on hard problems or easy problems, arithmetic or algebra, with triangles or circles, <u>anywhere</u>. They are powerful, versatile, and very, very easy.

We're going to show you three techniques for SAT Math problems: Plug In, Backsolve, and Guesstimate. Collectively, these three techniques can be used on about 40% of the math problems on the SAT. That's a lot. While each has its quirks and relative strengths, they all have the same fundamental principle—they turn **abstract** problems into **concrete** problems. The goal is to turn everything into arithmetic, to get rid of vague unknowns, intangible ideas, and long equations and make every problem into simple stuff you can punch into your calculator.

PLUG IN

Let's take a look at this problem:

9. **Bob has 4 dollars more than Lisa does. If Lisa has x dollars, how much would Bob have if he doubled his money?**

    (A) $x + 4$
    (B) $x + 8$
    (C) $2x$
    (D) $2x + 4$
    (E) $2x + 8$

Notice that this question is a number 9—not too hard, but not too easy, just in the middle of the pack. We can see what they want us to do here. They give us a word problem and expect us to translate from sentences into mathematical expressions. I don't want to do that.

Take a look at the answer choices here. They all have x's in them, and x is a variable. That means it can stand for any number. Let's say the answer turns out to be (A). We don't know it's (A), (and actually it isn't) but let's pretend. Well, if the answer is (A), then that's the answer. That's how much money Bob has: $x + 4$ dollars. So it will *always* be $x + 4$, *no matter what x is*. If x is 5, if x is 10, if x is 953,234,124.5255, the answer would always be (A).

So let's pick an x. If the answer comes out the same no matter what number x is, we can choose any value for x that we like and we'll always get the same thing.

This is *Plug In*. It has three steps.

1. Pick a number.

What should we choose? Something small, something manageable, preferably something that isn't already in the problem (to avoid confusion). Try to avoid weird numbers that have special properties like 0, 1, negatives or fractions. Just a nice easy counting number. I like 3. Let's say x is 3.

Once you choose a number, make sure you *write it down* and *put a box around it*, so we remember that's the number we made up.

$$\boxed{x = 3}$$

2. Do the problem with your number.

Read the problem again, but instead of x, we'll use 3.

9. Bob has 4 dollars more than Lisa does. If Lisa has **3 dollars**, how much would Bob have if he doubled his money?

Lisa has x dollars, so now we'll say Lisa has 3 dollars. Bob has 4 more, so Bob has 7 dollars. So if Bob doubled his money, he'd have **14 dollars**. That's our answer. 14. Once you have an answer, circle it.

Wait, but 14 isn't an answer choice. Ah, one more step:

(14)

3. Put the numbers into the choices.

Our answer isn't a choice, all the choices have x's. Aha! But we have an x now. Let's put 3 in for x in the choices and see which one comes out to 14.

(A)	$x + 4$	$3 + 4 = 7$ ✗
(B)	$x + 8$	$3 + 8 = 11$ ✗
(C)	$2x$	$2(3) = 6$ ✗
(D)	$2x + 4$	$2(3) + 4 = 6 + 4 = 10$ ✗
(E)	$2x + 8$	$2(3) + 8 = 6 + 8 = 14$ ✓

Only (E) works. That's our answer. We got the problem by adding one-digit numbers.

Think of the problem as a little function, a series of steps. If I put in this number, I get out that number. When I put in 3, I got 14. The right answer choice should give me the same function. When I put in 3, I should get out 14.

Don't believe me? Try a different number for x. You should still get (E) as your answer.

Frequently Asked Questions about Plug In

1. Do I have to test every choice?

Yes, just to be safe. It is possible that two answer choices both give you the answer you're looking for. This could happen if you choose a number with special properties (like 1) or a number that was already in the problem. Or it could happen purely by chance. So you should check all the choices to make sure there aren't two that both work.

2. So what do I do if I get two choices that work out?

First of all, eliminate everything else. You know it's going to be one of those two. Worst-case scenario, guess one; you've got a 50-50 chance.

> If a question asks what "MUST" be true, that's a sign you might want to try several different numbers.

But before you guess, why not try a different number? If two choices work, it's probably because you happened to pick a weird number. Pick a different one and test the choices that are left. Try different *kind* of number. If you picked a small one before, try a big one now, and vice versa.

If you *keep* getting the same two answers, try a *weird* number, like 0, 1, a fraction, or a negative.* These numbers have special properties, so they can help you notice scenarios that you might miss otherwise.

3. Why do I have to do this? That seemed like a lot of work for a #9.

First of all, we're demonstrating the technique on an easier problem so you can see how it works. The problems only get harder from here, yet Plug In is still little more than adding one-digit numbers. Heck, we already saw a Plug-In question in the Intro lecture—the Fool's Gold example about Scott driving to Bob's house. Try doing *that* sucker with algebra. It ain't pretty.

Second, Plug In may seem weird because it's new for you. The more you do it, the more you'll get the hang of it. Pretty soon, you'll be able to churn out problems in a fraction of the time.

Third, algebraic methods are fraught with possible careless mistakes—even on #9.

Let's try some algebra on that #9 just for kicks. Bob has 4 more than Lisa, so Bob has $x + 4$. Multiply it by two, you get $2x + 4$, right? That's (D), right? Of course not. It's not $2x + 4$; it's $2(x + 4)$. That comes out to $2x + 8$, which is (E), just like we got with Plug In. As brilliant as we all are with algebra, it's *really* easy to make a small stupid mistake like forgetting the parentheses. But with Plug In, you're *much* less likely to make that mistake because you're working with concrete numbers. You understand what all these terms represent; they're not just abstract letters on the page. (D) is no more tempting than any other wrong choice; it's just another choice that doesn't come out to 14.

---

* Conveniently, Fraction, One, Negative, and Zero spell *FONZ*.

There are other ways you can mess this up, too. If you forget to double Bob's money, you get (A). If you double Lisa's money instead of Bob's, you get (C). None of these mistakes are likely with Plug In because all you're doing is simple arithmetic.

So it's not just that Plug In is faster or easier than algebra; it's also _safer_ than algebra. You're much less likely to make an RTFQ or Fool's Gold mistake with Plug In.

Types of Plug In Problems

1. Explicit Variables

As we've already seen, having a _variable in the answer choices_ is the first sign of a Plug In problem. But it also works when there is _more than one variable_.

Sometimes, you can Plug In for each variable **independently**:

10. **How many hours are there in d days and h hours?**

    (A) $24h + d$
    (B) $h + 24d$
    (C) $24(h + d)$
    (D) $\dfrac{h+d}{24}$
    (E) $h + \dfrac{d}{24}$

Because there's no relationship between h and d here, we can come up with totally different numbers for each of them. To make things easy, let's use $d = 1$ and $h = 3$.[*] One day has 24 hours, plus 3 gives a total of **27 hours**. Which choice matches 27?

(A)	$24h + d$	$24(3) + 1 = 73$ ✗
(B)	$h + 24d$	$3 + 24(1) = 27$ ✓
(C)	$24(h + d)$	$24(3 + 1) = 96$ ✗
(D)	$\dfrac{h+d}{24}$	$\dfrac{3+1}{24} = \dfrac{1}{6}$ ✗
(E)	$h + \dfrac{d}{24}$	$3 + \dfrac{1}{24}$ ✗

On the other hand, sometimes the problem will give you some **restrictions** on the variables. In these cases, you can Plug In for one variable, and then use that value to figure out the other variable:

9. **If $x + 5$ is 3 less than y, then $x - 2$ is how much less than y?**

    (A) 2
    (B) 3
    (C) 7
    (D) 8
    (E) 10

Here we have two variables, but this time, if we pick an x, we can use that number to find y. Let's say $x = 4$. Read the beginning of the problem with our number for x: "If $4 + 5$ is 3 less than y". $4 + 5 = 9$. That means "9 is 3 less than y," so y is 3 more than 9. So $y = 12$. Picking an x allowed us to find y.

---

[*] Picking 1 makes things really nice and quick on a problem like this. But because multiplying and dividing by 1 each give you the same answer, picking 1 can sometimes give you two choices that work. Therefore, if your question has a lot of division in the choices, particularly if you see the variable on the bottom of the fraction, you probably shouldn't pick 1. And _any_ time you get more than one choice that works, just eliminate and pick a different number.

We're not done yet. The question asks "$x - 2$ is how much less than y?" $4 - 2 = 2$. So 2 is how much less than 12? 2 is **10** less than 12. That's **choice (E)**.

Notice also that we could still use Plug In even though there weren't any variables in the answer choices.

2. Implicit Variables

Take a look at this problem. It's a *Grid In* question, so there are no answer choices:

12. **Larry cuts a piece of paper into two equal
     pieces. He takes one of those pieces and cuts it
     into three equal pieces. The area of one of the
     smallest pieces is what fraction of the area of
     the original piece of paper?**

There's no variable anywhere in the problem or the answer choices—there aren't any answer choices at all! So we can't use Plug In, right?

Wrong! Even though no variable was explicitly mentioned, there is an **implicit** variable. There's no way for us to find the area of the original piece of paper, right? It doesn't tell us the length or width or any numbers at all (we don't even know whether it's a rectangle!), but we're still expected to get an answer. So it *must not matter* what the starting area is—we'll get the same answer no matter where we start.

Let's say the original piece has an area of **12**.

-   He cuts it into *two* pieces, so each has an area of 6. ($12 \div 6 = 2$)

-   He cuts one of those into *three* pieces, so each of the smaller pieces has an area of **2**. ($6 \div 3 = 2$)

-   So each smaller piece is $\dfrac{2}{12}$ or $\dfrac{1}{6}$ of the original.

We already saw one of these kinds of problems in the Fool's Gold section. Remember this?

20. **Scott drives to Bob's house at a speed of 30
     miles per hour and drives back at a speed of
     50 miles per hour. If he takes the same route
     both ways, what was his average speed, in
     miles per hour, for the whole trip?**

   (A) 35
   (B) 37.5
   (C) 40
   (D) 42.5
   (E) It cannot be determined from the
        information given

Even though there are no variables at all, we can still do the problem by making up a value for the distance of the trip. That's Plug In.

3. Geometry

Take a look at this problem:

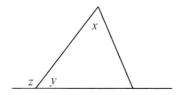

Note: Figure not drawn to scale.

10. **In the figure above, if $y = 90 - x$, what is z in terms of x?**

    (A) $90 + x$
    (B) $90 - x$
    (C) $90 - 2x$
    (D) $180 + x$
    (E) $180 - x$

Geometry can be scary for a lot of kids, and we'll talk a lot more about it in a later chapter. But look: we've got variables in the answer choices! That means we can Plug In for *x*, just like any other normal problem.

Let's say **$x = 30$**. We know $y = 90 - x$, so **$y = 60$**.

We can tell from the picture that *z* and *y* make a straight line; that means $z + y = 180$. Since $y = 60$, we know **$z = 120$**. So when $x = 30$, $z = 120$. Put 30 in for *x* in the answer choices and see which gives you 120:

(A)	**$90 + x$**	$90 + 30 = 120$	✓
(B)	$90 - x$	$90 - 30 = 60$	✗
(C)	$90 - 2x$	$90 - 60 = 30$	✗
(D)	$180 + x$	$180 + 30 = 210$	✗
(E)	$180 - x$	$180 - 30 = 150$	✗

Don't be scared off by figures. If you're confused, don't worry: we'll talk about geometry rules soon enough. But at its heart, this problem is no different than any other Plug In. As soon as you see all those variables in the choices, you know you can Plug In.

And keep in mind that Geometry Plug Ins come in all the same flavors that we've already seen: there may be explicit variables or implicit variables; sometimes you plug in for different variables separately, sometimes you plug in for one and figure out the others (as we just did in #10).

5. If p, q, r, and s are consecutive even integers such that $p < q < r < s$, then how much greater is $s - p$ than $r - q$?

(A) 0
(B) 1
(C) 2
(D) 3
(E) 4

8. Garth has x books, which is 20 more books than Henrietta has. If Garth gives Henrietta 7 books, how many books does Henrietta now have?

(A) $x - 27$
(B) $x - 20$
(C) $x - 13$
(D) $x - 7$
(E) $x + 6$

9. If $a^2 b = c$ and $b \neq 0$, then $\dfrac{1}{b} =$

(A) $a^2 c$

(B) $\dfrac{a^2}{c}$

(C) $\dfrac{c}{a^2}$

(D) $\dfrac{1}{a^2 c}$

(E) $\dfrac{1}{c - a^2}$

11. A number p is divided by 3 and the result is increased by 3. This result is then multiplied by 3. Finally, that result is decreased by 3. In terms of p, what is the final result?

(A) p
(B) $p + 6$
(C) $p - 6$
(D) $3p$
(E) $3p + 6$

12. Lisa uses 2 pieces of copper wire, each 9 feet long, for each robot she builds. If she started with a 500-yard roll of copper wire, which of the following represents the number of <u>yards</u> of wire left on the roll after Lisa built r robots? (3 feet = 1 yard)

(A) $500 - \dfrac{1}{6} r$

(B) $500 - \dfrac{1}{3} r$

(C) $500 - 2r$
(D) $500 - 6r$
(E) $500 - 9r$

14. Hot dogs cost h dollars and pretzels cost p dollars. How much would it cost, in dollars, to buy $h + 1$ hot dogs and $p - 1$ pretzels?

(A) $h + p$

(B) $hp - h + p - 1$

(C) $h^2 + p^2$

(D) $h^2 + 2hp + p^2$

(E) $h^2 + h + p^2 - p$

15. The sum of 3 consecutive integers is s. What is the greatest of these integers, in terms of s?

(A) $\dfrac{s}{3} - 1$

(B) $\dfrac{s}{3}$

(C) $\dfrac{s}{3} + 1$

(D) $\dfrac{s}{3} + 2$

(E) $\dfrac{s}{3} + 3$

16. If $t \neq 0$ and $s = \dfrac{1}{t}$, which of the following must be true?

(A) $s < t$

(B) $s > t$

(C) $st < 1$

(D) $st > 1$

(E) $st > 0$

19. If Leslie gives away k celery sticks, she will have $\dfrac{1}{n}$ times as many as she had originally.

In terms of k, and n, how many celery sticks did Leslie have originally?

(A) $k + \dfrac{1}{n}$

(B) $k + n$

(C) $kn + k$

(D) $\dfrac{kn}{n - 1}$

(E) $\dfrac{k}{n + 1}$

w decreased by 40% of w yields x
x increased by 50% of x yields y
y decreased by 10% of y yields z

20. According to the information above, z is what percent of w?

(A) 27%

(B) 60%

(C) 81%

(D) 90%

(E) 100%

BACKSOLVE

Take a look at this one.

11. Gerry's age is 5 more than three times Carol's age. If the sum of their ages is 45, how old is Carol?

    (A) 10
    (B) 12
    (C) 14
    (D) 16
    (E) 18

Here, we can't just make up a number for Carol's age because that's the whole point of the question. The value *does* matter—there's only one number that works for Carol's age. So Plug In is out.

However, like we did with Plug In, we can still turn this into a simple arithmetic problem. But instead of picking *random* numbers, let's use the numbers *in the answer choices*. We know one of these 5 numbers is Carol's age, so let's try them until we find one that works.

That's **Backsolve**. It also has three steps.

1. Make Choice (C) the answer

Why (C)? Because it's in the middle. When there are numbers in the answers like this, they always put the choices in order. So if we try Choice (C) and it doesn't work, we can figure out if it was too small or too big and eliminate three answer choices in one fell swoop.

Okay. So let's say that **(C)** is the answer. (C) is **14**. So what does that mean? What's 14? Well, 14 is the answer to the question. In this case, the question is "how old is Carol?" That means if (C) is right, then Carol is 14.

2. Do the problem and see if it fits

What else do we know? We know that Gerry's age is 5 more than three times Carol's age. Again, we're saying Carol is 14, so:

(C)   **Carol = 14.**

      $3 \times 14 = 42$ "Gerry's age is 5 more than 3 times 14."

      $42 + 5 = \mathbf{47} = \textbf{Gerry}.$ So if Carol is 14, then Gerry is **47**.

How do I know if (C) is the right answer, then? Well, what *else* does the problem tell us? Their ages should add up to 45. Do they? Of course not. Gerry's age *alone* is bigger than 45. So (C) is too big.

3. If (C) fails, figure out if you need a bigger or smaller number and repeat

Well, (C) was definitely too big, so we'll need a smaller number. So we'll move on to **(B)**

(B)   **Carol = 12.**

      $12 \times 3 + 5 = \mathbf{41} = \textbf{Gerry}.$

      $12 + 41 = \mathbf{53}$ ✗

Still too big. Their ages should add up to 45. Let's move on to **(A)**

(A)   **Carol = 10.**

      $10 \times 3 + 5 = \mathbf{35} = \textbf{Gerry}.$

      $10 + 35 = \mathbf{45}$ ✓

Bingo! (A) is our answer.

That was a word problem. Just like we saw before when we were discussing Plug In, this problem didn't have any explicit variables mentioned, but it did have **implicit** variables. There were no actual letters assigned to Carol or Gerry's age, but we could still put numbers in for them all the same. That's one of the strengths of these techniques. We don't need to worry about variables; we can work directly with the underlying concepts in the problem.

But Backsolve works just as well when there are **explicit** variables. Observe:

14. **If** $a + b = 9$ **and** $a^2 + ab = 36$ **then** $b =$

    (A) 3
    (B) 4
    (C) 5
    (D) 6
    (E) 7

Any time a problem asks for the value of a variable, we can Backsolve. Just put the numbers in the choices in for the variable and see if it works.

We'll start with **(C)**, that's 5. They're asking for b, so we'll say $b = 5$. Okay, fine. We know that $a + b = 9$. Since $b = 5$, $a = 4$. So far, so good. Now let's put a and b into that giant equation and see if it comes out to 36.

$$a^2 + ab = 4^2 + 4(5) = 16 + 20 = 36 \quad \checkmark$$

It works! Since (C) worked, I don't even have to look at anything else. The answer is (C). I'm done!

Let's take a minute to think about how to do this problem with algebra. First of all, you could solve one equation for a, and then substitute that into the other equation. Ugh. I guess we could do that, but it's a lot of work and easy to mess up. Backsolve is much quicker and easier.

Now, if you've got a really good eye, you might notice this:

$a + b = 9$ and $a^2 + ab = 36$	We're given two equations.
$a(a + b) = a^2 + ab$	The second equation is just the first equation times a.
$a(9) = 36$	So we can just substitute the values we know,
$a = 4$	And our answer is 4. That's (B).

Wait a minute: 4? (B)? Didn't we get (C)? Isn't (C) 5? Aha! $a = 4$; they're asking us for b. RTFQ! So even if we're really clever with our algebra, the algebra easily leads to an RTFQ. You're much less likely to make an RTFQ mistake with Backsolve because you're working *directly* from the question. You pick (C), and then make (C) *the answer to the question*. It's the first step!

So there are basically two algebraic ways of doing this problem. One is slow and painful. The other almost inevitably leads you to an RTFQ mistake. Like Plug In, Backsolve is faster, easier, and *safer* than algebra.

Frequently Asked Questions about Backsolve

1. If (C) works on my first try, should I try the other choices to be safe?

No. Unlike Plug In, with Backsolve there's no way that more than one choice will work out. Once you find a choice that works, stop. That's your answer.

2. What if I'm not sure whether I want a higher or lower number?

Then just pick one! Don't go crazy trying to deduce which way to go. Part of the point of Backsolve is to work quickly and methodically. If (C) fails and you're not sure whether you should go to (B) or (D), just pick one. You're just doing simple math here. The worst-case scenario is that you go the wrong way and wind up having to test all five choices. But really, that's not very much work. And you know that eventually you'll find the answer.

3. If $\dfrac{x+10}{12} = \dfrac{8}{3}$, then $x =$

    (A)   10
    (B)   22
    (C)   54
    (D)   66
    (E)   96

5. If the average of 2 and p is equal to the average of 1, 6, and p, what is the value of p?

    (A)   3
    (B)   5
    (C)   6
    (D)   7
    (E)   8

7. Allen is reviewing his receipts from three different visits to a spa, trying to determine the individual costs of his favorite spa treatments. From his receipts he knows:

    A manicure and a back rub together cost $18.
    A back rub and a facial together cost $19.
    A manicure and a facial together cost $21.

What is the cost of a back rub?

    (A) $7
    (B) $8
    (C) $9
    (D) $10
    (E) $11

9. If $(x+4)^2 = 49$ and $x < 0$, what is the value of x?

    (A) -53
    (B) -45
    (C) -11
    (D) -3
    (E)   3

10. The product of four consecutive odd integers is 9. What is the least of these integers?

    (A) -3
    (B)   1
    (C)   3
    (D)   5
    (E)   7

11. Erica had a stack of firewood on Monday. On Tuesday she used $\dfrac{1}{2}$ of the logs, and on Wednesday she used 110 logs, leaving Erica with $\dfrac{1}{3}$ of her original supply. How many logs of firewood did Erica originally have on Monday?

    (A)   220
    (B)   440
    (C)   500
    (D)   570
    (E)   660

13. Vladimir sold 18 books on Monday. He sold paperback books for $7.50 each and hardcover books for $15 each. If he made a total of $210, how many paperback books did he sell?

(A) 12
(B) 11
(C) 10
(D)   9
(E)   8

15. The sum of five consecutive integers a, b, c, d, and e is 55. What is the median of the set $\{a, b, c, d, e\}$?

(A)   9
(B) 10
(C) 11
(D) 12
(E) 13

17. Marion brought some biscuits to a tea party. If everyone at the party takes 5 biscuits, there will be 10 remaining. If 4 people do not take any and everyone else takes 8, there will be none remaining. How many biscuits did Marion bring to the party?

(A)   56
(B)   70
(C)   80
(D)   95
(E) 104

18. It took Adam 6 hours to canoe upstream from his campsite to the lake and back again. While paddling upstream, he averaged 2 miles per hour; while paddling back, he averaged 4 miles per hour. How many miles was it from his campsite to the lake?

(A)   4
(B)   8
(C) 10
(D) 12
(E) 16

GUESSTIMATE

Take a look at this problem:

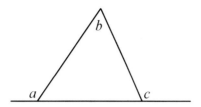

19. In the figure above, *c* is equal to 5 less than twice *b*. What is the value of *a* + *b*?

    (A)   60
    (B)   90
    (C) 100
    (D) 135
    (E) 185

Okay, this is a pretty hard one—19 out of 20. There are all sorts of Geometry rules that you could use here to set up equations and cancel out variables. Those can get pretty nasty, though. Plus we haven't talked about Geometry rules yet. Let's not do that. Let's find an easier way.

One thing you can do here is Plug In. Make up a number for *b*, say, and use it to find all the other angles. That's a pretty good way to do it, but I want to show you a third option.

If you've ever done a full SAT before, you've probably occasionally noticed a Geometry problem that has the words "<u>Note</u>: Figure not drawn to scale" under the picture. That means that the lines and angles don't necessarily have the values that they appear to. It might look like a square, but maybe its dimensions are actually 8 by 97.

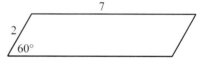

<u>Note</u>: Figure not drawn to scale.

The first drawing *looks* like a square, but because it says it's not to scale, we can't assume it's a square. In fact, we know it's definitely *not* a square because it has a 60° angle and 2 by 7 dimensions. The second drawing is the same figure drawn to scale. That means that if we measured that angle with a protractor it would come out to 60°, and if we measured those sides with a ruler, they would be in a 2 to 7 ratio.[*]

So if the problem says "<u>Note</u>: Figure not drawn to scale", then you can't use the size and shape of the figure to get information. You *can* use the numbers they tell you, but the picture won't necessarily look right.

However, *if the problem doesn't say "not drawn to scale", you can assume that it is drawn to scale.* The figure on the right above has no comment below it, so the figure really will measure the way it looks. If it looks like two lines are the same length, then they really are. If it looks like an angle is 60°, then it *is* 60°, or at least really close to 60°.

This is **Guesstimate**. It has one step.

---

[*] Note that we don't know the units, just the dimensions. The sides aren't two *inches* by seven *inches*. They're just in a 2 to 7 ratio.

1. Look at the picture and guess the values you want.

In our example above, they're asking us for $a + b$. So let's take a look at those angles. Angle a is pretty big. Let's say… 120? 130? Let's say **130**. Angle b is smaller, maybe 50 or 60. Let's say **60**. So $a + b$ must be about $130 + 60$ or about $\boxed{190}$. So our answer should be pretty close to 190. Hmm, 190 isn't a choice, but 185 is! That's pretty darn close. We'll take it. The answer is (E).

Look how easy that was! We didn't do a darn thing other than just looking at the picture. I got #19 in all of 10 seconds and all I did was add two numbers.

Frequently Asked Questions about Guesstimate

1. **That's all well and good, but how do I know that's right? I just made up those numbers. I could have been wrong.**

That's true, but you didn't *randomly* make up those numbers; you measured the angles in the problem, the angles they give you.

Seriously, just look at the other choices they give you. (A)? 60? Could $a + b$ be 60? Angle a is *obtuse!* Angle a <u>alone</u> has to be bigger than 90! So (A) and (B) are out right away. (C) is still too small—angle a is still probably bigger than 100, and when you add b to the mix, there's no way the two of them come out that small. (D) still looks too small. Think of it this way: the unmarked angle next to a looks to be about the same size as b. They're not exactly the same size, but they're close. And a makes a straight line with that unmarked angle, so together they're 180. So $a + b$ must be pretty close to 180. None of these choices make *any* sense at all. Only (E).

And here's the thing: if you do this problem algebraically, there are ways you can mess it up that will make you pick one of those wrong answers. If you add instead of subtract or forget to distribute across parentheses, you could think that (A) is a plausible answer because of your flawed algebra. But if you look at the picture, you can see there's no way those angles add up to 60. It just doesn't make sense.

2. **Okay, I see that. But what's the *real* math way to do this problem?**

Are you kidding? *This is real math.* There's nothing mathematically illegitimate about doing this. In math, as in all the sciences, there are two ways of solving any problem: *analytically*, by using pure logic and deducing (that's algebra), or *empirically*, by gathering evidence and measuring (that's Guesstimate).

Say you have a dining-room table and you want to figure out how tall it is. Well, one way I could figure out the height of the table is to construct a line from my eye to the top of the table and a line from my eye to the bottom of the table, measure the angle of declination, and use the law of cosines to find the third side of the triangle. *OR I COULD GET A @#%$!*& RULER AND MEASURE IT!*

Here are your choices for how tall the table is:

> (A) 2.5 inches
> (B) 3 feet
> (C) 7.8 miles

But how do I *know* the table isn't 7.8 miles tall? Because it's in my living room. And I'm looking at it.

And here's the thing: the College Board *wants* you to do this. If they didn't want you to do this, they could very easily make every figure on the SAT not to scale. But they *do* draw figures to scale. In fact, *most* figures they give you are drawn to scale—about 75% of them. That's a lot of figures. That's a lot of Guesstimate.

3. **Does this only work with angles?**

Of course not! You can use this on just about any problem that has a picture, as long as it's drawn to scale. Take a look at this one:

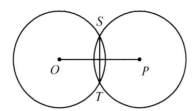

19. **In the figure above, $\overline{ST}$ is a chord and $\overline{OP}$ connects the centers of the two circles with equal radii. If $ST = 4$ and $OP = 4\sqrt{3}$, what is the radius of circle O?**

   (A) 2
   (B) $2\sqrt{3}$
   (C) 4
   (D) $4\sqrt{3}$
   (E) 8

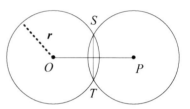

What do we want? The radius of O. Hmm, we don't have a radius there. So let's draw one in. Just draw a line from the center to anywhere on the side.

So that r is the length we're looking for. Let's compare that to the lines we know. Well, it definitely looks smaller than OP, which we know is $4\sqrt{3}$ (or about 6.92). So (D) and (E) are out. Good so far.

We also know that ST is 4, so let's compare r to *ST*. Hey, they look the same. Maybe $r = 4$. Wait a minute—they're *exactly* the same! How do I know? **Measure them**. Take a piece of paper (try your answer sheet) and lay the side of the paper against r and mark off its length. Then lay that paper you marked off against *ST*. What do you find? **They're the same!** We're done! So the radius is 4. So the answer is (C).

At the very least, if we go purely by our eyes, we know right away that the radius should be *close* to 4, so only (B) and (C) make sense ($2\sqrt{3}$ is about 3.46, which is close). If we actually measure it out, we can see that the radius is *exactly* 4. Perfect.

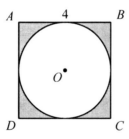

14. **In the figure above, square *ABCD* is circumscribed about circle *O*. If square *ABCD* has sides of length 4, what is the area of the shaded region?**

   (A) $4-2\pi$
   (B) $4-4\pi$
   (C) $16-2\pi$
   (D) $16-4\pi$
   (E) $16-16\pi$

Let's try to get in the ballpark of what we're looking for.

What do we know? The only value we're given is that the side of the square is 4.

What can we do with that? We can find the area of the square: $4 \times 4 = $ **16**.

How does that help us answer the question? The shaded area is much smaller than the square so our answer must be **a lot less than 16**. Okay, let's eliminate.

But how can we eliminate? All the choices have that stupid π thingy. What do we do? Ah, but wait! What *is* that stupid π thingy? It's not a variable—***it's a number!*** So we can punch all those choices out on our calculators and see which ones come close to what we want.

Even better, let's approximate: π is approximately 3, so we can just do out the choices with 3 instead.

(A) $4 - 2\pi$	$\approx$	$4 - 2(3)$	$= -2$	✗ That's negative! Areas can't be negative!
(B) $4 - 4\pi$	$\approx$	$4 - 4(3)$	$= -8$	✗ That's even more negative!
(C) $16 - 2\pi$	$\approx$	$16 - 2(3)$	$= 10$	✗ Too big. This is more than half of 16.
(D) $16 - 4\pi$	$\approx$	$16 - 4(3)$	$= 4$	✓ Okay, that might work.
(E) $16 - 16\pi$	$\approx$	$16 - 16(3)$	$= -32$	✗ That's *hugely* negative!

Look! Choice (D) is the only one that made sense.

4. Will Guesstimate work on 3-D figures?

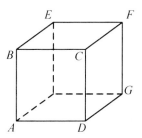

Not exactly. Three-dimensional figures like cubes are drawn using *perspective*, so we can't literally measure the lines as they're drawn to see which one is bigger. In the cube shown here, segment *BE* is literally shorter than segment *BC* as the figure is drawn. But we know that in a cube, the top face is supposed to be a square. Therefore, *BE* = *BC*, even though the lines on the page are not actually equal.

However, if you have a good eye, you might be able to use your imagination to figure this stuff out. Some of you may be good at imagining 3-D objects in your head. For example, you may be able to see that *ED* = *AF*, even though they're not equal in the drawing. If you can, that's great. Remember: the point of Guesstimate is to use what you know about the figure along with your common sense.

5. Does Guesstimate always work?

Unfortunately, Guesstimate isn't always going to work as beautifully as it did on these questions. You're not always going to be able to zero in on the right answer like this. However, you can often eliminate *something*, even if it's only one choice. And once you eliminate something, your odds of getting the problem increase. Even if you can't figure out any other solution, you can guess from what's left,

So *any time* you see a problem with a diagram that's drawn to scale, ***try Guesstimate first***. Before you do anything else, try to get a ballpark figure for the thing they're asking for.

GUESSTIMATE DRILL

Use Guesstimate for every question in this drill. *To help, we've taken normal SAT questions and blacked out most of the information given. That means you have no choice but to Guesstimate!*

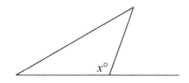

2. In the figure above, ▮▮▮▮▮▮▮▮▮▮
▮▮▮. What is the value of *x*?

    (A)   30
    (B)   50
    (C)   70
    (D)   110
    (E)   150

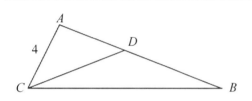

6. ▮▮▮▮▮▮▮▮▮▮▮▮▮▮▮▮▮
▮▮▮▮▮▮▮▮▮. What is the length of *AD*?

    (A)   4
    (B)   6
    (C)   8
    (D)   10
    (E)   12

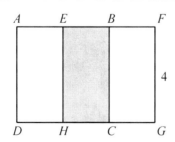

9. The figure above shows ▮▮▮▮▮▮▮
▮▮▮▮▮▮▮▮▮▮▮▮▮▮▮▮▮▮▮
▮▮, what is the area of the shaded region?

    (A)   6
    (B)   8
    (C)   12
    (D)   16
    (E)   24

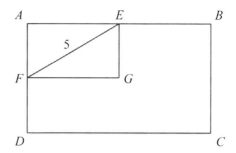

13. In the figure above, ▮▮▮▮▮▮▮▮▮
▮▮▮▮▮▮▮▮▮▮▮▮▮▮▮
▮▮▮▮▮▮▮▮ and ▮▮▮▮▮▮. What is
the length of *DC*?

    (A)   5
    (B)   5√3
    (C)   10
    (D)   10√3
    (E)   12

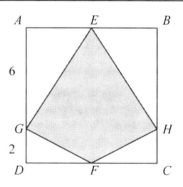

15. In the figure above, ▮▮▮▮▮▮▮▮▮
▮▮▮▮▮▮▮▮▮▮▮▮▮▮▮▮▮▮
▮▮. What is the area of the shaded region?

    (A)   12
    (B)   16
    (C)   32
    (D)   52
    (E)   64

IV. USING THE TECHNIQUES

It's one thing to understand how these techniques work. It's another to be able to use them and use them effectively in a real-test situation. We can't tell you how many times we've taught bright, eager young students who understand, love, and sing praises to the techniques, only to take a practice test and use none of them. Not surprisingly, they show little to no score improvement on these tests.

It's incredibly difficult to change your habits. These techniques are a fundamentally different approach than what you're used to doing in school. Therefore, you have to make a *conscious* effort to use them on your practice tests. *Every* time you do a problem from here on out, your *first* thought should be "Can I use a technique here?" Even if you see another way of doing the problem. Even if you think that other way is better than the technique. **You must try to use the techniques every chance you get**.

We can already hear you complaining, but trust us: it's for your own good. Clearly, your old ways of doing problems aren't working for you—if they were, you wouldn't be reading this now. Your old methods have gotten you the score you have now. If you want a different score, you have to try different things.

Every time you do a problem from here on out, your *first* thought should be "Can I use a technique here?" Sometimes, of course, the answer will be "no"; you can't use the techniques on every single problem you see. And sometimes, there will be problems where the algebra isn't so bad and you can get the problem without the techniques. But here's the thing: *you're not qualified to make that call yet*. The techniques are still new for you, so you don't know whether or not they're the best method on this or that problem. The only way you can *become* qualified is to try to use the techniques every time you possibly can.

This is no different from any time you learn something new. In sports or in music, the only way to get good at something is to do it a thousand times in a row. The more you practice, the better you become.

Techniques and Target Numbers

The more you use the techniques, the better you'll get at them. As we've seen already, the techniques can turn a really hard problem into a really easy problem. And techniques can be used on *a lot* of the hard problems.

But techniques can't be used on every question. There will be some legitimately tough questions that can't be done with Plug In, Backsolve, or Guesstimate. Luckily, a lot of those tough questions will be past your target numbers, so you'll never see them. But it's not unusual for the last question in your target numbers to be a legitimately tough non-technique question.

Therefore, we give you a little bit of leeway on your Target Numbers. If the last question in your assigned set is *not* a technique question, and you see a question past your target numbers that's *obviously* a technique question, you may do the technique question instead of one of your target questions.

Note this exception is *only* for technique questions. If you see a non-technique problem—even if you think you can do—it's not worth your time. Remember that one of the dangers of the harder questions is the possibility of a Fool's Gold choice, a wrong choice that looks like an easy answer. But we've already seen that using the techniques actually *reduces* your chances of making those mistakes.

And this doesn't mean you can do *all* technique questions past your target numbers. Remember: the goal of target numbers is *do fewer questions*. Your first goal should still be to do your target questions and *only* your target questions. But at the end of the section, if you notice a Plug In past your assignment, it's okay to swap it with one of your assigned questions.

So how can you tell if you can use a technique on a problem? Glad you asked.

Identifying Techniques

Circle the Question

This bears repeating. It's quite remarkable, but a simple act like circling the question—that is, the thing they're actually asking you to solve for—can do wonders for your performance.

We already saw how it can help you avoid RTFQ mistakes. Circling the question helps you remember what the point of the problem is, and will clear your mind on everything you do. But more importantly, it can help you decide *which* technique, if any, is applicable on a question.

> ## If the question asks for a *VALUE*, use Backsolve.
> ## If the question asks for a *RELATIONSHIP*, use Plug In.

The more you use Plug In and Backsolve, the more you'll be able to spot this. While it may seem like they ask you about a million different things on the test, they actually repeat the same kinds of question over and over again. The more questions you do, the easier it is to spot the techniques.

Okay, so let's recap some common characteristics of the Three Fundamental Techniques:

Plug In

This is the one where you make up a number.

Here are some common characteristics of Plug-In problems, with examples from problems we've seen:

➤ Any time you see a problem that has *variables in the answer choices*, you can definitely use Plug In. Because if the answer is $x + 4$, it will always be $x + 4$, no matter what x is.

➤ In particular, look out for questions that ask for "x in terms of y". That's a big sign that Plug In is possible.

➤ Sometimes you can also use Plug In when there are variables in the question but not in the choices. Sometimes if you plug in for one variable you can figure out the other variables.

➤ You can use Plug In on problems with *implicit* variables. You can use Plug In any time there's some concept in the problem and:

1. You don't know its value

2. There's no way to figure out its value

3. They still expect you to get an answer

4. So it doesn't matter what that value is; you'll get the same answer no matter what.

9. Bob has 4 dollars more than Lisa does. If Lisa has x dollars, how much would Bob have if he doubled his money?

(A) $x + 4$
(B) $x + 8$
(C) $2x$
(D) $2x + 4$
(E) $2x + 8$

9. If $x + 5$ is 3 less than y, then $x - 2$ is how much less than y?

(A)   2
(B)   3
(C)   7
(D)   8
(E)   10

20. Scott drives to Bob's house at a speed of 30 miles per hour and drives back at a speed of 50 miles per hour. If he takes the same route both ways, what was his average speed, in miles per hour, for the whole trip?

(A)   35
(B)   37.5
(C)   40
(D)   42.5
(E)   It cannot be determined from the information given

Backsolve

This is the one where you use the numbers in the choices.

Some common characteristics of Backsolve problems:

➤ There are whole numbers in the answer choices. Any time you need to find some kind of single value or quantity, you've got five options for that value right here. Four of them are wrong, one of them is right. Test them.

➤ If they're asking you for the *value of a variable* (i.e., what number does *x* equal), you can usually use Backsolve. They want to know *x*? Well, here are five options. Try 'em until you find one that works.

11. Gerry's age is 5 more than three times Carol's age. If the sum of their ages is 45, how old is Carol?

(A) 10
(B) 12
(C) 14
(D) 16
(E) 18

14. If $a + b = 9$ and $a^2 + ab = 36$ then $b =$

(A) 3
(B) 4
(C) 5
(D) 6
(E) 7

Often, Backsolve questions have *two pieces of information*. When you test an answer choice, you run the choice through one piece of information and see if it matches the other. In #11 above, we started with "5 more than three times" and checked that the resulting sums were 45. In #14, we started with the first equation and checked that the second came out to 36.

Guesstimate

This is the one where you look at the picture.

Any time you see a problem that has a picture drawn to scale your *first* instinct should be Guesstimate.

➤ Obviously, there has to be a picture. Duh.

➤ The picture has to be to scale. If you see "Note: Figure not drawn to scale" then you can't Guesstimate because, obviously, the picture isn't actually what it looks like.

➤ Use the numbers you're given and look at the picture to get an approximate value for the thing you're looking for.

➤ You can do this for any kind of value: angles, lengths, or areas.

➤ Try to eliminate as many implausible answers as you can. Maybe you can eliminate four choices, maybe only one. But get rid of any choice that doesn't make sense. Start with a broad guess and then try to get more precise.

➤ Remember that you are guessing here, so you can't eliminate choices that are too close together. If you guess an angle is 60 but 55, 57, 60, 63 and 65 are all choices, don't just pick 60. Those choices are too close to make a call; you're not that good at guessing.

➤ For three-dimensional figures, you can't literally measure the figure as it's drawn, though you may still be able to judge relative values if you have a good eye for figures.

BIG TECHNIQUE EXERCISE

Please enjoy this Big Technique Exercise! **You must use one of the three Techniques—Plug In, Backsolve, or Guesstimate—on every problem on this exercise.** *If you get a question right, but did not use a technique, you will get no credit.*

$$\begin{array}{r} \triangle 1 \\ \triangle 5 \\ \triangle 7 \\ + \triangle 9 \\ \hline 182 \end{array}$$

1. In the correctly worked addition problem above, each $\triangle$ represents the same digit. What is the value of $\triangle$?

   (A) 3
   (B) 4
   (C) 5
   (D) 6
   (E) 7

2. If $a \neq 0$, then 25% of $12a$ equals

   (A) $3a$
   (B) $4a$
   (C) $8a$
   (D) $9a$
   (E) $12a$

3. Rita has 5 fewer than 4 times the number of peaches that Sal has. If R represents the number of Rita's peaches and S represents the number of Sal's peaches, which of the following expressions correctly relates R and S?

   (A) $R = 4S - 5$
   (B) $R = 4(S - 5)$
   (C) $R = 5(S - 4)$
   (D) $R = 5S - 4$
   (E) $R = 5S + 4$

4. What is the <u>greatest</u> of four consecutive integers whose sum is 26?

   (A) 5
   (B) 6
   (C) 7
   (D) 8
   (E) 9

5. If x is a positive integer and $\dfrac{x+3}{2^x} = \dfrac{1}{4}$, then $x =$

   (A) 2
   (B) 3
   (C) 4
   (D) 5
   (E) 6

6. In the figure above, one side of the rectangle lies on the diameter of the circle. If C is the area of the circle and R is the area of the rectangle, which of the following *must* be true?

(A) $C < R$
(B) $C = R$
(C) $C > 2R$
(D) $C = 2R$
(E) $C < 2R$

7. Last month Company A sold 200 more copy machines than Company B. This month, Company A sold 75 fewer than Company B. Which of the following must be true about Company A's total sales for the two months compared to Company B's?

(A) Company A sold 275 fewer machines than Company B.

(B) Company A sold 125 fewer machines than Company B.

(C) Company A sold 125 more machines than Company B.

(D) Company A sold 275 more machines than Company B.

(E) Company A sold $\dfrac{3}{10}$ as many machines as Company B.

8. To steam rice, Paul uses m cups of water for every p cups of rice. In terms of m and p, how many cups of water are needed to steam $p + 2$ cups of rice?

(A) $m + 2$

(B) $m(p + 2)$

(C) $\dfrac{m}{p + 2}$

(D) $\dfrac{m(p + 2)}{p}$

(E) $\dfrac{p}{m(p + 2)}$

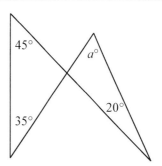

9. In the figure above, what is the value of a?

(A) 90
(B) 70
(C) 60
(D) 35
(E) 20

$$A = \left\{ \frac{5}{8}, 1, \frac{11}{8}, 3, \frac{9}{2}, 6 \right\}$$

$$B = \left\{ \frac{5}{8}, \frac{8}{5}, 3, 6 \right\}$$

10. If j is a member of both set A and set B, which of the following must be true?

      I. $j > 1$
      II. $j < 1$
      III. $j = 3$

(A) None
(B) I only
(C) II only
(D) III only
(E) I and III only

11. The width of a rectangular rug is one-sixth of the length. If the perimeter is 56, what is the rug's width?

(A)   4
(B)   7
(C)   12
(D)   15
(E)   24

12. The combined price of a pair of pants and a shirt is 100 dollars. If the pants cost 14 dollars less than 2 times the shirt, what is the price, in dollars, of the shirt?

(A)   28
(B)   38
(C)   46
(D)   62
(E)   70

13. If $4^a = b$, which of the following equals $16b^2$?

(A) 4^{4a}
(B) 4^{a^4}
(C) 4^{2a+2}
(D) 4^{2a^2}
(E) 16^a

14. Let j, k, and m be integers, where $j > k > m > 1$. If $j \times k \times m = 120$, what is the greatest possible value of j?

(A)   15
(B)   20
(C)   30
(D)   60
(E)   120

15. Which of the following would yield the same result as multiplying by $\frac{6}{7}$ and then dividing by $\frac{2}{7}$?

(A) Multiplying by 3
(B) Multiplying by $\frac{1}{3}$
(C) Multiplying by 2
(D) Dividing by 2
(E) Dividing by $\frac{1}{2}$

17. If $x \neq 0$, what is the value, in terms of x, of

$$\frac{3}{\frac{2}{x}} + \frac{1}{\frac{4}{10x}}?$$

(A) $\dfrac{1}{4x}$

(B) $\dfrac{4}{x}$

(C) $\dfrac{x}{4}$

(D) $\dfrac{15x}{4}$

(E) $4x$

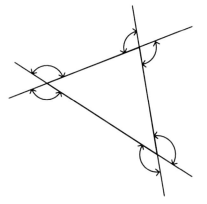

16. In the figure above, what is the sum of the measures of the marked angles?

(A) 180
(B) 360
(C) 540
(D) 720
(E) 900

18. At a certain gym, 18 people take an aerobics class and 24 people take a karate class. If 32 people take only one of the two classes, how many people take both classes?

(A) 5
(B) 10
(C) 13
(D) 15
(E) 19

19. The length and width of a rectangle are both reduced by 60%. Its length and width are then both increased by 50%. The area of the rectangle is what percent of its original area?

(A) 10%
(B) 36%
(C) 40%
(D) 81%
(E) 90%

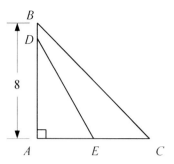

20. In the figure above, $AB = AC$ and E is the midpoint of $\overline{AC}$. If $\angle AED = 60°$, what is the length of $\overline{DE}$?

(A) 4
(B) $4\sqrt{3}$
(C) 8
(D) $8\sqrt{2}$
(E) $8\sqrt{3}$

MATH FUNDAMENTALS

We already talked about the 3 major techniques—Plug In, Backsolve, and Guesstimate. These are powerful techniques that can be applied to a lot of different problems. However, the techniques won't work on every problem. We need to talk about *content*—the actual rules of math you have to know on the SAT. So we're going to begin at the beginning, as one should. In this chapter, we're going to talk about the nuts and bolts, all the essential rules of arithmetic and algebra that you're going to need.

Since we're talking about the basics here, most of this will probably not be new to you. As such, there's a temptation to skip over this part. "This is so boring! Why do we have to talk about fractions? We did this in, like, seventh grade! I hate you!" Ah, but it's because this is stuff we've seen before that we must make sure we know it well. Remember: the problem most people have with the SAT *isn't* that they don't know enough math; it's that they're missing questions that they know how to do. Therefore, we've got to make sure we know all this stuff backwards and forwards.

I. ARITHMETIC

1. Number Concepts and Definitions

Let's get some terminology out of the way to avoid confusion down the line.

Integer: Any number that does not have a fraction or decimal part: ... –3, –2, –1, 0, 1, 2, 3...

Factor: An integer that can be divided into another integer without a remainder. For example, 3 is a factor of 12 because 12 ÷ 3 = 4. We say the larger number "*is divisible by*" the smaller number, so here 12 is divisible by 3.[*]

> Note that zero is an even integer but it is neither positive nor negative.

Multiple: An integer that has another integer as a factor. For example, 12 is a multiple of 3 because 3 × 4 = 12.

Prime Number: A number that is divisible only by 1 and itself. 1 is not a prime number. The only even prime number is 2. Examples of prime numbers include 2, 3, 5, 7, 11, and 13.

Remainder: The integer left over when an integer is divided by an integer that is not its factor. For example: 13 ÷ 5 = 2 with a *remainder of 3*. That means you can fit two fives in 13, but there will be 3 left over: 5 × 2 = 10, and 10 + 3 = 13.

Remainders are whole numbers, **NOT** decimals. If you punch "13 ÷ 5" on your calculator you'll get 2.6. The remainder is NOT 6.

Say a question asks you to find a number that gives a remainder of 3 when it's divided by 4. Just take a multiple of 4 and add 3 to it. Any these numbers would fit:

$$4 + 3 = 7 \qquad 8 + 3 = 11 \qquad 12 + 3 = 15 \qquad 16 + 3 = 19$$

Properties of Positive and Negative numbers:

Bigger digits give smaller negative numbers. That is, –10 is *smaller* than –2.

$$(\text{Pos}) \times (\text{Pos}) = \text{Pos} \qquad (\text{Neg}) \times (\text{Pos}) = \text{Neg} \qquad (\text{Neg}) \times (\text{Neg}) = \text{Pos}$$

Properties of Odd and Even Integers:

(Even) × (Even) = Even	Even + Even = Even
(Even) × (Odd) = Even	Even + Odd = Odd
(Odd) × (Odd) = Odd	Odd + Odd = Even

---

[*] Here's a trick to help you find factors: if the sum of the number's digits is divisible by 3, then the number is divisible by 3. 12 is divisible by 3 because 1 + 2 = 3. And 945 is divisible by 3 because 9 + 4 + 5 = 18, and 18 is divisible by 3. The rule is true for 9, too: if the sum of the digits is divisible by 9, the number is divisible by 9.

Decimal places: In the number **25.97**

- 2 is the "tens digit" and is in the "tens place"
- 5 is the "units digit" and is in the "units place"
- 9 is the "tenths digit" and is in the "tenths place"
- 7 is the "hundredths digit" and is in the "hundredths place"

Prime Factors

As we said above, integers can be broken down into *factors*, and a *prime number* is one that can't be broken down into factors. Therefore, a *prime factor* is a factor that can't be broken down into smaller factors. Any number that isn't prime can be reduced to a unique set of prime factors. And *all* that number's factors are just different combinations of its prime factors.

➤ **What are the prime factors of 12?**

All we have to do is break 12 up into any factors, then keep splitting up the factors until we can't anymore.

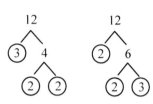

- ➤ We know 3 × 4 = 12, so 3 and 4 are factors of 12.

- ➤ 3 is prime, so it can't go any further.

- ➤ 4 is not prime, so we can break it up into 2 and 2.

- ➤ 2 is prime, so it can't go any further.

- ➤ So the prime factors of 12 are **3, 2, and 2**. (Because we found two 2's, we list both of them in our list of prime factors.)

If we had started with a different pair of factors—say, 2 and 6—we'd still get the same set of prime factors. All the factors of 12 can be produced by multiplying the prime factors together:

Factor	2	3	4	6	12
Prime factors	2	3	2 × 2	2 × 3	2 × 2 × 3

The branching diagram shown here makes it easy to find the prime factors of any integer. Split up the number into any factors. If one of the factors is prime, circle it. Otherwise, keep factoring. It helps to start with a small prime numbers on the left, so you only have to expand the tree on the right branch. The diagram to the right shows that the prime factors of 180 are 2, 2, 5, 3, and 3.

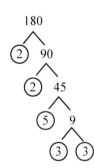

📌 In the number 379.045, what digit is in the units place?

📌 If x is an odd positive integer, which of the following expressions must be *even*?

    I. $2x$

    II. $x + 2$

    III. $3x + 1$

📌 If x has a remainder of 5 when divided by 6 and $x > 10$, what is the smallest possible value of x?

📌 If j is the largest prime factor of 42, and k is the largest prime factor of 36, what is the value of $j + k$?

📌 If x and y are integers such that $xy = -12$ and $x > 0$, what is the greatest possible value of y?

2. Fractions

A fraction is nothing more than one number divided by another. As such, to convert a fraction to a decimal, just divide the numbers. The top number is called the *numerator*; the bottom number is called the *denominator*.

$$\frac{3}{4} = 3 \div 4 = 0.75$$

An *improper fraction* is one in which the numerator is larger than the denominator. A *mixed number* contains a whole number and a fraction.

$$3\frac{1}{4} \text{ (Mixed number)} = \frac{3 \times 4}{4} + \frac{1}{4} = \frac{12}{4} + \frac{1}{4} = \frac{13}{4} \text{ (Improper fraction)}$$

You must know how to add, subtract, multiply and divide fractions.

To **add or subtract** fractions, you must find a *common denominator*. This just means that you can't add or subtract fractions that have different numbers on the bottom.

$$\frac{3}{4} - \frac{2}{3} = \frac{3 \times 3}{3 \times 4} - \frac{4 \times 2}{4 \times 3} = \frac{9}{12} - \frac{8}{12} = \frac{1}{12}$$

To **multiply** fractions, you don't have to do any preparation. Just multiply *straight across*: top × top; bottom × bottom.

$$\frac{2}{9} \times \frac{3}{4} = \frac{(2 \times 3)}{(9 \times 4)} = \frac{6}{36} = \frac{1}{6}$$

Notice that our answer could be reduced because the top and bottom had a common factor. We could also have taken out the common factors before we multiplied:

$$\frac{\overset{1}{\cancel{2}}}{9} \times \frac{3}{\underset{2}{\cancel{4}}} = \frac{1}{\underset{3}{\cancel{9}}} \times \frac{\overset{1}{\cancel{3}}}{2} = \frac{1}{3} \times \frac{1}{2} = \frac{1}{(3 \times 2)} = \frac{1}{6}$$

To **divide** fractions, you must take the *reciprocal* of the second fraction, and then multiply. "Reciprocal" just means to flip the fraction over.

$$\frac{3}{10} \div \frac{2}{5} = \frac{3}{\underset{2}{\cancel{10}}} \times \frac{\overset{1}{\cancel{5}}}{2} = \frac{3}{2} \times \frac{1}{2} = \frac{3}{4}$$

A *compound fraction* is one in which the numerator and/or denominator contain fractions. This is equivalent to dividing fractions. Remember: fractions just mean "divide".

$$\frac{\frac{1}{3}}{\frac{1}{2}} = \frac{1}{3} \div \frac{1}{2} = \frac{1}{3} \times \frac{2}{1} = \frac{2}{3}$$

Manipulating fractions is a lost art. With the advent of calculators, a lot of problems that used to require knowledge of fractions can now be done quickly with decimals, since fractions can be easily converted to decimals on your calculator.

That's fine. We're all for doing problems quickly. But don't forget about fractions. Often, using fractions effectively can actually make a problem *faster* than typing the problem out on your calculator.

- First of all, some fractions become repeating decimals, so the calculator will give *approximate* answers—this can be deadly if you have a long computation.

- Secondly, you must be careful of parentheses. If you try to do $(1/3) \div (1/2)$ by typing in "$1 \div 3 \div 1 \div 2$", you'll get it wrong. You must type "$(1 \div 3) \div (1 \div 2)$". [*]

- Third, using fractions is often easier than it seems because you can often cancel out common factors, thus turning hard math into easy math.

- Finally, you may see some algebra problems with fractions composed of variables. You won't be able to do those on your calculator, so you'd better know how to deal with fractions.

TRY SOME:

- $\dfrac{5}{4} + \dfrac{10}{3} = ?$

- $\dfrac{1}{3} + \dfrac{5}{6} = ?$

- $2\dfrac{2}{5} - \dfrac{1}{2} = ?$

- $\left(\dfrac{28}{15}\right)\left(\dfrac{3}{7}\right) = ?$

- $\dfrac{\dfrac{9}{4}}{\dfrac{3}{10}} = ?$

---

[*] Fun fact: the technical name for a division symbol ($\div$) is an *obelus*.

3. Ratios

A ratio is just a relationship between two or more quantities. Ratios are usually expressed as fractions, but there are many ways of describing them. All of the following mean the same thing:

The ratio of boys to girls is 2:3.

The ratio of boys to girls is 2 to 3.

The ratio of boys to girls is $\dfrac{2}{3}$.

There are two boys for every three girls.

Take a look at this problem:

> ☛ **A recipe calls for 3 cups of sugar for every 7 cups of flour. If Bill uses 28 cups of flour, how many cups of sugar should he use?**

You can set this up as two fractions equal to each other, then solve the equation by cross-multiplying the terms across the equals sign.[*]

$$\frac{x \text{ sugar}}{28 \text{ flour}} = \frac{3 \text{ sugar}}{7 \text{ flour}}$$

$$\frac{x \text{ sugar}}{28 \text{ flour}} \diagdown \frac{3 \text{ sugar}}{7 \text{ flour}}$$

$$7x = 28 \times 3$$

$$7x = 84$$

$$x = 12$$

The only tricky thing about ratios is that you must make sure your *units match*.

> ☛ **A certain park contains only maple and elm trees in a ratio of 2 to 3, respectively. If there are a total of 40 trees, how many maple trees are there in the park?**

The temptation is to set up the ratio like this:

✗ $\qquad \dfrac{x \text{ maple}}{40 \text{ total trees}} = \dfrac{2 \text{ maple}}{3 \text{ elm}}$

But look: the units in the denominators don't match. The right ratio is "maple" to "elm" but the left ratio is "maple" to "total trees". That's bad.

Luckily, we can fix the right ratio rather easily—just add. If there are 2 maple trees and 3 elm trees, then there are 5 total trees. So there are 2 maple trees for every 5 total trees.

✓ $\qquad \dfrac{x \text{ maple}}{40 \text{ total trees}} = \dfrac{2 \text{ maple}}{5 \text{ total trees}}$

> To avoid mismatching units, always **write the fraction with the quantity you're looking for FIRST.** Then set up a second fraction with matching units.

Now we can cross-multiply:

$$5x = 2 \times 40$$

$$5x = 80$$

$$x = 16$$

---

[*] Another way to solve equations like this is to look across the equals sign. Notice that 28 is *four times* 7, therefore x will be *four times* 3. Which is 12. This doesn't always work easily, but when it does it can save you some time.

Once again, circling the end of the question will help you on ratio problems. Here, the question is "If there are a *total* of 40 trees, how many *maple* trees are there in the park?" That tells us the ratio we're looking for is "maple" to "total trees", so we should set up our fractions using those units.

Direct and Inverse Proportions

Ratios like the ones above are called "direct proportions". That means that *x* **divided by** *y* always comes out to the same number, so we can set two fractions equal to each other, like in the problems we just did.

$$\textbf{\textit{Direct Proportion}} \qquad \frac{x}{y} = c \qquad \frac{x_1}{y_1} = \frac{x_2}{y_2}$$

In a direct proportion, the variables go in the **same direction**: as the value of *x* goes up, the value of *y* also goes up.[*] For example, consider the direct proportion $\frac{x}{y} = \frac{1}{2}$:

x	y	x/y = 0.5
1	2	$1 \div 2 = 0.5$
2	4	$2 \div 4 = 0.5$
3	6	$3 \div 6 = 0.5$

As *x* increases (1, 2, 3, …),

y also increases (2, 4, 6, …)

On the other hand, you may also encounter "inverse proportions". That means that *x* **times** *y* always comes out to the same number, so we can set two *products* equal to each other.

$$\textbf{\textit{Inverse Proportion}} \qquad xy = c \qquad x_1 y_1 = x_2 y_2$$

In an inverse proportion, the variables go in **opposite directions**: as the value of *x* goes up, the value of *y* goes *down*. For example, consider the inverse proportion $xy = 12$.

x	y	xy = 12
1	12	$1 \times 12 = 12$
2	6	$2 \times 6 = 12$
3	4	$3 \times 4 = 12$

As *x* increases (1, 2, 3, …),

y decreases (12, 6, 4, …)

---

[*] Legal disclaimer: it's actually the *absolute value* of the variables that go in the same direction. If the fraction equals to a negative constant, the values go in opposite directions. But you'll never see that on the SAT, so don't worry.

✍ Bob makes some fruit punch that contains apple juice and mango juice in a 1:5 ratio. If he uses 15 pints of the mango juice, how many pints of apple juice will he need?

✍ An animal shelter has 2 cats for every 3 dogs. If there are 45 animals in the shelter, how many dogs are there?

✍ At a certain school, the ratio of boys to girls in the seventh grade is 3 to 5. If there are 56 total seventh-graders, how many of them are girls?

✍ Two numbers x and y are in a direct proportion such that when $x = 2$, $y = 9$. What is the value of y when $x = 7$?

4. Percents

By now, we should all at least be familiar with percents. The simplest way to do percents is by pure division.

➤ **8 is what percent of 32?**

All you do is divide, then multiply by 100:

$$\frac{8}{32} = 0.25 \qquad\qquad 0.25 \times 100 = \textbf{25\%}$$

Do you want to know a secret? Percents are really nothing more than glorified ratios. Percent literally means "out of one hundred". So you're just converting a ratio into another ratio out of 100. This problem is the same thing as cross-multiplying:

$$\frac{8}{32} = \frac{x}{100}$$

"8 out of 32" is the same thing as "25 out of one hundred", or 25 "percent".

Of course, percent problems on the SAT are more complicated than that. Because of the nature of some of these problems, we've devised the following table for percent problems:

Read	Write
what	n
is	$=$
percent	$\overline{100}$
of	$\times$ (multiply)

Whenever you see one of the words in the left column, write the corresponding symbol in the right column. If you see a number, just write the number. For example:

➤ **12 is 40% of what number?**

becomes $\quad 12 = \dfrac{40}{100} \times n$

You know, a lot of students freak out about word problems. But really, the language we use to describe problems is really the same stuff as all the signs and symbols we use in equations. So as long as you can speak English, you can write equations; the words mean exactly what you think they mean.

The advantage of using the table is that it makes percent problems automatic and robotic. You can go directly from words to an equation without thinking about anything.

There are other similar ways of doing percent problems (some of you may know the "is-over-of" method), but this table is particularly effective on harder SAT problems. Take a look at this problem:

➤ **If 25 percent of 12 percent of s is 18, s = ?**

This can be really nasty with other ways of doing percents. But with the table, we don't care. Do it robotically; when you see a word, write its symbol. So this question becomes:

$$\frac{25}{100} \times \frac{12}{100} \times s = 18$$

Now we have a one-variable equation and we can solve for *s*. We didn't have to think about a darn thing. The equation came almost instantly.

Here's another toughie:

➤ **If x is $\frac{1}{2}$ percent of 600, $x = ?$**

Oh, well half of 600 is 300. Right?

WRONG! It doesn't say x is <u>half</u> of 600; it says x is <u>one-half percent</u> of 600. That is, half of one percent. RTFQ!

With the table, we don't make this mistake because we just write what we see:

$$x = \frac{\frac{1}{2}}{100} \times 600$$

Because we aren't *thinking* about the problem—we're just automatically writing down what we read—we're much less likely to make the RTFQ.

Percent Increase and Decrease

A percent increase or decrease just means:

> **The amount of the *change* is what percent of the *original* amount?**

Or:

$$\text{Percent Change} = \frac{\text{Change}}{\text{Original}} \times 100$$

➤ **Joe made 150 dollars last week and 180 dollars this week. What was the percent increase in his pay?**

In this problem, the amount of the change is **30** (that's $180 - 150$) and the original amount is **150**. So the question is "30 is what percent of 150?" Now we can just use the table to set up an equation:

$$30 = \frac{n}{100} \times 150$$

You can also think of percent change as just the *change* divided by the *original*.

$$\frac{30}{150} = \frac{1}{5} = 0.2 = \frac{20}{100} = \textbf{20\%}$$

TRY SOME:

➤ What is 42% of 50?

➤ 18 is what percent of 200?

➤ 5 is what percent of 4?

➤ 21 is 35% of what number?

➤ What is 15% of 75% of 80?

➤ A school had 30 reported absences one week
and 27 reported absences the following week.
What was the percent decrease in the number
of absences between the two weeks?

5. Exponents

Exponents tell you how many times to multiply a number or term by itself. The number that is being multiplied is called the "base".

$$base \rightarrow 4^2 \leftarrow exponent$$

There are a few rules for dealing with exponential numbers that you should know:

1. To multiply exponential numbers with the same base, add the exponents.

$$2^5 \times 2^3 = 2^{5+3} = 2^8$$

2. To divide exponential numbers with the same base, subtract the exponents.

$$\frac{2^5}{2^3} = 2^{5-3} = 2^2$$

3. To raise an exponential number to another exponent, multiply the exponents.

$$\left(2^5\right)^3 = 2^{5 \times 3} = 2^{15}$$

WARNING: You can add variables with the same exponent, but you **cannot** add bases with different exponents:

OK: $2x^2 + 7x^2 = 9x^2$ NOT OK: $2^5 + 2^3 \neq 2^8$

WARNING: All these rules only apply to exponential numbers *with the same base*. If you're given exponential numbers in different bases, try to get them in the same base.

There are some other weird properties of exponents that may show up on some of the harder problems.

- Any number to the zero power equals one.

$$x^0 = 1$$

- A fractional exponent is the same as a root.

$$x^{\frac{1}{2}} = \sqrt{x}$$

- A negative exponent is the same as 1 over the base with a positive exponent.

$$x^{-3} = \frac{1}{x^3}$$

If you have trouble remembering these rules, don't sweat it. When you do see something like, say, a fractional exponent on a problem, you usually don't actually have to know what that means. For example:

- $\left(3^4\right)^{\frac{1}{2}} = ?$

You don't actually have to know that taking a number to the ½ power means the same thing as taking the square root. Just treat the fraction like any other number and use rule number 3 above:

$$\left(3^4\right)^{\frac{1}{2}} = 3^{4 \times \frac{1}{2}} = 3^2 = 9$$

➤ $a^5 \left(a^3\right)^2 = ?$

➤ $\dfrac{x^4 x^3}{x^5} = ?$

➤ $9^{-\frac{1}{2}} = ?$

➤ **If** $8^{13} = 2^x$ **, then** $x = ?$

➤ $\dfrac{15^{100} - 15^{99}}{15^{99}} = ?$

6. Averages

There are three types of calculations that concern us here:

Arithmetic Mean

This is what we mean when we say **average**. Find the average by taking the **sum of the numbers** divided by the **number of terms**.

> ✐ **What is the average (arithmetic mean) of 2, 4, 7, 9 and 18?**

The sum is $2 + 4 + 7 + 9 + 18 = 40$. The average is $40/5 = $ **8**.

Median

The median is the **middle** number, <u>when you put the terms in order</u>.[*]

> ✐ **What is the median of 7, 18, 4, 9 and 2?**

You must put the terms in numerical order before finding the median.

Write them in order, you get 2, 4, 7, 9, 18. The one in the middle is 7, so the median is **7**.

If there are an *even* number of terms, such that there is no one number in the middle, the median is **the average of the two middle numbers**.

> ✐ **What is the median of 9, 2, 7, 8, 4 and 18?**

Write them in order and you get 2, 4, 7, 8, 9, 18. The two middle numbers are 7 and 8, so the median is **7.5**.

Mode

The mode is the number that occurs **most frequently**.

> ✐ **What is the mode of 5, 2, 7, 2 and 9?**

Each number occurs once, except for 2, which occurs twice. So the mode is **2**.

Using the Sum

Let's take a closer look at arithmetic mean (which we'll just call "average"). We all know pretty well how to take the average of a list of numbers they give us. *If you're given a list of numbers*, just add them all up and divide by how many there are. As we already saw:

> ✐ **What is the average (arithmetic mean) of 2, 4, 7, 9 and 18?**

The sum is $2 + 4 + 7 + 9 + 18 = 40$. There are 5 terms. So the average is $40/5 = $ **8**.

But often on SAT questions *we don't know what the individual numbers are*. Let's look at one:

> ✐ **The average of 5 numbers is 15. If the average of 3 of those numbers is 19, what is the average of the other two numbers?**

It looks like we don't have enough information. Since we don't know the terms, we can't add them up. What do we do??

Ah, we know more than we think. Let's look again at the definition of average:

$$\text{Average} = \frac{\text{Sum of terms}}{\text{How many terms}}$$

If we multiply both sides of this equation by the number of terms, we get:

(How many terms) × (Average) = Sum of the terms

---

[*] Note that the value of the median doesn't change if you make the highest term higher or the lowest term lower. For example, if we changed the sequence above to 2, 4, 7, 9, 157, the median would still be 7.

This equation is very important. Even if we don't know the *individual* numbers, we can still work directly with their sum. In our problem, we know we have 5 numbers that have an average of 15, so their sum *must* be 5 × 15 = 75. Regardless of what the individual numbers are, they must have a sum of 75.

We can fill out a chart to help us organize this information:

How many terms	Average	Sum of terms	
5	15	75	5 numbers with an average of 15, so their sum is 5(15) = 75
– 3	19	– 57	3 numbers with an average of 19, so their sum is 3(19) = 57
2		**18**	There are **2** numbers we don't know, so their sum must be **18**.

First, we multiplied across each row. The number of terms times the average gives you the sum of the terms.

Then, as we can see in the first column, we should subtract to find the two remaining terms. Since we subtracted in the first column, we'll subtract the sums as well. (Don't try to subtract the average column; just focus on the sum.)

Once we know that those two numbers have a sum of 18, we can find the average:

$$\text{Average} = \frac{\text{Sum of terms}}{\text{How many terms}} = \frac{18}{2} = 9$$

This type of question is very common on the SAT, and this chart is incredibly useful. But again, you only need to use it when you don't know the individual terms involved. If you're given a list of numbers, just add them up and divide by how many there are.

$$\{ 4, 6, 9, 17, 24 \}$$

➤ What is the average (arithmetic mean) of the numbers in the set above?

➤ A set contains 3 consecutive integers that have a sum of 78. What is the median of the set?

➤ The 12 trees in John's backyard have an average height of 135 inches. If 7 of the trees have an average height of 100 inches, what is the average height of the other 5 trees?

➤ In a certain class, a student's final grade is determined by taking the average of his or her scores on six tests, each of which is scored on a scale from 0 to 100. If Bob got an average score of 85 on his first 4 tests, what is the highest possible final grade he can get in the class?

II. ALGEBRA

1. Basic Manipulation

The main goal of simple algebra is to get the variable by itself. You can do this by doing the opposite of any function you see:

> ✐ **If $3x + 5 = 23$, $x = ?$**

$$3x + 5 - 5 = 23 - 5 \qquad \text{Subtract 5 from each side}$$

$$3x = 18$$

$$\frac{3x}{3} = \frac{18}{3} \qquad \text{Divide both sides by 3}$$

$$\boxed{x = 6}$$

This, my friend, is all that algebra is.[*] To get x by itself, just do the opposite to both sides. We'll see more complicated concepts, of course, but at heart, this is pretty much it.

Not every algebra problem will just deal with numbers. Observe:

> ✐ **$y = 5x + 3$. What is x in terms of y?**

The phrase "x in terms of y" just means that we want to get x by itself on one side of the equation and nothing but y's and numbers on the other side. We do this exactly the same way we did the last problem:

$$y = 5x + 3$$

$$y - 3 = 5x + 3 - 3$$

$$y - 3 = 5x$$

$$\frac{y - 3}{5} = \frac{5x}{5}$$

$$\boxed{\frac{y - 3}{5} = x}$$

TRY SOME:

> ✐ **If $4 + (a - 4) = 9$, $a = ?$**

> ✐ **If $\dfrac{5x + 6}{6} = 11$, $x = ?$**

> ✐ **If $x = 5$ and $y = 4$, what is the value of $3x - 4y$?**

---

[*] Why is x always the first variable we use? There are several theories, but this is my favorite. This notation started in 1637 with the French mathematician and philosopher René Descartes in his book *La Géométrie*. Originally, he wanted to use z as the first variable, y as the second, x as the third, etc. But when the book went to be published, the publisher didn't have enough z's (back then, books were printed using individual blocks of metal for each letter). He had plenty of x's though—very few French words use x. So we use x as our variables because the French language uses too many z's.

2. FOIL

Take a look at this:

➢ $(x + 5)(x + 4) = ?$

Each of the terms in parentheses is called a *binomial*, an expression that has a variable plus or minus a number. To multiply binomials, remember the acronym "FOIL". Multiply:

First two terms	$x \times x$
Outside terms	$x \times 4$
Inside terms	$5 \times x$
Last terms	5×4

Then add all the terms together.

$$= x^2 + 4x + 5x + 20$$
$$= x^2 + 9x + 20$$

TRY SOME:

➢ $(a - 7)(a - 2) = ?$

➢ $(2y + 3)(y - 4) = ?$

3. Solving Directly for Expressions

Take a look at this problem:

➢ If $4x - 3y = 13$ and $x + 2y = 3$, then $5x - y = ?$

There are some *very painful* ways to do this with normal algebra. You could try to solve one equation for x, then substitute your answer in for x in the other equation, solve for y, then put y back into the first equation and solve for x, then stick x and y into the expression they're asking for and you're done:

1. Solve Equation 2 for x (that is, get x in terms of y).

   $x + 2y = 3$

   $x = 3 - 2y$

2. Substitute that expression into Equation 1 and solve for y.

   $4x - 3y = 13$

   $4(3 - 2y) - 3y = 13$

   $12 - 8y - 3y = 13$

   $12 - 11y = 13$

   $-11y = 1$

   $$\boxed{y = -\frac{1}{11}}$$

3. Substitute y into Equation 2 and solve for x.

   $$x = 3 - 2\left(-\frac{1}{11}\right)$$

   $$x = 3 + \frac{2}{11} = \frac{33 + 2}{11}$$

   $$\boxed{x = \frac{35}{11}}$$

4. Substitute x and y into the expression they are asking for.

   $$5x - y = 5\left(\frac{35}{11}\right) - \left(-\frac{1}{11}\right) = \frac{175}{11} + \frac{1}{11} = \frac{176}{11}$$

   $$\boxed{5x - y = 16}$$

Ugh. I mean, we could do it, but that wasn't fun. No one wants that.

Wait a minute—take another look at this question.

> ✎ If $4x - 3y = 13$ and $x + 2y = 3$, then $5x - y = ?$

They're <u>not</u> asking you for x or y individually; they're asking for an *expression*: $5x - y$. So instead of solving for x or y, let's try to solve directly for $5x - y$.

To make it easier, let's write the equations on top of each other so the x and y values line up:

$$
\begin{array}{r}
4x - 3y = 13 \\
+\quad x + 2y = 3 \\
\hline
5x - y = 16
\end{array}
$$

Aha! If we **add** the equations, we get $5x - y$! That's what we're looking for. It's just $13 + 3$! It's 16!

Wait, what about x? How do we find x? Forget x! They're not asking me for it, so I don't care.

Any time they ask you for an *expression*, don't solve for individual variables; try to solve directly for the expression. Try adding equations, multiplying by two, whatever it takes. Try to play with what they give you until it looks like what they're asking for. Why do you think they're asking for *that* expression, anyway? Why specifically $5x - y$? They didn't come up with that randomly; they're asking you for that *because* that's what you get when you add the equations.

Once again, this is another reason circling the question will help you. If you see they're asking you for an *expression*, don't worry about the individual variables; try to solve directly for the expression.

| TRY SOME: |

> ✎ If $3p + 2q = 8$ and $4p + 3q = 11$, then $7p + 5q =$

> ✎ If $4a + b = 13$ and $a + 3b = 22$, then $\dfrac{5a + 4b}{5} =$

> ✎ If $2x + y = 23$ and $x + 2y = 17$, then $3x - 3y =$

> ✎ If $xy = 11$ and $x + y = 7$, then $x^2 y + xy^2 =$

4. Some Identities

Take a look at this:

> ✍ **If $x + y = 5$ and $x - y = 7$, then $x^2 - y^2 = ?$**

Yeesh. Well, we could try some experimental Plug In here; we could try to come up with some numbers that work in both the first two equations, and then stick them in the big nasty guy that they're asking for.

But let's hold off on that. Notice that they're asking for an *expression* here—not x or y—so let's try to get that expression directly. Well, adding or subtracting won't get it—we need to get some squares in there. Let's try *multiplying* the first two equations instead.

$$(x + y)(x - y) = x^2 - xy + xy - y^2 = x^2 - y^2$$

What the—? That's what we're looking for! So that means

$$(x + y)(x - y) = x^2 - y^2$$

$$(5)(7) = \mathbf{35}$$

This equation is called an *identity*. That just means it's an equation that shows up a lot that's always true for any variables. If we have any two parts of the identity, we can easily solve for the third.

Here's another:

> ✍ **If $x^2 + y^2 = 29$ and $xy = 10$, then $(x + y)^2 = ?$**

Again, let's solve for the expression. Rather than playing with the stuff they've given us, let's work backwards and FOIL out: $(x + y)^2$

$$(x + y)^2 = (x + y)(x + y) = x^2 + xy + yx + y^2 = x^2 + y^2 + 2xy$$

Once again, we can just combine the stuff we have to get what we want.

$$(x + y)^2 = x^2 + y^2 + 2xy$$

$$(x + y)^2 = 29 + 2(10)$$

$$= 29 + 20$$

$$\boxed{= 49}$$

These identities won't show up a whole lot, and would only appear on the harder questions. However, they are handy to know and can help you get out of some jams.

IDENTITIES
$(x + y)(x - y) = x^2 - y^2$
$(x + y)^2 = x^2 + 2xy + y^2$

5. Inequalities

Inequalities work just like equations for the most part. You can solve for variables just like you do with equations. The only difference is that **if you multiply or divide by a negative number, you have to flip the inequality**.

Permit us to demonstrate:

$$7 - 3x > 16$$

$$7 - 3x - 7 > 16 - 7$$

$$-3x > 9$$

$$\frac{-3x}{-3} < \frac{9}{-3} \qquad \leftarrow \text{Watch out here. This is where the sign flips.}$$

$$\boxed{x < -3}$$

TRY ONE:

✎ **If $7 - 4x \leq 35$, which of the following could NOT be the value of x?**

(A)   −9

(B)   −7

(C)   0

(D)   2

(E)   7

1. Which of the following numbers has the digit 4 in the thousandths place?

   (A) 0.004
   (B) 0.040
   (C) 0.400
   (D) 4.0
   (E) 40.0

2. What is the value of $\frac{1}{2} \times \frac{2}{3} \times \frac{3}{4} \times \frac{4}{5}$?

   (A) $\frac{1}{5}$

   (B) $\frac{5}{6}$

   (C) $\frac{4}{5}$

   (D) 1

   (E) $\frac{51}{30}$

3. If $3x - 5 = 5x + 3$, then $x =$

   (A) 4
   (B) 1
   (C) −1
   (D) −4
   (E) −8

$$\frac{x}{30}, \frac{x}{22}, \frac{x}{15}$$

4. If each of the above fractions is in its most reduced form, which of the following could be x?

   (A) 3
   (B) 4
   (C) 5
   (D) 6
   (E) 7

5. Which of the following is equivalent to $(x - a)(x + b)$?

   (A) $x^2 - (b - a)x - ab$

   (B) $x^2 + (b - a)x - ab$

   (C) $x^2 + (a - b)x + ab$

   (D) $x^2 + (a + b)x - ab$

   (E) $x^2 + (a + b)x + ab$

6. If as many 5-inch strips of ribbon as possible are cut from a ribbon that is 4 feet long, what is the total length of the ribbon that is left over? (12 inches = 1 foot)

   (A) 1 inch
   (B) 2 inches
   (C) 3 inches
   (D) 4 inches
   (E) 5 inches

7. If $9x - 15 < 2x + 6$, which of the following must be true?

    (A) $x > 3$
    (B) $x > 0$
    (C) $x < 0$
    (D) $x < 3$
    (E) $x < 9$

8. If $(x + 4)(x - 4) = 9$, then $(2x + 8)(2x - 8) =$

    (A) 5
    (B) 9
    (C) 18
    (D) 25
    (E) 36

9. If $5^{2x+1} = 125$, what is the value of x?

    (A) 1
    (B) 2
    (C) 3
    (D) 4
    (E) 5

10. If a is directly proportional to b and if $a = 30$ when $b = 21$, what is the value of a when $b = 10\frac{1}{2}$?

    (A) $\dfrac{20}{3}$
    (B) $\dfrac{147}{20}$
    (C) 10
    (D) 15
    (E) 30

11. What number is 175 percent of 16?

    (A) 12
    (B) 20
    (C) 24
    (D) 28
    (E) 32

12. If $a = b^2 c^3$ and $c = j^2 k^5$, which of the following is a correct expression for a in terms of b, j, and k?

(A) $b^2 j^2 k^8$

(B) $b^2 j^2 k^{15}$

(C) $b^2 j^5 k^8$

(D) $b^2 j^5 k^{15}$

(E) $b^2 j^6 k^{15}$

13. Loretta had 60 roses and 80 daffodils. If she sold 40% of her roses and 75% of her daffodils, what percent of her flowers remain?

(A) 40%
(B) 50%
(C) 56%
(D) 60%
(E) 80%

14. The average of three numbers is 10. The average of just two of them is 6. What is the third number?

(A) 2
(B) 6
(C) 10
(D) 18
(E) 20

15. A multi-colored candy is sold in a ratio of 7:3:2 of blue, red, and brown candies, respectively. How many pounds of red candies will be found in a 4-pound bag of this multi-colored candy?

(A) $\dfrac{1}{2}$

(B) $\dfrac{2}{3}$

(C) 1

(D) 2

(E) 3

16. If $x^2 - y^2 = 36$, and $x + y = 9$, what is the value of $x - y$?

(A) 4
(B) 6
(C) 9
(D) 12
(E) 18

17. The average (arithmetic mean) of a, b, c, d, e, f, and g is 50. If the average of a, b and c is 30, what is the average of d, e, f, and g?

(A) 40
(B) 44
(C) 55
(D) 65
(E) 70

19. There are 15 consecutive numbers in a list. Which of the following operations would change the value of the median?

(A) Decreasing the smallest number by 5
(B) Decreasing the largest number by 5
(C) Increasing the smallest number by 7
(D) Increasing the smallest number by 8
(E) Increasing the largest number by 8

$$x + y = 5$$
$$y + z = 11$$
$$x + z = 8$$

18. Based on the system of equations above, what is the average of x, y, and z?

(A) 4
(B) 5
(C) 8
(D) 11
(E) 12

20. A certain car cost c dollars in August. In September, the price was cut by 20 percent. In October, the price increased by 40 percent of the previous month's price. The price of the car at the end of October was what percent of the price in August?

(A) 48%
(B) 80%
(C) 100%
(D) 112%
(E) 120%

GEOMETRY

Geometry is a love-it-or-hate-it world. Some students can't get enough of it. Some students freeze up and wet themselves at the very thought of it. You're going to have to do some geometry on the SAT. Whether this is good news or bad news is up to you.

Geometry was one of the first segments of math to be really studied in depth, starting with the ancient Greek mathematicians like Euclid. In fact, Euclid actually used geometry for *all* math, even stuff that today we use algebra for, like solving quadratic equations. We won't bore you with the history of Greek geometry, but it is worth mentioning *the way* Euclid went about his work. He started with a few simple rules and used them to prove everything else.

Similarly, we're going to show you a few simple rules and not much else. Now, if you've had a rigorous geometry class in school, you probably had to learn a lot of theorems—little rules about angles and lengths and relationships between all sorts of weird things. On the SAT, you don't need all those rules. All you need is the stuff in this chapter and *only* the stuff in this chapter. Any other theorems or rules that you may have heard about are only true *because of* the stuff in this chapter. For the most part, the basic rules really are all you need. But if you do need a more complicated rule, you can figure it out from the basic rules.

Of course, if you haven't had a rigorous geometry class in school, don't worry. All you need is the stuff in this chapter. Learn it, and you're good to go on every geometry question on the SAT. We promise.

I. INTRODUCTORY REMARKS

A few quick remarks before we get started:

A. Techniques

Don't forget about **Guesstimate**. If you see a question with a picture, *before you do anything else*, check that it's to scale, guess the value they're asking for, and then eliminate any implausible choices.

In this chapter we're going to be talking about a lot of straight math content (rules and formulas). But that doesn't mean you should forget about the techniques. And not just Guesstimate, either. You can use Plug In and Backsolve on geometry problems, too. So stay alert.

B. Not sure of a formula?

We're going to talk about a lot of little rules and formulas throughout this lecture. However, you don't even *really* have to know a lot of them. They **tell you** many of the facts and formulas you'll need. On the first page of every math section, you'll see this:

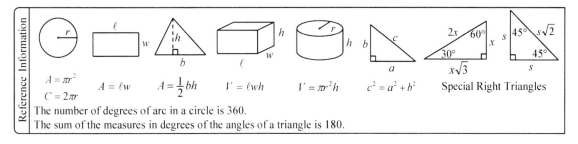

It's astounding how little math you actually have to know on this test.

Obviously, you'll work a lot more quickly if you know all this stuff by heart. But if you're ever unsure of a formula, take a few seconds to check the front. Better safe than sorry.

C. General Strategy for Geometry

While the number of rules you need on the test is relatively small, it may still seem burdensome to you. I mean, how do you know which rule to use on which question? Where do you even begin?

Just like we saw before, there are two questions to ask yourself:

1. What do I *want*? **2. What do I *know*?**

The goal of every geometry problem is to connect these two questions, to play with what you *know* in order to get what you *want*.

Take a look at this problem:

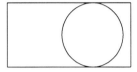

6. **In the figure above, a circle is tangent to two sides of a 12 by 6 rectangle. What is the area of the circle?**

> If a geometry problem doesn't already have a picture, **DRAW A PICTURE!** It doesn't have to be perfect; even a rough sketch can help you understand the problem and catch careless mistakes.

    (A) 3π
    (B) 6π
    (C) 9π
    (D) 12π
    (E) 36π

1. **What do we want?** The area of the circle.

According to the formulas at the beginning of the section, that's $A = \pi r^2$. So to find the area, we'll need the radius of the circle (or the diameter, which is just double the radius).

2. **What do we know?** The length of the rectangle is 12 and the width is 6.

So the real key to this problem is: *how can I use the length or width of the rectangle to find the radius or diameter of the circle?*

Aha! The width of the rectangle is equal to the diameter of the circle! How can I tell? By Guesstimate! Don't worry about the weird "tangent" stuff: they *look* equal.

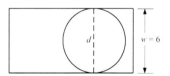

The width of the rectangle is 6, so the diameter of the circle is 6. So the radius is 3, and the area of the circle is 9π, which is (C).[*]

The point here is that *you should never be absolutely stuck on a geometry question.* There's always *something* that you know, something that you can figure out. Don't be scared of the figures, just put down what you know and try to connect it to what you want.

---

[*] Note that we could also use Guesstimate to get the area of the circle directly. The rectangle is 12 by 6, so its area is 72. The circle looks like a bit less than half the rectangle, so its area should be a bit less than 36. All the answers are in terms of π, so we'll multiply the choices by 3.14 (or use the "π" button if your calculator has one) and see which is closest. (D) and (E) are more than 36. (A) is way too small. (B) is 18.84, and (C) is 28.27. (C) is closest. Bam.

II. ANGLES

There are five things you have to know about angles.

1. A straight line equals 180°.

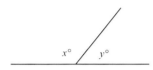

When angles form a straight line, the sum of their measures is 180°. In this diagram, $x + y = 180$.

2. A triangle equals 180°.

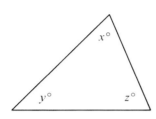

The three angles of a triangle add up to 180°. In this diagram, $x + y + z = 180$.

Here's an example of using one rule to figure out another: An *equilateral triangle* has three equal sides and three equal angles. If all angles are equal, and they add up to 180°, each angle of an equilateral triangle is $180 \div 3 = 60°$.

So we have a new rule: every equilateral triangle has three 60° angles.

3. An isosceles triangle has two equal sides and two equal angles.

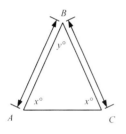

An *isosceles triangle* is one in which two of the sides are equal in length. The angles opposite the equal sides will also be equal to each other. (Similarly, an *isosceles trapezoid* has two pairs of equal angles.)

In this triangle, since we know that $\angle BAC = \angle ACB$ (both are x) we know $AB = BC$. Conversely, if we know that the sides AB and AC are equal, we can assume that the angles are equal.

4. Vertical Angles are equal.

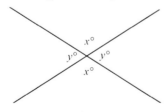

When two straight lines cross, four angles are formed. The angles that are directly across from each other are called "vertical angles" and they are equal to each other.

In this diagram, the angles marked "x" are equal to each other, and the angles marked "y" are equal to each other.

5. Parallel lines with a transversal produce a bunch of equal angles.

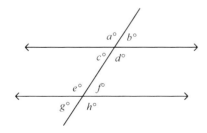

When a third line (a "transversal") cuts through two parallel lines, eight angles are formed. The four at the top are collectively the same as the four at the bottom. Basically, we've got two types of angles: big ones and little ones. All the big ones are equal, and all the little ones are equal. Any big one plus any little one is 180°.

Here, $a = d = e = h$ and $b = c = f = g$. Any of the big ones (a, d, e, h) plus any of the little ones (b, c, f, g) equals 180°.

Note that this is *only* true for parallel lines. If we know that the lines above are *not* parallel, then we know that these rules are not true (e.g., $c \neq f$).

This one's a little bit more complicated than the other four, but it's a great demonstration of what we were saying before about knowing the basic rules. If we just look at the top four angles, we know that $a = d$ and

$b = c$ because of rule #4: vertical angles are equal. Similarly, we know that $a + c = 180$ because of rule #1: a straight line equals 180. The only new information we're adding here is that because the lines are parallel, $c = f$. Everything else we can say here is simply a logical conclusion of the rules we already know. So once you know the small rules, you can figure out the larger rules.

Of course, there are other rules that exist about angles, but they're only true *because of* these rules. For example, take a look at this problem:

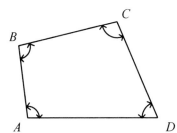

➤ **What is the sum of the marked angles in quadrilateral *ABCD* show to the left?**

What? They don't tell us anything about this thing! Whatever shall we do?[*]

Fear not. We didn't learn any rules about angles of quadrilaterals. But we *do* know that a triangle has 180°. Let's split this guy up into triangles!

The quadrilateral is made up of two triangles. Each triangle has 180°. So the quadrilateral has 2 × 180 or **360°**. That's it. We're done!

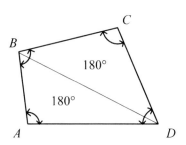

Some of you may have already known that the angles of any quadrilateral add up to 360°. But we can do this with any shape. Draw triangles using only the shape's existing vertices. We can see that a pentagon contains 3 triangles, so its angles add up to 3 × 180 = 540°. And a hexagon contains 4 triangles, so its angles add up to 4 × 180 = 720°. [†]

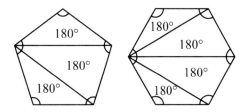

Our point is not to get you to memorize the number of angles in every polygon. the point is that you don't have to memorize a bunch of rules like that. Just know these five, and you can figure out anything else you need to know about angles.

You should never be totally stuck on a problem that deals with angles, because there's always *something* you know. More often than not, just putting down what you know based on these rules will lead you to what you're trying to find—even if you don't see where you're going with it. "Okay, I really don't know how to find what they want, but I know that's a triangle, so its angles add up to 180. And I know that's a straight line, so those angles add up to 180..." Et cetera. Just play with these rules and see where it takes you.

And remember: **when in doubt, draw triangles**.

---

[*] If we had answer choices, this would be a great Guesstimate problem.

[†] If you're interested here's the formula: the angles a polygon with *n* sides will add up to $(n - 2)180$ degrees. That's because $n - 2$ is the number of triangles you can draw in the shape. When drawing triangles, remember to only connect points in the polygon—don't use the center of the shape as a triangle's vertex.

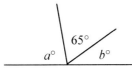

5. In the figure above, what is the value of
a + b?

(A)   25
(B)   115
(C)   125
(D)   295
(E)   305

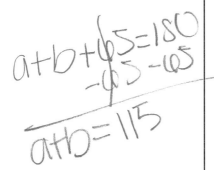

$a + b + 65 = 180$
$-65 \quad -65$

$a + b = 115$

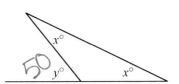

6. In the figure above, if y = 50, then x =

(A)   20
(B)   25
(C)   30
(D)   50
(E)   65

$2x = 50$

$x + x = y$

$x + x = 50$

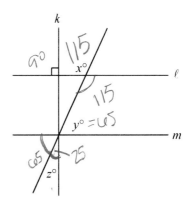

10. In the figure above, line *k* is perpendicular to
line ℓ and lines ℓ and *m* are parallel. If *x* =
115, what is the value of *y* – *z*?

(A)   25
(B)   40
(C)   65
(D)   90
(E)   115

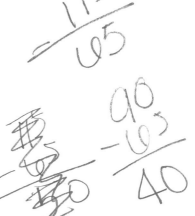

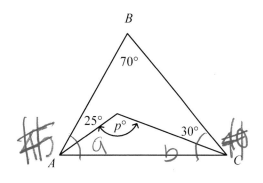

15. In the figure above, $p =$

(A) 110
(B) 115
(C) 120
(D) 125
(E) 130

D

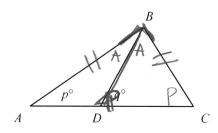

Note: Figure not drawn to scale

20. In $\triangle ABC$ above, $AB = BC$ and $\overline{BD}$ bisects $\angle ABC$. If $q = 4p$, what is the measure of $\angle ABC$?

(A) 22.5°
(B) 45°
(C) 70°
(D) 90°
(E) 135°

E

O

Handwritten work (left):

$-\dfrac{\begin{array}{r}70\\80\end{array}}{40}$

$70 + 25 + 30 + a + b = 180$

$125 + a + b = 180$
$-125 \qquad -125$

$a + b = 55$

$\begin{array}{r}17\,\cancel{8}\cancel{0}10\\ -55\\\hline 125\end{array}$

Handwritten work (right):

$p + 2a + p = 180$

$2p + 2a = 180$

$p + a = 90 \rightarrow p = 90 - a$

$4p + p + a = 180$
$5p + a = 180$

$2a = 135$

$5(90 - a) + a = 180$
$450 - 5a + a = 180$
$450 - 4a = 180$
$+450 \qquad +450$

$-4a = -270$
$\dfrac{-4a}{4} \quad \dfrac{-270}{4} \qquad a = 67.5$

III. TRIANGLES

We already talked a bit about triangles and their angles, but there's still more to be said. Triangles are the key to a lot of SAT questions; you'll see a lot more triangles than any other shape. In fact, if you're confronted with an odd shape you don't understand, try drawing in a triangle. We already saw an example of that in the quadrilateral problem in the last section. We didn't know anything about quadrilaterals, but we know a lot about triangles, so we drew some triangles. Triangles are your best friend. Trust us.

1. The Pythagorean Theorem*

The Pythagorean Theorem is a way to find the third side of **a right triangle**.

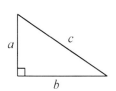

$$a^2 + b^2 = c^2$$

The sum of the squares of the legs of a right triangle is equal to the square of the hypotenuse.

By the way, if you forget the Pythagorean Theorem, look at the front of any math section: *they give it to you.* You don't even have to

> A *right triangle* is a triangle with a right angle (a 90° angle). The side opposite the right angle is called the *hypotenuse*. The two sides next to the right angle are called *legs*.

actually know it! Things will obviously go more swiftly if you know it by heart (and many of you probably do), but even if you're *slightly* unsure about it, check the front. Better safe than sorry.

Try this one:

> ☞ **If a right triangle has legs of length 3 and 4, what is the length of the hypotenuse?**

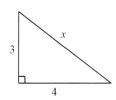

$$3^2 + 4^2 = x^2$$

$$9 + 16 = x^2$$

$$25 = x^2$$

$$\boxed{5 = x}$$

Some of you may have recognized the triangle in the problem above. It's a "Pythagorean Triple". Because the Pythagorean Theorem has all those "squares" in it, most right triangles don't have integer values for all the sides. So the triangles that *do* have all integers show up a lot. The 3-4-5 is the most common.[†] If you see a triangle that has legs of length 3 and 4, you know immediately that the hypotenuse must be 5.

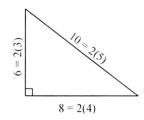

Be on the lookout for multiples of the 3-4-5, as well. For example, a 6-8-10 triangle is just a 3-4-5 triangle with each side multiplied by two.

Being able to spot a 3-4-5 triangle can save you some time. If you see a triangle with legs 6 and 8, you know immediately the hypotenuse is 10, without having to do out the Theorem. But spotting this is really just a bonus; if you can't see the 3-4-5 triangle, don't worry. You can always use the Pythagorean Theorem to find the dimensions of a right triangle.

Warning: Don't be too quick to declare a triangle 3-4-5. The hypotenuse <u>must</u> be the largest side of a triangle. If a triangle has *legs* of 4 and 5, the hypotenuse is *not* 3.

---

[*] The theorem is named for the Greek philosopher Pythagoras and his cult, the Pythagoreans, but the fundamentals of the theorem were known hundreds of years before him by the Babylonians, Indians, and Chinese among others. There is little evidence that he or his followers ever proved the theorem. Why it was named for him, we have no idea. The Pythagoreans did a lot of important work in mathematics, but they also thought eating beans was sinful.

[†] There are other Pythagorean Triples, such as the 5-12-13, 7-24-25, 8-15-17, and more (to say nothing of the multiples of each). Don't worry—those rarely if ever show up on the SAT. 3-4-5 is plenty.

2. The Isosceles Right Triangle (45-45-90)

An *isosceles* right triangle has two legs of equal length, and two 45° angles.[*] The dimensions of these triangles are always in the same proportion:

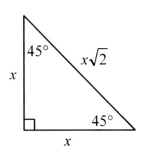

$$a^2 + b^2 = c^2$$

$$x^2 + x^2 = c^2$$

$$2x^2 = c^2$$

$$\sqrt{2x^2} = \sqrt{c^2}$$

$$\left(\sqrt{2}\right)x = c$$

This means that if you know the length of a leg of the triangle, you can immediately find the hypotenuse— it's just the leg multiplied by $\sqrt{2}$.

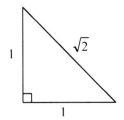 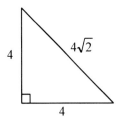 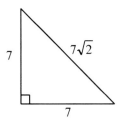 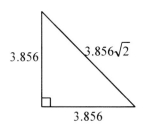

Notice that we know all of these triangles are 45-45-90 even though they didn't tell us the angles are 45°. That's because we know each has two equal sides—and that alone is enough to make them isosceles.

3. The 30-60-90 Triangle

Any triangle with angles of 30°, 60°, and 90° will always have the same dimensions.

It's the same concept as the 45-45-90 triangle: if I know just a few things about the triangle, I can just fill in all the values for the rest of the triangle without doing a lot of calculations or bothering with the Pythagorean Theorem.[†]

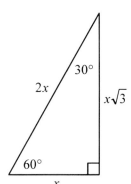

Remembering these triangles

It can be tough to remember all these dimensions. The 45-45-90 is a bit easier since two of the sides are the same. But in the 30-60-90 since each side has a different value and it's easy to mix up where everything goes. Here's a tip for remembering which angle and which length goes where:

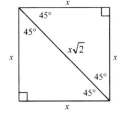

➤ The 45-45-90 triangle is **half a square**. The diagonal of the square cuts two right angles into 45° angles. The two *x*'s are the sides of the square and the hypotenuse is the diagonal.

➤ The 30-60-90 triangle is **half an equilateral triangle**. A line divides one of the 60° angles into two 30° angles, and then cuts the opposite side in half as well.

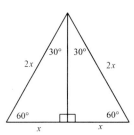

---

[*] Plus a 90° angle. Thus, "right triangle".

[†] You could prove these dimensions with the Pythagorean Theorem the same way we did above with the 45-45-90 triangle. We didn't, because we don't feel like it and we don't think any of you care. But if you do, knock yourself out.

But again, if you're not sure where to put everything—*check the front of the section*. They *give* you this. You don't have to remember it.

Sometimes, it may not be obvious that a triangle in a problem is 30-60-90 or 45-45-90. But notice that these triangles involve two **happy magic numbers**: $\sqrt{2}$ and $\sqrt{3}$. These numbers don't show up very often in other situations. In fact, they rarely show up in other situations. So if you're doing a problem and notice $\sqrt{3}$ in the answer choices, there's a pretty good chance that there's a 30-60-90 triangle in the problem. The same goes for $\sqrt{2}$; if you see it in the answers, there's a good chance there's a 45-45-90 triangle in the problem. Of course, this isn't *always* true. But if you're stuck on a problem, look for these happy magic numbers. They could help you spot something you would have missed otherwise.[*]

4. Similar Triangles

If all the angles of one triangle are equal to all the corresponding angles of a second triangle, then they are *similar triangles*. That means that all their sides are in the same ratio with each other.

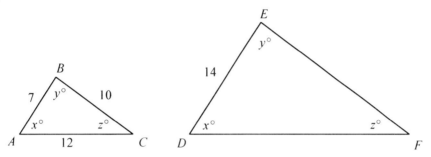

Here, $\triangle ABC$ has all the same angles as $\triangle DEF$, so they are similar triangles. $AB = 7$ and $DE = 14$, so DE is double AB. Since the triangles are similar, each side of $\triangle DEF$ will be double the corresponding side of $\triangle ABC$. So $EF = 2(10) = 20$, and $DF = 2(12) = 24$.

When dealing with similar triangles, it's important to keep track of which side is which. AB will be proportional to DE because each of them is across from the "z" angle.

This, by the way, is exactly why we can do that stuff with the 30-60-90 triangles we just saw. All 30-60-90 triangles have the same angles, therefore their sides are in the same ratio—$1:\sqrt{3}:2$.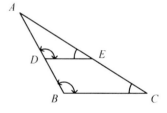

Similar triangles don't have to be next to each other. Often these questions will feature *a triangle inside of a triangle*. In the figure to the left, if DE is parallel to BC, then $\angle ADE = \angle ABC$. Therefore $\triangle ABC$ is similar to $\triangle ADE$ because all of their corresponding angles are equal.

5. Lengths of the sides of a triangle

There are several additional points to be made about the relationship between sides in a triangle.

> ☛ **The hypotenuse must be the longest side of a right triangle.**

Well, that makes sense, since the Pythagorean Theorem says a and b together contribute to c. So if someone tells you a right triangle has sides of 7, 24, 25, you know right away that the hypotenuse is 25 and the legs are 7 and 24.

---

[*] $\sqrt{2}$ is certainly a magic number. It was the first "irrational number"—a decimal that can't be expressed as a fraction. It was first discovered by Hippasus of Metapontum, a Pythagorean mathematician. He was at sea when he discovered it, and some of his Pythagorean shipmates were so angered and offended by the idea of an irrational number, they threw him overboard and drowned him. The Pythagoreans were nuts. If you know any Pythagoreans, don't mention $\sqrt{2}$ to them.

In a right triangle, the 90° angle must always be the largest angle, so the side opposite (the hypotenuse) must be the longest side. But this same rule holds for *any* triangle:

> ➤ **The largest angle of a triangle must be opposite the longest side.**

Or, more generally, "the larger the angle, the larger the opposite side." There's a definite relationship between the lengths of the sides of a triangle and the angles opposite them.[*] That's exactly why an isosceles triangle has two equal sides *and* two equal angles opposite.

Let's look at this in action:

As you can see from these figures, when we make angle *A* bigger, side *BC* opposite it also becomes bigger. Ditto, when *A* is smaller, *BC* is smaller.

But are there limits to how big or small that third side can get? Yes, there are:

> ➤ **The third side of a triangle must be *smaller* than the *sum* of the other two sides.**

$$BC < AC + AB$$

> ➤ **The third side of a triangle must be *larger* than the *difference* of the other two sides.**

$$BC > AC - AB$$

Let's see how far we can stretch these triangles. On the left, we'll make angle *A* bigger and bigger; on the right, we'll make angle *A* smaller and smaller. Let's see what happens to side *BC*.

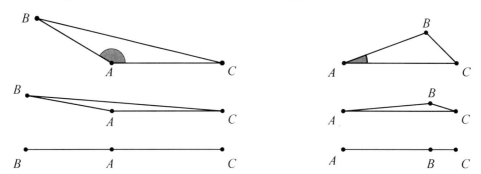

We can keep stretching angle *A* until it reaches 180° — a straight line. In that case, *BC* is exactly equal to *BA* and *AC* combined. But if we do that, *it's not a triangle.* It's just a straight line now. So if we want it to be a triangle, angle *A* has to be less than 180°, so the third side has to be less than the sum of the other two.

On the right, we can see the same thing happening in the opposite direction. Angle *A* can keep shrinking until it gets to 0°. Now we have a straight line again, this time with *AB* lying on top of *AC*. So *BC* is equal to the difference of the other two: *AC − AB*. But again, if we do that, *we don't have a triangle.* So if we want it to be a triangle, angle *A* has to be greater than 0°, so the third side has to be greater than the difference of the other two.

We can see that if the third side were bigger than the sum of the other two, the two smaller sides wouldn't be able to reach each other:

---

[*] We can actually define that relationship more specifically if you want to do some trig. Do you want to do some trig? I don't. Don't ever do trig on the SAT. Just know that big angles are opposite big sides.

4. What is the area of a square that has a
diagonal of length $3\sqrt{2}$?

(A) 3
(B) 4
(C) 9
(D) $9\sqrt{2}$
(E) 18

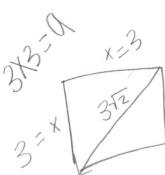

$3 \times 3 = 9$

$x = 3$

$3\sqrt{2}$

$3 = x$

3

10. Mariano lives 12 miles due south of school
and Nancy lives 16 miles due west of
school. If Chris walks in a straight line from
Nancy's house to Mariano's house, what is
the distance, in miles, that he will have
walked?

(A) 12
(B) 16
(C) 20
(D) 25
(E) 28

C

$16^2 + 12^2 = C^2$

$3, 4, 5$

$12 \quad 16 \quad \boxed{20}$

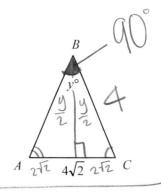

Note: Figure not drawn to scale.

11. In the figure above, the measure of $\angle BAC$
equals the measure of $\angle ACB$. If $\overline{BC} = 4$,
what is y?

(A) 30
(B) 45
(C) 60
(D) 75
(E) 90

E

GO TO THE NEXT PAGE

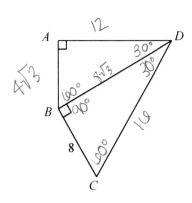

18. In quadrilateral *ABCD* above, $\angle ABC = 150°$ and $\overline{BD}$ bisects $\angle ADC$. What is the perimeter of *ABCD*?

(A) $8 + 24\sqrt{3}$

(B) $24 + 8\sqrt{3}$

(C) $32 + 8\sqrt{3}$

(D) $36 + 4\sqrt{3}$

(E) $36 + 12\sqrt{3}$

D

$$\begin{array}{r} 12 \\ +16 \\ 8 \\ \hline 34 \end{array}$$

$36 + 4\sqrt{3}$

$\sqrt{3}X$ $2X$ X

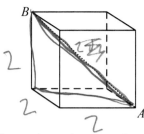

20. The figure above shows a cube with edges of length 2. What is the length of diagonal *AB*?

(A) $\sqrt{2}$

(B) $2\sqrt{2}$

(C) $\sqrt{6}$

(D) $2\sqrt{3}$

(E) 4

D

2

$2\sqrt{2}$

$\sqrt{4+8} = \sqrt{12} =$

$2\sqrt{3}$

IV. PERIMETER, AREA & VOLUME

Let's start with a few definitions and formulas. Note that this is *all* you need to know for the SAT about perimeter, area, and volume. If you want to find the area or volume of a shape that isn't listed here (like a pentagon or a pyramid), either

   (a) you can find it by using some combination of the shapes listed here, or

   (b) you don't actually need that area (you only *think* you do).

A. Perimeter

The perimeter of any figure is the sum of the lengths of all the sides.

Okay? Okay.

B. Area

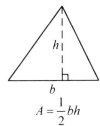 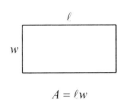 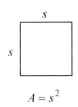

AREA:

Triangle: $A = \frac{1}{2}bh$

Rectangle: $A = \ell w$

Square: $A = s^2$

Hey, don't they tell us these formulas? Yeah, I'm pretty sure they do.

Some notes:

- In a triangle, the **base** is just whatever side happens to be lying flat on the ground. The **height** is a line from the topmost point of the triangle extending perpendicular to the base. Sometimes that's just a side of the triangle, sometimes it's inside the triangle, sometimes it's outside the triangle. All three of the following triangles have identical areas, because they have the same base and height:

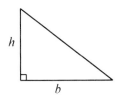 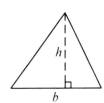 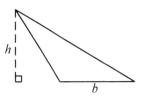

- The formulas for squares and rectangles say the same thing. A square is just a rectangle with equal sides, so $s = \ell = w$.

- Notice that the area of a triangle is half the area of a rectangle. Imagine cutting a rectangle in half along the diagonal; you'd get two right triangles. And for each triangle, the base and height are equal to the length and width of the original rectangle.

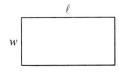 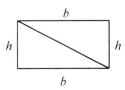

- You can also use triangles to find the area of other shapes that aren't shown here. For example, the area of a parallelogram is base times height (that's the *height*; *not* the side). You can see this by drawing in two triangles, as we do below. Again, we use the rules we know to figure out the rules we don't.

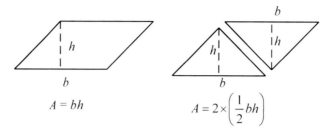

$$A = bh \qquad\qquad A = 2 \times \left(\frac{1}{2}bh\right)$$

Shaded Area Problems

Shaded area problems are best done by **subtraction**. Find the area of the whole figure and take away what you don't need.

Take a look at this one:

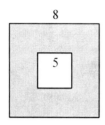

Note: Figure not drawn to scale.

> ☞ **In the figure above, a small square is inside a larger square. What is the area of the shaded region?**

It may be tempting to try to find the area directly by dividing up the shaded region into four rectangles. But we can't find those areas because we don't know all of their dimensions. Plus it's kind of tedious.

Instead, let's just find the area of the **whole** square and subtract the area of the **unshaded** square. Whatever's left will be the area of the shaded region.

$$A_{whole} = s^2 = 8^2 = 64$$
$$A_{unshaded} = 5^2 = 25$$
$$A_{shaded} = A_{whole} - A_{unshaded}$$
$$= 64 - 25 \boxed{= \mathbf{39}}$$

C. Surface Area

We find the "surface area" by finding the *area* of the *surfaces.*[*] That means we have to find the areas of all the shapes on the outside of the box. A box is made up of a bunch of rectangles; we'll find the area of the rectangles and add them all up. That's it.

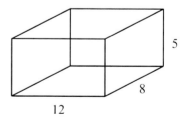

This box has dimensions 12, 8, and 5. To find the surface area, we'll take the areas of all the rectangles on the outside and add them up.

---

[*] Brilliant.

We can see that there are three types of rectangles in this box:

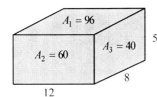

$A_1 = 12 \times 8 = 96$

$A_2 = 12 \times 5 = 60$

$A_3 = 8 \times 5 = 40$

BUT, each of these sides shows up *twice* in the box (top and bottom, front and back, side and side.)

$SA = 2(A_1 + A_2 + A_3)$ $SA = 2(96 + 60 + 40) = 2(196)$ $\boxed{SA = 392}$

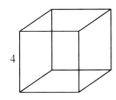

Again, a cube is just a special type of box. Since it's made up of 6 squares, we'll just find the area of one face and multiply by 6. This square has edges of length 4.

$SA = 6(A_\square)$

$SA = 6(s^2) = 6(4^2) = 6(16)$

$\boxed{SA = 96}$

D. Volume

$V = \ell w h$ $V = s^3$ $V = \pi r^2 h$

VOLUME:

Box: $V = \ell w h$

Cube: $V = s^3$

Cylinder: $V = \pi r^2 h$

- Just as the area of a rectangle is found by multiplying its two dimensions, the volume of a box is found by multiplying its three dimensions.[*]

- Just as a square is a rectangle with equal sides, a cube is a box with equal sides.

- Notice that the volume of a cylinder works under the same principle as the volume of a box. For a box, the base is a rectangle, so its area is length times width; get the volume by multiplying that by the height. For a cylinder, the base is a circle, so its area is πr^2; get the volume by multiplying that by the height.

$V = (\ell w) \times h$ $V = \left(\pi r^2\right) \times h$

---

[*] In a sense, it doesn't really matter which side you call length, width, or height, since the volume comes out the same no matter what ($1 \times 2 \times 3 = 2 \times 3 \times 1$), but there are some conventions about what to call them. In a rectangle, the length is usually the longer side and the width is the shorter one. In a box, the height will always be the side that goes *up*, away from the face lying flat on the ground. Thus if the box is, say, a tank filled with water, the height will correspond to the *depth* of the water.

PERIMETER/AREA/VOLUME DRILL

2. The width of a rectangular quilt is 1 foot less than its length. If the width of the quilt is 3 feet, what is the area of the quilt in square feet?

(A) 4
(B) 6
(C) 7
(D) 10
(E) 12

12. Orestes has a rectangular block of cheese with dimensions 15 inches by 21 inches by 24 inches. If he cuts this block entirely into cubes with a side of length 3, how many such cubes are produced?

(A) 27
(B) 42
(C) 96
(D) 280
(E) 480

14. What is the area of a right triangle whose sides are x, $x + 4$, and $x - 4$ and whose perimeter is 48?

(A) 48
(B) 96
(C) 144
(D) 192
(E) 210

GO TO THE NEXT PAGE

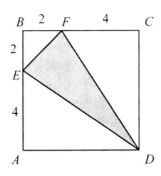

15. In the figure above, △*EFD* is an isosceles triangle inscribed in a square of side 6. What is the area of the shaded region?

[For a change of pace, here's a Grid-in. No choices. Deal with it.]

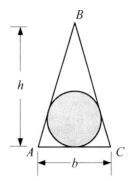

Note: Figure not drawn to scale.

16. In △*ABC* above, the area of the shaded region is given by $\frac{\pi bh}{9}$. If the area of the shaded region is 6π , what is the area, to the nearest whole number, of the unshaded regions of △*ABC*?

(A)   5
(B)   8
(C)   19
(D)   27
(E)   54

V. CIRCLES

Circles are a wee bit different from other shapes, so they get their own section.

A. Definitions

Some fun circle facts:[*]

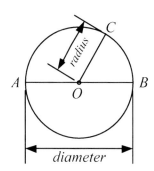

- A circle has **360°**. In the figure to the left, all angles surrounding point O will add up to 360°.[†]

- The **diameter** of a circle is a line segment from one end of the circle to the other, passing through the center. In the figure, AB is a diameter. The diameter by definition is the longest segment you can draw through a circle.

> Circles are named for their center points, so this circle is circle O. A lot of circles are named "O". Can you guess why?

- The **radius** of a circle is a line segment from the center to the end of a circle. The radius is half of the diameter. In the figure, OA, OB, and OC are all radii. All radii of a circle are equal.

Almost everything we do with a circle requires knowing its radius (or diameter, which is just double the radius). If you're given a circle and you don't know its radius, before you do anything else **try to find the radius**. You'll probably need it, even if you don't yet know why.

- When a line is **tangent** to a circle, that means it touches the circle at exactly one point. In the figure to the right, segment AB is tangent to circle O at point C. Note that a tangent line is always perpendicular to the radius of the circle at the point of intersection. Here, radius OC is perpendicular to segment AB.

- When one shape is **inscribed** inside another shape, that means it fits exactly within the larger shape, touching its edges at one point on each side.[‡] If you encounter a question involving circles and inscribed shapes, the radius or diameter of the circle likely corresponds with a key element of the other shape. In the first figure to the right, the circle's diameter is the same length as the side of the square. In the second, the diameter is the same as the diagonal of the square.

A circle inscribed in a square   *A square inscribed in a circle*

B. Formulas

- The perimeter of a circle is called its **circumference (C)**. The circumference is equal to the diameter times π, which is the same as two times the radius times π (since the diameter equals two radii).

- Note that the distance a wheel travels in one revolution is equal to the circumference of the circle.

$$C = \pi d = 2\pi r$$
$$A = \pi r^2$$

- The **area** of a circle is equal to the radius squared times π.

- π (pronounced "pie") stands for a special number whose value is approximately 3.14. For most SAT problems, you don't have to calculate the number; you can just leave it as the symbol π.

---

[*] Well, not *that* fun.

[†] Actually, we can already figure this out from our angle rules. The diameter is a straight line, so the angles above it add up to 180° and the angles below it add up to 180°. Put them together and you've got 360°.

[‡] The opposite of inscribed is *circumscribed*. To say that a circle is inscribed within a square means the same thing as saying the square is circumscribed about the circle.

In the circle shown here, the radius is 3, so

$$C = 2\pi r \qquad\qquad A = \pi r^2$$

$$C = 2\pi(3) \qquad\quad A = \pi\left(3^2\right)$$

$$\boxed{C = 6\pi} \qquad\qquad \boxed{A = 9\pi}$$

C. Slices

A wedge or slice of a circle is nothing more than a *part* of a circle. Problems dealing with them can be done with simple ratios. Take a look at this circle:

Obviously, the shaded section is one fourth of the circle. How can I tell? First of all, because it *looks* like a fourth of the circle (Guesstimate!)

That central angle, $\angle AOB$, is $90°$. 90 is one fourth of 360. So that central angle is one fourth of the whole angle (360).

Let's say the circle has a radius of 10. So its area is 100π. The area of the slice is one fourth of that: 25π.

If the radius is 10, its circumference is 20π. The length of minor arc AB is one fourth of that: 5π.

This is pretty easy to see. Since that slice is one fourth of the circle, everything about that slice is one fourth of the corresponding characteristic of the circle: the angle is one fourth of 360, the area is one fourth of the circle's area, and the arc length is one fourth of the circumference.

$$\frac{1}{4} = \frac{90°}{360°} = \frac{25\pi}{100\pi} = \frac{5\pi}{20\pi}$$

This is true of *all* slices. The slice shown to the left is 1/60 of the circle, so that angle is 1/60 of 360, the arc is 1/60 of the circumference, and the area of the slice is 1/60 of the whole area.

So if you know any one thing about a slice, you can figure out what fraction of the circle it is. Once you know what fraction of the circle it is, you can find anything else about that slice.

You can set up any such problem with a series of ratios:

$$\frac{\text{part}}{\text{whole}} = \frac{\text{angle}}{360°} = \frac{A_{\text{slice}}}{A_{\text{O}}} = \frac{\text{arc}}{C}$$

TRY ONE:

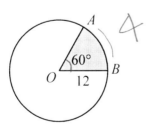

✎ **Circle O has a radius of 12. If $\angle AOB$ is $60°$, what is the length of minor arc AB?**

$$\frac{60}{300} = \frac{1}{6}$$

$$2\pi r = 24\pi \leftarrow \text{circmfr.}$$

$$\frac{24\pi}{6} = \boxed{4\pi}$$

CIRCLE DRILL

6. If the radius of a circle is doubled, by what factor does the circle's area increase?

(A) 2
(B) 4
(C) 6
(D) 8
(E) 16

$$Area = \pi r^2$$
$$\pi (2r)^2$$
$$\pi \cdot 4 r^2$$

---

10. Through how many degrees does the hour hand of a clock turn from 4:00 pm to 8:00 pm of the same day?

(A) 20
(B) 40
(C) 80
(D) 90
(E) 120

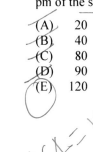

$$\frac{360}{12} = 30 \times 4 = 120$$

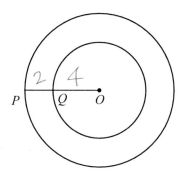

14. In the figure above, two circles have their centers at point O, with radii OP and OQ. If $OQ = 4$ and $PQ = 2$, what is the ratio of the circumference of the smaller circle to the circumference of the larger circle?

(A) 1:3
(B) 1:2
(C) 2:3
(D) 3:5
(E) 4:5

C

smaller: larger

$$\frac{2\pi 4}{2\pi 6} = \frac{2}{3}$$

GO TO THE NEXT PAGE

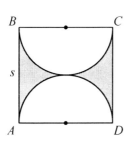

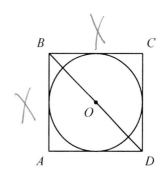

16. In the figure above $ABCD$ is a square with sides of length s and AD and BC are both diameters of semicircles inscribed in square $ABCD$. What, in terms of s, is the area of the shaded region?

(A) $s^2 - \pi s^2$

(B) $\dfrac{s^2 - \pi s^2}{4}$

(C) $s^2 \left(1 - \dfrac{\pi}{4}\right)$

(D) $s^2 \left(1 - \dfrac{\pi}{16}\right)$

(E) $2s^2 \left(1 - \dfrac{\pi}{4}\right)$

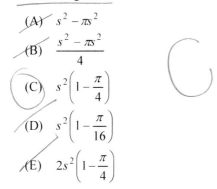

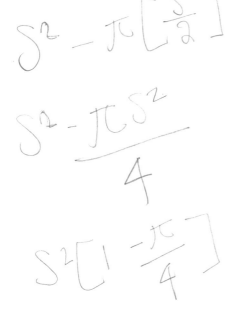

20. The circle in the figure above with center O is inscribed in square $ABCD$. Which of the following measures for the figure would be sufficient by itself to determine the area of the circle?

    I. The perimeter of square $ABCD$
    II. The area of square $ABCD$
    III. The length of diagonal BD

(A) None
(B) I only
(C) III only
(D) I and II only
(E) I, II, and III

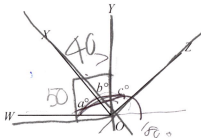

1. In the figure above, $\overline{OZ} \perp \overline{OX}$ and $\overline{OY} \perp \overline{OW}$. If $a = 50$, what is the value of c?

50+b+c=180

(A) 50
(B) 45
(C) 40
(D) 35
(E) 30

A ✓

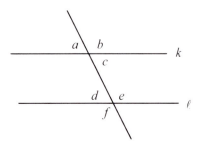

2. In the figure above, if line k is parallel to line ℓ, the sum of which of the following pairs of angles must equal $180°$?

(A) a and c
(B) a and d
(C) b and d
(D) c and d
(E) e and f

C ✓

3. A rectangle has a perimeter of 200 and a width of 40. What is the length of the rectangle?

(A) 40
(B) 50
(C) 60
(D) 70
(E) 80

C ✓

P = 200
2l + 2w = 200
2l + 2(40) = 200
2l + 80 = 200

4. Circles O and P have radii of 3 and 4 respectively. How much greater is the area of circle P than the area of circle O?

(A) π
(B) 3π
(C) 5π
(D) 7π
(E) 9π

$O = 9\pi$
$P = 16\pi$

X C

Correct ans: D

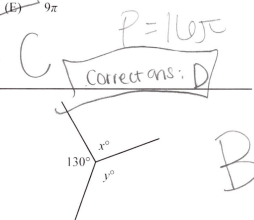

5. In the figure above, what is the value of $x + y$?

(A) 260
(B) 230
(C) 210
(D) 180
(E) 130

360
x+y+130 = 180
-130 -130
x+y = 230

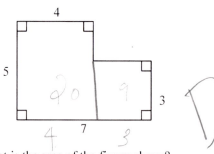

6. What is the area of the figure above?

(A) 20
(B) 24
(C) 26
(D) 29
(E) 35

7. How many more degrees of arc are there in $\frac{1}{3}$ of a circle than in $\frac{1}{4}$ of a circle?

(A) 15°
(B) 20°
(C) 25°
(D) 30°
(E) 35°

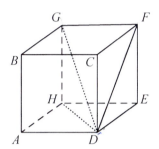

8. In the cube shown above, the length of $\overline{DF}$ is equal in length to which of the following?

(A) $\overline{AH}$
(B) $\overline{DE}$
(C) $\overline{DG}$
(D) $\overline{DH}$
(E) $\overline{EH}$

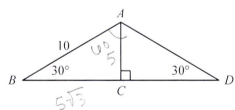

9. In $\triangle ABC$ above, what is the length of AC?

(A) 5
(B) $5\sqrt{3}$
(C) 10
(D) $10\sqrt{3}$
(E) 20

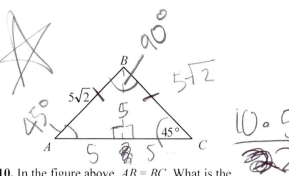

10. In the figure above, $AB = BC$. What is the area of $\triangle ABC$?

(A) 5
(B) 10
(C) 15
(D) 20
(E) 25

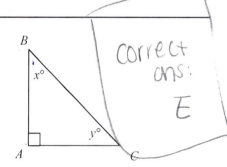

Note: Figure not drawn to scale

11. In $\triangle ABC$ above, $AB > AC$. Which of the following must be true?

(A) $AB > BC$
(B) $AC > BC$
(C) $x = 45$
(D) $x > y$
(E) $x < y$

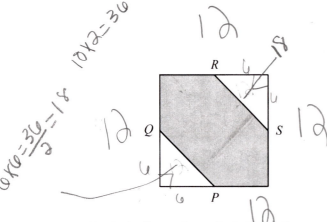

12. In the figure above, *P*, *Q*, *R*, and *S* are midpoints of the sides of the square. If the square has sides of length 12, what is the area of the shaded region?

   (A)   144
   (B)   126
   (C)   108
   (D)   72
   (E)   36

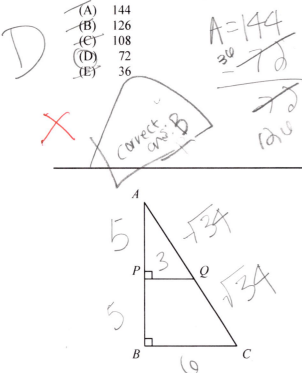

13. In the figure above, *P* is the midpoint of $\overline{AB}$ and *Q* is the midpoint of $\overline{AC}$. If $\overline{AP}$ is 5 and $\overline{PQ}$ is 3, what is the area of $\triangle ABC$?

   (A)   7.5
   (B)   8
   (C)   15
   (D)   30
   (E)   60

14. What is the volume of a cube that has a surface area of 54?

   (A)   3
   (B)   9
   (C)   27
   (D)   36
   (E)   81

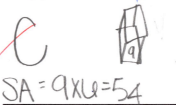

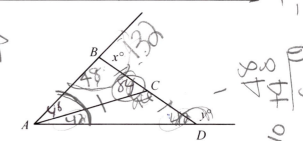

Note: Figure not drawn to scale.

15. In the figure above, if *x* = 132, and *BC* = *AC* = *CD*, then *y* =

   (A)   148
   (B)   138
   (C)   132
   (D)   116
   (E)   96

16. A right circular cylinder has a volume of 64π. If the height of the cylinder is 4, what is the circumference of the base?

   (A)   8π
   (B)   12π
   (C)   16π
   (D)   20π
   (E)   24π

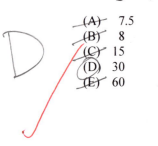

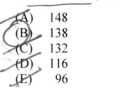

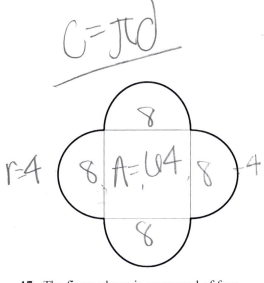

$C = \pi d$

r=4

8

8 A=64 8 -4

8

$r=4$

17. The figure above is composed of four semicircles on the sides of a square. If the square has an area of 64, what is the length of the darkened outline of the figure?

(A) 8π
(B) 16π
(C) 24π
(D) 32π
(E) 64π

B

$C = \dfrac{8\pi}{2} = 4\pi$

$4\pi \cdot 4 = 16\pi$

18. The longest and shortest sides of a non-isosceles triangle are 10 and 2 respectively. Which of the following could be the length of the third side?

(A) 12
(B) 11
(C) 10
(D) 9
(E) 8

E ✗

correct ans: D

$10 - 2 = 8$

$10 + 2 = 12$

10

2

$8 < x < 12$

longest

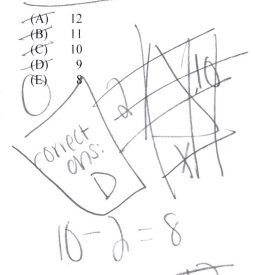

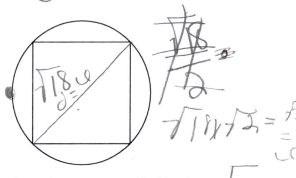

$C = \pi d$

$\sqrt{18} \cdot d$

$\sqrt{18} + \sqrt{18} = \sqrt{36} = 6$

E

19. In the figure above, a square with side of length $\sqrt{18}$ is inscribed in a circle. What is the circumference of the circle?

(A) 3π
(B) 6π
(C) 9π
(D) 18π
(E) 36π

$C = 2\pi r$

correct ans: B

18
+18

36π

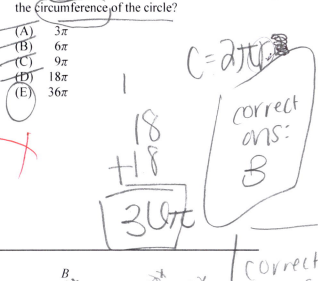

20. In the figure above, $BQ = PQ = RQ$ and $AP = PR$. If $\overline{PQ}$ is parallel to $\overline{AC}$, what is y in terms of x?

(A) $180 - 2x$
(B) $180 - 4x$
(C) $2x - 180$
(D) $2x - 360$
(E) $4x - 180$

A

correct ans: E

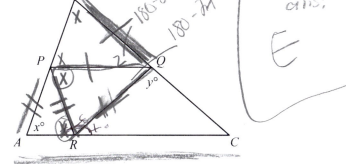

$x + x + y = 180$

$2x + y = 180$
$\quad\quad -2x$
$y = 180 - 2x$

$2x + 2 = 180$
$2 = 2x - 180$
$180 - 2x + 180 - 2x + y$
$360 - 4x + y = 180$
$y = 4x - 180$

FUNCTIONS

Okay, we've covered most of the stuff you need. We've got the techniques. We've got Arithmetic, Algebra, and Geometry. However, we haven't yet talked about *Functions*. Functions appear all over the test, but they don't really fall into any of the above categories. They're part algebra, part geometry, and you can certainly use the techniques on them. But they're really a category all on their own.

So let's talk about them.

I. FUNNY SYMBOLS

Look at this:

$$5^2$$

What does that mean? Duh. Obviously:

$$5^2 = 5 \times 5$$

The little "2" tells us to multiply the big number times itself. We all know that.

Similarly:

$$7^2 = 7 \times 7$$

$$(-23)^2 = (-23) \times (-23)$$

$$y^2 = y \times y$$

$$\Omega^2 = \Omega \times \Omega$$

$$(\text{donkey})^2 = (\text{donkey}) \times (\text{donkey})$$

This should not be news to you. Any time you see a little "2" next to *anything*, multiply it by itself.

That's a function. It's a symbol (the "2") with a rule attached to it (multiply by self). *Everything* we do in math is a kind of function: a symbol with a rule attached to it.

On the SAT, sometimes there will be new, made-up symbols. Take a look at this problem:

9.   **Let ♥x be defined for all numbers x such that**
     ♥x = 2x + 5. What is ♥7 − ♥6 ?

   (A)   1
   (B)   2
   (C)   6
   (D)   7
   (E)   9

Some of you are thinking, "Huh? What's up with the little heart? I've never seen a little heart symbol before. So how am I supposed to know what the little heart means?"

Because they just told you what it means! It's the first thing they say in the problem! Do you really think you're expected to know what ♥ means before the test? Can you show me the ♥ button on your calculator? Of course not. They just made it up. It's a random, arbitrary function, and they *tell you* exactly what it means.

The little heart is a new symbol they made up to stand for this function. The only difference between this and 5^2 is that the exponent is a common math function, while ♥ is just one they made up randomly.

So. Don't worry about the weird language in the question ("all numbers x such that" blah blah blah). All that matters is the function itself. The function they give us is defined as:

$$\heartsuit x = 2x + 5$$

The x here is just a placeholder; it's a variable that stands for *any number*, an example of how to use the function. Just as the little "2" meant "multiply the number by itself", the little heart here means "multiply by 2 and add 5".

That means: $\heartsuit 2 = 2(2) + 5$

and: $\heartsuit 3 = 2(3) + 5$

therefore: $\heartsuit 18 = 2(18) + 5$

so: $\heartsuit 1979 = 2(1979) + 5$

also: $\heartsuit y = 2y + 5$

ergo: $\heartsuit (omg) = 2(omg) + 5$

this too: $\heartsuit \pi = 2(\pi) + 5$

why not: $\heartsuit (\smiley) = 2(\smiley) + 5$

one more: $\heartsuit (fluffybabypandabear) = 2(fluffybabypandabear) + 5$

Get the point? Whatever you see next to the $\heartsuit$, stick it in for x in $2x + 5$.

Now, let's get back to the original problem:

9. Let $\heartsuit x$ be defined for all numbers x such that $\heartsuit x = 2x + 5$. What is $\heartsuit 7 - \heartsuit 6$?

(A) 1
(B) 2
(C) 6
(D) 7
(E) 9

So let's just stick 7 and 6 into the function and subtract our answers.

$$\heartsuit 7 = 2(7) + 5 = 14 + 5 = \mathbf{19}$$

$$\heartsuit 6 = 2(6) + 5 = 12 + 5 = \mathbf{17}$$

$$\heartsuit 7 - \heartsuit 6 = 19 - 17 = \boxed{2}$$

So our answer is **2**. That's (B).

The only trick to functions is to *FOLLOW DIRECTIONS*. <u>Don't take shortcuts</u>, just do exactly what the function says.

Here, they're asking us for $\heartsuit 7 - \heartsuit 6$. You CANNOT assume that's the same thing as $\heartsuit 1$. Maybe it is, maybe it isn't. You must *do the function FIRST*.

Look what would happen if we didn't do the function first:

✗ $\heartsuit 7 - \heartsuit 6 = \heartsuit 1 = 2(1) + 5 = 7$ ✗

See that? We got a different answer. You have to do the *function first*. Start by doing whatever the funny symbol tells you to do, and then do any other arithmetic they ask you for. You can't assume that $7^2 - 6^2 = 1^2$, so you also can't assume that $\heartsuit 7 - \heartsuit 6 = \heartsuit 1$.

Take a look at this problem:

12. **Let the operation @*x* be defined for all numbers *x* by $@x = x^2 + 4$. Which of the following is equal to $\dfrac{@6}{@2}$?**

   (A) @1
   (B) @2
   (C) @3
   (D) @4
   (E) @5

As always, we mustn't take shortcuts.[*] We'll do @6, then @2, then divide our answers.

$$@6 = 6^2 + 4 = 36 + 4 = \mathbf{40}$$

$$@2 = 2^2 + 4 = 4 + 4 = \mathbf{8}$$

$$\frac{@6}{@2} = \frac{40}{8} = \mathbf{5}$$

So the answer is 5. That's (E). Right? WRONG! 5 is correct, but look: choice (E) says **@5**—that's $5^2 + 4$. All the answers here are @-functions; we must do out the choices and see which one comes out to 5. That's going to be (A):

(A): $@1 = 1^2 + 4 = 1 + 4 = \mathbf{5} \checkmark$

Think of it this way. There are two elements to the function: you put in one number, you get out another number. You could easily have written the same function using *x* and *y* instead of the weird symbols. Instead of:

$$@x = x^2 + 4$$

We could have said

$$y = x^2 + 4$$

So to say that @1 = 5 is the same as saying that *y* = 5 when *x* = 1.

_____

[*] Don't just jump to choice (C) because 6/2 = 3. Do the function first!

Questions 8 - 9 refer to the following function:

$$x \, \aleph \, y = x^2 + y$$

8. If $2 \, \aleph \, h = 11$, then $h =$

    (A) 2
    (B) 5
    (C) 7
    (D) 11
    (E) 15

C

$2^2 + h = 7$

$h = 7$

_____

9. $(3 \, \aleph \, 4) \, \aleph \, 5 = ?$

    (A) 12
    (B) 18
    (C) 60
    (D) 149
    (E) 174

E

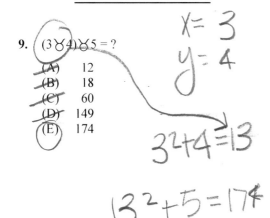

$x = 3$
$y = 4$

$3^2 + 4 = 13$

$13^2 + 5 = 174$

_____

10. For any number x, the symbol $\circlearrowleft x$ represents the number obtained when the digits of x are reversed, dropping any zeroes at the end of the original number. For example:

    $\circlearrowleft 3251 = 1523$
    $\circlearrowleft 470 = 74$

    For which of the following values of x would $\circlearrowleft x < 200$?

    (A) 109 → 901
    (B) 202 → 202
    (C) 318 → 813
    (D) 1400 → 41
    (E) 1820 → 281

D

15. For all positive integers x and y, let $\diamond$ be defined by $x \diamond y = x^2 - y^2$. If a and b are positive integers, which of the following CANNOT be the value of $a \diamond b$?

    (A) 0
    (B) 1
    (C) 3
    (D) 5
    (E) 8

B

II. $f(x)$ NOTATION

We've just seen some examples of new functions being defined with funny symbols:

$$\heartsuit x = 2x + 5$$

But in reality, they don't use funny symbols all that often on the SAT. More often, they simply use a letter.

$$f(x) = 2x + 5$$

This means *exactly* the same thing as the little heart did. The only difference is that here they used an "f" instead of a "$\heartsuit$". The function itself behaves in exactly the same way. This means that:

$$f(2) = 2(2) + 5$$

$$f(-5) = 2(-5) + 5$$

$$f(q) = 2(q) + 5$$

$$f(g(k)) = 2(g(k)) + 5$$

$$f(x + 1) = 2(x + 1) + 5$$

You get the picture: "$f(x)$" doesn't mean "multiply f by x". The f isn't a variable; it's the name of a *function*.

We can do a lot with functions, but it all comes down to **substitution**:

> ## Take whatever you see inside the parentheses and stick it in for *x*.

Take a look at this problem:

> ☛ **If $g(x) = 3x + 4$ and $h(x) = g(x) - 7$, what is $h(2)$?**

This may look nasty, but remember: the key to functions is to just follow directions. They want $h(2)$. So just take the equation for h and stick a 2 wherever you see an x.

$$h(2) = g(2) - 7$$

We know that $g(x) = 3x + 4$. So $g(2) = 3(2) + 4$. Stick that in there:

$h(2) = [3(2) + 4] - 7$ ←Put 2 in for x in the formula for $g(x)$

$h(2) = [6 + 4] - 7$

$h(2) = 10 - 7$

$\boxed{h(2) = 3}$

F(X) DRILL

9. If $f(x) = \dfrac{2x-5}{x^2}$ for all nonzero values of x,

 then $f(3) =$

 (A) $\dfrac{11}{6}$

 (B) $\dfrac{11}{9}$

 (C) $\dfrac{1}{6}$

 (D) $\dfrac{1}{9}$

 (E) -1

D

$f(x) = \dfrac{2(3)-5}{3^2}$ $\dfrac{1}{9}$

11. When Troy jumps off a bridge, the distance d, in feet, that he travels from his starting point after t seconds is given by the function $d(t) = 25t - 2t^2$. How far will Troy have traveled after 2 seconds?

 (A)   8 feet
 (B)   17 feet
 (C)   42 feet
 (D)   50 feet
 (E)   58 feet

C

$d(t) = 25(2) - 2(2)^2$

$50 - 8 = 42$

12. The profit, P, in dollars that Milton makes selling staplers can be determined by the function $P(s) = 5s - 300$, where s is the number of staplers he sold. How many staplers must Milton sell in order to make a profit of $1000?

 (A)   200
 (B)   260
 (C)   300
 (D)   1300
 (E)   4700

B

$1000 = 5s - 300$
$300 \qquad\qquad + 300$

$\dfrac{1300 = 5s}{5} \quad \dfrac{}{5}$

$\begin{array}{r} 260 \\ 5\overline{)1300} \\ 10 \end{array}$

14. Let $f(x)$ be defined by $f(x) = 4x - 2$. If $2f(a) = 6$, what is the value of a?

 (A) $\dfrac{1}{4}$

 (B) $\dfrac{5}{4}$

 (C) $\dfrac{5}{2}$

 (D) $\dfrac{7}{4}$

 (E) $\dfrac{7}{2}$

B

$4a - 2 = 3$
$\quad +2 +2$

$\dfrac{4a}{4} = \dfrac{5}{4}$

$\dfrac{2(4 \times a) = 6}{2}$

$\dfrac{2f(a)}{2} = \dfrac{6}{2}$

$f(a) = 3$

III. Graphing

A. What's the *xy*-plane?

This is the *xy*-coordinate plane (or "*xy* grid", or "coordinate plane" or whatever you want to call it).

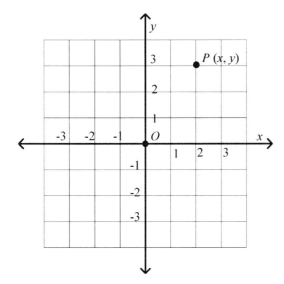

A lot of you probably know your way around this guy, but here are some definitions for those who are confused:

The **x-axis** is the horizontal line; it tells you the *x* value of a point. Values of *x* are positive to the right and negative to the left.

The **y-axis** is the vertical line; it tells you the *y* value of a point. Values of *y* are positive at the top and negative at the bottom.

Points on the graph are given as (*x*, *y*). So point *P* is (2,3), since it has an *x* value of 2 and a *y* value of 3. You can tell the *x* and *y* values by looking at where the point lies with respect to the axes.

The **origin** is the point where the axes* cross (labeled "*O*" here); it has a value of (0,0).

Before we go any further, it's important to emphasize that graphs are *pictures*. Therefore, **you can use *Guesstimate* on graph problems**. In fact, you'd be astounded how many graphing problems can be done just by looking at the picture they give you. If this line looks equal to that line, then they are equal.

If you want to find the ***distance*** between two points on a graph, just use the Pythagorean Theorem:

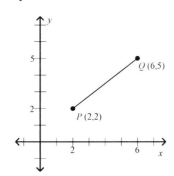

Say we want to find the distance between points *P* and *Q*. We don't have a good way of measuring diagonal lines like that directly. But we *do* have a good way of measuring horizontal and vertical lines— that's the whole point of the grid! So we can draw a triangle that has $\overline{PQ}$ as its hypotenuse. We can easily measure its legs because we know the coordinates of the points.

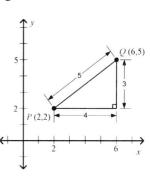

The base is 4 [that's 6 – 2] and the height is 3 [that's 5 – 2]. My stars! It's a 3-4-5 triangle. The hypotenuse is 5, so the length of $\overline{PQ}$ is 5.†

B. So how do you graph functions?

A graph on the *xy*-coordinate plane is nothing more than *a picture of a function*.

Take the equation **y = 2x**. We could plug in any number we like for *x* and we'll get a value for *y* as a result. Below we have a table of *x*'s and their respective *y*'s, along with a graph of those points plotted on the grid

---

* Yes, the plural of "axis" is "axes". It rhymes with "taxis", not with "faxes".

† Hey, remember when we said that drawing triangles can help you? Good times.

x	y
-3	-6
-2	-4
-1	-2
0	0
1	2
2	4
3	6

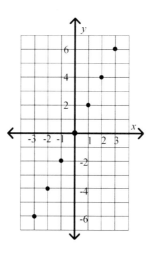

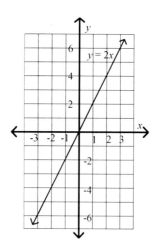

We can see that the points we chose start to make a straight line. If we fill in *all* the possible *x*'s and their corresponding *y*'s, including all the nasty decimal numbers, that's exactly what we'd get: a straight line. So our graph of $y = 2x$ is a picture of all the possible solutions to the equation—every *x* paired with its corresponding *y*.

Remember that in function notation, the "$f(x)$" dealie is basically the same thing as *y*. Rather than defining our equation as $y = 2x$, we could easily have defined it as $f(x) = 2x$ and said that $y = f(x)$ in the graph. Don't get bogged down with all the different letters. It's all the same thing.

The most important thing to remember is: **If a point lies on the graph of a function, the coordinates of that point will satisfy the function's equation.** And vice versa. Even if you don't know the equation of the function, you can learn a lot just from the picture. For example:

☛ **The figure below shows the graph of $y = f(x)$. What is the value of $f(1)$?**

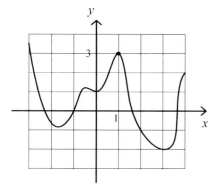

If they'd given you an equation for $f(x)$, you could find $f(1)$ by substituting "1" for "*x*" in the formula. No problem.

But here they don't give us an equation. Hmm. Now that's a crazy, crazy looking function. You will never be able to write an equation for it.

But we don't need an equation because we have a graph of the function! A graph is a picture of the function. Every point on that squiggly line is a set of numbers that satisfies the equation, whatever that may be.

They want the value of $f(1)$. So all we have to do is find the value of *y* when $x = 1$. That's 3! The squiggly line crosses point (1, 3). So when $x = 1$, $y = 3$. So $\boxed{f(1) = 3}$.

This is an important point, so it bears repeating.

If the point (a, b) is on the graph of f, then $f(a) = b$.

If $f(a) = b$, then the point (a, b) is on the graph of f.

TRY SOME : *Try to find some more points on this graph:*

☛ $f(-1) = ?$ ☛ $f(2) = ?$

☛ $f(0) = ?$ ☛ $f(3) = ?$

A lot of people get confused by this notation, so here's a trick to help you remember. If you <u>draw in some parentheses</u>, the equation looks just like a coordinate pair. So:

$$f(1) = 3 \qquad\qquad f(x) = y$$

becomes

$$f\big(1, \ 3\big) \qquad\qquad f\big(x, \ y\big)$$

C. Lines

The main equation to remember about straight lines is $y = mx + b$. Let's look at what that means:

Slope (*m*)

As the name implies, slope (abbreviated "*m*" for some reason[*]) is a way to measure the "steepness" of a line. Looking from left to right, a *positive* slope goes <u>up</u> and a *negative* slope goes <u>down</u>. As you can see from the examples below, the more the line goes up, the larger its slope; the more the line goes down, the smaller its slope.

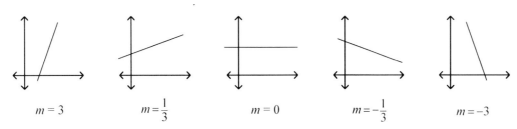

$$m = 3 \qquad m = \frac{1}{3} \qquad m = 0 \qquad m = -\frac{1}{3} \qquad m = -3$$

There are many ways to define slope, but they all mean the same thing:

$$\frac{\text{change in } y}{\text{change in } x} \qquad \frac{\text{rise}}{\text{run}} \qquad \frac{\Delta y}{\Delta x} \qquad \frac{y_2 - y_1}{x_2 - x_1}$$

If you know two points on a line, you can find the slope of the line. All you have to do is take the difference of the *y*'s over the difference in the *x*'s:

Here, $(x_1, y_1) = (1,2)$ and $(x_2, y_2) = (6,4)$

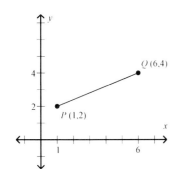

$$m = \frac{y_2 - y_1}{x_2 - x_1} = \frac{4 - 2}{6 - 1} \qquad \boxed{m = \frac{2}{5}}$$

Don't get bogged down by all those letters. We're just picking which point to go first and which to go second. In fact, it doesn't matter which point we use first. We could say that $(x_1, y_1) = (6,4)$ and $(x_2, y_2) = (1,2)$ and...

$$m = \frac{y_2 - y_1}{x_2 - x_1} = \frac{2 - 4}{1 - 6} = \frac{-2}{-5} = \frac{2}{5}$$

...we get the same thing.

> When the axes of a graph measure distance and time, the slope of a line gives the speed of the object.

Some things to remember when calculating slope:

- ☛ Make sure *y* is on top. We repeat: make sure $\boxed{Y}$ is on top. They do <u>not</u> tell you the formula for slope. You have to remember it.

- ☛ Be consistent with the *x* and *y*. In the example above, if I use the 4 first on the top, I have to use the 6 first on the bottom.

- ☛ *Parallel* lines have equal slopes.

- ☛ The slopes of *perpendicular* lines are the "negative reciprocals" of one another. Take the first slope, make it negative, and flip the fraction to get the second slope.

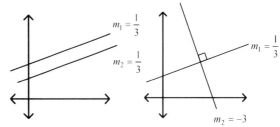

---

[*] No one knows how "*m*" became the symbol for slope. Over the years, different people in different countries have used *a, k, l, p,* and *s* for slope. Descartes, who invented "*x*", did not use "*m*". Sometimes this stuff is just random.

y-intercept (*b*)

An "intercept" is just the point at which the line crosses one of the axes. So the *x-intercept* is the point at which the line crosses the x-axis. And the *y-intercept* is the point at which the line crosses the y-axis

In the figure to the right, the line has a *y*-intercept of 3, since it crosses the *y*-axis at the point (0,3). The *y*-intercept always has an <u>x-value of zero</u>.

In the figure to the right, the line has an *x*-intercept of 2, since it crosses the *x*-axis at the point (2,0). The *x*-intercept always has a <u>y-value of zero</u>.

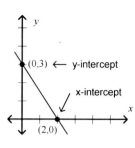

Equations

The standard form for an equation for a line is $y = mx + b$. The "*m*" stands for slope. The "*b*" stands for the *y*-intercept. And the "*x*" and "*y*" stand for the coordinates of any and all points on the line.

Let's see this stuff at work:

➤ **Line *ℓ* passes through the points (4,4) and (2,3) . What is the equation of line *ℓ*?**

To find the equation of the line, we need the *slope* and the *y-intercept*. First, since we know two points, we can find the slope.

$$m = \frac{y_2 - y_1}{x_2 - x_1} = \frac{4-3}{4-2} \qquad \boxed{m = \frac{1}{2}}$$

Now we know *m*, so our equation so far is $y = \frac{1}{2}x + b$. To find *b*, let's just stick one of the points we know in for *x* and *y*. Then we can solve for *b*.

$$y = \frac{1}{2}x + b$$

$$3 = \frac{1}{2}(2) + b$$

$$\boxed{2 = b}$$

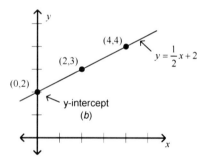

So our equation is $\boxed{y = \frac{1}{2}x + 2}$. The graph of the line can be seen at right.

Reflections

☞ **What is the equation for the line that results when the line $y = \dfrac{1}{2}x + 1$ is reflected across the *x*-axis?**

Reflecting a line across an axis is exactly what it sounds like. Imagine the axis is a *mirror*, and draw the original line's mirror image across the axis.

First, since we don't have a figure, let's draw it. We know the slope and the *y*-intercept, so it should be easy to sketch out quickly. We can label a few points on the line to make things a bit clearer.

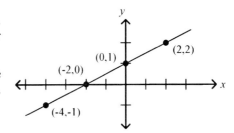

We want to reflect that line across the *x*-axis (the horizontal line). So we're going to take every point shown and **move it to the other side of the axis**, to the "mirror image" point on the other side.

☞ Points above the axis will now be below it.

☞ Points below the axis will now be above it.

☞ Points on the axis will stay on the axis.

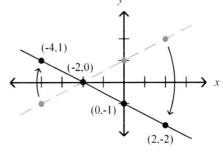

That means the *x*-values will stay the same, but the *y*-values will be multiplied by −1.

How does this affect the equation? Look at our picture. Now the *y*-intercept is −1, and the slope is $-\dfrac{1}{2}$. So both the slope and the *y*-intercept change signs, and the equation of the new line is $\boxed{y = -\dfrac{1}{2}x - 1}$.

Note that our resulting equation is equivalent to taking the original equation and multiplying *y* by −1. Similarly, if you want to reflect a line across the *y*-axis, just multiply *x* by −1 in the original equation. That means that the slope will change signs, but the *y*-intercept will not.

TRY SOME:

☞ What is the slope of the line that passes through the points (2, 6) and (4, 1)?

☞ What is the slope of the line that passes through the points (−2, −3) and (−1, 5)?

☞ What is the equation of the line that passes through the points (−1, 2) and (1, 6)?

☞ What are the coordinates of the _x-intercept_ of the line $y = 4x - 10$?

☞ The equation of line ℓ is $y = 3x + 5$. If line k is perpendicular to line ℓ and passes through the point (0, −3), what is the equation of line k?

☞ The equation of line ℓ is $y = -2x + 3$. If line k is the reflection of line ℓ across the x-axis, what is the equation of line k?

D. Parabolas

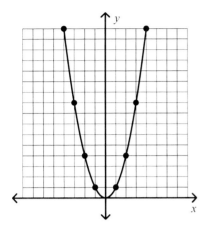

A *parabola* is the graph of an equation that contains the square of x. This is the graph of $y = x^2$. You can see that the marked points fit the equation: the y value of each point is the square of the x value:

x	–4	–3	–2	–1	0	1	2	3	4
y	16	9	4	1	0	1	4	9	16

Parabolas always fit into the following equation:

$$y = ax^2 + bx + c$$

where a, b, and c are constants.[*] For $y = x^2$, $a = 1$, $b = 0$, and $c = 0$.

Some of you may recognize this form as what's called a "quadratic equation". Some of you may also know that there is a complicated formula (the "quadratic formula") that you can use to solve quadratic equations. *You will **not** need the quadratic formula on the SAT.* We repeat: *You will **not** need the quadratic formula on the SAT.* If you have no idea what we're talking about, GOOD. Ignore this paragraph. But if you're tempted to use the quadratic formula on the SAT—*DON'T.*

Here are some properties of parabolas:

- Notice that this parabola is *symmetrical*. That's because the square of a negative comes out positive (in our example: $y = 4$ when $x = 2$ *and* when $x = –2$.) *All* parabolas are symmetrical, though they may not be centered on the axis like this.

- If a (the number in front of the "x^2") is *positive*, the parabola will point <u>up</u>. If a is *negative*, the parabola will point <u>down</u>.

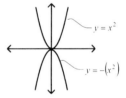

- The value of c (the number that doesn't have any x's next to it) will be the *y-intercept* of the parabola. Just like in a straight line, the *y*-intercept is the value of y when $x = 0$. Because c is the only term in the equation that doesn't come with an x next to it, if $x = 0$, all that's left is c.[†]

E. Transformation of Functions

Here are some examples of how functions can move depending on what you do to them:

- **For any $f(x)$, the graph of $f(x) + c$ is the graph of $f(x)$ shifted c places UP.**

- **For any $f(x)$, the graph of $f(x) – c$ is the graph of $f(x)$ shifted c places DOWN.**

Subtracting a number from the end means you'll lower the y value by that number, so the graph will shift down. Adding will increase the y value, so the graph will shift up. This is true of all functions, no matter what the equation looks like.

---

[*] Constants are numbers that don't change at all *within a given equation.* You can stick in any numbers you want for x and y and it'll still be the same equation. If you change the values of a, b, or c, it's no longer considered the same equation.

[†] Don't be confused by the fact that c is the y-intercept for parabolas, while b is the y-intercept for lines. The letters are entirely arbitrary. We could call them p and q for all it matters. Heck, we don't even have to put it last; we could say $y = b + xm$. What does matter is that it's the number that stands by itself. In each case, the y-intercept is the number that doesn't have an x next to it.

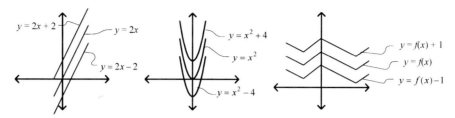

Okay, this next one is a bit weird, so bear with us.

- ☛ **For any $f(x)$, the graph of $f(x + c)$ is the graph of $f(x)$ shifted c places to the LEFT.**

- ☛ **For any $f(x)$, the graph of $f(x - c)$ is the graph of $f(x)$ shifted c places to the RIGHT.**

Before, we were adding to or subtracting from the *end* of the function. Here, we're adding or subtracting from *inside* the parentheses. Think of the space *inside* the parentheses as *Bizarro World*: adding to the x moves the graph toward the negatives, subtracting from the x moves the graph toward the positives.

If you have a graphing calculator, you can try this out yourself. Type these equations into "Y="

$$Y_1 = (x)^2 \qquad Y_2 = (x+1)^2$$

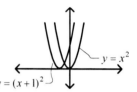

You can see that the graph of the second equation looks just like that of the first equation, but shifted to the left by one space.

This can be confusing, and it isn't really that important, so if you're still confused, just move on. But if you're curious and really must know why this is true, let's explain. Take a look at these:

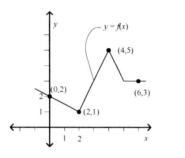 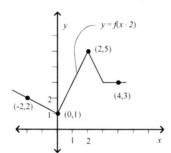

Man, that's a funny-looking function. We certainly don't know the equation for it. But no matter what the original equation for $f(x)$ is, we know that $f(x + 2)$ will make the graph shift 2 places *to the left*.

To understand, let's look at some points.

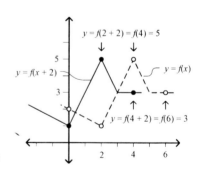

x	$f(x)$	point	$f(x + 2)$	point
$x = 0$	$f(0) = 2$	$(0,2)$	$f(0 + 2) = f(2)$	$(0,1)$
$x = 2$	$f(2) = 1$	$(2,1)$	$f(2 + 2) = f(4)$	$(2,5)$
$x = 4$	$f(4) = 5$	$(4,5)$	$f(4 + 2) = f(6)$	$(4,3)$

When x is 0 in $f(x + 2)$, the y value will be the same as $f(2)$ in the first graph, which is 1. So $f(0+2) = 1$, so the graph will touch $(0,1)$. When $x = 0$, $y = 1$

When x is 2 in $f(x + 2)$, the y value will be the same as $f(4)$ in the first graph, which is 5. So $f(2 + 2) = 4$, so the graph will touch $(2,5)$. When $x = 2$, $y = 5$.

So every point in $f(x + 2)$ takes its y value from the point two spaces to the right. That means $f(x + 2)$ is two spaces to the left of $f(x)$.

GRAPHING DRILL

9. The vertices of a rectangle are at $(-1, 5)$, $(5, 5)$, $(5, -2)$, and $(-1, -2)$. What is the perimeter of this rectangle?

(A) 13
(B) 26
(C) 28
(D) 36
(E) 42

13. What is the slope of a line that passes through the origin and the point $(-3, 2)$?

(A) 3/2
(B) 2/3
(C) 0
(D) $-2/3$
(E) $-3/2$

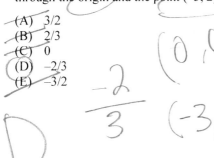

14. Let the function f be defined by $f(x) = ax^2 + bx + c$ where a, b, and c are constants. If $b < 0$ and $c > 0$, then which of the following could be the graph of f?

(A)

(B)

(C)

(D)

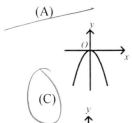 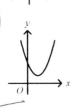

(E)

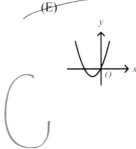

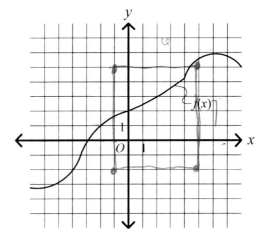

15. The figure above shows the graph of $f(x)$. If $g(x) = f(x + 4)$, what is $g(-2)$?

(A) -2
(B) 1
(C) 2
(D) 3
(E) 4

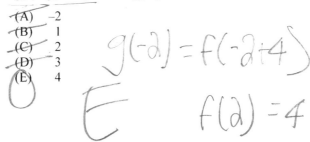

16. In the xy-coordinate plane, $(a, 5)$ is a point of intersection of the graphs of $y = x^2 + 1$ and $y = k - x^2$, where k is a constant. If $a > 0$, what is the value of k?

(A) 1
(B) 2
(C) 5
(D) 7
(E) 9

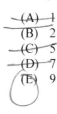

© A-List Services LLC

– 115–

BIG FUNCTION EXERCISE

1. Which of the following could be the graph of a line with a positive slope and a negative y-intercept?

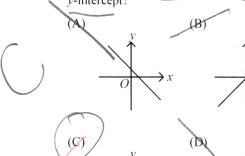

(A)

(B)

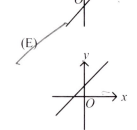

(C)

(D)

(E)

2. For all integers a and b, let $a \ast b = 3a + b$. What is the value of $3 \ast 2$?

(A) 8
(B) 9
(C) 10
(D) 11
(E) 12

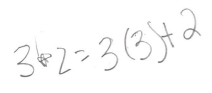

$3 \ast 2 = 3(3) + 2$

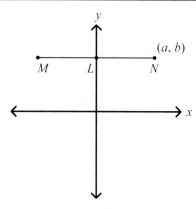

(a, b)

M   L   N

3. In the figure above, $\overline{MN}$ is parallel to the x-axis. If $ML = LN$, what are the coordinates of point M?

(A) (b, a)
(B) $(b, -a)$
(C) $(a, -b)$
(D) $(-a, b)$
(E) $(-a, -b)$

x	$f(x)$
-1	-1
0	-2
2	2
3	7

4. The table above gives values of the function f. Which of the following equations defines f?

(A) $f(x) = x - 2$
(B) $f(x) = x^2 - 2$
(C) $f(x) = x^2 + 1$
(D) $f(x) = 2x - 2$
(E) $f(x) = 3x - 2$

Questions 5 and 6 refer to the following function:

Let ↑x refer to the greatest prime factor of x.

5.   What is the value of ↑60?

   (A)   2
   (B)   3
   (C)   5
   (D)   10
   (E)   20

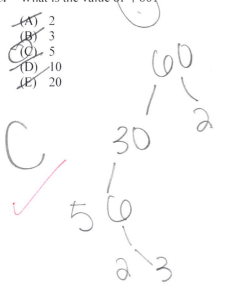

6. If ↑k = 3, which of the following could be k?

   (A)   15
   (B)   24
   (C)   30
   (D)   42
   (E)   45

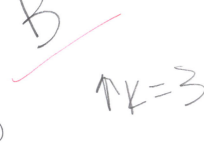

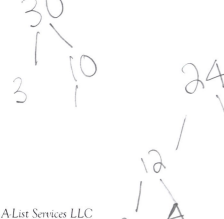

7.   For which of the following functions is it true that $f(-3) = f(3)$?

   (A) $x^3 + 2$
   (B) $2x^2$
   (C) $x + 2$
   (D) $3 - x$
   (E) $\dfrac{x}{3}$

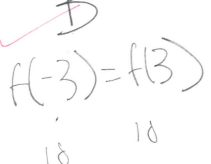

8.   If the function $k(x)$ is defined by $k(x) = x^3 + 2x$, what is $k(-2)$?

   (A)   −12
   (B)   −6
   (C)   0
   (D)   6
   (E)   12

9. Let the operation ▼ be defined by
    $x \blacktriangledown y = y - \dfrac{1}{x}$. What is the value of $1 \blacktriangledown 5$?

    (A) -4

    (B) 1

    (C) $\dfrac{4}{5}$

    (D) $\dfrac{5}{4}$

    (E) 4

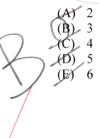

$1 \triangledown 5 = 5 - \dfrac{1}{1}$

10. For all values of x, let the function f be
    defined by $f(x) = 5x - 3$. If $f(a) = 12$, what is
    the value of a?

    (A) 2
    (B) 3
    (C) 4
    (D) 5
    (E) 6

$f(x) = 5x - 3$

$f(a) = 12$

11. If the function f is defined by $f(x) = 2x + 2$,
    then $2f(x) + 2 =$

    (A) $2x + 4$
    (B) $4x + 2$
    (C) $4x + 4$
    (D) $4x + 6$
    (E) $4x + 8$

12. For all values of x, the function f is defined
    by $f(x) = 7x$, and the function g is defined by
    $g(x) = f(x) + 7$. What is the value of $g(10)$?

    (A)   7
    (B)   10
    (C)   17
    (D)   70
    (E)   77

13. For all values of x, let $x℗$ be defined by $x℗ = 3x + 2$. Which of the following is equivalent to $(x℗)℗$?

(A) $6x + 4$
(B) $6x + 8$
(C) $9x + 2$
(D) $9x + 4$
(E) $9x + 8$

$x℗ = 3x + 2$

14. The equation of line ℓ is $y = 3x - 2$. if line m is the reflection of ℓ across the x-axis, what is the equation of line m?

(A) $y = -3x - 2$
(B) $y = -3x + 2$
(C) $y = 3x + 2$
(D) $y = -\dfrac{1}{3}x + 2$
(E) $y = -\dfrac{1}{3}x - 2$

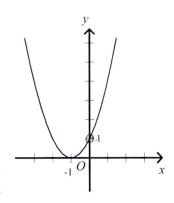

15. Which of the following could be the graph of the function f, shown above?

(A) $f(x) = x^2 - 2x - 1$
(B) $f(x) = x^2 - x - 1$
(C) $f(x) = x^2 + 2x + 1$
(D) $f(x) = x^2 + 2x - 2$
(E) $f(x) = x^2 + 3x - 2$

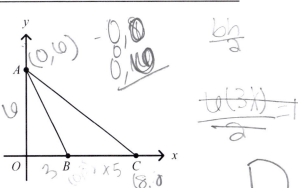

16. In the xy plane above, the area of $\triangle ABC$ is 15, the length of $\overline{OB}$ is 3 and the coordinates of point A are $(0, 6)$. What is the slope of segment $\overline{AC}$?

(A) -2
(B) $-\dfrac{4}{3}$
(C) $-\dfrac{6}{5}$
(D) $-\dfrac{3}{4}$
(E) $-\dfrac{1}{2}$

$\dfrac{6(x)}{2} = 15$

$x = 5$

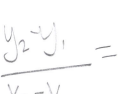

$\dfrac{y_2 - y_1}{x_2 - x_1} =$

17. The graph of function f in the xy-plane is a line. If $f(1) = 9$ and $f(4) = 3$, what is the slope of the line?

(A) −2
(B) −1
(C) 2
(D) 6
(E) 8

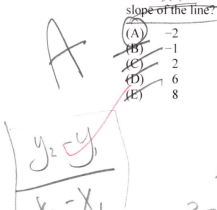

$$f(1) = 9$$

$$f(4) = 3$$

$$\frac{3-9}{4-1} = \frac{-6}{3}$$

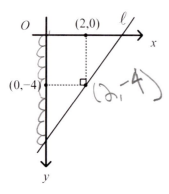

Note: Figure not drawn to scale.

18. In the figure above, if line ℓ has a slope of 3, what is the y-intercept of ℓ?

(A) −7
(B) −8
(C) −9
(D) −10
(E) −11

19. In the xy-coordinate plane, the distance between point A (7,7) and point B (1, k) is 10. Which of the following is a possible value of k?

(A) −3
(B) −1
(C) 1
(D) 8
(E) 17

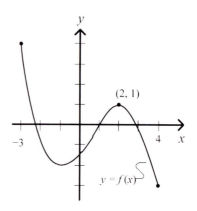

20. The function $y = f(x)$, defined for the interval $-3 \leq x \leq 4$, is shown in the graph above. For how many values of x does $f(x) = -1$?

(A) None
(B) One
(C) Two
(D) Three
(E) More than three

MISCELLANY

We're almost at the end. There are a few more concepts left that don't quite fit into any of the topics we've covered so far. So we just threw them all together into the grab bag of math that follows. Note that all of the following topics are at the bottom of the SAT Math totem pole: they don't appear very often, and a lot of it you could probably figure out on your own without our help. They might appear on one question per test. If you're going for an 800, you'll need to know this stuff backwards and forwards. Otherwise, don't lose sleep over it.

I. COMBINATORICS

Combinatorics is a fancy word that just refers to the mathematics of possible arrangements. There are several different kinds of problems that deal with possible arrangements.

A. Two separate groups

Take a look at this problem:

> ✐ **An ice cream shop is having a sale on a cup of one flavor of ice cream with one topping. If the shop sells 4 flavors of ice cream and 3 kinds of toppings, how many different combinations of flavor and topping are possible?**

There are four options for the flavor, and each of those has three options for the topping. So all you have to do to solve this problem is multiply 4 × 3. That's **12**.

If you get confused by problems like this, it sometimes helps to list all the possible arrangements that can be made. Let's say the flavors are *vanilla, chocolate, strawberry,* and *pistachio*. And let's say the options for toppings are *sprinkles, chocolate syrup,* and *cookies.* So here are all the possible combinations, as in the figure to the left.

For each of the four flavors, there are three options for toppings. Therefore, we can get the total number of combinations simply by multiplying 4 times 3.

So if you're just pairing members of one group with members of another group, just multiply the groups together to get the total number of possible combinations.

B. Single group: order matters

> ✐ **Roberto has three paintings he wants to hang in a straight horizontal line on his bedroom wall. How many different arrangements of the paintings are possible?**

Here, instead of pairing together two groups, we're putting a single group of things into a certain order. As in the last problem, we could count all the possible arrangements. Since the paintings don't have names, let's just call them A, B, and C. Write them out: there are **six** possible arrangements:

As in the last problem, we could count all the possible arrangements. Since the paintings don't have names, let's just call them A, B, and C.

ABC	BAC	CAB
ACB	BCA	CBA

There are *6* possible ways to order the paintings.

Think about these problems according to **SLOTS**. There are three slots that we want to fill: first, second, and third.

Start with the first slot. There are **3** possible paintings for the first slot.

Let's say we put painting A in the first slot. Now, there are **2** options left for the second slot, B and C.

Let's put painting B in the second slot. Now, there's only **1** option left for the third slot, painting C.

We can figure out how many possible orders there are by **multiplying** the options for each slot: $3 \times 2 \times 1 =$ **6 options**.

First	Second	Third
A, B, C		
3 options		
A	A̶, **B, C**	
	2 options	
A	B	A̶, B̶, **C**
		1 option
3 options $\times$	**2 options** $\times$	**1 option**

Try another one:

➤ **A school club wants to appoint a president and a vice president. If there are 5 students in the club and no student can hold both positions, how many different assignments of students to positions are possible?**

This problem works just like the last one. There are **five** candidates for president. Once we choose a president, there are **four** candidates for vice president. $5 \times 4 = 20$. There are **20** total possibilities.

C. Single group: order doesn't matter

➤ **At a certain detective agency, each case is handled by a team of two detectives. If a total of four detectives work at the agency, how many different teams are possible?**

> Problems where order matters are sometimes called *Permutations*, while problems where order doesn't matter are called *Combinations*. But don't worry, you don't have to know these terms.

This problem is a lot like the last two, but with one important difference: *order doesn't matter*.

This is pretty easy to do if we just write out all the possible teams. To make things easier, let's give them names: **Andre**, **Bob**, **Carlos**, and **Dietrich**.

Andre–Bob	Bob–Carlos
Andre–Carlos	Bob–Dietrich
Andre–Dietrich	Carlos–Dietrich

There are **6 possible teams**.

Wait a minute. Six? If we do the multiplication we did before, we would get 4 options for the first slot and 3 for the second, and 4×3 is 12. How did we get 6?

This problem is different because unlike the painting problem, *order doesn't matter*. In the previous problem, having Andre as president and Bob as vice president was different than having Bob president and Andre vice president, so we want to count each scenario separately. Here, a team of Andre–Bob *is the same* as a team of Bob–Andre, so we don't want to count them separately.

If we multiply 4×3, this is what we're doing:

Andre–Bob	B̶o̶b̶–̶A̶n̶d̶r̶e̶	C̶a̶r̶l̶o̶s̶–̶A̶n̶d̶r̶e̶	D̶i̶e̶t̶r̶i̶c̶h̶–̶A̶n̶d̶r̶e̶
Andre–Carlos	Bob–Carlos	C̶a̶r̶l̶o̶s̶–̶B̶o̶b̶	D̶i̶e̶t̶r̶i̶c̶h̶–̶B̶o̶b̶
Andre–Dietrich	Bob–Dietrich	Carlos–Dietrich	D̶i̶e̶t̶r̶i̶c̶h̶–̶C̶a̶r̶l̶o̶s̶

We are counting each team *twice*; we're counting Andre–Bob *and* Bob–Andre. Since that gives us 12 possibilities, if we divide that by two, we'll get our answer. $12/2 = 6$. There are **6 possible teams**.

II. PROBABILITY

"Probability" means exactly what it sounds like: how "probable" is this event. The probability of an event is defined as:

$$\frac{\text{number of "winners"}}{\text{total possible events}}$$

Say the probability of winning the lottery is "one in a million". That just means there's *one* winning number out of *a million* possible numbers. Since probabilities are just glorified fractions, you can think of probability as basically *the same thing as percents*. People talk this way all the time; when the weatherman says there's a 60% chance of rain, that's the same thing as a probability of 3/5. So most probability questions just boil down to: what **part of the whole** is the thing you're looking for?

➤ **A certain jar with 32 marbles contains only red marbles and blue marbles. If the jar contains 8 red marbles, what is the probability that a marble chosen from the jar will be blue?**

We're looking for the probability of choosing a blue marble. So all we have to find is:

$$\frac{\text{number of blue marbles}}{\text{total number of marbles}} = \frac{\text{blue}}{32}$$

We know there are 32 total marbles, so 32 will go on the bottom. We don't know how many blue marbles there are, but we do know there are 8 red marbles, and there are only red and blue marbles. So if we subtract the red from the total, we'll be left with the blue.

$$\frac{32-8}{32} = \frac{24}{32} = \frac{3}{4}$$ We're done! The probability of choosing a blue marble is 3/4.

Note that instead of solving for the blue marbles, we could've found the probability of choosing a red marble and subtracted from 1.

$$\frac{\text{red}}{\text{total}} = \frac{8}{32} = \frac{1}{4}$$ There's a 1/4 chance of picking a red marble…

$$1 - \frac{1}{4} = \frac{3}{4}$$ …so there's a 3/4 chance of picking a blue marble.

We can see from this that *the probabilities of all events surrounding a given problem must add up to 1*. Just like all percents of a whole add up to 100%, all probabilities add up to 1.

➤ **Gerald has a deck of five playing cards each with a different integer from 1 to 5. He draws three cards and lays them in order on a table to produce a three-digit number. What is the probability that the number he produces is 235?**

Probability is the number of *winners* over the *total possibilities*. Here, there's only *one* winner: the number 235. So the question is really: how many total possible numbers could be produced?

We can find the total possible arrangements the same way we did before. Since the order matters, we'll multiply all the options for each slot: **Five** options for the first card drawn, then **four** for the second (since one was already used), then **three** for the third (since two were used). $5 \times 4 \times 3 = 60$ *possibilities*.

So the probability of choosing 235 is $\frac{1}{60}$.

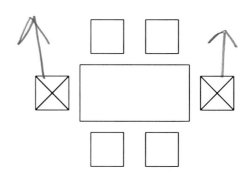

A,B,C,D,T,F

COMBINATORICS DRILL

3. Four randomly chosen employees at Dave's company will win large cash prizes. If there are 100 employees at the company, what is the probability that Dave will not win?

(A) $\frac{1}{100}$

(B) $\frac{1}{25}$

(C) $\frac{1}{4}$

(D) $\frac{24}{25}$

(E) $\frac{99}{100}$

[handwritten: D]

[handwritten: P(win) $\frac{4}{100} = \frac{1}{25}$]

[handwritten: P(not win) $= \frac{24}{25}$]

20. The figure above represents the seating arrangements at a dinner table, which are to be determined randomly among six guests. If Bill and Ted are two of the guests, what is the probability that each will be seated in a position marked with an X?

(A) $\frac{1}{36}$

(B) $\frac{1}{30}$

(C) $\frac{1}{15}$

(D) $\frac{1}{12}$

(E) $\frac{1}{3}$

[handwritten: C]

12. Four people live on a city block and each person has exactly one car. If there are four parking spots on the street, how many different assignments of cars to parking spots are possible?

(A) 10
(B) 12
(C) 16
(D) 24
(E) 256

[handwritten: D]

[handwritten: ABCD]

[handwritten: 4X3X2X1]

19. A box contains a shipment of stuffed bears, of which 14 are red, 30 are green, 40 are blue and the rest are yellow. If the probability of selecting a yellow bear from this box at random is $\frac{1}{4}$, how many yellow bears are in the box?

(A) 21
(B) 28
(C) 31
(D) 56
(E) 168

[handwritten: B]

[handwritten: 14-R, 30-G, 40-B, X-Y]

[handwritten: $\frac{x}{40+30+40+x} = \frac{1}{4}$]

[handwritten: $\frac{x}{84+x} = \frac{1}{4}$]

*[handwritten:
A 6
B 5
C 5
D 5
T 5
F 5]*

[handwritten: $\frac{2}{30} = \frac{1}{15}$]

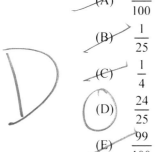
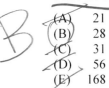
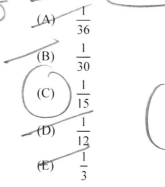

III. Sequences

3, 5, 9, …

> **In the sequence above, the first term is 3. Each term after the first is obtained by doubling the previous term and subtracting 1 from the result. What is the 7th term in this sequence?**

This is a sequence. That just means it's a list of numbers. But it's not a random sequence—there's a rule here. Every next term in the sequence is determined by applying that rule to the previous term.

Wait a minute—following a rule. Didn't we do this already? Heck, yeah, we did! This is just like a function. All we have to do is apply the rule until we get what they want. This question involves nothing more than following directions.[*] They want the 7th term in the sequence? Just keep applying the rule until you get 7 terms.

$$3 \leftarrow 1^{st} \text{ term} \qquad\qquad 17(2) - 1 = 33 \leftarrow 5^{th} \text{ term}$$

$$3(2) - 1 = 5 \leftarrow 2^{nd} \text{ term} \qquad 33(2) - 1 = 65 \leftarrow 6^{th} \text{ term}$$

$$5(2) - 1 = 9 \leftarrow 3^{rd} \text{ term} \qquad 65(2) - 1 = \boxed{129} \leftarrow 7^{th} \text{ term}$$

$$9(2) - 1 = 17 \leftarrow 4^{th} \text{ term}$$

That's it. Just follow directions, like you do with a function. Take a look at this one:

0.37829378293…

> **In the repeating decimal above, the digits 37829 repeat in that order infinitely. What is the value of the 404th digit?**

What?? The four hundred and fourth digit?!? I don't know about you, but I don't want to write that many numbers. What are we supposed to do??

Calm down, kitty cat. We'll tell you what you're NOT supposed to do: you're not supposed to write out 404 digits. Seriously, do you *really* think that's the "right" way to do this problem? They give you, like, two inches of space to do each problem!

So there must be a trick. There must be some kind of *pattern*, so we can tell what that digit is without doing it all out. We're telling you right now:

> **Any time you need a really large term in a sequence, try to find the pattern.**

Instead of doing out 404 terms, let's **write out a *few* terms** and look for a repeating pattern.

term	1st	2nd	3rd	4th	5th	6th	7th	8th	9th	10th	11th	12th	13th	14th	15th
digit	3	7	8	2	9	3	7	8	2	9	3	7	8	2	9

Five numbers are repeating, so let's focus on the last one in the list. That's **9**. So the **5th** digit is 9, the **10th** term is 9, the **15th** digit is 9: *Every digit that's a multiple of 5 is 9.* So the **20th** digit is 9, the **100th** digit is 9, the **105th** digit is 9, the **200th** digit is 9, and the **400th** digit is 9.

Now that we know the 400th digit is 9, we can just count to the one we want:

term	400th	401st	402nd	403rd	404th	405th
digit	9	3	7	8	2	9

So the 404th digit is **2**.

---

[*] Man, you *really* don't need to know any math for this test.

Sequence questions are like function questions; they're all about following rules.

➤ If the question asks for a small term—less than 10—just do out the sequence until you get there.

➤ If the question asks for an large term, *don't do it out*. Look for some kind of *pattern* or rule to find that term directly. If you can't see the pattern, try taking the sequence out a few terms until you can. Don't worry: we promise there will be a pattern.

SEQUENCE DRILL

5, 6, 8, …

5. In the sequence above, the first term is 5, and each term after the first is obtained by subtracting two and then multiplying by two. What is the 8th term in the sequence?

(A) 33
(B) 48
(C) 68
(D) 132
(E) 256

handwritten D

handwritten table:
n |
1 | 5
2 | 6
3 | 8
4 | 12
5 | 20
6 | 36
7 | 68
| 132

12. The nth term of a sequence is defined to be $6n - 4$. The 25th term is how much less than the 30th?

(A) 5
(B) 10
(C) 20
(D) 24
(E) 30

handwritten E

$6n - 4$

$6(25) - 4 = 146$

$6(30) - 4 = 176$

15. Each person who comes to the circus gets a balloon in one of four colors: red, purple, green, or yellow. If balloons are always handed out in that order, and the first person gets a red balloon, what color balloon will the 93rd person get?

(A) Red
(B) Purple
(C) Green
(D) Yellow
(E) It cannot be determined from the information given.

handwritten A

R 1
P 2
G 3
Y ←4

18. The first term of a sequence is –2 and every term after the first is 5 more than the term preceding it. What is the 75th term?

(A) 360
(B) 363
(C) 368
(D) 370
(E) 373

handwritten C

$-2, 3, 8, 13 \ldots$

$a, +(n-1)d$

$= -2 + (75-1)5$

$= -2 + (74)5$

20. In a certain sequence, each even numbered term is obtained by adding 4 to the previous term, and each odd numbered term after the first is obtained by multiplying the previous term by –1. If the first term is 9, what is the sum of the first 34 terms?

(A) –123
(B) 13
(C) 22
(D) 141
(E) 145

handwritten C

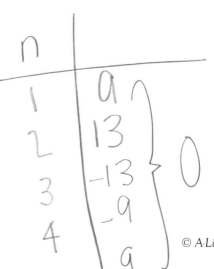

handwritten table:
n | a
1 | 9
2 | 13
3 | –13
4 | –9
5 | 9

} 0

IV. ABSOLUTE VALUE

Take a look at this:

☞ $|x| = 7$

Those straight lines on either side of the x mean we're taking the "absolute value" of x. The absolute value of a number is its numerical value, ignoring its sign:

$$|5| = 5 \qquad\qquad |-5| = 5$$

If there's a positive number between the lines, just repeat the number. If there's a negative number between the signs, make it positive.

So in this equation:

☞ $|x| = 7$

x could equal 7 or –7.

The key to absolute value problems is ***DON'T FORGET ABOUT THE NEGATIVES.***

☞ **If $|n - 12| = 7$, what is one possible value of n?**

If $|n - 12| = 7$, then we have two options:

$n - 12 = 7$ or $n - 12 = -7$

$\boxed{n = 19}$ $\boxed{n = 5}$

It's sometimes helpful to think of absolute value as **distance**: *The absolute value of a difference gives the distance between the two points.* That is:

$$|\text{Point A} - \text{Point B}| = \text{distance between points}$$

Think about that problem above. The expression "$|n - 12| = 7$" means that "point n and point 12 are a distance of 7 away from each other". The use of absolute value means n could be a distance of 7 in either direction: n could be 7 more than 12, or 7 less than 12.

With that in mind, take a look at this problem:

15. **Scott is using rocks to build a wall. In order to fit in the wall, each rock must be between 9 and 11 inches wide. Which of the following expressions can be used to determine whether the width w of a certain rock can be used in his wall?**

(A) $|w - 10| < 1$

(B) $|w + 10| < 1$

(C) $|w - 10| = 1$

(D) $|w + 10| = 1$

(E) $|w - 10| > 1$

First of all, this problem is begging to be solved with Plug In. Let's say $w = 10$. A rock that's 10 inches wide can be used in the wall—it's right in the middle of our range. So let's put 10 in for w in all the choices; whichever choice gives us an expression that's true will be our answer.

(A) $\quad |10-10| = |0| = 0 < 1$ ✓ $\qquad$ **Zero is less than 1.**

(B) $\quad |10+10| = |20| = 20 < 1$ ✗ $\qquad$ 20 is <u>not</u> less than 1.

(C) $\quad |10-10| = |0| = 0 = 1$ ✗ $\qquad$ Zero does <u>not</u> equal 1.

(D) $\quad |10+10| = |20| = 20 = 1$ ✗ $\qquad$ 20 does <u>not</u> equal 1.

(E) $\quad |10-10| = |0| = 0 > 1$ ✗ $\qquad$ Zero is <u>not</u> greater than 1.

Only (A) works. That's our answer.

But what the heck is going on? What's with all this absolute value stuff?

Remember what we just said: absolute value is a way to find **distance**. This problem says that each rock must be between 9 inches and 11 inches wide. That means each rock must be no more than a distance of 1 inch away from 10. Look at this number line:

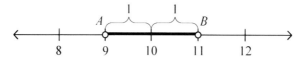

The dark line represents all the values of w that are allowed; 9 and 11 are the endpoints—w must be between 9 and 11. The points 9 and 11 are centered around the point 10. That is, each point is a distance of 1 away from the point 10. So any point we choose within that dark line will be closer to the middle, or *less than 1 away from 10.*

Therefore, the distance from w to 10 will be less than 1, or $|w - \mathbf{10}| < \mathbf{1}$

So any time you have a problem that asks you for a range like this, just remember this expression:

$$|\text{variable} - \text{midpoint}| < \text{half the total range}$$

$$|9 - x| = 8$$
$$|x - 5| = 12$$

3. What value of x satisfies both of the two equations above?

(A) −7
(B) −1
(C) 1
(D) 7
(E) 17

[handwritten: E]
[handwritten: X = 17]
[handwritten: X − 5 = 12]
[handwritten: X − 5 = −12]
[handwritten: X = −7]

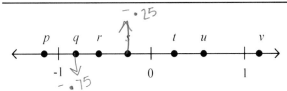

[handwritten: −.25]
[handwritten: −.75]

9. Which of the points on the number line above corresponds to $|q - s|$?

(A) p
(B) r
(C) t
(D) u
(E) v

[handwritten: D]

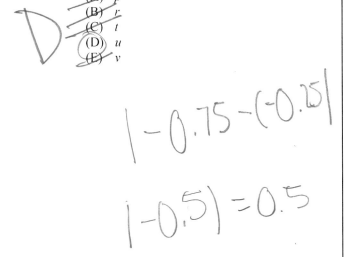

[handwritten: $|-0.75 - (-0.25)|$]
[handwritten: $|-0.5| = 0.5$]

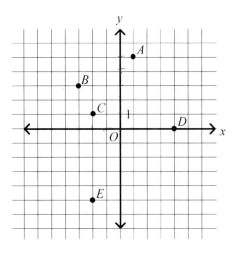

10. Which of the lettered points in the figure above has coordinates (x, y) such that $|x| + |y| = 7$?

(A) A
(B) B
(C) C
(D) D
(E) E

[handwritten: E]
[handwritten: A = (1, 5)]
[handwritten: B = (−4, 3)]
[handwritten: C = (−2, 1)]
[handwritten: D =]
[handwritten: E = (−2, −5)]

15. In order to make a bracelet, a jeweler can only use emeralds that weigh between 120 and 140 milligrams. Which of the following expressions can be used to determine whether a stone that weighs m milligrams satisfies the jeweler's restriction?

(A) $|m - 100| < 40$
(B) $|m - 120| < 20$
(C) $|m - 125| < 5$
(D) $|m - 130| < 10$
(E) $|m - 140| < 20$

[handwritten: D]
*[handwritten: *plug in method*]*
[handwritten: 120 < X < 140]
[handwritten: 110]
[handwritten: 150]
[handwritten: 130]

WRITING

INTRODUCTION TO WRITING

Welcome to Writing! The Writing section is everyone's least favorite section on the SAT.[*] It's often the most difficult because it's the one you've had the least exposure to in school. Sure, you have to write essays in school all the time, but not many students get explicit classes in grammar. So some of this will be unfamiliar to you.

We've got a lot of little rules to get through, but remember that you instinctively know a lot of them already. If you speak fluent English, *by definition* you know the rules of English. That's what "fluent" means. I mean, when you speak, you make sense.[†] People understand what you say. You don't go around pointing at things, grunting, and shouting "Car hat donkey donkey whiffleball McCoy!"

It's not that easy, of course. The SAT tests Standard Written English, whose rules may differ sometimes from those you use every day. Furthermore, you may not be *aware of* the rules you do know. In long, complicated sentences, it's easy to overlook an obvious error. So when you do these questions, you get lost. Everything sounds right. Everything sounds wrong. You freak out and start weeping softly. That's bad.

Our job here is to make you *aware* of the rules, to tell you what they expect you to know. Once you know what's coming, you'll be able to spot errors much, much more easily. It may seem that there are a lot of rules to learn, but each rule isn't very complicated. More importantly, the rules *make sense.* There's a reason that each of them came about. And once you understand why they work, it'll be that much easier to spot them when they show up.

For example, subject-verb agreement is a basic rule that we follow every day when we talk. But on SAT questions, it's easy to miss a verb agreement error. The sentences are so long and complicated that we lose track of the subject. HOWEVER, once we know that verb agreement is the most common error on the test, we can actively look for it and easily spot violations. So once you know what to look for, it's much easier to do well.

FORMAT

The format for the three Writing sections is always the same, and sections are always in the same order:

Time	Content
25 minutes	1 one- to two-page essay
25 minutes	11 Sentence Improvement questions 18 Error Identification questions 6 Paragraph Improvement questions
10 minutes	14 Sentence Improvement questions
60 minutes	**49 multiple-choice questions plus 1 essay**

The essay will always be the very first section of the test, and the 10-minute section will always be the last. The middle section will be mixed up with the Math and Critical Reading sections in any order.

Sentence Improvement and Error Identification questions are ordered by difficulty *within the section.* That is, the difficulty resets with the new question types: question #11 will be a hard Sentence Improvement, while question #12 will be an easy Error ID. Paragraph Improvement questions are not ordered by difficulty. Like passage-based questions in the Critical Reading, Paragraph Improvement questions are given in the order they appear in the passage (questions about paragraph 1, then questions about paragraph 2, etc.).

---

[*] Tied with Math and Reading.

[†] Usually.

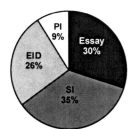

As mentioned before, you will actually get three Writing scores on the SAT. Besides the final Writing score (on a 200 to 800 scale), you will get an Essay score (0 to 12) and a multiple choice component score (20 to 80). The Essay score will account for about 30% of your overall Writing score, while the multiple choice accounts for 70% of your score. Since Sentence Improvement questions make up 50% of the multiple choice, they account for 35% of your final Writing score. Error IDs are not far behind—they're 37% of the multiple choice, thus 26% of your final Writing score.

So Sentence Improvement is the most important question type and Error ID is only third. Yet this book starts with the Error Identification section and spends two chapters on it. Why?

You can think of these sections as testing different kinds of relationships. In general:

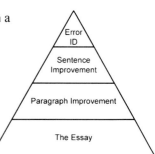

- ☞ Error Identification tests the relationship between **individual words** within a sentence.

- ☞ Sentence Improvement tests the relationship between **parts of a single sentence**, like clauses and phrases within a sentence.

- ☞ Paragraph Improvement tests the relationship between **separate sentences and paragraphs** within an essay.

- ☞ The Essay tests the **overall coherence** of the ideas in a text.

The sections build up larger and larger sections of language. Errors and concepts that appear on the more basic level may also appear on the levels after it, but not before it. That is, common Error ID concepts like subject-verb agreement also appear on Sentence Improvement questions, but common Sentence Improvement concepts like run-on sentences will likely not appear on Error ID questions.

Let's look at what these sections entail:

Error Identification

There will be **18 Error Identification Questions**. These present a sentence with four words or short phrases underlined. Students must decide which choice contains an error in grammar or usage. If there is no error, pick choice (E). Here's an example provided by the SAT:

The other delegates and him immediately
    A   B   C
accepted the resolution drafted by the
                           D
neutral states. No error   *Answer: B.*
           E

Error Identification questions are ordered by difficulty. Questions do not form a larger passage; each question will be its own distinct sentence.

Strategies

Most students rely too heavily on their natural intuition (their "ear") when determining whether a sentence is grammatical. This often means that they miss a lot of errors and choose choice (E) too frequently. These sentences are designed to fool your ears if you read carelessly.

That's not to say you should never trust your ears. Because the questions are ordered by difficulty, you can trust your ears in proportion with how far along in the section you are. Earlier, easier questions are likely to have easy-to-spot errors, while later, harder questions are likely to trick you.

But thankfully, this section is not trying to pull out obscure rules: *the same basic errors are tested frequently*. Once you know what these errors are, you can actively analyze the sentences to look for these errors and identify them more easily. Here are the three most common issues on Error Identification questions:

- ✐ **Subject-verb agreement.** Make sure an underlined verb agrees in number with its subject.

- ✐ **Pronoun agreement.** Make sure an underlined pronoun agrees in number with its antecedent.

- ✐ **Parallelism.** Make sure words expressing parallel ideas use parallel forms.

Once you know to look out for them and *actively check* for them on every question, you'll start to notice them more frequently in cases when your ear otherwise would have tricked you.

Sentence Improvement

There will be **25 Sentence Improvement Questions**, split across two sections. These present a sentence with a long phrase underlined. Students will be given five choices for how to word the underlined phrase, correcting for grammar, usage and style. Choice (A) is always identical to the original underlined phrase. Here's an example provided by the SAT:

Laura Ingalls Wilder published her first book
<u>and she was sixty-five years old then</u>.

(A)   and she was sixty-five years old then
(B)   when she was sixty-five years old
(C)   at age sixty-five years old
(D)   upon the reaching of sixty-five years
(E)   at the time when she was sixty-five   *Answer: B.*

Sentence Improvement questions are ordered by difficulty within each section. Questions do not form a larger passage; each question will be its own distinct sentence.

Strategies

One of the biggest obstacles in these questions is the time constraint for the amount of reading. Students tend to take each of the five choices back into the context of the sentence and end up reading the full sentence over and over. To save time, **eliminate quickly**. Use structural clues in the sentence to identify the error in one choice, and then quickly scan the other choices and eliminate any that make the same error.

Like on Error Identification questions, the same basic errors are tested frequently on Sentence Improvements. Once you know these errors, you can *actively* analyze the sentences to look for these errors and identify them more quickly and easily. In addition to the errors from the Error Identification section, Sentence Improvement errors include:

- ✐ **Sentence fragments.** Make sure each sentence has one independent clause with a main subject and verb.

- ✐ **Run-on sentences.** Avoid comma splices and link independent clauses appropriately.

- ✐ **Dangling modifiers.** Make sure all modifying phrases are appropriately connected to the sentence.

- ✐ **Big sentences.** Choose the most concise and direct phrasing of a sentence.

Paragraph Improvement

There will be **6 Paragraph Improvement questions.** This section presents a short essay, usually two or three paragraphs, followed by questions about grammar, development, and organization of the sentences in the context of the passage. Unlike other sections, students may be asked about more than one sentence in the same question or about a sentence's relationship with the rest of the passage.

Some Paragraph Improvement questions are basically variations of Sentence Improvement questions, addressing many of the same concepts and error types. However, because this section works with multiple sentences in a larger passage, some other types of questions may appear. For example, there may be questions asking you to combine sentences, move a sentence somewhere else in the passage, or delete sentences that do not contribute to the paragraph.

Essay

The Essay will always be the first section of the test. It will be graded for the strength and development of the your argument as well as the clarity and effectiveness of your language. You are given a maximum of two pages on which to write about the given topic. Essay readers understand that the essay is intended as a first draft and that the result will not be as polished as a school assignment would be.

Scoring

The essay will be holistically scored by two readers, each of whom will give it a score from 1 (bad) to 6 (good). If their scores differ by two points or more, the essay will go to a third reader to resolve the discrepancy. So the final essay score will be from 2 (two 1's) to 12 (two 6's). An essay that is off-topic or written in ink will get a zero.

There are several key things that readers look for when grading the essay: *Development*, *Organization*, *Language*, *Sentences*, *Grammar*, roughly in descending order of importance. They boil down to two main questions:

- ☞ **Can you make a convincing argument?** (Development and Organization)

- ☞ **Do you use English properly?** (Language, Sentences and Grammar)

In general, it's easier to improve your essay through better development and organization than with better language.

Here's a sample essay topic from the SAT:

Think carefully about the issue presented in the following excerpt and the assignment below.

> Many persons believe that to move up the ladder of success and achievement, they must forget the past, repress it, and relinquish it. But others have just the opposite view. They see old memories as a chance to reckon with the past and integrate past and present.
>
> Adapted from Sara Lawrence-Lightfoot,
> *I've Known Rivers: Lives of Loss and Liberation*

Assignment: Do memories hinder or help people in their effort to learn from the past and succeed in the present? Plan and write an essay in which you develop your point of view on this issue. Support your position with reasoning and examples taken from your reading, studies, experience, or observations.

Strategies

Note that the topic is worded to be generally *content free*. That is, you do not need any *particular* knowledge in order to effectively write on the topic. You can write about virtually anything, as long as you tie it into the topic. One side effect of this format is that you will not be penalized for making factual errors in your essays. You are being tested on their writing skills, not your knowledge of facts.

The biggest hurdle is timing: 25 minutes is simply not very much time to write an essay. The first thing you can do to help is to **practice writing these essays under timed conditions.** The more you practice, the more comfortable you will be with the format.

Secondly, it's often difficult to decide what to write about. Because the topics are so open-ended, students freeze up and can't decide where to begin. But *because* the topics are so open-ended, *almost any example* can be used for any topic. Therefore, you should come up with a few examples ahead of time, topics you know well enough to be able to write about at length. These could be books, movies, historical figures, or even personal experiences. Once you have 4 or 5 different examples, chances are one or two of them will be relevant to just about any topic you might encounter.

TIMING

Timing on the SAT Writing section is relatively straightforward. Although there are three question types that seem very different in form, in practice you should be spending roughly the same amount of time on each question. For a 25-minute section with 35 questions, that works out to **about 45 seconds per question**. For the section as a whole, the timing works out like this:

Section	Questions	Timing
Sentence Improvement	11 questions	9 minutes
Error Identification	18 questions	12 minutes
Paragraph Improvement	6 questions	4 minutes
Total	35 questions	25 minutes

We don't formally give target numbers for the Writing the way we do for the math, but for some students they may be a good idea. If you really struggle with these questions, the hardest Sentence Improvement questions could take *forever* to read and understand. But remember that these questions are ordered by difficulty *separately*. So what comes right after those hard Sentence Improvements? *Easy* Error IDs! If you have trouble with these questions or have trouble timing, consider skipping the last few Sentence Improvements and moving on to the Error IDs.

The last Writing section is easy for timing, since it only contains one type of question. Again, the timing works out to about 45 seconds per question:

Section	Questions	Timing
Sentence Improvement	14 questions	10 minutes

PARTS OF SPEECH

Before we begin, it's useful to take a minute to familiarize ourselves with a few basic parts of speech. This is not an exhaustive list. There are other parts of speech we'll talk about later,[*] but these are the basics that will give us the foundation we need get us started.

Nouns

Nouns include words that refer to a person, place or thing, though there are abstract nouns, too. Frankly, you may see more abstract nouns than any of the other categories.

- **Person:** *girl, chef, researcher, Doug, Phil Collins*
- **Place:** *house, hospital, dining room, Belgium, Cleveland*
- **Thing:** *stapler, horseshoe, broccoli, foot, water, fire*
- **Abstract:** *odor, justice, love, manslaughter, emancipation, action, indecision, illusion, despair*

They can be the subject or object of a verb, as well as the object of a preposition:

- **The <u>dog</u> ate a <u>donut</u> with <u>sprinkles</u>.**
   - "dog" is the subject of the verb "ate" (the dog performed the eating).
   - "donut" is the object of the verb "ate" (the donut was the thing that was eaten).
   - "sprinkles" is the object of the preposition "with".

---

[*] And some we won't talk about at all. There's no reason to talk about "determinatives" on the SAT.

Verbs

Verbs include words that refer to concrete actions, but some are also more abstract. Anything that something can *do* is a verb.

- ☞ **Concrete actions:** *jump, play, kick, move, speak, poke, smolder*

- ☞ **Abstract actions and states:** *stand, live, believe, assume, develop, hire, fire, despair*

Some words can be either nouns or verbs depending on the context—notice that "fire" and "despair" appeared in our lists for both.

There are a number of "auxiliary" (or "helping") verbs. These usually appear along with other verbs in order to change their tense.

- ☞ **Auxiliary verbs:** *is/are/was/were, have/has/had, will/would, can/could*

Verbs show **tense** that indicate the time the action occurred. Some tenses require auxiliary verbs.

- ☞ **Yesterday the dog <u>ate</u> a donut.**
- ☞ **The dog <u>is eating</u> a donut right now.**
- ☞ **The dog <u>will eat</u> a donut tomorrow.**

The **main verb** in a clause is directly tied to its subject.[*] The main verb must have a subject associated with it. But there may be other verbs in a sentence as well.[†]

- ☞ **After <u>leaving</u> home, Bob <u>went</u> to the store <u>to buy</u> a kite.**
  - o "went" is the main verb, with subject "Bob"
  - o "leaving" and "to buy" are also verbs. They do describe actions Bob did, but they are not the main verb in the sentence.

Prepositions

A preposition is a small word that often shows direction or location (like "in" or "out"). Some prepositions can also be more abstract (like "of").

- ☞ **Prepositions:** *of, in, on, to, at, with, from, towards, upon*

Prepositions usually take a noun as an object. Together they form a prepositional phrase. That prepositional phrase in turn often describes another noun.

- ☞ **The dog [<u>in</u> the yard] ate a donut [<u>with</u> sprinkles]**
  - o "in" is a preposition whose object is the noun "the yard"
  - o "in the yard" is a prepositional phrase describing the noun "dog"
  - o "with" is a preposition whose object is the noun "sprinkles"
  - o "with sprinkles" is a prepositional phrase describing the noun "donut"

There are other parts of speech, too, you know. This is but a small taste of what you'll see on the SAT. Shall we begin?

---

[*] Note that some auxiliary verbs can also appear alone as the main verb in a sentence, like *John <u>is</u> fat* or *John <u>has</u> a gut*, whereas other auxiliary verbs, like *will/would* or *can/could* cannot be main verbs.

[†] Verb forms that are not a main verb are called "nonfinite verbs".

ERROR IDENTIFICATION
PART I: THE BASICS

Error Identification questions make up 18 of the 49 multiple-choice questions on the SAT. Each question consists of a sentence that has four words or short phrases underlined. Your task is to determine which underlined choice is grammatically incorrect. If all choices are correct, choose (E), No error.

Before we get into specific concepts, let's take a look at a few general points to keep in mind on the Error ID questions.

First: **DON'T PANIC**. It's true that few schools these days teach grammar in a thorough and rigorous way, so many of you will naturally be worried about how little you know about the subject. It's also true that a hard-core study of grammar can be very complicated and scary. HOWEVER, the SAT does not expect you to know and understand every little rule of English. In fact, they repeat the same basic concepts over and over again. So once you know which concepts are tested, you can *actively* look for them.

> We've broken up the Error IDs into two lectures. Here, we'll discuss all the *most common errors* on the section. You **absolutely must** get these questions right every time they show up.
>
> So pay attention.

Fortunately, you actually know more grammar than you think you do. Language is an innate skill. If you're a fluent English speaker, you've got the rules of English subconsciously programmed into your brain, even if you don't know all the fancy words like "antecedents" and "infinitives". So sometimes you'll simply *know* that a sentence has an error. You may not know exactly why, but you can tell that it just... *sounds* wrong.

Unfortunately, the SAT is prepared to fool you. Sentences are often intentionally constructed so that they will *sound* correct, even though they contain errors. That's why it's important that you don't *just* trust your ear, but that you *actively* check each choice for the errors that appear most frequently.

In fact, one of the most common problems students have on the Error IDs is **choosing choice (E) too often**. Because the errors are hidden, a lot of *incorrect* sentences will *sound* perfectly fine. Choice (E) will show up no more frequently than any other answer choice. If the choices were evenly distributed, each choice would be correct about 20% of the time. In fact, our research shows that (E) is correct *less* frequently than other choices: about 15% of the time. That means that on an 18-question section, (E) will be the correct answer on 2–4 questions. If you find yourself picking (E) on more than 4 questions, you probably missed some errors.

Your Error ID procedure:

1. Read the sentence and look for anything that seems wrong.
Just like Math and Sentence Completion questions, Error ID questions are roughly arranged by difficulty. Early questions are easy; late questions are hard. So if something jumps out at you as obviously wrong on an *early* question, there's a good chance that's the answer. If this happens on a *late* question, you should be skeptical of your intuition. But either way, don't stop there:

2. Check every underlined choice for the common types of errors.
This is the most important step. We're going to show you the errors that show up most frequently. It's not enough just to be aware that they show up—you must *actively* check each choice for these errors. If you find one, that's your answer. Even if there was a different choice that sounded weird. These errors trump anything else that seems wrong.

3. If you still don't see an error, choose (E).
But only after you've checked every underlined word. And don't pick it too often: there should be 2–4 (E)'s per section.

So what are the most common errors? Glad you asked.

I. SUBJECT-VERB AGREEMENT

Every sentence has a *subject* and a *verb*. A verb is generally an action word, like *jump*, *go*, or *bake*.* The *subject* is usually the word that performs the action of the verb. The verb will be in a different form depending on whether the subject is singular or plural. That is, the subject and verb must *agree in number*:

✓	The *dog* <u>is</u> barking.	✗	The *dog* <u>are</u> barking.
✓	The *dogs* <u>are</u> barking.	✗	The *dogs* <u>is</u> barking.

The singular subject "dog" takes the verb "is" while the plural subject "dogs" takes the verb "are".[†]

Subject-Verb Agreement is the most frequently tested concept on the test. *Any time* you see a verb underlined, your first mission is to find the subject and see whether it agrees with the verb. Start by asking:

Who is performing the action?

Sound easy? Well, it's not. There are a number of ways they can *hide* the subject. Even though the sentence sounds okay, the subject may not be what you think it is. Here are some tips to help you find the subject.

1. Find the core sentence.

The subject may not be the word immediately in front of the verb. In fact, it probably isn't. They often stick a bunch of extra words between the subject and the verb. So how can you tell which word is the subject?

In real life, sentences are rarely simple statements like "The dog is barking" or "Bob is cool". There are usually a lot of extra words that modify, describe, or elaborate on the words and concepts. But in every sentence, you can strip away all the extra descriptive stuff and find a *core sentence*; that is, a simple statement composed of just the subject and verb. Once you pull out the subject and the verb, you can easily tell whether the verb agrees with the subject.

a. *Phrases surrounded by commas*

First, if you see a phrase surrounded by commas, the subject won't be in there. Take a look at this sentence:

> ✎ **The Queen, who has absolute power over her subjects as well as all the dukes and other aristocrats, <u>are</u> rich.**

All that stuff between the commas doesn't affect the core sentence. It's like a footnote, an extra chunk of information they threw in the middle of the sentence.[‡] But it doesn't affect the *core sentence*. So let's get rid of it.

> ✗ *The Queen,* ~~who has absolute power over all her subjects as well as all the dukes and other aristocrats,~~ *<u>are</u> rich.*

Now we can see that the core sentence is "The Queen are rich". Does that agree? Of course not. It should say "The Queen *is* rich".

This is important because the stuff in the comma phrase may *sound* like part of the subject:

> ✎ **Dave, along with Bob and Scott, <u>have</u> qualified for the next round of the tournament.**

Each sample sentence in the lecture will be marked with an "X" if it's wrong, a check (✓) if it's right, and a chili pepper (✎) if we don't know yet.

---

* Technically, not every verb is an "action". These underlined words are also verbs: *I <u>like</u> cats; I <u>decided</u> to get married; Pittsburgh <u>is</u> in Pennsylvania.* But a lot of verbs are actions, and this definition will help you develop a sense of which words are verbs.

† The "-ing" words are verbs, too; the whole phrase "is barking" is a verb phrase. However, only the first word will be affected by the subject; "barking" is the same in all the examples. Since "-ing" words are not an issue for verb agreement, we're mostly going to ignore them for now.

‡ This is a footnote. It's like one of these.

Here's a case where your intuition will trick you. Who qualified? Dave, Bob, and Scott. They're three people. That's plural, so they *have qualified*, right? Ah, but look—Bob and Scott are stuck inside the commas. They *can't* be a part of the subject. If we get rid of them, we can see the verb does not agree:

✗   *Dave,* ~~along with Bob and Scott,~~ <u>have</u> qualified for the next round of the tournament.

Now the core sentence is "Dave have qualified". That's bad. It should say "Dave *has* qualified".

b. *Prepositional phrases*

Second, the subject cannot be the *object of a preposition*. For example:

✓   The *Queen* of England <u>is</u> rich.

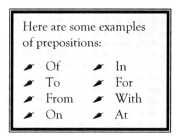

Here are some examples of prepositions:

- Of
- To
- From
- On
- In
- For
- With
- At

"Of" is a preposition, and "England" is its object, so the phrase "of England" is a prepositional phrase. "Of England" *describes* the Queen—it tells us which Queen we're talking about. *The Queen* is the subject of this sentence, not *England*. She's the one that's rich.

The preposition "of" shows up in a lot of verb agreement questions. When you're looking for the subject, look for the word "of". If you see it, the subject will probably be the word *before* "of", not after it.

This holds true for *all* prepositional phrases—the subject of the sentence will never be the object of a preposition. This is the same concept that we saw with the commas. Prepositional phrases only give you additional information; they are not part of the core sentence. So if you see a prepositional phrase, cross it out; the subject *cannot* be in there:

✓   The *dogs* ~~in the yard~~ <u>are</u> barking.   ✓   The *man* ~~with three children~~ <u>is</u> married.

✓   *All flights* ~~to Denver~~ <u>have</u> been delayed.   ✓   The *movie* ~~about vampires~~ <u>is</u> scary.

Of course, there may not be just one prepositional phrase. There could be a whole string of them.

✐   The *construction* of several groups of townhouses across the street from the complex of office buildings <u>have improved</u> the neighborhood.

What improved the neighborhood? The groups? The townhouses? Let's cross out all the prepositional phrases:

✗   The *construction* ~~(of several groups)~~ ~~(of townhouses)~~ ~~(across the street)~~ ~~(from the complex)~~ ~~(of office buildings)~~ <u>have improved</u> the neighborhood.

Our core sentence is "the *construction* have improved". That doesn't agree, so the verb is wrong. You can see how they tried to fool you: the actual subject is singular, but they put a plural word right before the verb, so the verb sounded okay. Don't be fooled. The subject will not be in a prepositional phrase.

2. The subject might come *after* the verb

Take a look at this sentence:

✐   At the front of the building <u>stands</u> two bronze statues.

What is the subject of the verb "stands"? What is doing the standing? The building? The front? No: the *statues* <u>stand</u>. Here, the subject comes *after* the verb, so it's easy to miss the fact that they don't agree. But look: "at the front" and "of the building" are prepositional phrases. The subject *can't* be in there. Sometimes you can see the verb agreement error more easily if you play with the order of words in the sentence. What the sentence really *means* is

✓   *Two bronze statues* <u>stand</u> at the front of the building.

It's perfectly alright to put the subject after the verb. You probably do it all the time. Look:

✐   There <u>is</u> two people from Portugal in my math class.

Does the verb agree? Hmm. "There is" sounds okay, doesn't it? Ah, but "there" isn't the subject. "Two people" is the subject. The sentence should read:

✓ There <u>are</u> *two people* from Portugal in my math class.

Any time you see the phrase "there is" underlined, alarms should go off.* Look *after* "there is" to find the subject. It should come right after the verb.

3. "Neither" gives you a singular subject.

Sometimes a sentence will have a compound subject:

✓ *Scott and Bob* <u>are</u> at the movies.

The subject here is "Scott and Bob". Since they are two people, we have a plural subject, so it takes a plural verb. However, if the subject has two parts that are connected with *neither*, the verb should be *singular*:

✓ *Neither* Scott *nor* Bob <u>is</u> Portuguese.

✓ I have two friends, but *neither* of them <u>is</u> Portuguese.†

In the second example, "neither" occurs by itself. Here, "of them" is a prepositional phrase, so "them" can't be the subject. If "neither is" sounds weird to you, imagine that the word "friend" comes after "neither":

✓ I have two friends, but neither (*friend*) <u>is</u> Portuguese.

Of course, **either** works exactly the same way:

✓ *Either* Scott *or* Bob <u>is</u> going to win the election.

There are a few other words that also seem plural but are actually singular, like **each**, **every**, and **any**:

✓ I have many friends, and *each* of them <u>is</u> Portuguese.

✓ *Every* shirt that Jerry owns <u>is</u> red.

✓ *Any* student who fails this class <u>is</u> not going to graduate.

Again, it may seem like we're talking about multiple friends, multiple shirts, and multiple students. But in each case, the actual subject is singular and takes a singular verb.

All of these words might appear with the subject on an Error Identification question, but "neither" is the most common. Beware of all of them, but keep an extra eye out for "neither".

VERB AGREEMENT SUMMARY

When a verb is underlined, **find its subject** to see if they agree in number, singular or plural. To find the subject:

➤ Ask yourself: who is **performing** the action of verb?

➤ Find the **core sentence**. Cross out:
   - o   phrases separated by commas
   - o   prepositional phrases

➤ The subject might come **after the verb**. Look out for **"there is"**.

➤ **"Neither"** gives you a singular subject.

---

* In your head.

† This may sound weird to you. In fact, in general use it's quite common to use a plural verb with "neither" (as in "Neither of them are Portuguese.") But in formal English, the rule says that "neither" must be singular here. This is a case in which Standard Written English follows different rules than those you might use every day. Since the SAT tests the formal stuff, we're stuck with the rule. If you don't know it already, learn it.

Now that you know all about subjects and verbs, you will never be tricked by verb agreement questions. But, just to be safe, try these questions. We'll give you a hint: all these questions have either a verb agreement error, or no error. Look for an underlined verb, and then find its subject.

1. <u>Although</u> the police department has <u>drastically cut</u>
      A   B

   the city's murder rate, the number of car thefts in

   suburban areas <u>are</u> <u>still rising</u>. <u>No error</u>
              C   D   E

2. A joint organization of teachers <u>and</u> library workers
                              A

   <u>has agreed</u> to sponsor a fundraiser <u>in order</u> <u>to raise</u>
     B   C   D

   money for the poverty-stricken museum. <u>No error</u>
                                   E

3. The activist, <u>having launched</u> several initiatives to
                 A

   bring fresh produce to inner-city areas, <u>were</u> awarded
                              B

   a grant that <u>would expand</u> her programs <u>to</u> other
               C   D

   parts of the country. <u>No error</u>
                  E

4. Neither of the professors I spoke with <u>were</u>
                          A

   <u>familiar with</u> the text <u>that</u> I <u>mentioned in</u> my thesis.
     B   C   D

   <u>No error</u>
     E

5. Images on the Standard of Ur, an artifact <u>discovered</u>
                                A

   by British archeologists in 1927, <u>suggests</u> that ancient
                          B

   Sumerian chariots may have <u>been pulled</u> <u>by</u> wild
                       C   D

   donkeys. <u>No error</u>
           E

6. Dr. Watanabe has <u>already</u> acquired all the materials
                 A

   he <u>needs for</u> the experiment, but there <u>is</u> still several
       B   C

   calculations he <u>has yet to</u> perform before he can
                D

   begin. <u>No error</u>
         E

7. The depiction <u>of natural</u> and architectural scenes
                A

   portrayed <u>with</u> wide brushstrokes in vivid colors <u>is</u>
           B   C

   what most people <u>associate with</u> the art of Monet.
                  D

   <u>No error</u>
     E

8. The existence of objects so massive <u>that</u> even light
                         A

   itself cannot escape <u>their</u> gravitational pull, objects
               B

   we now call black holes, <u>were</u> first <u>proposed by</u> the
                 C   D

   geologist John Michell. <u>No error</u>
                 E

9. The investigation <u>has</u> <u>suggested that</u> a certain genetic
                 A   B

   mutation, <u>rather than</u> dietary and environmental
           C

   factors, <u>cause</u> this previously unknown illness.
           D

   <u>No error</u>
     E

10. <u>Within the walls</u> of this ancient city <u>lies</u> the ruins <u>of</u> a
      A   B   C

   temple <u>dedicated to</u> the goddess of the harvest.
          D

   <u>No error</u>
     E

II. PRONOUN AGREEMENT

Pronouns are words like *they*, *it*, or *her* that take the place of nouns. They work like abbreviations; they refer to some other noun in the sentence so you don't have to repeat the noun. The noun that a pronoun refers to is called the "antecedent".

> For some reason, a lot of pronoun agreement questions are about animals. I don't know why.

    ✓   *The snake* **swallows <u>its</u> prey whole.**

"Its" is a pronoun and "the snake" is its antecedent; "its" refers to "the snake."

Just like with subject/verb agreement, a pronoun must agree in number with its antecedent: match singular to singular and plural to plural.

  ✓ *The snake* **swallows <u>its</u> prey whole.**   ✗ *The snake* **swallows <u>their</u> prey whole.**

  ✓ *Snakes* **swallow <u>their</u> prey whole.**   ✗ *Snakes* **swallow <u>its</u> prey whole.**

So *any* time you see a pronoun underlined, find its antecedent and make sure they agree in number. The best way to find the antecedent is to use common sense. Just ask yourself:

> ### *Who or what does the pronoun refer to?*

That is, if you replaced the pronoun with another word in the sentence, which would you use?

    ✗   **This new mobile phone looks great, but <u>they</u> can break very easily.**

"They" is a pronoun, so let's find the antecedent. What does "they" refer to? *What* "can break"? *The phone* can break. "The phone" is singular, so we must say "it".

Here are some examples of pronouns that appear most frequently on pronoun agreement questions:

    Singular pronouns: *it, its, he, him, his, she, her*

    Plural pronouns: *they, them, their*

> Note that "he or she" and "his or her" are *singular*, not plural.

You may be confused about all these different forms. That's okay; we'll talk more about the difference between them later. Right now all we care about is whether the pronoun is singular or plural.

Pronoun agreement can be tricky. Here are some tips to help you:

1. Don't confuse Pronoun Agreement with Verb Agreement.

The subject of the verb may or may not be the same word as the antecedent of a pronoun.

    ✓   **The *age* of some *trees* <u>is</u> determined by counting <u>their</u> rings.**

Here, the subject of the verb "is" is "age", but the antecedent of the pronoun "their" is "trees". Note that unlike the subject, the antecedent *can be* inside a prepositional phrase. **The antecedent can be anywhere in the sentence.** Usually it comes before the pronoun, but it can also come after. It's important that you keep the search for the subject distinct from the search for the antecedent. Take it slow and think about the *meaning*. What *is determined*? The *age* is determined. But what has *rings*? *Trees* have rings.

2. Watch out for singular words that seem plural.

Take a look at this:

    ✗   *Italy* **is well known for <u>their</u> excellent food.**

Who has excellent food? *Italy*. We may think of Italy as a culture or a group of people, so it's tempting to think of it as plural. But the sentence doesn't say "the Italian people". It says "Italy". Italy is a country, one country. It is *singular*—we can tell because it uses a *singular verb*, "is". So we must say "its". When looking for the antecedent, we must look only at the words that *literally appear* in the sentence, not the *implied meaning* of the words.

Similarly, look out for the words **each**, **every**, or **any**:

✓ *Each potato* **was thoroughly washed before** <u>it was</u> **added to the pot.**

Here, the antecedent of "it" is *each potato*. It sounds like we're talking about multiple potatoes, but remember what we said in the Verb Agreement section: words like "each" are *singular*. There may well be a lot of potatoes, but "each" means we're only talking about one at a time.

It's easier to see in this example because the word that follows "each" is *potato*. That's singular and is followed by a singular verb, *was*, so it makes sense that we'd use a singular pronoun. But words like "each" will *always* be singular, even if the word that follows it is plural:

✓ *Each* **of these potatoes was thoroughly washed before** <u>it was</u> **added to the pot.**

You might be more tempted to use "they" in this sentence because we have a plural noun "potatoes". But "each" makes the entire phrase "each of the potatoes" singular.[*]

3. Watch out for *vague pronouns*.

Take a look at this:

✗ **Scott and Bob were partners until** <u>he</u> **quit.**

Here we have two options for the person who quit: Scott or Bob. How can you tell which it is? You can't, and that's the problem: *he* is a **vague pronoun**. In this case, we can't use a pronoun at all. We have to specify who quit.

✓ **Scott and Bob were partners until** <u>Bob</u> **quit.**

Of course, if they *both* quit, then we'd have to say "they".

4. Watch out for *mystery pronouns*.

Take a look at this:

✗ **In gymnastics,** <u>they</u> **take off points for bad dismounts.**

Sounds fine? Well, it's not. Who's "they"? Gymnastics? *Gymnastics* take off points? Are you kidding me? No. Absolutely not. The problem here is that there isn't any word in the sentence that could possibly be the antecedent of the pronoun. "They" is a **mystery pronoun**—we have no idea who or what it refers to. The only way to correct it is to not use a pronoun at all: we must specify who we're talking about:

✓ **In gymnastics,** <u>judges</u> **take off points for bad dismounts.**

5. Watch out for *pronoun shifts*.

There are special cases when it's okay for a pronoun to lack a specific antecedent. For example, "one" is a pronoun that basically means "anyone" or "someone".

✓ **If** <u>one</u> **is sick,** <u>one</u> **should go to the hospital.**

✓ **If** <u>you</u> **are sick,** <u>you</u> **should go to the hospital.**

These sentences mean the same thing; the only difference is that "one" is more formal than "you". Neither "one" nor "you" has an actual antecedent—you can't point to anything in the sentence that they refer to. That's okay; they refer to any person in general. Thus we call them **generic pronouns**.

> This concept doesn't show up all that often, but once you know about it, it's one of the *easiest* errors to spot. Don't ever, ever miss this. Seriously.

---

[*] This may seem weird; isn't *potatoes* the antecedent? We just said that the antecedent of a pronoun can come inside a prepositional phrase. The short answer is to just remember that "each" is always singular. Words like "each" belong to a special class of words that uses special rules. The long answer is that the pronoun here is a "bound variable". Would you like to talk about bound variables? No? Then just remember that "each" is singular.

In these cases, "one" and "you" are equivalent; either is fine. However, you cannot use *both* of them in the same sentence:

    ✗   **If <u>one</u> is sick, <u>you</u> should go to the hospital.**

Here, we started the sentence with the pronoun "one" and then shifted to the pronoun "you".[*] That's not okay. If "one" and "you" show up in the same sentence, chances are one of them is wrong.

Of course, this rule doesn't just apply to "one" and "you". You must be consistent with all such pronouns:

    ✗   **If *we* examine this painting closely, <u>one</u> can tell that the artist was left-handed.**

    ✗   **When *people* spend all day typing, <u>your</u> hands get tired quickly.**

In the first example, the sentence starts with "we", so it should repeat "we" in the second half. In the second, the sentence starts with "people"— not even a pronoun. The second half should say "their".

PRONOUN AGREEMENT SUMMARY

When a pronoun is underlined, **find its antecedent** to see if they agree, singular or plural.

To find the antecedent:

- ➤ Ask yourself: **who or what does the pronoun refer to?**
- ➤ Watch out for singular words that **seem plural.**
- ➤ There may be **vague pronouns** that have **more than one** option for the antecedent.
- ➤ There may be **mystery pronouns** that have **no** option for the antecedent.
- ➤ Watch out for **pronoun shifts**: be consistent with **generic pronouns** like "one" or "you".

---

[*] Thus the term "pronoun shift".

PRONOUN AGREEMENT DRILL

Try some on your own. Again, every question in this exercise will have either a pronoun agreement error or no error. So don't get distracted: find an underlined pronoun, and then look for its antecedent.

1. Some paleontologists <u>now believe</u> that the
    A
    Tyrannosaurus <u>was</u> a scavenger, primarily
    B
    <u>eating</u> animals that were already dead rather than
    C
    hunting <u>their</u> own prey. <u>No error</u>
    D   E

2. Although <u>they are</u> still experiencing financial
    A
    difficulties, the investment firm <u>has shown</u>
    B
    <u>significant</u> growth in the <u>past</u> year. <u>No error</u>
    C   D   E

3. Medieval authors believed unicorn horns <u>had</u> the
    A
    ability <u>to cure</u> illness and guard <u>against</u> poison if
    B   C
    <u>it was</u> ground up and sprinkled over food. <u>No error</u>
    D   E

4. <u>In the event of</u> a fire drill, all employees must
    A
    immediately evacuate the building <u>and</u> should not
    B
    return to <u>his or her desk</u> until the alarm
    C
    <u>stops ringing.</u> <u>No error</u>
    D   E

5. The maned wolf, <u>found</u> primarily in the grasslands
    A
    of South America, <u>has</u> long, stilt-like legs that
    B
    enable <u>them</u> to see prey <u>hiding</u> in tall grass. <u>No error</u>
    C   D   E

6. <u>When</u> one <u>listens to</u> the music of early rock bands,
    A   B
    <u>you</u> can hear the influence of the blues in <u>their</u> guitar
    C   D
    melodies. <u>No error</u>
              E

7. Some people believe modern golf <u>descended</u> from the
    A
    ancient Roman game of paganica, in which <u>they used</u>
    B   C
    a bent stick <u>to hit</u> a ball stuffed with feathers.
    D
    <u>No error</u>
    E

8. Certain groups are <u>concerned about</u> the injuries that
    A
    an airbag can <u>inflict</u> from the force with which
    B
    <u>they are</u> deployed, but safety experts argue that
    C
    <u>incidents of</u> airbag-related deaths are extremely rare.
    D
    <u>No error</u>
    E

9. <u>While</u> many people find hobbies <u>such as</u> painting or
    A   B
    figure drawing <u>to be</u> relaxing, others find <u>it</u> to be a
    C   D
    waste of time. <u>No error</u>
                  E

10. Marie Curie performed <u>many</u> experiments <u>on</u>
    A   B
    radioactive elements <u>without realizing</u> that her
    C
    exposure to <u>it</u> was slowly killing her. <u>No error</u>
    D   E

III. PARALLELISM

Verb agreement and pronoun agreement both deal with *matching*: match singular to singular, match plural to plural. *Parallelism* is a term that is probably foreign to you, and it applies to several different concepts, but the overall point is the same: matching. When we have similar elements in a sentence, we must match their structures.

Parallelism can sometimes be a bit trickier to spot than the other errors we've seen so far. Verb agreement and pronoun agreement are easy to look for: if a verb is underlined, find the subject; if a pronoun is underlined, find its antecedent. Parallelism doesn't always have an obvious warning sign like that, but there are some things you can look out for.

1. Lists

The point of parallelism is to get a balanced sentence. When you have two or more elements in a sentence that are similar to each other in some way, you must put them in the same form.

It's easy to see this when you have a list of three items.

> ✓ **I like jogging, fishing, and hiking.**
>
> ✓ **I like to jog, to fish, and to hike.**[*]
>
> ✗ **I like *jogging*, *fishing*, and <u>to hike</u>.**

Either the "to" form or the "-ing" form can be okay here. What's not okay is mixing them up: if we start a list using one form, we must *repeat* that form for every element of the list.

Similarly, don't repeat the subject if you don't have to:

> ✗ **Fred Astaire could *sing*, *dance*, and <u>he could act</u>.**
>
> ✓ **Fred Astaire could sing, dance, and <u>act</u>.**

This doesn't apply just to verbs, but to any type of list.

> ✗ **This book is about patience, hard work, and <u>how to be a leader</u>.**
>
> ✓ **This book is about patience, hard work, and <u>leadership</u>.**

We started the list using nouns (*patience* and *hard work*), so we must end with another noun (*leadership*).

Why do we have to do this? Because when things aren't parallel, they sound nasty. Parallelism makes your sentences beautiful and catchy. I mean, which of these sounds better?

> ✗ **A government of the people, by the people, and <u>it is meant for those people, too</u>...**
>
> ✓ **A government of the people, by the people, and <u>for the people</u>...**

See? We didn't make this up. Parallelism has been around for a while.

This also doesn't apply just to lists of three terms. If a sentence has two elements that are of equal weight, they must have parallel forms.

> ✓ **It is better *to give* than *to receive*.**
>
> ✓ **_Reading_ a book is not as easy as *understanding* it.**
>
> ✓ **The government both *protects* freedoms and *restricts* them.**

It's a bit trickier to spot the need for parallelism in these examples, since they aren't obvious lists. But in all these examples, the ideas in question are directly connected somehow. That's the key: Use parallel forms *for parallel ideas.*

---

[*] We repeated the "to" here to make the parallelism more obvious, but when all items of a list take the same preposition, you don't have to repeat it. We could also say "I like to jog, fish, and hike."

2. Special pairs

There are certain pairs of words that are big warning signs for parallelism.[*] Here are a few:

either...or	*Either* Chicago *or* Houston will win the pennant.
neither...nor	*Neither* Chicago *nor* Houston will win the pennant.
not only...but also	This cereal is *not only* delicious *but also* nutritious.
both...and	This cereal is *both* delicious *and* nutritious.
between...and	I must choose *between* the green one *and* the red one.
more/less...than	The movie is *more* tragic *than* comic.
as...as	The movie is not *as* good *as* the book.

First of all, these words must go together. In each case, the first word must be followed by the second.[†]

  ✗ *Neither* the book <u>or</u> the movie was good.   ✓ *Neither* the book <u>nor</u> the movie was good.

  ✗ *Both* the book <u>as well as</u> the movie were awful.   ✓ *Both* the book <u>and</u> the movie were awful.

Secondly, these pairs must be followed by parallel structures.[‡]

    ✗   I use this credit card *not only* for business expenses *but also* <u>when buying personal things</u>.

    ✓   I use this credit card *not only* for business expenses *but also* <u>for personal expenses</u>.

The first part of the pair, "not only", is followed by a prepositional phrase. Therefore the second part, "but also", should also be followed by a prepositional phrase.

If you see these expressions in a sentence, first make sure the right words are paired off. Then make sure they're followed by nicely parallel forms.

3. Comparisons

Notice that several of the examples we've seen involve *comparisons*:

    ✓ **It is better to give than to receive.**

    ✓ **The movie is more tragic than comic.**

Almost any sentence that makes a comparison must contain some kind of parallel structure. Since comparisons by definition directly link two things, those two terms must be in the same form.

> These words usually indicate there's a comparison in the sentence:
> - Than
> - As
> - Like/unlike
> - Differs from
> - Similar to

But comparisons also require a special kind of parallelism. You don't just have to compare things that are *in the same form*, you also have to compare *the same type of thing*. You can't compare apples and orangutans. Observe:

    ✗ **Scott's apples taste better than Bob.**

This sentence says that Scott's apples taste better than *Bob himself*. That's no good. I mean, you *could* say that. I should hope they do taste better than Bob. But that's not what we meant to say. What we mean is:

---

[*] These pairs are sometimes called "correlative expressions" but you don't need to know that. It'll be our secret.

[†] They don't necessarily have to show up *as pairs*. Sometimes one of them might appear by itself: "I saw two movies, but *both* of them were awful." The point is that if they *do* appear as pairs, they have to appear as *these* pairs.

[‡] The exception to this is "as...as", which uses a somewhat more complicated sentence structure. Don't worry; you won't be tested on that structure. But first rule still applies, and you will be tested on correctly pairing "as" with another "as".

✓ *Scott's apples* taste better than <u>Bob's apples</u>.

Here, we're not just making the grammatical *forms* parallel; we're making the *concepts themselves* parallel.

As always, when the sentences get more abstract, it becomes more difficult to spot.

✗ **Professor Starsky's** *explanation* **of Feynman's principles of subatomic particles was much more lucid than** <u>his colleague</u>.

In this sentence, we're comparing the "explanation" to the "colleague". That doesn't match. There are three main ways to correct this type of error.

✓ **...than** <u>his colleague's explanation</u>. **(Repeat the thing you're comparing.)**

✓ **...than** <u>his colleague's</u>. **(Use a** *possessive*; **the object of comparison is implied.)**

✓ **...than** <u>that of his colleague</u>. **("that" is a pronoun referring to "explanation".)**

Please note that in the last correction, the word "that" is a kind of *pronoun*. That means it must *agree with its antecedent*. In this sentence, the antecedent of "that" is *explanation*, which is singular. However, if the object of comparison was plural, we'd use "those":

✓ *Scott's apples* taste better than *<u>those</u>* <u>of Bob</u>.

In this sentence, the object of comparison is "apples". That's plural, so we need a plural pronoun, "those".

PARALLELISM SUMMARY

Use **parallel structures** for **parallel ideas**. If two or more similar ideas are equated, compared, or related, they should be in the same grammatical form.

- All elements of a **list** must be in the same form.
- Remember that **special pairs**
  - must appear as the pairs shown
  - must be followed by parallel structures.
- When making a **comparison**, you must compare similar *concepts*, not just similar forms.

All these questions deal with parallelism. Look out for lists, special pairs, and comparisons.

1. After three years of medical school, neither Frank or
   <u> </u>
   A
   Harry <u>wants</u> to work <u>in</u> medicine <u>anymore</u>. <u>No error</u>
      B   C   D   E

2. If Christopher Marlowe <u>had not been</u> murdered at the
                        A
   age of 29, <u>perhaps</u> his career <u>would have been</u> even
             B   C
   more impressive <u>than William Shakespeare</u>. <u>No error</u>
                     D   E

3. John must <u>prepare</u> for football season by attending
           A
   two practices a day, <u>working out</u> in the weight room
                   B
   with the rest of the team, and <u>run</u> at least ten miles a
                        C
   week <u>in</u> his spare time. <u>No error</u>
        D   E

4. <u>Every year</u>, Herb inevitably <u>misses</u> several early
      A   B
   morning meetings either by <u>sleeping</u> too late <u>and</u> by
                     C   D
   getting stuck in traffic. <u>No error</u>
              E

5. Her <u>performances</u> at the Olympia music hall <u>in</u> the
        A   B
   1950s <u>made singer</u> Edith Piaf famous not only in
          C
   France <u>and also</u> around the world. <u>No error</u>
          D   E

6. The mayoral candidate <u>has promised</u> to cut taxes,
                  A
   reduce crime, and <u>he will raise</u> the standard <u>of</u> living
                  B   C
   <u>for</u> all citizens. <u>No error</u>
    D   E

7. The Noguchi Museum <u>may be</u> small, but <u>its</u> selection
                 A   B
   of sculptures is <u>as exquisite</u> and beautiful as
                 C
   <u>any other museum</u> in the city. <u>No error</u>
          D   E

8. <u>Like those of</u> Stanley Kubrick, the films of David
      A
   Lynch often <u>contain</u> strange events <u>and</u> abstract
           B   C
   images <u>that are</u> not overtly explained in the films
           D
   themselves. <u>No error</u>
           E

9. <u>To develop</u> a theory about the nature of an abstract
    A
   concept <u>like</u> political justice <u>is</u> easier than proving
          B   C
   <u>that theory</u> to be true. <u>No error</u>
      D   E

10. The texture of applesauce <u>made from</u> sweet apples
                  A
    <u>tends</u> to be coarser than <u>applesauce</u> made from
     B   C
    <u>sour ones</u>. <u>No error</u>
      D   E

EVERY QUESTION HERE HAS ONE OF THE THREE TYPES OF ERRORS DISCUSSED ABOVE OR NO ERROR.

Identify which type of error occurs in each question and provide a corrected version of the choice. Enjoy!

1. The room was a mess: the desk <u>was</u> <u>covered with</u>
   A   B
   unfinished assignments, <u>and</u> a pile of dirty clothes
                            C
   <u>were lying</u> on the floor. <u>No error</u>
   D   E

2. The detectives were <u>certain that</u> this suspect was the
                         A
   murderer, but since neither the murder weapon

   <u>or</u> even the body of the victim <u>had been</u> found, <u>they</u>
   B   C   D
   were forced to release him. <u>No error</u>
                               E

3. Because of <u>its</u> magnificent plumage and exotic
              A
   origins, peacocks <u>were</u> often <u>kept in</u> the gardens of
                     B   C
   European palaces <u>in order to</u> flaunt the opulence of
                    D
   the king. <u>No error</u>
             E

4. <u>Although</u> this restaurant has a reputation <u>for serving</u>
   A   B
   fatty food, <u>there is</u> actually <u>several</u> low-fat items on
               C   D
   the menu. <u>No error</u>
             E

5. The <u>development of</u> a method for measuring degrees
       A
   of longitude <u>was</u> an important step <u>toward</u> the
                B   C
   creation of an accurate <u>map of</u> the oceans. <u>No error</u>
                           D   E

6. The New York City subway system, <u>with over</u> six
                                     A
   hundred miles of track <u>and</u> more than four hundred
                          B
   stations, <u>is</u> more extensive than <u>any other city</u> in the
             C   D
   United States. <u>No error</u>
                  E

7. While his propensity <u>for committing</u> violent acts
                        A
   <u>make</u> him a threat to society, aggressive
   B
   psychological treatment may <u>be able to help</u> him
                               C
   <u>to control</u> his destructive urges. <u>No error</u>
   D   E

8. Very young children <u>can easily</u> become <u>fluent in</u> any
                       A   B
   language <u>to which</u> <u>he or she is</u> exposed on a regular
            C   D
   basis. <u>No error</u>
          E

9. <u>Central to</u> the proposed new contract <u>is</u> <u>higher</u> wages
   A   B   C
   for <u>employees who have</u> worked at the company for
       D
   over three years. <u>No error</u>
                     E

10. This automotive company <u>is currently</u> working on
                            A
    <u>designs for</u> a car that will run on a vegetable-based
    B
    fuel and <u>be powerful</u> enough <u>to satisfy</u> the car-buying
             C   D
    public. <u>No error</u>
            E

11. <u>Exposure to</u> fumes from cars and trucks <u>have been</u>
    A   B
    shown <u>to be</u> as detrimental to the respiratory system
          C
    <u>as</u> exposure to tobacco smoke. <u>No error</u>
    D   E

12. Although <u>they</u> defeated the Spanish Armada in 1588,
             A
    England <u>was</u> mostly <u>unsuccessful in</u> the subsequent
            B   C
    twenty-year war <u>with</u> Spain. <u>No error</u>
                    D   E

13. Both players <u>have had</u> great seasons, but Patrick
                  A
    deserves <u>to win</u> the most valuable player award
              B
    because his <u>role on</u> the team was more substantial
                 C
    <u>than Alex</u>. <u>No error</u>
         D   E

14. The terms of <u>his plea</u> agreement <u>state</u> that he must
                  A   B
    spend three weeks <u>in jail</u>, do one hundred hours of
                       C
    community service, and <u>has to pay</u> a fine of one
                            D
    thousand dollars. <u>No error</u>
                        E

15. Elegant photography, as well as a <u>captivating</u>
                                      A
    screenplay, <u>are</u> the difference <u>between</u> a movie that is
                 B   C
    merely good and a movie that becomes <u>a classic</u>.
                                          D
    <u>No error</u>
    E

16. The television network, <u>trying</u> to expand its
                            A
    programming into other media, <u>is developing</u> <u>one</u> that
                                   B   C
    will <u>be broadcast</u> over the Internet. <u>No error</u>
         D   E

17. <u>What is</u> truly impressive about the painting is the
    A
    accuracy <u>with which</u> the artist <u>has rendered</u> the
              B   C
    <u>minutest</u> details of his subject. <u>No error</u>
    D   E

18. <u>Like Beckett</u>, Ionesco's plays are <u>so</u> absurd <u>in both</u>
    A   B   C
    language and plot that audiences often find <u>them</u>
                                                 D
    incomprehensible. <u>No error</u>
                       E

ERROR IDENTIFICATION

PART II: THE FINER POINTS

Okay, so we covered the basics. Verb Agreement, Pronoun Agreement, and Parallelism are the most common errors; they will collectively show up on about 35% of the Error ID questions. That's why we spent so much time on them. So if those three take up 35% and 15% have no error, that's already 50% of the questions. But what about the other half? That's what we're about to cover. In this part of the lecture, we'll look at some additional concepts that individually don't show up often, but collectively cover a lot of ground.

Okay, enough stalling. On to the grammar:

I. VERB TENSE

A verb's *tense* tells us *when* the action takes place. Tense can be really scary sometimes; if you've ever taken a foreign language, you've probably been through some of the misery of studying tenses. However, tense questions on the SAT are usually fairly straightforward. The main goal is *consistency*. When events happen in the past or future, the verbs should reflect that. If events happen at the same time, the verbs should be in the same tense. There are several clues that will tell you tense will be an issue.

> Words that refer to time might be a clue that verb tense is an issue, such as:
>
> ☞ when   ☞ before
> ☞ during   ☞ after
> ☞ while   ☞ since

First, look for words that **literally refer to the past or future**. If you see any such words, the tense of the verb should match the time they refer to.

   ✗   *In 1776,* America <u>is declaring</u> independence.   ✓   **In 1776, America <u>declared</u> independence.**

   ✗   *Next year,* **our team <u>has won</u> 30 games.**   ✓   **Next year, our team <u>will win</u> 30 games.**

"In 1776" tells us the first sentence should be in the past; "next year" tells us the second sentence should be in the future.

Second, look at **the tense of any other verbs in the sentence**. Verbs should be *consistent* within the sentence; if events happen at the same time, the verbs should be in the same tense.

   ✗   **Dave <u>sees</u> several museums when he *went* to Belgium.**

   ✗   **Mrs. Jones <u>made</u> us sit in the corner whenever we *are* bad.**

In the first sentence, the verb "went" is in the past, so we know his trip to Belgium happened in the past. Since the museum trips occurred *while* he was in Belgium, "sees" must also be put into the past. Similarly, in the second sentence, "are" is in the present. The act of sitting in the corner happens *at the same time* as being bad, so "made" should be put into the present.

   ✓   **Dave <u>saw</u> several museums when he *went* to Belgium.**

   ✓   **Mrs. Jones <u>makes</u> us sit in the corner whenever we *are* bad.**

Given the weirdness of some tenses, it may not always be obvious how to *correct* the error.

   ✗   **Before we *ate* dinner, we <u>are going</u> to the zoo.**

Since "ate" is in the past and the trip to the zoo happened *before* dinner, "are going" should also be past. But should it be "went"? Or "had gone"? It doesn't matter. We only have to *find* the error; we don't have to *fix* it. All that matters is that "are going" should be in *some* kind of past form, so it's definitely wrong as is.

Perfect verbs

Most tense questions will be fairly straightforward. However, there are all sorts of other verb categories in English besides past/present/future; if you've ever studied a foreign language, you've probably had to study page after page of bizarre verb forms. Most weird forms are off-limits on the SAT, but every so often you might see something more complicated. Look at this:

✓ **Bob <u>was</u> class president in 2010.**

This sentence is the simple past. It refers to a specific time in the past and only the past. Compare to this:

✓ **Bob <u>has been</u> class president *since* 2010.**

This sentence is in the **present perfect**.[*] It means that not only was Bob president in the past, but he's *still* president now. The present perfect is used for time periods that extend *from the past up to the present*.

So if you see a reference to a specific time, look at whether it refers to a time *entirely* in the past, or whether the time period *includes the present*.

✗ *In* 1776, America <u>has declared</u> independence.	✓ *In* 1776, America <u>declared</u> independence.
✗ *Since* 1959, Hawaii <u>was</u> a U.S. state.	✓ *Since* 1959, Hawaii <u>has been</u> a U.S. state.

Additionally, you may see verbs in the **past perfect**.[†] This structure is used for *the past of the past*, when an event happened before another past event:

✓ **Lucas <u>had read</u> the book before he saw the film adaptation.**

Here, both the reading of the book and the watching of the movie are past events. But the reading of the book was further in the past, so "read" is in the past perfect.

The past perfect isn't tested very often on the SAT, in part because it's often interchangeable with the simple past. This sentence, for example, is also acceptable:

✓ **Lucas <u>read</u> the book before he saw the film adaptation.**

But the form is *used* often, and there's a pretty good chance that you'll see it somewhere. So don't freak out if you see it.

---

[*] The present perfect is formed with the verb "to have" in the present tense, plus the past participle of the main verb.

[†] The past perfect is formed with the verb "to have" is the past tense, plus the past participle of the main verb.

II. PRONOUN CASE

There's more to pronouns than singular vs. plural. There's also something we call the *case* of the pronoun:

   ✓ <u>I</u> **love Derek Jeter.**   ✓ **Derek Jeter loves** <u>me</u>**.**

In these two sentences, "I" and "me" refer to the same person, but in different roles. We use "I" when the person is *the subject* (performing the action) and "me" when the person is the *object* (receiving the action). Here's a chart outlining pronoun cases:

	SUBJECT		OBJECT
I	*I* love Jeter.	me	Jeter loves *me*.
he	*He* loves Jeter.	him	Jeter loves *him*.
she	*She* loves Jeter.	her	Jeter loves *her*.
we	*We* love Jeter.	us	Jeter loves *us*.
they	*They* love Jeter.	them	Jeter loves *them*.

> "You" and "it" aren't on the chart because they have the same form in both cases. (*You* love Jeter. Jeter loves *you*.) So don't worry about them.

So when you see a pronoun underlined, ask yourself: is the person *performing* the action (subject) or *receiving* the action (object).[*]

Of course, case questions can often be tricky when the pronoun is not by itself. Error ID questions involving pronoun case often involve *two* people. But it's easier to see which pronoun form to use if there's only one pronoun. So how can we get only one pronoun? There are two easy ways to do so:

1. Delete the other person.

   ☛ **The studio loved the screenplay that** <u>Roger and him</u> **wrote.**

It may be hard to hear whether "him" is correct because Roger is in the way. So let's ignore him.

   ✗ **The studio loved the screenplay that** ~~Roger and~~ <u>him</u> **wrote.**

   ✓ **The studio loved the screenplay that** <u>he</u> **wrote.**

"Him" is the subject of the verb "wrote", so we need the subject pronoun, "he".

2. Combine into one pronoun

   ☛ **Dave sat between** <u>Janet and I</u> **at the game.**

You can combine the two people into one plural pronoun: "Janet and I" would become either "we" or "us".

   ✗ **Dave sat between** <u>we</u> **at the game.**

   ✓ **Dave sat between** <u>us</u> **at the game.**

"Between *us*" sounds better than "between *we*". "Us" is the *object* of the preposition "between", so we need the object pronoun form in the chart above. Since "us" is an object, we would use the object "me".

   ✓ **Dave sat between** <u>Janet and me</u> **at the game.**

> The majority of questions involving pronoun case are about "I" versus "me". Be on high alert if you see "I" or "me" underlined.

They *love* to test this, so remember: **NEVER USE "I" WITH "BETWEEN"**. It's not "between Janet and I"; it's "between Janet and me". Remember: *there's no "I" in "between"*.

---

[*] By the way, this is also the difference between *who* and *whom*. *Who* is a subject and *whom* is an object. "That's the girl *who* likes me" ("who" is the subject of "like"). But: "That's the boy *whom* I like" ("whom" is the object of "like"). This will never be tested on the SAT. You might *see* the word "whom" on a question (used correctly), but you won't see a "who" that needs to be changed to "whom".

III. Diction

Most Error ID questions we've seen so far are based on rules of grammar that are independent of the actual words used. For example, in the sentence:

> ✗ The ontologist <u>refute</u> the postulate.

You don't have to know what these words *mean* in order to see that the verb "refute" doesn't agree with the subject "ontologist".[*] You have to be able to tell which word is a verb, but beyond that it doesn't matter.

However, sometimes it's not the structure that's the problem, it's the words themselves. "Diction" refers to the proper choice of words in your writing. There are several ways those can be tested on the SAT.

1. Idiomatic preposition use

Sometimes your choice of words is stylistic—you could phrase a sentence several different ways depending on your taste. However, there are certain English rules that are *specific* to the words used. These are called "idiomatic" rules. The word "idiomatic" means "particular to a certain language". That is, it refers to things that are simply quirks of a language. These rules are arbitrary: you have to use a certain word because, well, that's just how you say it.

Take a look at these:

> ✗ Dave is <u>listening at</u> the radio.   ✓ Dave is <u>listening to</u> the radio.

The verb "listen" must be followed by the preposition "to". Why? Because I said so. It's an arbitrary convention. Certain words must be paired with certain prepositions just because that's how you say it. Often you'll be able to "hear" the error—a preposition will sound weird in a certain sentence. But sometimes they can be hard to spot.

First of all, if you see a word followed by a preposition underlined together, be aware of it. Don't *automatically* pick it as an error, but treat it suspiciously. Secondly, any time you encounter an idiomatic convention like this on a practice test, remember it for future tests. The SAT loves to repeat itself. Here are a few more examples:

> ✗ This disease is <u>caused from</u> a virus.   ✓ This disease is <u>caused by</u> a virus.
>
> ✗ Dave is <u>a critic toward</u> the SAT.   ✓ Dave is <u>a critic of</u> the SAT.
>
> ✗ This book is a <u>protest on</u> the dictator.   ✓ This book is a <u>protest against</u> the dictator.

Sometimes, your choice of preposition **will affect the verb that follows it**. For example:

> ✗ In times of danger, an ordinary person is *capable* <u>to perform</u> extraordinary acts.
>
> ✓ In times of danger, an ordinary person is *capable* <u>of performing</u> extraordinary acts.

In this sentence, the word "capable" should be followed by the preposition "of". But if we make that change, we also have to change "perform" to "performing".[†] The key to determining which verb form to use here has nothing to do with the word "perform"; it depends on the word that comes before it: "capable".

Of course, some words work the other way; they *have* to take the "to" form, *not* the "-ing" form:

> ✗ Scott is *able* <u>of touching</u> his nose with his tongue.
>
> ✓ Scott is *able* <u>to touch</u> his nose with his tongue.

Notice that "capable" and "able" mean *exactly the same thing*, but one takes the "to" form and one takes the "-ing" form. Why? It's just a quirk of the language. Why are some words irregular? Why isn't "childs" the plural of "child"? That's just the way it is.

---

[*] This sentence doesn't even make sense! You can't refute a postulate!

[†] The "to" form is called the *infinitive* and the "-ing" form is (often) called a *gerund*. Ignore these terms.

2. Word Choice

Sometimes a sentence will use a word that simply doesn't mean what you think it does.

> ✗ **Dave saw so many movies that they all seemed <u>indifferent</u> from each other.**

We mean to say that they all seemed the same. But "indifferent" doesn't mean "not different". It means "unbiased" or "without preference". So this sentence is nonsense. We need a word like "indistinguishable". Of course, you don't have to come up with the corrected word, but if you can it will help. Often the question will replace the word we want with a word that kinda sounds like it, so the sentence may sound right when you first read it. Here are a few examples.

✗ **The use of typewriters has been <u>reclining</u> for the past 20 years.**	"*Re*cline" means "lean back". "*De*cline" means "decrease".
✗ **<u>Perspective</u> students are allowed to sign up for preview classes.**	"*Per*spective" means "point of view". "*Pro*spective" means "likely to become".
✗ **The price of milk has been <u>raising</u> in the past year.**	"Raise" is when you make something go up. "Rise" is when something goes up. That is, *raise* takes an object and *rise* does not. When I *raise* my hand, my hand *rises*.

These idiomatic concepts can be quite irritating; you just have to know them and if you don't, there's not much you can do. This can cause panic. *Do not panic.* First of all, knowing whether this preposition goes with that verb won't make or break your score. The grand majority of the test deals with the other rules we've already covered. Second, if you do see one of the other errors we talked about before, that error will trump any idiomatic concept you might see. For example:

> ✎ **Psychologists say <u>that</u> talking about your fears often <u>help</u> <u>to alleviate</u> <u>them</u>. <u>No error</u>**
>   A   B   C   D   E

Hmm. Do you say "help *to* alleviate"? Or should it just be "help alleviate"? Or "for alleviating"? And what exactly does "alleviate" mean? Maybe that's the wrong word there. Maybe it should be "*re*lieviate". Wait, is that even a word? I'm not sure. I don't know. I hate this test! I hate myself! I'm so stupid! Nobody loves me!

Okay, calm down. Don't worry about all that stuff until we've checked the basic rules we discussed. First, is there a verb underlined? Sure: "help". What's the subject of that verb? Fears? No, because "*about* your fears" is a prepositional phrase. *Talking* is the subject. Talking *help*? No: talking *helps*. So the verb doesn't agree with the subject. That's the error. Our answer is (B). We're done! We don't have to think about the rest of the sentence.

These diction rules can sometimes lead you to be too trigger-happy in picking out errors. On Error ID questions, we're looking for *errors*, not just the best way to say something.

Be *aware* that diction and idiomatic concepts will occur, but don't *worry* about them. First, check the main rules. If you don't find any errors, see if anything sounds wrong idiomatically. If you still don't find anything, pick (E) and move on.

IV. MISCELLANEOUS TOPICS

There are a few other rules that come up fairly regularly that are best demonstrated by example.

1. Adjective versus Adverb

An adjective describes a noun. An adverb describes a verb, adjective, or other adverb.

> **ADJECTIVE: This is an <u>easy</u> *test*.** ("Easy" describes "test")

> **ADVERB: I <u>easily</u> *passed* the test.** ("Easily" describes "passed")

If you see an adjective underlined, ask yourself what it's describing. If it's not describing a noun, it should be an adverb.

> ✗ **He died of a <u>previous</u> unknown disease.**

What is "previous" here? The disease? No. The disease was *previously unknown.* The adjective should be an adverb.

> ✓ **He died of a <u>previously</u> unknown disease.**

2. Noun Agreement

Just as pronouns must agree with antecedents, sometimes *nouns* have to agree with what they refer to.

> ✗ **Scott and Bob want to be <u>an astronaut</u>.**

Here, the subject "Scott and Bob" is plural, but "astronaut" is singular. They don't match. Scott and Bob don't want to be *one astronaut.* What we really mean is:

> ✓ **Scott and Bob want to be <u>astronauts</u>.**

3. *Which* versus *Who*

You cannot use "which" to refer to people. You must use "who".

> ✗ **Natalie is the woman <u>which</u> ate all the cookies.**

> ✓ **Natalie is the woman <u>who</u> ate all the cookies.**

Any time you see "which" underlined, check what word it's referring to. If it's supposed to refer to a person, it should be "who".

Additionally, "where" must refer to a *place*, and "when" must refer to a *time*.[*]

> ✓ **I went to the hospital <u>where</u> I was born.** (*where* refers to the hospital)

> ✓ **I went to the hospital <u>when</u> I got the flu.** (*when* refers to the time I got the flu)

4. Comparative versus Superlative

When you compare *two* people or things, use the *comparative*—either an "-er" word or the word "more".

> ✓ **Alaska is <u>larger</u> than Texas.**

> ✓ **Of the *two* candidates, Julio is <u>more qualified</u> for the position.**

When you compare *three or more* things, use the *superlative*—either an "-est" word or the word "most".

> ✓ **Alaska is <u>the largest</u> of the *fifty* states.**

> ✓ **Of the *three* candidates, Julio is <u>the most qualified</u> for the position.**

Don't mix up these forms. If a sentence uses a comparative or superlative form, check how many people or things it's talking about.

---

[*] Note also that the phrase "in which" is often synonymous with "where".

    ✗   Of the *two* candidates, Julio is <u>the most qualified</u> for the position.

And don't mix up the different ways of forming the comparative: use *either* "more" *or* "-er", not both.

    ✗   Alaska is <u>more larger</u> than Texas.

5. Irregular verbs

Most verbs form the past tense simply by adding "-ed". Some verbs, however, have special forms for the past. Others even use the same form for past and present. We call these verbs **irregular verbs**:

REGULAR:	✓	I <u>walk</u> the dog.	✓	I <u>walked</u> the dog.			
IRREGULAR:	✓	I <u>catch</u> the fish.	✓	I <u>caught</u> the fish.	✗	I <u>catched</u> the fish.
IRREGULAR:	✓	I <u>hit</u> the ball today.	✓	I <u>hit</u> the ball yesterday.	✗	I <u>hitted</u> the ball.

The "perfect" forms mentioned above were compound tenses that require more than one verb: a form of the verb "to have" plus the **past participle** of the verb. For regular verbs—and even some irregular verbs—the past participle looks exactly the same as the simple past:

    ✓ I <u>walk</u> the dog.   ✓ I <u>walked</u> the dog.   ✓ I <u>have walked</u> the dog.

    ✓ I <u>catch</u> the fish.   ✓ I <u>caught</u> the fish.   ✓ I <u>have caught</u> the fish.

    ✓ I <u>hit</u> the ball today.   ✓ I <u>hit</u> the ball yesterday.   ✓ I <u>have hit</u> the ball.

However, some irregular verbs have distinct past participles—they use *different* words in the simple past and perfect tenses. Here are a few examples:

PRESENT	SIMPLE PAST	PERFECT FORM
write	wrote	had/have *written*
rise	rose	had/have *risen*
arise	arose	had/have *arisen*
begin	began	had/have *begun*

When a verb has different forms like this, don't confuse the two. You can't use the simple past form in a compound tense:

    ✓ I <u>began</u> a new job.

    ✓ I <u>have begun</u> a new job.

Either of these is fine in different circumstances. But don't mix them up:

    ✗ I <u>begun</u> a new job.

    ✗ I <u>have began</u> a new job.

Now that we know everything there is to know about Error IDs, please enjoy this drill. There'll be a little bit of everything here, including the Big Three we saw in Part I. Identify which type of error occurs in each question and provide a corrected version of the choice. Have fun!

1. If <u>you want</u> to produce nature documentaries, one
      A

   must be prepared <u>to sit</u> <u>completely</u> motionless in
              B   C

   uncomfortable conditions for days <u>on end</u>.
                            D

   <u>No error</u>
    E

2. Before he wrote the children's books <u>for which</u> he
                         A

   is <u>so</u> famous today, Dr. Seuss <u>is making</u> training
      B   C

   films for the U.S. Army <u>during</u> World War II.
                  D

   <u>No error</u>
    E

3. Julia was very satisfied <u>with the work</u> Murray did
                  A

   on her car because he <u>not only</u> fixed the problem
                B

   but also <u>charging</u> less than <u>any other mechanic</u> in
         C   D

   town. <u>No error</u>
        E

4. <u>Although</u> Richard normally does not enjoy
    A

   <u>spending</u> time outdoors, <u>him</u> and Molly went for
    B   C

   a long hike in the forest in the hopes <u>of spotting</u>
                          D

   some spring birds. <u>No error</u>
             E

5. <u>Pleased with</u> his work <u>on the project</u>, Ms. Jenkins
    A   B

   rewarded Gary <u>with</u> a promotion <u>and</u> an extra
            C   D

   week of vacation. <u>No error</u>
             E

6. Recent studies <u>have shown</u> that the genetic
             A

   structure of whales <u>is</u> <u>surprising</u> similar to
               B   C

   <u>that of</u> pigs. <u>No error</u>
    D   E

7. Our chemistry teacher <u>reluctantly</u> gave my lab
                  A

   partner <u>and I</u> an extension on the report that
         B

   <u>was supposed</u> <u>to be finished</u> today. <u>No error</u>
      C   D   E

8. The dean of the college announced <u>that</u>, unless
                       A

   revenue from alumni donations <u>increases,</u> <u>they</u>
                     B   C

   will have <u>to raise</u> tuition next year. <u>No error</u>
         D   E

9. <u>Visiting</u> science museums <u>at</u> a young age can
    A   B

   often inspire children <u>to become</u> <u>a scientist</u> when
                 C   D

   they grow up. <u>No error</u>
            E

10. The proliferation of portable electronic devices

   <u>such as</u> mobile phones and laptop computers
      A

   <u>have</u> made it easier for companies <u>to do</u> business
      B   C

   <u>on the road</u>. <u>No error</u>
     D   E

11. The <u>discovery of</u> Uranus <u>radically transformed</u>
        A   B

   the world of astronomy, <u>for</u> no new planets
                 C

   <u>had been found</u> since ancient times. <u>No error</u>
      D   E

12. The programmers have noticed <u>that</u> <u>there is</u> a
                      A   B

   bug in the new software, <u>but neither</u> the cause of
                    C

   the problem nor its solution <u>are known</u>. <u>No error</u>
                    D   E

13. Because this school lacks the ability <u>for hiring</u>
$$\qquad\qquad\qquad\qquad\qquad\qquad\qquad\text{A}$$
    new teachers without permission <u>to do so</u> from the
$$\qquad\qquad\qquad\qquad\qquad\qquad\quad\text{B}$$
    city council, its average class size <u>is</u> still <u>far</u> too
$$\qquad\qquad\qquad\qquad\qquad\qquad\quad\text{C}\qquad\quad\text{D}$$
    high. <u>No error</u>
$$\qquad\quad\text{E}$$

14. The orangelo, a hybrid fruit <u>resulting from</u> a cross
$$\qquad\qquad\qquad\qquad\qquad\qquad\quad\text{A}$$
    <u>between</u> an orange and a grapefruit, <u>grow</u>
$$\quad\text{B}\qquad\qquad\qquad\qquad\qquad\qquad\quad\text{C}$$
    naturally <u>in the highlands</u> of Puerto Rico.
$$\qquad\qquad\quad\text{D}$$
    <u>No error</u>
$$\quad\text{E}$$

15. The restaurant <u>to which</u> Mr. Kaczynski <u>inferred</u> in
$$\qquad\qquad\quad\text{A}\qquad\qquad\qquad\qquad\text{B}$$
    his book is <u>long since</u> gone, but its owners
$$\qquad\qquad\quad\text{C}$$
    <u>have recently opened</u> a new French bistro across
$$\qquad\quad\text{D}$$
    town. <u>No error</u>
$$\qquad\quad\text{E}$$

16. <u>For the past</u> ten years, our school's basketball
$$\quad\text{A}$$
    team <u>was</u> awful, but the new coach has assured <u>us</u>
$$\qquad\quad\text{B}\qquad\qquad\qquad\qquad\qquad\qquad\qquad\text{C}$$
    that the team <u>will have</u> a winning season this year.
$$\qquad\qquad\qquad\quad\text{D}$$
    <u>No error</u>
$$\quad\text{E}$$

17. The universe is <u>teeming with</u> millions of <u>as yet</u>
$$\qquad\qquad\qquad\quad\text{A}\qquad\qquad\qquad\qquad\text{B}$$
    undiscovered solar systems, <u>any one</u> of which
$$\qquad\qquad\qquad\qquad\qquad\quad\text{C}$$
    may contain planets capable <u>of sustaining</u> life.
$$\qquad\qquad\qquad\qquad\qquad\quad\text{D}$$
    <u>No error</u>
$$\quad\text{E}$$

18. Indifference to violations of civil rights <u>are</u>
$$\qquad\qquad\qquad\qquad\qquad\qquad\qquad\text{A}$$
    dangerous to society's moral welfare, for ignoring
    crimes against humanity <u>is</u> tantamount to
$$\qquad\qquad\qquad\qquad\quad\text{B}$$
    <u>endorsing</u> <u>them</u>. <u>No error</u>
$$\quad\text{C}\qquad\quad\text{D}\qquad\quad\text{E}$$

SENTENCE IMPROVEMENT

Sentence Improvement questions make up the majority of the multiple-choice questions on the Writing section. You'll see them twice: there will be 11 of them in the 25-minute section and 14 of them all by themselves in the 10-minute mini-section, for a total of 25 Sentence Improvement questions. Here, you'll be given a sentence that has a long phrase underlined. You must decide which choice would produce the clearest and most effective sentence without violating the rules of grammar. Choice (A) will always be identical to the original underlined phrase—the Sentence Improvement equivalent of "No Error".

> All of "the Basics" from the Error ID may appear on Sentence Improvements, but in particular, watch out for "special pairs" of parallelism and "mystery pronouns".

The first thing to remember is that all the rules we discussed for the Error IDs still apply to the Sentence Improvements. We didn't make up those rules; they're the rules of grammar and they're always the same. So you'll still see verb agreement, pronoun agreement, parallelism, and all your other friends. Some of the more minor Error ID rules, like pronoun case, will appear much less frequently on Sentence Improvements, but keep an eye out for them nonetheless.

We're also going to add a few rules for the Sentence Improvements that you probably won't see on the Error IDs. Error IDs dealt with individual elements of the sentence; you can focus on just a pronoun and its antecedent without looking at the rest of the structure. Sentence Improvements, however, deal with large parts of sentences and the relationships between them. So we must now look at the rules for connecting large parts of sentences.

GENERAL STRATEGY: *ANTICIPATE*

A common difficulty that students have on Sentence Improvements is *time*. You've got a long sentence followed by five long choices to get through. If you're not careful, you could wind up reading the sentence five, six, maybe even ten times and still not be sure of your answer. That's bad.

First off, you have to eliminate answers *rigorously*. If a choice violates a rule that we've seen, cross it out—even if other parts of the choice sound okay. If four choices violate rules, but the fifth choice sounds kinda weird, don't hesitate. That fifth choice is your answer. You've got to reduce your options as quickly as possible. You must be on High Alert. Eliminate quickly.

More importantly, if you can *anticipate* the problem with the sentence, you can save yourself a whole lot of time. Look at the sentence as it's originally written and try to find what's wrong with it. Often, many or all of the wrong choices in a question will have the same type of error. So if you find an error, get rid of *all* choices that have the same error. Here's an example:

➣ **Because the technology has become more sophisticated, the popularity of digital cameras <u>have greatly increased over the past five years</u>.**

- (A) have greatly increased over the past five years
- (B) are greatly increasing for five years
- (C) have been increasingly great for five years
- (D) has greatly increased over the past five years
- (E) have, for five years, been greatly increasing for this reason

These choices have a lot going on in them. Several choices have verbs in different tenses. There are a couple of ways to deal with the "five years". Hmm. What's the difference? How can I tell? Ah, but look: the original underlined phrase starts with a verb, "have". What's the subject of that verb? "Digital cameras"? No—that pesky "of" means "cameras" cannot be the subject. *Popularity* is the subject. "The popularity have increased"? No. The verb does not agree with the subject. Look through the choices: which one has a verb that agrees with "popularity"? Only (D)! "The popularity *has* increased". That must be the answer. What about the tense issues? What about the "five years"? None of that matters. We know (D) is the only choice without a verb agreement error, so (D) is the answer. We can ignore everything else.

So as soon as you spot an error in one of the choices, check all the other choices for that same error and eliminate as you go. If you do, you will save yourself a lot of time.

Try getting your feet wet with a few sample problems. These questions only deal with errors we've already seen in the Error ID chapters.

1. The drummer's use of complex time signatures <u>were less impressive than the guitarist</u>.

   (A) were less impressive than the guitarist
   (B) were less impressive than those of the guitarist
   (C) was less impressive than the guitarist
   (D) was less impressive than that of the guitarist
   (E) was less impressive than those of the guitarist

2. Oscar, Laura, and Gerald assiduously worked together to pass their organic chemistry exam because <u>it was his desire to become a physician</u>.

   (A) it was his desire to become a physician
   (B) they wanted to become a physician
   (C) they wanted to become physicians
   (D) of their wanting to become physicians
   (E) becoming a physician was his desire

3. Each one of the prehistoric paintings that the researchers discovered on the cave walls <u>have been categorized according to their</u> size, shape, and color.

   (A) have been categorized according to their
   (B) have been categorized according to its
   (C) has been categorized according to its
   (D) has been categorized according to their
   (E) were categorized according to their

4. The testing showed that the new drug inhibits the virus's growth and activity more effectively in adults <u>instead of children</u>.

   (A) instead of children
   (B) than when children use them
   (C) over inhibiting children
   (D) rather than when it is used by children
   (E) than in children

5. <u>Speaking fluent Spanish and familiarity with the region's history, along with excellent physical fitness, are</u> prerequisites for anyone who wishes to become a tour guide at the archeological site.

   (A) Speaking fluent Spanish and familiarity with the region's history, along with excellent physical fitness, are
   (B) Fluency in Spanish, familiarity with the region's history, and excellent physical fitness are
   (C) Knowledge of fluent Spanish and the region's history and being excellently physically fit are
   (D) Everyone must speak fluent Spanish and know the region's history, also excellent physical fitness is
   (E) Fluency in Spanish, as well as being familiar with the history of the region and in excellent physical fitness, is

PROLOGUE: FANCY GRAMMATICAL TERMS

Normally we shy away from boring you with fancy grammatical terms. However, several of the common errors on the Sentence Improvements deal with the same concepts, so everything will go much more smoothly if we lay some groundwork first. If you get lost, don't worry. All will become clear soon enough.

Sentences are made up of **clauses**. A clause is any phrase that contains a subject and a verb. There are two flavors of clauses:

An **independent clause** is a clause that can stand alone as a complete sentence:

> ✓ **Chapman is a doctor.**

The subject is "Chapman" and the verb is "is". It's "independent" because it doesn't *need* anything else; it sounds fine as it is.

> ✓ **Chapman is a doctor, and he cured my acne.**

This sentence has two independent clauses, linked together with the word "and". We happened to put them together in the same sentence, but either of the underlined phrases would sound fine all by itself.

> ✓ **Chapman is a doctor. He cured my acne.**

A **dependent clause** is a clause that *cannot* stand alone as a complete sentence.

> ✓ **Chapman is the doctor <u>who cured my acne</u>.**

In this sentence, "who cured my acne" is a dependent clause. Its subject is "who" and its verb is "cured". It's *dependent* because "who cured my acne" cannot stand alone as a sentence.[*] It's not a complete thought; it's a description of someone. Thus it *depends* on the independent clause "Chapman is a doctor" to tell us what it's talking about. Here, we cannot split this into two separate sentences.

> Dependent clauses usually begin with words like *WHO, WHICH,* or *THAT.*

> ✗ **Chapman is the doctor. Who cured my acne.**

The first clause sounds fine as a sentence, but the second does not. So the first is *independent* and the second is *dependent*.

Sentence	Independent Clause	Dependent Clause
I want to meet a woman <u>who loves fishing</u>.	I want to meet a woman	who loves fishing
Harold got a new bike, <u>which he really liked</u>.	Harold got a new bike	which he really liked
The team <u>that scores the most points</u> wins.	The team wins	that scores the most points
You can have dessert <u>when you finish your broccoli</u>.	You can have dessert	when you finish your broccoli

Notice that in each of these examples, the independent clause would sound fine as a sentence all by itself, but the dependent clause would not—each needs the independent clause to tell us what it's talking about.

Not every chunk of words in a sentence is a clause. Take a look at this:

> ✓ **<u>A brilliant doctor</u>, Chapman cured my acne.**

"A brilliant doctor" is not a clause. It's just a noun phrase without a verb. It's just a description of Chapman. There are all sorts of names for these things, but let's just call it a **modifier**, because it modifies the word "Chapman".[†]

---

[*] Unless it's a question: "Who cured my acne?" But that's a whole different issue. Don't worry about questions.

[†] "Modifies" is just a fancy grammar word for "describes".

Similarly, a modifier can be a verb without a subject:

✓ <u>**Using advanced medical techniques,**</u> **Chapman cured my acne.**

This sentence contains an independent clause, "Chapman cured my acne," and a separate opening phrase, "Using advanced medical techniques". The opening phrase has a verb ("using") but no subject. It's a modifier describing "Chapman". So any bunch of words that isn't a clause we'll call a modifier.

So there are three things of interest to us: independent clauses, dependent clauses, and modifiers.

I. SENTENCE FRAGMENTS

As we mentioned earlier when we were talking about verb agreement, every sentence must have a subject and a verb. If it *doesn't* have a verb, it's not a sentence—it's a *sentence fragment.*

✗ **Riding the bus.**

See that? That's not a sentence. First of all, it has no subject. Who's riding the bus? We don't know. Okay, so let's add a subject:

✗ *Bob* **riding the bus.**

Hmm. That's better, but it's still not a sentence. It sounds like something a caveman would say. This is a fragment because it has no main verb. That's bad. *This* is a sentence:

✓ **Bob** *is* **riding the bus.**

So if you see a sentence that doesn't have a main verb, it's a fragment and cannot be the correct choice. Of course, SAT questions get more complicated than this. Take a look at this sentence:

> Wait, isn't "riding" a verb? **No**; it's only *part* of a verb. The "-ing" form can't stand by itself, so it doesn't count as the *main* verb.

➤ **Dr. Steve, who is a research scientist trying to develop new cancer drugs.**

Hmmm. It kinda sounds like a sentence. And we do have a verb: "is". So what's wrong here? The problem is that the "is" is stuck behind "who". Everything after the comma is a *dependent clause.*

➤ **who is a research scientist trying to develop new cancer drugs**

See that? It can't stand alone as a sentence. That means it's a dependent clause.

Back in the Error ID lecture, we talked about the idea of a *core sentence*—the main subject and verb of a sentence stripped of all the extra descriptive stuff. We found the core sentence by deleting prepositional phrases and phrases set off by commas.[*] The same idea applies here: dependent clauses are not part of the core sentence. So let's get rid of the dependent clause and see if we're left with a sentence.

✗ **Dr. Steve,** ~~**who is a research scientist trying to develop new cancer drugs.**~~

"Dr. Steve" is definitely not a sentence. So this is a fragment. There are a number of ways we can fix it:

✓ *Dr. Steve,* **who is a research scientist,** *is trying* **to develop new cancer drugs.**

✓ *Dr. Steve is* **a research scientist trying to develop new cancer drugs.**

Both of these are complete sentences. Excellent.

So what's really going on here, grammatically speaking? The point here is that _**EVERY SENTENCE MUST HAVE AT LEAST ONE INDEPENDENT CLAUSE.**_ That's what we really mean by "core sentence". And that's why we ignore dependent clauses and modifiers when we try to find the core sentence—what we're really looking for is an independent clause.

Sentences can often have very complicated structures, jumbles of commas and modifiers and clauses. But no matter how long and complicated a sentence is, if you can't find a core sentence with a subject and a verb buried in there, it's a fragment.

---

[*] We talked about this in Part I of the Error ID lecture. Don't you remember? Of course you don't. Look it up.

FRAGMENT DRILL

Take a look at these examples and see if they are complete sentences or sentence fragments. If it is a complete sentence, circle the subject and verb of each independent clause.

1. I am going to the library to study, and I will be back at six.

2. Sacramento, which is the capital of California but is only its seventh largest city.

3. The motorcycle, weaving from lane to lane and quickly darting between cars, was being followed by a pack of police cruisers.

4. Moe Berg, who held degrees from two Ivy League schools, an education that was, to say the least, unusual for a baseball player of his era.

5. The double agent, running up and down the labyrinthine hallways of the National Security Agency, while keeping a tight grip on the flash memory card holding the schematics of the doomsday machine.

6. The nineteenth-century French writer Gustave Flaubert, author of the novel *Madame Bovary*, which took him almost six years to write because of his meticulous method of composition.

7. Despite the recent surge in interest in earlier thinkers such as Heraclitus and Empedocles, Plato and Aristotle are still the most widely read ancient Greek philosophers on college campuses today.

8. Eddy Merckx, who is perhaps the greatest cyclist of all time and is one of the most famous people in Belgium.

9. Having already revolutionized the scientific world with his theory of relativity, Albert Einstein, spending the remainder of his life searching for a unified field theory, which he ultimately was unable to discover.

10. Upset by the barrage of news stories about recent scandals at Harvard, Mr. Bennett, who has been one of the most generous donors to the University since he graduated from its undergraduate engineering school in 1982, began to have doubts about the amount of his annual donation.

II. RUN-ON SENTENCES

We said that every sentence must have *at least one* independent clause. But what if we have two independent clauses in the same sentence? Take a look at these sentences:

    ✓ **I am going to the game. Scott will meet me there.**

These two sentences are fine; each has a subject and verb. However, if you want to combine them into *one* sentence, there's one main rule you must follow: *you cannot combine independent clauses with a comma alone.*

    ✗ **I am going to the game, Scott will meet me there.**

This is a *run-on sentence.* That's bad. You cannot combine complete sentences with a comma alone.[*] There are two main ways you can fix it.

1. Add a conjunction

First, you could put a *conjunction* after the comma.[†]

    ✓ **I am going to the game, <u>and</u> Scott will meet me there.**

We saw this construction earlier when we were talking about independent clauses, remember?

    ✓ **Chapman is a doctor, <u>and</u> he cured my acne.**

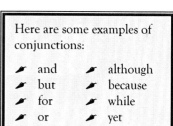

Here are some examples of conjunctions:

- and
- but
- for
- or
- although
- because
- while
- yet

2. Use a semicolon

Or, you can connect them directly with a *semicolon*:

    ✓ **I am going to the game; Scott will meet me there.**

A semicolon is basically the same thing as a period. They follow the same rules. Why bother with the semicolon, then? Well, it puts the two clauses into the same sentence, so it connects the ideas more strongly than if they were separate sentences with a period.

In fact, a semicolon is exactly what it looks like—a combination of a period and a comma. It separates independent clauses as a period does, but it separates parts of a single sentence as a comma does.

> Run-on sentences on the SAT are more commonly corrected with a semicolon than with a conjunction.

Because a semicolon works just like a period, whatever follows a semicolon *must* be an independent clause; it cannot be a fragment.

    ✗ **I am going to the game; <u>Scott meeting me there.</u>**

"Scott meeting me there" is a fragment. That's bad.

Okay, so that's not so hard. Let's try a practice problem.

    ☞ **James Joyce was indisputably one of the greatest writers of the twentieth <u>century, he was never awarded</u> the Nobel Prize for Literature.**

    (A)   **century, he was never awarded**
    (B)   **century, he had never been awarded**
    (C)   **century; never having won**
    (D)   **century, however he was never awarded**
    (E)   **century; however, he was never awarded**

---

[*] This type of error is also called a "comma splice" or "comma fault".

[†] Can I use a conjunction *without* a comma? Well, sometimes. It's not against the rules (in fact, sometimes people prefer it) but on the SAT, a choice like that is usually wrong (albeit for other reasons). If you see independent clauses joined with a conjunction and no comma, there's probably a better choice somewhere else.

This problem is testing us on the ways to link clauses in a sentence. Let's go through the choices and look for run-ons.

Let's start with the full sentence as written (which is identical to choice (A)). It's a run-on. There are two sets of subject and verb: "James Joyce *was*" and "he *was* never awarded". Therefore, there are two independent clauses. And they're linked with only a comma. That's bad. Choice (B) has the same problem; they just changed the tense of the verb. Choice (C) has a semicolon—that's good. But everything after the semicolon is a fragment: "Never having won" has neither a subject nor a verb. That's bad. So we got rid of three choices pretty quickly.

What about (D) and (E)? Aren't they the same thing? The only difference is the punctuation. Which is correct?

Here's a hint: (E) is right. (D) is wrong. To explain this, let's look at a simpler sentence.

> ✗   I like mangoes, <u>however</u> Scott does not.

This is still a run-on. Why? Because *however is not a conjunction*. You cannot link independent clauses with "however". You can start a sentence with however. You can put however in the middle of a sentence. But you cannot *link* clauses with however.* If you want to use a linking word, you must use one of those small conjunctions we saw earlier.

> ✓   I like mangoes, *but* Scott does not.

"However" is an adverb, like "easily" or "slowly".† That means you can use "however" anywhere within a sentence by itself.

> ✓   **However, Scott does not.**

> ✓   **Scott, however, does not.**

> ✓   **Scott does not, however.**

That also means you can use "however" after a semicolon, just like choice (E) above.

> ✓   **I like mangoes; however, Scott does not.**

> Here are some examples of
> adverbs, which CANNOT
> be used to link clauses:
>
> ✒   however
> ✒   therefore
> ✒   consequently
> ✒   moreover

3. Change one independent clause

We said there are two main ways to fix run-ons, but there is a third option. The run-on rule deals with the connection between two independent clauses. Therefore, another way to fix a run-on is to *get rid of* one of the independent clauses.

> ✗   I went to a game at Wrigley Field, <u>it is one of the oldest stadiums in America.</u>

This is a run-on because it has two independent clauses linked with a comma. We could fix it with a semicolon or a conjunction. But instead, let's change the second independent clause:

> ✓   I went to a game at Wrigley Field, <u>which is one of the oldest stadiums in America.</u>

> ✓   I went to a game at Wrigley Field, <u>one of the oldest stadiums in America.</u>

In the first sentence, the second half is a dependent clause. In the second, it's a modifier describing "Wrigley Field". In both cases, we avoid the run-on issue because there simply aren't two independent clauses anymore.

---

*   Well, technically you *could* link clauses with "however" if you want it to mean "any way", as in "You can do it *however* you want." This is unlikely to show up on the test.

†   This doesn't really look anything like the adverbs we talked about in the Error ID chapter, but don't worry about it. All you have to know is that you can't link clauses with these words the way you can with words like "and". If you really want to learn more about adverbs, you could read the book *The Syntax of Adjuncts* by Thomas Ernst. The book is 567 pages long. What, you haven't read it? Then don't worry about adverbs.

Take a look at each of the following examples and see if it is a run-on. For each sentence, circle the subject and verb of each independent clause, and circle the connection between the clauses (either the punctuation or the words used to connect the clauses). If it is a run-on, come up with a suggestion for how to fix it.

1. I tried to go to the library, it was closed.

2. The mayor attended the opening of the new hospital, but the governor stayed home.

3. Having just returned home from a long day of running errands, Karl had to immediately run back out again, he had left his wallet at the grocery store.

4. Professor Wellingham teaches the introductory course on thermodynamics, it is one of the hardest classes in the department.

5. While hiking on a mountainous trail through the state park, Frank noticed a strange type of flower with bright blue petals; he had never seen anything like it before.

6. In the fifteenth century, Johannes Gutenberg invented the first mechanical printing press, a device that would vastly change the course of history.

7. The football team and the soccer team both use the same small facilities, therefore we have to make sure that we don't schedule games for both teams on the same day.

8. Although the bicycle was not the color she wanted, Lauren bought it anyway because it was the last one in stock, and the next shipment would not arrive until December.

9. The new director of marketing, who had just been hired by our company after having successfully run a major advertising campaign for one of our competitors, had some radical ideas about how to promote our main product line, our sales in the first year of implementation almost doubled as a result.

10. New research has confirmed that the medication is effective, according to the scientists who conducted the study, proper dosages of the serum can both relieve symptoms and treat the underlying cause of the disease.

III. DANGLING MODIFIERS

We've talked about clauses, both independent and dependent, but what about modifiers? Remember: modifiers are those phrases that aren't clauses, but describe something else in the sentence. Often, a sentence will open with a modifier. Whenever this happens, the thing that phrase describes must come immediately after the comma. Otherwise, it's a *dangling modifier*. Observe:

> ✗ **Sitting close to the field, *a foul ball* hit Bob.**

Who is sitting close to the field? *Bob*. The opening phrase is supposed to describe "Bob". But here, "a foul ball" comes after the comma. So the modifier is "dangling"—it's not connected to the thing it should be describing. That's bad. We need "Bob" to be the subject of the main clause

> ✓ **Sitting close to the field, *Bob* was hit by a foul ball.**

The modifier dangles no more. So any time a sentence begins with a modifier like this, *anticipate* the error: ask yourself what the modifier describes. Whatever it describes *must* come immediately after the comma.

Dangling Modifiers are the most common error on the Sentence Improvements. But thankfully, they're also one of the easiest errors to spot and fix. It's basically the same process we use for pronoun agreement. The opening phrase refers to something, so all we have to do is find out what it refers to and put it after the comma.

Take a look at this:

> ☛ **Visiting our history class, Professor Feldman's speech was about the Battle of Gettysburg.**

Who was visiting our class? *Professor Feldman*. So this is okay, because Professor Feldman comes after the comma, right? Wrong. That's *not* Professor Feldman after the comma; it's *Professor Feldman's speech*. That's bad. The speech was not visiting our class. We should say:

> ✓ **Visiting our history class, Professor Feldman spoke about the Battle of Gettysburg.**

¡Perfecto!

Once you spot a Dangling Modifier, you can ignore everything else that's going on in the sentence. By itself, "a foul ball hit Bob" might sound better than "Bob was hit by a foul ball". It's shorter, more direct, and active instead of passive. But none of that matters; "Bob" *must* come after the comma since the modifier is describing "Bob", end of discussion.

> Notice that all three of these errors—Fragments, Run-ons, and Dangling Modifiers—involve COMMAS. If you see a comma in or near the underline, there's a 50-50 chance the sentence has one of these three errors.

Take a look at this:

> ☛ **Worried about losing everything he owns, <u>fire insurance seemed like the best way for Gary to protect his assets</u>.**
>
> **(A)** fire insurance seemed like the best way for Gary to protect his assets
> **(B)** getting fire insurance seemed to Gary to be the best way to protect his assets
> **(C)** his assets would best be protected with fire insurance, Gary decided
> **(D)** Gary decided that getting fire insurance would best protect his assets
> **(E)** Gary's decision to get fire insurance was to protect his assets best

Who was worried about losing everything he owns? Gary, of course. So "Gary" should come right after the comma. Which choice works? Only (D). *Look how fast we did that!* By spotting the Dangling Modifier right away, we jumped right to the correct choice. We didn't even have to read all that other stuff. Granted, not every Dangling Modifier question will be this easy, but a lot of them are. This is what we meant by "*anticipating*": if you spot the error in (A) quickly, you can eliminate every choice that makes the same error.

DANGLING MODIFIER DRILL

1. When shopping for a new car, <u>safety and fuel efficiency should both be considered by the consumer</u>.

    (A)   safety and fuel efficiency should both be considered by the consumer
    (B)   safety, as well as fuel efficiency, are among the concerns of the consumer
    (C)   a consumer should consider both safety and fuel efficiency
    (D)   considerations should include safety and fuel efficiency
    (E)   the safety of the car as well as its fuel efficiency should concern consumers

2. An outspoken supporter of American Independence, <u>the pamphlet *Common Sense* by Thomas Paine was</u> a harsh denouncement of British rule over the colonies.

    (A)   the pamphlet *Common Sense* by Thomas Paine was
    (B)   Thomas Paine wrote the pamphlet *Common Sense* as
    (C)   Thomas Paine, author of the pamphlet *Common Sense*, which was
    (D)   Thomas Paine's pamphlet *Common Sense* was
    (E)   *Common Sense* was a pamphlet by Thomas Paine, written as

3. Filmed thirty years after the original movie, <u>the sophisticated computer technology used in the sequel was a recent development</u>.

    (A)   the sophisticated computer technology used in the sequel was a recent development
    (B)   the sequel was made with sophisticated computer technology that has only recently been developed
    (C)   only recently has the sophisticated computer technology in the sequel been developed
    (D)   the technology used in the sequel involved sophisticated computers that were only developed recently
    (E)   it was only recently that the sophisticated computer technology with which the sequel was made was developed

4. Having never been out of the country before, <u>Allie's upcoming trip to Paris was the cause of her excitement</u>.

    (A)   Allie's upcoming trip to Paris was the cause of her excitement
    (B)   the upcoming trip to Paris excited Allie greatly
    (C)   Allie was going on a trip to Paris and this was the cause of her great excitement
    (D)   Allie was very excited about her upcoming trip to Paris
    (E)   her excitement was caused by her upcoming trip to Paris

IV. AVOIDING BS

"BS" stands for "Big Sentences". In the Error ID section, the goal is to find specific grammatical rule violations, and there were three main rules we mentioned. That's true of Sentence Improvements as well; we just looked at three more rules that are frequently tested here. However, a lot of the time, a Sentence Improvement choice will be wrong because, well, it's just a bad way to write a sentence. Look at choice (C) in question #4 above:

✗ **Allie was going on a trip to Paris and this was the cause of her great excitement.**

I mean, *structurally* there's nothing wrong with this choice; it's not a dangling modifier, it's not a run-on, it's not a fragment. It's just awful. It's awkward, it's wordy, and it's unnecessarily complicated. We get across the *exact same meaning* with choice (D):

✓ **Allie was very excited about her upcoming trip to Paris.**

Doesn't that sound better? Why use two clauses when you only need one? This one gets right to the point.

BS can be found *all over* the Sentence Improvements. That's both good and bad. It's good because you can rely on your ear and your natural capacity for language to help you—to a much greater extent than on the Error IDs. On the Error IDs, if a sentence sounds weird but doesn't violate any rules, then there's no error. Here, if a choice sounds weird, you can look for another one that sounds better.

On the other hand, it's bad because you can second-guess yourself too much when you're relying purely on your own judgment. With rule violations, there's no debate: if a choice is a Dangling Modifier, it is wrong, period. With BS, you might doubt yourself: "Well, *I* think choice (B) sounds better, but maybe someone else would prefer choice (C)." Don't worry. Here are some guidelines to help you.

1. Check the shortest choice

A shorter sentence is always preferable to a longer sentence, as long as it has the same meaning and doesn't violate any rules. The whole point of BS is that they're BIG sentences. That's what all these different phenomena have in common: they make the sentence longer than it has to be.

> The word "being" is a big clue here. It's almost always unnecessary. If you see "being" in a choice, there's a 95% chance it's wrong.

✗ **The owning of pets is being done by people who are great in number.**

What the heck is that? Is that even English? It sounds like a subtitle from a kung fu movie. What does this sentence really mean?

✓ **Many people own pets.**

That's it! So if you see a bunch of choices that are jam-packed with words, jump down to the shortest choice. *If it doesn't violate any other rules*, it's probably correct.

1. <u>**Being that he is such an excellent cook,**</u> **Dave is now head chef at one of the most popular restaurants in town.**

   (A)   **Being that he is such an excellent cook**
   (B)   **In being an excellent cook**
   (C)   **An excellent cook**
   (D)   **A cook of an excellent nature**
   (E)   **Having excellence in cooking**

2. **Although Manjula had studied all week,** <u>**the number of the score she got was the lowest of all those in the class**</u> **on the history test.**

   (A)   **the number of the score she got was the lowest of all those in the class**
   (B)   **her score was lower in number than those of her classmates**
   (C)   **she was scoring the lowest among all those in the class**
   (D)   **she got the lowest score in the class**
   (E)   **but she scored lowest in the class**

2. Eliminate Redundancies

Take a look at this sentence:

> ✗ Greek geometry was more advanced than <u>earlier forms of mathematics that came before it</u>.

The underlined part here is pretty wordy, but there's a specific problem here: why does it say "that came before it" at the end? We already said that we're talking about "earlier" forms of math. That's what "earlier" *means*: that they "came before"! So this phrase is *redundant*—it unnecessarily repeats itself. That last phrase doesn't add any new information to the sentence. So let's get rid of it.

> ✓ Greek geometry was more advanced than <u>earlier forms of mathematics</u>.

Much simpler; much better. Here's another common redundancy:

> ✗ <u>Because the price of gas is so high is the reason why</u> Scott bought a fuel-efficient car.

Do you see it? The underlined phrase starts with "because" and ends with "is the reason why". Those expressions mean the same thing! Don't say it twice. Just say this:

> ✓ <u>Because the price of gas is so high</u>, Scott bought a fuel-efficient car.

"Because" is a much more concise way to say what we mean. So we axed "is the reason why". Perfect.[*]

> Like "being", the phrase "is the reason why" (or variations of it) is almost *never* right. Treat it as a big warning sign that says "THIS CHOICE IS WRONG."

3. Active is better than passive

An "active" sentence is one in which the person or thing doing the action is the actual subject of the sentence. A "passive" sentence is one in which the person or thing receiving the action is the subject.

ACTIVE: A car <u>hit</u> Chapman.   **PASSIVE: Chapman <u>was hit by</u> a car.**

See the difference? Both these sentences *mean* the same thing: the car *did* the hitting, and Chapman *received* the hitting. But in the first sentence, the "car" is the subject, and in the second, "Chapman" is the subject. You can usually spot a passive sentence easily; the verb will contain a "to be" word like "was", "are", or "is" followed by a past tense verb form.

In general, active sentences are better than passive sentences. Take a look at this:

> ➤ Federico was chosen for the team by Paolo.

The phrase "by Paolo" tells us that Paolo is the one who did the choosing ("by" is a big clue that a sentence is passive). Since he did the action, why not make "Paolo" the subject?

> ✓ Paolo chose Federico for the team.

Nice. Now look at this:

> ✗ Swimming is unable to be done *by* Gretchen.

Ugh. That's terrible. Who talks like that?[†] I can't even look at this sentence. But there's that "by" again, so let's make "Gretchen" the subject of the sentence:

> ✓ Gretchen cannot swim.

Ahh. That's much better.

Passive sentences are *not wrong*; they're just frowned upon. As we can see with Gretchen, the passive can often make a sentence icky. But often the passive is perfectly acceptable and beautiful. In fact, sometimes you're *forced* to use the passive. For example, if there's an opening modifier:

---

[*] Certain people may have told you that you should never start a sentence with "because". That is a lie. Ignore these people.

[†] Robots, maybe?

✓ *While crossing the street*, **Chapman** <u>was hit by</u> a car.

Here, we need "Chapman" to be the subject of the sentence or else we'd have a dangling modifier.

Or if we don't know who performed the action:

✓ **Scott** <u>was fired</u> yesterday.

But as long as no rules are being violated, pick an active sentence over a passive sentence.

V. MISCELLANEOUS TOPICS

Here are a few additional concepts that don't show up as often but are good to remember nonetheless.

Double Subjects

Take a look at this sentence:

🖝 **The team's star quarterback, having just made an amazing play, he waved at the applauding crowd.**

What's going on in this sentence? It kinda sounds okay, but there is a problem. Let's simplify it by ignoring that modifier in the middle of the sentence:

✗ <u>**The team's star quarterback,**</u> ~~having just made an amazing play,~~ **he** waved at the applauding crowd.

When the sentence begins, it sounds as if "the team's star quarterback" is going to be the subject of the sentence. But in the last part, it seems like "he" is the subject. We don't need two subjects; the "he" is unnecessary:

✓ **The team's star quarterback,** ~~having just made an amazing play,~~ **waved at the applauding crowd.**

Connectors

We've seen plenty of examples of sentences that are made up of multiple parts. And we've seen examples of errors in the way we link those parts. But sometimes, it's not enough to look at the structure of the sentence; we have to look at the *meaning* of the parts to figure out what word or words we should use to connect the parts. Let's look at a few examples:

1. Contrast

When the parts of the sentence have *contrasting* meanings, the connecting word should reflect that contrast.

✗ **Johnny has never been a very good athlete, <u>and</u> he has won his last five races.**

Obviously, the two parts of these sentences are different: if Johnny's not a good athlete, we wouldn't expect him to win races. So we want to connect the parts with a contrast word.

✓ **Johnny has never been a very good athlete, <u>but</u> he has won his last five races.**

✓ **Johnny has never been a very good athlete, <u>yet</u> he has won his last five races.**

✓ **<u>Although</u> Johnny has never been a very good athlete, he has won his last five races.**

> Here are some examples of contrast words:
>
> 🖝 but 🖝 nor
> 🖝 yet 🖝 while
> 🖝 although 🖝 however
> 🖝 even though

These three sentences have slightly different connotations, but any of them would show proper contrast.

2. Causation

If one part of a sentence is the *cause* of another, use a connector like "because"

✓ **I bought the large box of crayons <u>because</u> I needed a lot of different colors.**

Conversely, don't use "because" if causation is inappropriate:

✗ **Johnny has never been a very good athlete <u>because</u> he has won his last five races.**

3. Coordination

Sometimes, picking a connector is as easy as figuring out if the parts are the same or different. But sometimes it's not enough to notice that two parts are similar: you have to look at *how* they're similar.

The word "**and**" is called a *coordinator*. "Coordination" means that the two parts of the sentence are *distinct* and of *equal importance:*

✓ **Dave went to the zoo, <u>and</u> Jerry went to the movies.**

Here, we're making two separate statements referring to two separate events. One guy did this and the other guy did that. That's coordination.[*] Compare that to this sentence:

✗ **Dave went to the zoo, <u>and</u> he saw an elephant.**

This makes it sound as if going to the zoo and seeing an elephant were two totally separate events. Instead, we should *link them directly*:

✓ **Dave went to the zoo, <u>where</u> he saw an elephant.**

By using "where" instead of "and", the sentence is clearer. Now, the second half is just a part of the first half. The sentence is referring to one overall event instead of two separate events.[†]

It's not *incorrect* to use "and" in this sentence; it's just not the *best* way to get across your meaning. Using "and" arouses the possibility that he didn't see the elephant at the zoo. Maybe he saw it somewhere else. Maybe it's just a list of things Dave did on Thursday: he went to the zoo, had lunch at Taco Bell, and saw an elephant.

But if he saw the elephant at the zoo, we should link the clauses directly.

SENTENCE IMPROVEMENT SUMMARY

➤ Every sentence must have at least one **independent clause**. If it doesn't, it's a **fragment**.

➤ If a sentence has **two independent clauses**, they *cannot* be connected with **a comma alone**; that's a **run-on**. You *may* connect independent clauses with:

   ○ a comma and a **conjunction** (and, but, because, although…)

   ○ a **semicolon** alone.

➤ If a sentence starts with a **modifier**, the thing that it describes must be the subject of the main clause, **directly after the comma**. If it doesn't, it's a **dangling modifier**.

➤ Don't put up with **BS**. Keep your sentences **short and direct**.

---

[*] This is similar to the concept behind *parallelism* that we discussed in the Error ID chapter.

[†] This is the difference between those clause types that we saw at the beginning of the chapter. At first, we had two *independent clauses* linked by a conjunction: two separate (or "independent") events. Now, the second half is a *dependent clause*: the second event is a part of (or "dependent on") the first event.

SENTENCE IMPROVEMENTS: BIG EXERCISE

1. Hoping to impress the notoriously demanding director, <u>the song Pamela chose for her audition was extremely difficult</u>.

   (A) the song Pamela chose for her audition was extremely difficult
   (B) the audition song chosen by Pamela was extremely difficult
   (C) Pamela's audition song was an extremely difficult choice
   (D) Pamela's choice of audition song was difficult and extreme
   (E) Pamela chose an extremely difficult song for her audition

2. Among the Congressional powers granted by the Constitution is the power to impeach the President, but <u>it has only done that</u> twice.

   (A) it has only done that
   (B) it has only exercised that power
   (C) they have only done that
   (D) Congress only will do so
   (E) Congress has only exercised that power

3. At first Portia had been very concerned about David's lack of experience, <u>and she eventually came to appreciate</u> his contribution to the project.

   (A) and she eventually came to appreciate
   (B) eventually coming to appreciate
   (C) but she eventually came to appreciate
   (D) however she came to an appreciation of
   (E) eventually she appreciated

4. By pasting a piece of cloth onto a painting in 1912, Picasso invented <u>collage and it is a technique in which</u> different materials and images are assembled into a new artwork.

   (A) collage and it is a technique in which
   (B) collage, it is a technique in which
   (C) collage, it is when
   (D) collage, a technique in which
   (E) collage; and that is

5. Professor Simmons thinks that this documentary about the Sudanese civil war is important not only for its educational value <u>and because it has</u> artistic merit.

   (A) and because it has
   (B) but also for its
   (C) but also its
   (D) as well as its
   (E) and it also has

6. Some people believe the proposed transportation bill will improve the city's subway and bus <u>service, others believe</u> it will only plunge the city further into debt.

   (A) service, others believe
   (B) service, however others believe
   (C) service; others believe
   (D) service; with others believing
   (E) service, but it is others who believe

7. <u>Born to a Haitian father and a Puerto Rican mother, Jean-Michel Basquiat incorporated Afro-Caribbean themes into much of his artwork.</u>

   (A) Born to a Haitian father and a Puerto Rican mother, Jean-Michel Basquiat incorporated Afro-Caribbean themes into much of his artwork.
   (B) Born to a Haitian father and a Puerto Rican mother, much of Jean-Michel Basquiat's artwork had Afro-Caribbean themes.
   (C) Jean-Michel Basquiat, who had a Haitian father and a Puerto Rican mother, and incorporated Afro-Caribbean themes into much of his artwork.
   (D) Jean-Michel Basquiat had a Haitian father and a Puerto Rican mother, who incorporated Afro-Caribbean themes into much of his artwork.
   (E) Afro-Caribbean themes were incorporated into much of Jean-Michel Basquiat's artwork, which had a Haitian father and a Puerto Rican mother.

8. Olivia's new <u>book, a comprehensive history of television, which is scheduled</u> to be published next spring along with a video containing actual footage of old programs.

   (A)   book, a comprehensive history of television, which is scheduled

   (B)   book, a comprehensive history of television, is scheduled

   (C)   book, a comprehensive history of television, being scheduled

   (D)   book is a comprehensive history of television, it is scheduled

   (E)   book, which is a comprehensive history of television, and which is scheduled

9. Our increasing consumption of fossil fuels <u>are severely polluting the air we breathe and are</u> accelerating the phenomenon of global warming.

   (A)   are severely polluting the air we breathe and are

   (B)   are causing severe pollution to breathable air, so

   (C)   is severely polluting the air we breathe and

   (D)   has caused the polluted air and

   (E)   thus causing severe pollution to the air we breathe and

10. Because this state park has become so <u>popular is why prospective visitors should reserve campsites</u> at least two weeks in advance.

   (A)   popular is why prospective visitors should reserve campsites

   (B)   popular being why prospective visitors should be reserving campsites

   (C)   popular, prospective visitors should reserve campsites

   (D)   popular, campsites should have been reserved for prospective visitors

   (E)   popular, campsites should be reserved by those who will be visiting

11. All new inductees to our organization must pledge both to obey the rules of membership <u>and also support all fellow members</u> in need of help.

   (A)   and also support all fellow members

   (B)   as well as supporting any fellow member

   (C)   and to support any fellow member

   (D)   with the support of all fellow members

   (E)   plus fellow members being supported

12. <u>Otis having invented the safety elevator in 1853</u>, much of the technology necessary for creating skyscrapers was already in place before the Civil War.

   (A)   Otis having invented the safety elevator in 1853

   (B)   Otis invented the safety elevator in 1853

   (C)   The safety elevator was invented by Otis in 1853

   (D)   Since Otis will invent the safety elevator in 1853

   (E)   Because of the safety elevator being an Otis invention of 1853

13. While working in Hong Kong in 1894, <u>that the bubonic plague is transmitted by fleas from rats was discovered by Alexandre Yersin.</u>

   (A)   that the bubonic plague is transmitted by fleas from rats was discovered by Alexandre Yersin

   (B)   the transmission of the bubonic plague by fleas carried by rats is what Alexandre Yersin discovered

   (C)   fleas from rats transmit the bubonic plague, Alexandre Yersin discovered

   (D)   Alexandre Yersin discovered that the bubonic plague is transmitted by fleas from rats

   (E)   Alexandre Yersin, who discovered fleas which are carried by rats transmitting the bubonic plague

14. The oceans are filled with millions of species of fish, some <u>of them live</u> so far beneath the surface that light cannot reach them.

   (A)   of them live

   (B)   of which live

   (C)   live

   (D)   are living

   (E)   having lived

PARAGRAPH IMPROVEMENT

So. There are three types of multiple-choice writing questions. We've covered Error Identification questions; these deal with the relationships between words (such as the verb and its subject). We've covered Sentence Improvement questions; these deal with the relationships between parts of a sentence (such as how to connect clauses). We're left with Paragraph Improvement questions; these deal with the relationship between entire sentences.

In this section, you will be presented with a short essay on some topic. Parts of the essay will be well written, parts will be poorly written. You will be asked six questions about the essay; these questions generally fall into one of two categories: 1) questions that ask you to fix grammatical and stylistic errors; 2) questions that ask you to describe the structure of the essay and the rhetorical tactics the author uses. Most questions will fall into the first category.

Paragraph Improvement is the least of your worries on the writing section. First of all, there are only six PI questions on the test. Since there are 49 total multiple-choice questions, to say nothing of the essay, how you do on six questions is not going to make or break your score. Second, as we'll see, these questions are often little more than glorified Sentence Improvement questions, so there's really nothing new we have to learn for them.

Some people might be a bit afraid of Paragraph Improvement because it brings back bad memories of Critical Reading passages. Let us assure you that this is *not* Critical Reading. This is much easier because:

- The passages are not very long—only 10–14 sentences on average.

- The passages are not weird. They aren't on obscure or subtle topics that you have to think about to understand. They are incredibly straightforward; they mean what they say.

- You're not being tested on what the passage *means* or even what it *says*; you're being tested on its grammar—*how* the passage says it.

- Did we mention there are only six questions?

As such, *don't* spend a lot of time reading the passage. Many of the questions will test you on individual sentences from the passage, *not* on the passage as a whole. Not only that, but usually they will *reprint the sentence in the question itself.* You don't even have to go back to the passage—the sentence is right there!

That's not to say that you shouldn't read the passage *at all.* You should; some questions will require you to understand the passage as a whole. And sometimes, the way to fix one sentence depends on the sentence before it. But read the passage quickly. Don't spend a lot of time trying to analyze the nuts and bolts of the passage. Just get a sense of what it's about, and then move on to the questions.

Paragraph Improvement is best explained by example, so let's try one.

(1) The Brooklyn Bridge is one of the most incredible things ever built. **(2)** It is not the first suspension bridge ever built. **(3)** There are other bridges today that are bigger and longer than it. **(4)** When it was built, it was the longest bridge in the world.

(5) The story of how it came to be constructed is very interesting, indeed. **(6)** The bridge being designed by John Augustus Roebling, an engineer who had previously built several other small bridges. **(7)** Just as they started building, he died suddenly after getting tetanus from a foot injury. **(8)** His son, Washington Roebling, took over the job of construction, but soon he became sick. **(9)** A strange disease caused by moving too quickly out of a pressurized area. **(10)** He was still alive, but he was forced to stay in bed, so he got his wife Emily to help. **(11)** She would give messages from Washington to the workmen and report back to him on the progress of the project. **(12)** She even learned some engineering so she could understand what was happening, this was a rare feat for a woman in the nineteenth century.

(13) The bridge finally opened to the public in 1883 after fourteen years of construction. **(14)** At the time that it opened, the bridge was over fifty percent longer than any other and was the first suspension bridge to use steel cables. **(15)** The bridge still stands today, a symbol of New York and the hard work and determination of a lot of people.

1. The primary effect of the first paragraph is to

(A) summarize the author's argument
(B) present a thesis that will be proven later
(C) introduce the topic to the reader
(D) refute a position that differs from the author's
(E) explain an apparent contradiction

2. In context, which is the best word to insert at the beginning of sentence 4?

(A) Furthermore,
(B) Therefore,
(C) Additionally,
(D) However,
(E) Consequently,

3. Which is the best way to deal with sentence 6 (reproduced below) ?

The bridge being designed by John Augustus Roebling, an engineer who had previously built several other small bridges.

(A) Leave it as it is.
(B) Change "being" to "was"
(C) Insert "he was" before "an engineer"
(D) Change "had" to "has"
(E) Insert "as well" after "bridges"

4. In context, which is the best version of the underlined portion of sentence 7 (reproduced below) ?

Just as they started building, he died suddenly after getting tetanus from a foot injury.

(A) (As it is now)
(B) When they started to build the bridge, he
(C) The construction of the bridge started, he
(D) They had just started when he
(E) Soon after the bridge's construction began, he

5. Which of the following is the best way to revise and combine the underlined portions of sentence 8 & 9 (reproduced below) ?

His son, Washington Roebling, took over the job of construction, but soon he became sick. A strange disease caused by moving too quickly out of a pressurized area.

(A) he became sick; a strange disease
(B) he became sick, it was a strange disease
(C) getting a strange disease
(D) he became sick from a strange disease
(E) the disease he got was

6. Of the following, which is the best version of the underlined portion of sentence 12 (reproduced below)?

She even learned some engineering so she could understand what was happening, this was a rare feat for a woman in the nineteenth century.

(A) (as it is now)
(B) happening, this is something a woman rarely does
(C) happening, because this was a rare feat for a woman
(D) happening; women will rarely do this
(E) happening, a rare feat for a woman

THE ESSAY

I t's really not that bad.

First of all, remember that everyone is in the same boat you're in. No one likes this. We're stuck with it, but we're all in this together.

Second, The Essay is only *ONE* (1) part of the Writing section. The Essay score will account for about 30% of your overall writing score, while the multiple choice accounts for 70% of your score. Since Sentence Improvement questions make up 50% of the multiple choice, they account for 35% of your score. That means that Sentence Improvement counts more towards your score than The Essay does. And Error IDs are not far behind—they're 37% of the multiple choice, thus 26% of your score.

These numbers aren't important. What is important is that **you should not freak out about The Essay**. It's only one section. In fact, depending on the scoring table, you could get a *zero* on The Essay—a score you can only get if you write off-topic—and still get as high as a 690 on the Writing Section if you nail the multiple-choice questions.[*]

Of course, that's not to say that The Essay isn't important. You're not going to be perfect on the multiple choice, so you'll need to score some points here as well. The great thing about The Essay is that doing well isn't nearly as hard as it sounds. They don't expect you to write something spectacular. They're not looking for a Pulitzer Prize-winning article here. They just want to see that you can string a series of coherent thoughts together.[†]

Let's talk about The Essay in general before we get into your strategies for doing well.

I. GENERAL POINTS

Scoring

Your essay will be read by two Official SAT Essay Readers.[‡] Each will give your essay a score from 1 (sad) to 6 (happy). So your total score will range from 2 to 12. If your essay is not on the given topic or if you write with a pen, you will get a zero.

These guys are good and know exactly what they're looking for, so in most cases you will get either two of the same score (such as a 3 and a 3) or two scores that are off by one (such as a 3 and a 4). If by some chance the two readers disagree by more than one point (such as a 3 and a 5), then your essay will go to a third reader who will determine your final score. This means that you will never get severely disparate scores. You'll never get a 1 and a 6.

---

[*] Hypothetically, that is. Please do not test this theory.

[†] Okay, maybe that is hard for some of you. Don't worry. We'll work on it.

[‡] While the essays are obviously scored by living human beings, they are scanned into a computer for various reasons. On the very first test that featured the essay (in March of 2005), some students' scores were delayed because they wrote their essays in pen instead of pencil, so the essays could not be scanned into the computer. Do not write your essay in pen. Why would you even *bring* a pen to the SAT? Don't use a pen.

What They're Looking For

There are several key things that the Official SAT Essay Readers look for when grading your essay:

1.	**Development**	How well do you make your point? Do your examples demonstrate the point you're trying to make? Do you effectively explain your examples? Or are you full of it?
2.	**Organization**	Is your essay well organized? Does the progression of ideas make sense? Is your essay well focused? Or does it madly jump from topic to topic in a seemingly random order?
3.	**Language**	Do you use baby words or grown-up words? If you use grown-up words, do you *really* know what they mean?
4.	**Sentences**	Do you use a varied sentence structure? Or does your essay read like a *Dick and Jane* book?
5.	**Grammar**	Did you make errors? Do your subjects agree with your verbs? Do your modifiers dangle?

These five categories are roughly in descending order of importance. But they boil down to two main elements:

➤ **Can you make a convincing argument? (Development and Organization)**

➤ **Do you speak English? (Language, Sentences and Grammar)**

The nitty-gritty language bits may seem like the fundamental element here. If you write well, if your sentences are beautiful and fully formed, then your argument will become stronger. However, we're going to focus on the Argument. From a preparation standpoint, it's much easier to change the way you construct your argument than it is to change the way you write.

II. THE ARGUMENT

A. Development

Before you do anything else, you have to figure out what you're going to say. Read the topic, and then choose some examples that best support your argument.

The Topic

The topic will consist of a quote expressing a point of view (or two quotes expressing contrasting points of view). This will be followed by a question (usually yes-or-no) that's relevant to the topic of the quote. Here's a sample:

> Charity and altruism are often considered the greatest goals of civilized people. But true selflessness is not only difficult, but nearly impossible to attain. Charitable acts can have obvious self-interested motives, such as good publicity or tax credits. Acts that benefit the public will likewise benefit the giver. And even charitable acts that seem to provide no benefit to the givers still are usually performed as a self-affirmation, to make the givers feel better about themselves.
>
> Adapted from Romulo Johannsen, "The Economics of Charity"

Assignment: Are people always motivated by selfish desires? Plan and write an essay in which you develop your point of view on this issue. Support your position with reasoning and examples taken from your reading, studies, experience, or observations.

Note that the question under the quote is what matters, not the quote itself. The quote is there to help you understand the question, and to give you ideas about how to get started. But you do not have to specifically address the quote in your essay.*

Choose Examples

You should give *TWO* examples that prove your point. Three would be nice, but you don't have time for three. One would be okay, theoretically, but you would *really* have to explain it well, which is hard. Two is perfect. So once you read the topic, try to think of two situations, events, or people that are relevant to the topic. So how do you choose your examples?

The topics are intentionally vague so that there is no right or wrong answer to the question. Remember: they're not testing your *knowledge*; they're testing your *writing*. You can write about pretty much anything you want as long as it demonstrates your point somehow.

Unfortunately, this openness can actually make your job harder. If you knew that you'd have to write an essay on, say, the Crimean War, you'd just learn everything you could about the Crimean War before the test. That's how you do things in school. Here, though, since *everything* is on the table, it's easy to blank out. You could wind up spending 20 minutes staring at the wall trying to think of something, *anything*, to write about. This is a very common problem, and many students don't have enough time to finish writing because they spent so much time deciding what to write about.

That's why you should **come up with FIVE all-purpose examples** *right now*. This way, you won't have to waste a lot of time coming up with something to write about. As soon as you read the topic, you can immediately pick the *two* of your five examples that are most relevant to the topic.

Know Something

So how do you pick examples? Think of some things that a) you know something about and b) are broad enough to be applied to a lot of different essay topics. Here are some possible examples. Obviously, we're not saying you have to know everything about all of these; we're just trying to get the ball rolling.

History: American Revolution, Civil War/slavery, World War II

Science/Technology: Industrial Revolution, the Renaissance, invention of the automobile, computers/the Internet

People: Hitler, Martin Luther King, Jr., Rosa Parks, Richard Nixon, Gandhi

Literature: What are you reading in English class right now? Chances are it's something in which the main character undergoes some kind of transformation. Discuss.

Other topics: You don't have to write about academic subjects. Personal examples are fine. Even pop culture examples are fine. If you want to write about *Star Wars* or *The Simpsons*—fine, go for it. As long as whatever you write is relevant to the topic.

Once you have your five examples, **pick two that are most relevant to the topic**. The key point here is *relevance*. Obviously, not every example will be relevant to every topic. Martin Luther King Jr. is a good example for topics about social justice, but a bad example for topics about technology. It's best to prepare an example from *each* of these five fields listed above. That way, you'll have a range of different examples, so you're more likely to be able to address a wide range of essay topics.

Give Details

The most important thing is to **prepare examples you know something about**. One of the biggest differences between a weak essay and an effective essay is *details*. The more concrete details you provide, the stronger your argument will be. So pick examples that you can comfortably provide details for. Why not start with whatever you're doing in school right now? Not what you did two years ago—you won't

---

* Some of you may be thinking that you can eat up some space in your essay by repeating the quote in your introduction. Please don't do that. It does not help your essay. The essay readers have been reading stacks of essays. They know what the quote is. You can refer to the quote if you like, but don't reproduce it in full.

remember it. Pick whatever you're doing *now*. Similarly, pick a book that you've *actually read*, not a book you were supposed to read but didn't.

Feel free to deviate from your five examples if inspiration strikes you. If your essay topic reminds you of something you've recently read or a movie you've recently seen, and you want to write about something new, that's great. As long as you know something about that example. Our goal here is to have a safety net, a backup. You should have some things that you're prepared to discuss *no matter what* so you won't blank out and stare at the wall for 20 minutes.

Facts

As we've said, you're not being tested on your knowledge here. As a result, you can actually make some factual errors without penalty. **Getting facts wrong will not count against you.** You can get character names wrong, mess up the plot of a book, even get historical facts radically incorrect and still do well, *as long as your essay is well written.*

That said, you should *try* to minimize factual errors. The test makers *say* that they won't count off for factual errors, but these essay readers are human—in fact, most of them are teachers. They know when you're wrong. And even if they say they overlook errors, subconsciously they may think less of you when you make them. And if you make *atrocious* errors, they can't help but take notice.

If you pick a subject you know something about, you'll be less likely to get stuff wrong. But if you're not sure of a fact, try to work around it. Not sure what year the Civil War started? Just say "mid-nineteenth century" or "the 1800's". Or don't mention the time period at all. Just do the best you can.

Similarly, it's perfectly fine to use personal examples, and obviously your reader won't know if your personal example is true or not. [*] So, can you just make up totally fictitious examples?

<u>No</u>. **Do not make up examples**. While in theory you're allowed to write about fictitious things, in practice *it's really hard to do that effectively*. Remember—effective essays have lots of *concrete details*. It's really hard to come up with made-up details on the spot. Also, fictitious examples often sound so absurdly fake that they actually weaken your argument. Personal examples are fine, but stick to things that actually happened.

Pick a Side

Remember that most topics will take the form of a yes-or-no question, so you will have to pick a side. Which one? **Pick the side that fits your examples**. You've already got five examples to draw from. First figure out which two are most relevant to the topic. *Then* decide which side those examples fit. If you start writing an outline and then decide the other side is a better fit, that's fine, go for it. Just pick a side.

It is *possible* to write an effective essay that argues both sides. These essays will show that both sides have merit depending on your perspective. However, *it's really hard to do that effectively*. Often when you try to argue both sides, you wind up contradicting yourself, which weakens your argument. You don't have to actually agree with the argument you're making. There's no right or wrong answer here, just good or bad arguments. So pick a side.

B. Organization

A lot of students don't bother much with planning the organization of their essays, but it's ***incredibly*** important. It's one thing to have brilliant ideas swimming around in your head and it's another to be able to communicate them to your readers. These essays are not little short stories—they're *arguments*. As such, you must pay close attention to how you present your case. ***You must write an outline before you begin***.

We know what you're thinking. "An outline? I've only got twenty-five minutes to write! I can't waste my time on an outline, fool!"

---

[*] It's also perfectly fine to write in the first person. The essay is meant to be your opinion, so feel free to write "I" as much as you want.

You can and will. An outline takes very little time and will help the actual writing process go much more quickly and coherently. You must write an outline. You must write an outline.*

Writing an outline is incredibly easy. In fact, we're going to tell you what your outline should look like right now. We're doing your work for you. Some English-teacher types often talk about "the five-paragraph essay" as the standard for student essays. That's too much. You don't have that kind of time. We endorse *the four-paragraph essay*. Here is your outline.

I. **Introduction**   Say which side you're going to take—your **thesis**—and what your examples will be.

II. **Example 1**   Discuss your first example and *why it proves your point.*

III. **Example 2**   Discuss your second example and *why it proves your point.*

IV. **Conclusion**   Summarize what you've just said.

That's it! There's your essay. In fact, if you're running out of time, the conclusion is optional. All that matters is that your examples are clearly defined and well argued. Really, your only job now is to figure out what your examples will be and which to use first.

Writing Your Examples

You must provide two things for each of your examples: its **Background** and its **Relevance**.

Background (who, what, when, and where)

Tell us *what the example is.* Give us the background. Who is this person? What happened in the book? What did he do? Why did he do it? What effects did it have? Where and when did these events occur? Provide **concrete details** about the example, all the *information*, like a reporter giving a news story.

Don't assume that your essay readers know what you're talking about. They may not have read this book or seen this movie. You have to give all the details so your audience knows the story.

Of course, you don't have to tell us *everything* you know about your example, only those details that are relevant to your point. Giving extra details that don't have anything to do with your thesis will weaken your argument. Your readers are not impressed by your knowledge, only your argument.

Relevance (why and how)

Tell us *why the example proves your point.* Given that this person did these things, what does that have to do with the topic? How does *this* example prove your thesis? As we said before, you want to make sure that you give details that are relevant to your point. But you also have to show us why they're relevant. It's not enough just to tell us what the happened. Don't assume your readers will automatically see how it proves your point. You have to tell them. BE SPECIFIC.

III. LANGUAGE

Again, improving your organization and development is a much more effective way of improving your essay score than trying to improve your language. First of all, it's really hard to change the language you write with. Secondly, it doesn't have as much of an effect on your score as you'd think.

Nevertheless, there are some things to keep in mind about the way you write.

A. Vocabulary

First of all, remember the box? Why not use some of those words in your essay? You'll be glad you did.

More important than vocabulary is using **concrete language**. This means being *specific* in everything you say. Give us details, give us examples, give us concrete words, not abstract ideas. Say *exactly* what you mean.

---

* You must write an outline.

Using concrete language is directly related to what we've already been preaching—give concrete details. One of the biggest problems that students have on their essays is that they don't know the difference between *saying* something and *proving* it. You can't assume that your reader will automatically understand why your examples support your point. You've got to *prove* it explicitly.

B. Sentences

If all your sentences sound the same, your writing becomes dull. Varying your sentence structure can help break up the monotony and make you sound like a big shot.

What does that mean? Glad you asked.

There are three different types of sentences (get ready, I'm about to use Fancy Grammatical Terms™):

1. **Simple**   Sentence has only one clause.

    ☛ I like cats.

    ☛ My science partner smells like onions.

2. **Compound**   Sentence has two or more independent clauses stuck together.

    ☛ I like cats, but John does not.

    ☛ My science partner smells like onions, and his clothes are dirty.

3. **Complex**   Sentence has an independent clause and a *subordinate* clause (a clause of lesser importance).

    ☛ Although I like cats, John apparently does not.

    ☛ My science partner, who sits next to me every day in Biology class, smells like onions.

Many students only write in simple and compound sentences. To shake things up, try to throw at least one complex sentence into your essay. Just make a point of using a sentence with the word "although". That's all you need.

C. Grammar

Believe it or not, your grammatical competence is probably the *least* important element of The Essay. The Essay is intended to be a first draft. That means it doesn't have to be totally polished. They know that you only have 25 minutes for this bad boy, so you've got some leeway here. They're not looking for Shakespeare here. You can make spelling and grammatical errors and still get a double-6. Your argument is more important than your grammar.

> Your essay doesn't have to be neat. You can cross words out or insert whole sentences with asterisks and arrows pointing here and there. But stay in the box—any text outside the box around the page will not be read.

That said, your mistakes should be within the limits of reason. Every little mistake adds up. A few scattered here and there are okay, but if you consistently butcher every sentence you write, it won't matter how good your examples are—no one will be able to understand what you're saying. So while grammar shouldn't be your *main* concern on The Essay, you should try to cut down on errors whenever possible.

We've already discussed pretty much all of the major rules of grammar, so we don't have to go over them all again.[*] Just know that all the grammatical rules we've talked about so far apply to you too.

One way to avoid grammatical problems is to **reread your work**. When you've got a strict time limit, you write quickly, so it's incredibly easy to lose track of what you've already written. In fact, many of the grammatical mistakes students make on the essay arise because they *literally forgot* what they had just written. Obviously, timing is an issue on the essay, so if you don't have time to re-read, that's okay. But giving your essay another read once you've finished can help you spot errors and clean things up a bit.

---

[*]   Well, we *shouldn't* have to go over them again.

IV. SAMPLE ESSAYS

Let's look at a few sample essays to see how everything we've been talking about translates to actual scores. Below, we'll find one representative essay for each score, from 0 to 6.

Keep in mind that **this is just one set of examples**. There are no strict rules about what an essay has to do to get a specific score. There are many reasons why an essay might get a particular score. There's no rule for what a 3 looks like. One essay might get a 3 if it's generally well written but has vague examples. Another if it had concrete examples but is poorly written. While there's no guarantee that doing any one thing will get you any particular score, there are certainly things you can do to improve any essay.

A note about scores: It's tempting to think of your essay scores in terms of the final score, 0 to 12, since that's what you see on your score report, but it's best to think about scores in terms of a single reader's grade instead. If you start thinking about it on a 12-point scale, you're going to start to make distinctions that are too fine. You'll look at an essay and think, "Hmm, is this a 7 or an 8? It's more of an 7.5..." But that's not how scores work: the 12 point scale already has that kind of indecision built into it. Getting a 7 means that readers couldn't decide between giving it a 3 and giving it a 4. There's no such thing as an essay that's "a 7"; there are only essays that one reader thought was a 3 and another thought was a 4.

Here's the prompt for our sample essays:

> Charity and altruism are often considered the greatest goals of civilized people. But true selflessness is not only difficult, but nearly impossible to attain. Charitable acts can have obviously self-interested motives, such as good publicity or tax credits. Acts that benefit the public will likewise benefit the giver. And even charitable acts that seem to provide no benefit to the givers still are usually performed as a self-affirmation, to make the givers feel better about themselves.
>
> Adapted from Romulo Johannsen, "The Economics of Charity"

Assignment: Are people always motivated by selfish desires? Plan and write an essay in which you develop your point of view on this issue. Support your position with reasoning and examples taken from your reading, studies, experience, or observations.

Essay A: Score of 0

I AM THE CHIPMUNK KING!

What's good about this essay:

It is free of errors in grammar, usage and spelling.

What's bad about this essay:

It does not address the prompt. Any off-topic essay will get a zero. Also, it is crazy.

How it can be better:

- Write on topic.
- Don't be crazy.

Essay B: Score of 1

> I belive people are always motivated by selfish desires. People are always saying to be nice and good, but in realty people only do what they want. Everyday people are dieing and suffering because there poor and starving. I think its important to help people when they need help, but they do not. The reason why I think people are motivated by selfish desire because we only care about ourselves and what makes us richer. The world would be better place if people stop worrying about money and learn to love each other.

What's good about this essay:

Ok, now we're rolling! This essay is on topic and clearly states a thesis: "People are always motivated by selfish desires."

What's bad about this essay:

Pretty much everything else.

First of all, it's simply **too short**. You have to write more than this.

This is a common question students ask: how important is it to write a lot?

Writing a long essay is *necessary* but not *sufficient*. If you only write one paragraph that's less than 100 words long, there's no way you can score above a 2 at best. This is supposed to be an essay, not a poem.

However, you don't automatically get a 6 just by filling two pages. If it's two pages of nonsense, you'll still do poorly. So you do have to write a lot to do well, but just writing a lot isn't enough.

Second, the essay simply states and restates that people are selfish, but it doesn't give any **evidence** to show that it's true. It has no examples or concrete details, only grand unsupported statements. Look at this sentence:

> ☞ **The reason why I think people are motivated by selfish desire because we only care about ourselves and what makes us richer.**

Besides missing a verb—we need an "is" before "because"—this sentence doesn't make sense. Caring only about yourself isn't a *reason* people are motivated by selfishness. Caring about yourself is *the definition* of selfishness. The author thinks he or she is giving support for the thesis, but this is just re-stating the thesis.

Third, the language is not good. The sentence structures are choppy, and the vocabulary is simple and repetitive. The word "people" is used in *every single sentence in the essay*. There are a number of spelling and grammatical errors. To name a few:

Error	Correction	Notes
realty	*reality*	Spelling error
dieing	*dying*	Spelling error
because there poor	*because they're poor*	Need a contraction: they *are* poor.
its important	*it's important*	Need a contraction: it *is* important
Everyday people	*Every day, people*	"Everyday" is an adjective meaning "ordinary" as in "everyday clothes"; we want to say something *happens* every day.
but they do not	[Needs greater revision; several corrections are possible.]	Vague pronoun. Does "they" refer to the people who need help, or the people who are supposed to help them?

How it can be better:

- ☞ Write more.
- ☞ Use specific examples to show why your thesis is true.
- ☞ Clean up the errors.

Essay C: Score of 2

Charity and altruism are often considered the greatest goals of civilized people. But true selflessness is not only difficult, but nearly impossible to attain. Charitable acts can have obviously self-interested motives, such as good publicity or tax credits. Acts that benefit the public will likewise benefit the giver. And even charitable acts that seem to provide no benefit to the givers still are usually performed as a self-affirmation, to make the givers feel better about themselves. Are people always motivated by selfish desires? I would have to say, no, people are not motivated by selfish desires. Sure, we all have selfish desires and want the best for our selves, but we also care about people too.

If you only do things that help yourself than you won't have a happy life. You can get money, cars, houses, and electonics but it wont make you happy.

People always get to the top by stomping on the little guy below them but does that make you happy? No, all you want is true hapiness and you can only get that with love. How many times does someone spend all their time trying to get all the money and then when they get old and die they realize they're all alone. They want love, not money and cars.

What's good about this essay:

Wow, that opening paragraph is really good! Complex sentences, sophisticated vocabulary. It almost sounds—hey, wait a minute. That's just the quote from the prompt copied into the essay! Nice try. You think we'd fall for that? The essay graders have been reading hundreds of essays on the same topic. You think they wouldn't recognize it?

We're going to ignore all that. For our purposes, this essay starts at the end of the first paragraph with "I would have to say, no."

There is some good stuff here. Even without all that padding, this essay is longer than essay B, though it's still a bit short. It has a clear thesis: "no, people are not motivated by selfish desires." It has separate paragraphs that appear to contain separate ideas.

What's bad about this essay:

The biggest problem is that the essay doesn't really provide any evidence or discussion of the thesis. It repeatedly says that money and cars won't bring happiness, but provides no examples or evidence of that, no way to prove it's true. It says over and over that love is better than money. How about an example of this?

It *begins* to gesture toward an example at the end, describing "someone" who tried "to get all the money" and died alone. But that's much too vague.

The reason we need evidence and details is this: *what if your reader disagrees with you?* How do we know you're right? You say people want love, not money. What if I don't? Surely there are some people out there who don't want love. Surely there are some people who really, really, really like money and cars. How about an example of someone who had money but no love? You can't just say "people do X" and leave it at that. Give me an example of someone doing X. *Show* me someone doing X.

Furthermore, this essay doesn't quite address the topic properly. The essay asks if people are motivated by selfish desires. Certainly, desire for money and cars would be an example of that. The opposite argument, that people are not motivated by selfish desires, would be that people are motivated by *unselfish* desires, by thinking of *other people*. This essay's example, desire for love, is still a selfish desire. Wanting love instead of money is still an example of *wanting* something *for yourself*.

Finally, the essay still has errors in spelling and grammar. Not as many as Essay B, but still enough to be noticeable: "than" should be "then"; "electonics" should be "electronics"; "wont" should be "won't". But the technical errors aren't as problematic as the general style. The prose is simple, repetitive, and rambling.

How it can be better:

- ☛ Don't copy the prompt into your essay. The time it takes you to do that is time you could spend on writing better examples or more details.

- ☛ Use specific examples with details.

- ☛ Clean up the writing.

Essay D: Score of 3

> People are always motivated by selfish desires. Certainly, it may sometimes seem like people in accordance with an altruistic desire to help others, but often they have hidden alterior motives. People only act for others when they have a selfish reason for it. For example, say a girl needs help with her math homework and asks a boy for help. The boy might agree and give her the help she needs. But he doesn't really care about her math grade, he just wants to be nice to her so she'll go out with him. If a successful lawyer takes a case for free, it might look like he's taking the case because he wants justice and wants an innocent man to go free. Even though it looks like he's doing a good thing, he really just wants to look good so people think he's a good person instead of a sleezy lawyer. Examples like these show that people are really motivated by selfish desires, even when they help others.

What's good about this essay:

Finally, we have some real examples now. This essay has two examples to support its point: a boy helping a girl with her math homework, and a lawyer taking a case for free. Both are clearly relevant to the thesis. And again, we have a clear thesis and a strong position taken on the topic.

The writing is a little better than we've seen: some better vocabulary, better sentence structures. Not perfect, but better.

What's bad about this essay:

First the obvious: *it's one big paragraph!* An essay without any paragraph breaks can be tough to read and tough to follow. This essay actually already has a nice internal logic to it that would lead to natural paragraph breaks without rewriting anything. Like this:

- some introductory sentences
- the first example about the math homework
- the second example about the lawyer
- the last sentence as a conclusion

We'd want to add some transitional language between the first and second examples. It doesn't have to be elaborate, just something like "As another example," would be fine.

Second, while we do have some examples here, they're not quite fleshed out enough. They're both hypothetical, meaning we're describing a generic situation instead of specific people. It's not impossible to write a hypothetical example well, but they're generally not as strong as real examples because they don't have any *details*.

It opens the example up to interpretation. Yes, maybe we can think of a situation in which the boy just wants to go out with the girl, but we can also think of a situation in which he doesn't. Maybe he already has a girlfriend. Maybe he likes helping people. Maybe he *really* likes doing math. We don't know because we don't have any details. The essay starts by strongly saying "people are *always* motivated by selfish desires," but the examples are saying 'well, here's a situation where it might happen.'

If instead the essay used, say, a personal anecdote describing a girl the author actually liked, there would be less room for ambiguity. As an added bonus, when you write about concrete situations, you know more about them, so you can give more details and paint a more vivid picture: Who is this girl? What class was it? Has the boy always liked her? Did his plan work? Did she go out with him? Did going out with her lead him to start actually caring about her and make him less of a selfish jerk?

Finally, while the language is better than we saw in the previous essays, there are still some errors scattered throughout.

- The word is "ulterior" not "alterior". But kudos for trying to use sophisticated vocabulary.
- "Sleezy" should be spelled "sleazy".

How it can be better:

- Split the essay into separate paragraphs.
- Use more concrete examples with concrete language.

Essay E: Score of 4

> No one is ever truly unselfish. Selfishness is an inherent trait of human nature and all actions can ultimately be traced back to some human desire. Whether helping a friend or giving money to charity, most supposedly "unselfish" acts have selfish motivations.
>
> Rosa Parks was an African American woman who lived in the time of segregation, a bleak time for African Americans. They could not use the same facilities as whites, and were forced to use separate bathrooms and water fountains. One day, Rosa Parks was riding a bus when a white woman wanted her to move to the back. Parks was tired and did not want to move, so she refused to go, and she was thrown in jail as a result. This simple act of defiance sparked a movement that eventually resulted in the end of segregation. Her great contribution to the movement was motivated by the selfish desire to stay where she was sitting.
>
> In the movie Star Trek: First Contact, a group of aliens called the Borg go back in time to prevent humans from inventing the warp drive, and Captain Picard and the USS Enterprise follow and try to stop them. The warp drive was invented by a man named Zefram Cochrane, whose flight would cause Vulcans to make contact with Earth. This "first contact" launched a new era of peace and exploration. The Enterprise crew considers Cochrane to be a great hero for his invention. However, he turns out to be a drunk and only created the warp drive to make money.
>
> These two examples show that, in life, even when you act unselfishly, there are often selfish motivations for your actions, even for the greatest heroes throughout history.

What's good about this essay:

Structurally, this essay is pretty solid. We have clearly delineated paragraphs and two concrete examples with background details, each clearly relevant to the thesis.

The writing is generally good. Fewer mistakes, fewer ugly sentences. There's some nice vocabulary (e.g. *inherent* and *bleak*), and a few elegant sentences ("This simple act of defiance sparked a movement that eventually resulted in the end of segregation.")

What's bad about this essay:

The first problem here is a complete lack of transitions between paragraphs. Each paragraph is totally separate from the others—they might as well be four separate essays. You have to connect your examples into a coherent whole.

Transitional language doesn't have to be elaborate. It can be as basic as "One example of this is", or "In contrast". Really any sentence that directly connects each paragraph to the one before would be better than this. It's especially jarring in an essay that jumps from the Civil Rights era to a Star Trek movie without even acknowledging the change of topic.

Some students like to mention their examples in the introduction itself. That can help set the tone for the essay, but don't spend too much time talking about them in the introduction. Get to the body of your essay.

Both examples here show a good amount of detail, but both also have the same problem—they have too much *background* and not enough *discussion*. In the Rosa Parks example, we get a decent description of the world of segregation and the events of her arrest, but only one sentence talking about her selfish desire. The idea that Rosa Parks' actions were somehow selfish is very counterintuitive (not to mention somewhat offensive!), and requires much more explanation. The selfish desire is the whole point of the essay; *that's* where you should be spending your time.

The Star Trek example has the same problem. Writing about Star Trek is fine, nerd; there's no requirement that your example must be high literature, as long as it's relevant, which this clearly is. But the essay glosses over the point—that Cochrane changed human history accidentally for a purely selfish reason. That's where you should focus your discussion. Why mention the Borg or Picard at all? Sure, they're important to the movie, but not to your essay. We need some set up about going back in time and the invention of the warp drive, but we don't need the plot of the whole movie. *Don't spend time on things that aren't relevant to your argument.*

How it can be better:

- Add transitional language between paragraphs.
- Spend more time on *discussion* of examples, not just background.

Essay F: Score of 5

There is so much greed in the world, from Hollywood to Wall Street and through all of Middle America in between. In every town and city we see people who think only of themselves and their immediate needs. As pervasive as greed is, people do not always act on selfish motivation. Sometimes, when a person truly does act selflessly, it's a remarkable and noteworthy event.

One of the most selfless people of the 20th century was Martin Luther King, Jr. He grew up in Atlanta, GA eventually becoming a pastor. While slavery had previously been outlawed 100 years earlier, segregation and Jim Crow laws guaranteed that African Americans still had virtually no rights. Martin Luther King, Jr., changed that. Through his work as the leader of the SLSC, he advocated nonviolent solutions, organizing protests and boycotts to spur people both black and white to come together and end the injustice. His work culminated in his famous "I have a dream" speech during a massive march on Washington DC, a short speech, but one that crystalized the goals of the movement. One may argue that King's actions were selfish in a way, since he himself was also the victim of the inequality he fought. But he always fought injustice, in word and deed, and worked tirelessly to help others without demanding compensation. He even eventually gave his life for the cause, as he was assassinated for his work. Putting your own life in danger in order to help others is the ultimate selfless act.

We can see selfless acts in literature as well. In the book <u>The Great Gatsby</u> by F. Scott Fitzgerald, Jay Gatsby is a playboy millionaire given to throwing lavish parties at his mansion. But his only true desire is his love for Daisy Buchannan. So great is his love for her that he takes credit for a fatal crash that Daisy was responsible for, which eventually would lead to his being murdered by the husband of the woman who was killed. He literally gave his life to save hers.

Truly selfless acts may be rare, but they do occur.

What's good about this essay:

The thesis here is interesting: the essay agrees that *most* people are selfish, but disagrees that people are *always* selfish. That's a good thesis. If you try to argue that people are always selfish, you can give examples of selfishness, but the reader may still think there are also other examples of selflessness that we haven't thought of. Here, we only need to show one example of a selfless act in order to prove that *sometimes* people can be selfless.

As with Essay E, this essay has a good structure, clearly laying out its thesis and examples into discrete paragraphs. Unlike Essay E, this essay has better transitional language: notice how the beginning of the second paragraph specifically refers to the selflessness that was mentioned at the end of the first paragraph. Similarly, the beginning of the third paragraph again mentions selflessness while explicitly introducing the shift to a literary example.

Both examples have lots of details, particularly the King example. And both have discussion as well as background; they are explicitly tied back to the idea of selflessness. (Note that the King example has an error—the organization is called the SCLC, not SLSC. But that's a factual error, so the essay will not be penalized for it.)

The language is generally good. There is some good vocabulary (e.g. *pervasive* and *culminated*) and some elegant sentences.

What's bad about this essay:

The second example is clearly weaker than the first. It's well chosen—giving your life to save someone else is certainly a selfless act—but it's too bare. There are fewer details and less discussion.

It's also more awkwardly written. Look at the second to last sentence:

> **So great is his love for her that he takes credit for a fatal crash that Daisy was responsible for, which eventually would lead to his being murdered by the husband of the woman who was killed.**

Yeesh. It's a garden path of confusion. The problem seems to be that the author is trying to get too much plot information (that there was a car crash, that a woman died, that Daisy was driving, that Gatsby took responsibility, that Gatsby was murdered) into a single sentence. It needs to be split into at least two sentences, if not more.

One possible explanation is that the writer simply ran out of time. She did good work with the King example, looked up and saw she had only a few minutes left for Gatsby. That would also explain the more awkward writing and the cursory one-sentence conclusion. You can help prevent this by practicing writing essays and pacing yourself. Be aware of how much time has passed. Some of the background of the King example could probably have been cut in order to give the writer more time for Gatsby. Remember what we said in Essay E: you only need as much background as is relevant to your thesis.

Another explanation is that the writer simply knew more about King than she knew about Gatsby. If you've got one strong example and one weak example, you might consider just focusing on the strong one and cutting the weak one. There's no rule that says you have to have two examples, as long as you can write at length on the one you choose. The King example here could probably have been stretched out into two paragraphs to fill a whole essay.

How it can be better:

- Pay attention to both examples. Try to get both to be the same quality.

- Pace yourself. Practice writing timed essays to get used to the time constraint.

- Trim the first example to give more time for the second, OR cut the second altogether and spend more time on the first.

Essay G: Score of 6

No matter how much we may think that we're all charitable people, the fact is that most of us act primarily on selfish desires most of the time. However, this doesn't mean that nobody does unselfish things. Even when people have selfish motivations, the goodness of their acts is more important than the motivation behind them.

I can see this at work in my own life. One of my proudest accomplishments has been my volunteer work at a children's hospital. Every week, I spend a few hours on the floor talking to the children and their families. My job is to give them a little break from the stress of their illnesses. I read stories, do art projects, play games, sing songs, or do anything I can to cheer them up. This has a palpable effect on both the children who are sick or dying and the parents who spend all their time wracked with worry.

But the truth is that I only started going there for a selfish reason. My school gives extra credit for performing community service, and I thought it would be an easy way to improve my GPA. Through most of high school I had gotten straight A's, but a few tough classes made my average slip into the B range. I was desperate for an easy A. It worked: I only had to go for a few hours a week and I got an A in an elective credit.

A more cynical person might think that this selfishness somehow diminishes the value of the work I'm doing. I admit that I used to feel guilty about the fact that this personal reward underlies my charity work. But I no longer see it that way. I am doing good rewarding work for these families, work that I wouldn't have done it without this motivation—and I'm still doing it even after getting the credit. What matters isn't <u>why</u> I started helping these families, but that I <u>am</u> helping these families, and will continue to do so. Thomas Edison invented the lightbulb to get rich, not to make the world a better place, but the world is a better place nontheless. My school created this community service credit in order to get students involved in the community. It worked: I'm involved in my community and I couldn't be happier.

What's good about this essay:

Hey, this essay only has one example, but we said before you need two. What gives? As we said for Essay F, the two-example essay is just a guideline, not a rule. If you can write at length on a single example, great! *But doing this effectively is **really hard**.* Most kids have trouble coming up with enough to say and need the second example to fill out their argument.

This essay takes one example and looks at it *in depth*. Instead of putting a distinct example with background and discussion in each paragraph, it takes one example and separates the background and discussion into separate paragraphs. After the introduction, the essay spends two full paragraphs on the background details of the situation and another full paragraph on discussing its relevance to the thesis. That gives us a complete, thoughtful discussion that does a better job arguing its point that two cursory examples would.

Like Essay F, this essay's thesis has an interesting take on the topic. It argues that people are selfish, but the selfishness of the motivation doesn't matter as much as "the goodness of their acts". Some students feel that they have to take a strong "yes" or "no" stance on the topic question, but nuances like this can produce interesting essays—if you can pull it off.

Thankfully, this essay does pull it off, particularly because the writing is also good. There's some good vocabulary ("a palpable effect") and sophisticated sentences ("A more cynical person might think that this selfishness somehow diminishes the value of the work I'm doing").

What's bad about this essay:

The essay isn't perfect. The introduction is a little choppy. There are a few spelling errors ("nontheless" should be "nonetheless"; "lightbulb" should be two words). The mention of Thomas Edison seems thrown in, and probably should either be expanded into a full example or omitted entirely. None of these problems are enough to distract from the overall quality of the work.

How it can be better:

I'm sure if the author went back to edit this essay there are a dozen things that could be changed. But remember the test uses a *holistic* grading system, judging the essay on the overall impression of its quality. An error here and there is fine if it doesn't affect the overall impression. The essay is intended to be a first draft written quickly, so even the best essays will be expected to have some errors.

Reminder again: these sample essays are just examples, not rules. Just because Essay G got a 6 with one long example does not mean that you have to use one example to get a 6. You can get a 6 with two or even three examples. Nor does it mean that writing one long example will guarantee you a 6. You could write one long example and get a 5, or a 3, or even a 1. There's no one definition of what a 6 looks like, or a 4, or a 2. It's a holistic grading system based on the reader's overall impression of the quality of the essay. Some people may disagree about that quality. You may even disagree with the grades given to the samples above. That's okay—that's why there are two readers giving you two grades.

ESSAY SUMMARY

1. Scoring

- Essay will get two scores, each 1 to 6. The scores cannot differ by more than 1 point.
- Essay is graded in 5 categories: Development, Organization, Language, Sentences, and Grammar.
- It's generally easier to improve your development and organization skills than your language, grammar or sentence structure.

2. Development

- The topic will ask a generic question that generally has two sides. **Choose a specific side.** It doesn't have to be the side you actually believe.
- Pick **two concrete examples** to support your point. These can be things from school, personal experiences, or pop culture like movies or TV shows.
- Before you take the test, **choose 5 all-purpose examples** that can be applied to a variety of topics.
  - Choose examples from **different areas**: history, literature, science/technology
  - Choose examples that you **know something about** so you can give details.
- **Facts don't matter**: you will not be penalized for factual errors. But don't actively try to make stuff up—it's really hard.
- Pick a side to argue that **best fits your examples**. Don't force your examples into an argument where they don't fit.

3. Organization

- Make an **outline** of your essay
  - Introduction
  - Example 1
  - Example 2
  - Conclusion
- For each example you write about, you should include two things:
  - **Background** of the example (who, what, when, where)
  - **Relevance** to the topic (why, how)

4. Language

- Include **vocabulary** you learned for the Critical Reading section.
- Make sure you use **concrete language** whenever possible.
- Use **complex sentences** with a varied structure
- Watch out for **grammatical mistakes** (like those we discussed in the other chapters).

SAMPLE ESSAY TOPICS

Okay, enough talk. Let's try some samples! Here are some sample essay topics. Think about the prompts, come up with some examples, and write your outlines using the worksheets on the following pages. We've already filled one out for Sample Essay E above.

ESSAY ONE

> We are at the very beginning of time for the human race. It is not unreasonable that we grapple with problems. But there are tens of thousands of years in the future. Our responsibility is to do what we can, learn what we can, improve the solutions, and pass them on.
>
> Adapted from Richard Feynman

Assignment: Is it the responsibility of the younger generations to set an example for future generations? Plan and write an essay in which you develop your point of view on this issue. Support your position with reasoning and examples taken from your reading, studies, experience, or observations.

ESSAY TWO

> 1. We cannot enjoy our accomplishments when envy is in our hearts. Too often our successes are tempered by our longing after the greater successes of our neighbors. Our successes should be valued for their own sake, not because we beat the Joneses.
>
> 2. Complacency is an impediment to true progress. Competition ensures that any success, no matter how great, is not enough. Comparing ourselves to our peers drives us to constantly improve ourselves, which is the very essence of growth.

Assignment: Is it useful to compare our accomplishments to the success of others? Plan and write an essay in which you develop your point of view on this issue. Support your position with reasoning and examples taken from your reading, studies, experience, or observations.

ESSAY THREE

> People often limit their view of culture solely to the humanities—art, literature, history—but a society's identity is necessarily intertwined with its technology. Technology determines not only the social identity, but also the cultural identity of every people around the world. The societies with the greatest technological achievement have subsequently created the greatest arts.
>
> Murray J. Siskind, *Science of Culture, Culture of Science*

Assignment: Is culture determined by technology? Plan and write an essay in which you develop your point of view on this issue. Support your position with reasoning and examples taken from your reading, studies, experience, or observations.

I. Introduction

Thesis: Most supposedly "unselfish" acts have selfish motivations.

Example 1: Rosa Parks

Example 2: Star Trek: First Contact

II. First Example

Background: Describe the example (Who? What? When? Where?)

Lived during segregation, blacks and whites used separate facilities

Forced to move to the back of the bus because she was black.

Refused and was thrown in jail

Relevance: Connect to your thesis (Why and How does it prove your point?)

Important contribution to civil rights movement

But she did it for selfish reasons: because she was tired and didn't want to move

III. Second Example

Background: Describe the example (Who? What? When? Where?)

Borg travels back in time, Picard & co follow.

Borg want to prevent Zephram Cochrane from inventing warp drive

Cochrane's invention of warp drive would cause first contact,

Relevance: Connect to your thesis (Why and How does it prove your point?)

Enterprise crew thinks Cochrane is a great hero, launched new era of humanity

But he was a drunk and didn't care. Only invented warp drive for selfish reasons (to get rich).

IV. Conclusion

Unselfish actions can have selfish motivation

Even actions by heroes that change the course of history.

I. Introduction

Thesis: _____

_____

Example 1: _____

Example 2: _____

II. First Example

Background: Describe the example (Who? What? When? Where?)

_____

_____

_____

Relevance: Connect to your thesis (Why and How does it prove your point?)

_____

_____

_____

III. Second Example

Background: Describe the example (Who? What? When? Where?)

_____

_____

_____

Relevance: Connect to your thesis (Why and How does it prove your point?)

_____

_____

_____

IV. Conclusion

_____

_____

I. Introduction

Thesis: _____

_____

Example 1: _____

Example 2: _____

II. First Example

Background: Describe the example (Who? What? When? Where?)

_____

_____

_____

Relevance: Connect to your thesis (Why and How does it prove your point?)

_____

_____

_____

III. Second Example

Background: Describe the example (Who? What? When? Where?)

_____

_____

_____

Relevance: Connect to your thesis (Why and How does it prove your point?)

_____

_____

_____

IV. Conclusion

_____

_____

I. Introduction

Thesis: _____

_____

Example 1: _____

Example 2: _____

II. First Example

Background: Describe the example (Who? What? When? Where?)

_____

_____

_____

Relevance: Connect to your thesis (Why and How does it prove your point?)

_____

_____

_____

III. Second Example

Background: Describe the example (Who? What? When? Where?)

_____

_____

_____

Relevance: Connect to your thesis (Why and How does it prove your point?)

_____

_____

_____

IV. Conclusion

_____

_____

CRITICAL
READING

INTRODUCTION TO CRITICAL READING

Welcome to Critical Reading! The Critical Reading section is everyone's least favorite section on the SAT.[*] It's tedious because there's a lot of, you know, *reading* on it. Ugh. Reading. So much reading. But that's okay! There's *so* much you can do to improve your score, by getting better at reading and getting better at answering the questions.

FORMAT

There are two types of questions on the Critical Reading section: **Sentence Completions** and **Passage-based Questions**. Each section will have both types of questions, with the Sentence Completions always coming first.

There will be **19 Sentence Completions** split across the three sections. These questions present a sentence containing one or two blanks. Students must choose the word or set of words that best fits the meaning of the sentence as a whole. Here's an example provided by the SAT:

Hoping to ------- the dispute, negotiators proposed
a compromise that they felt would be ------- to both
labor and management.

    (A) enforce. . useful
    (B) end. . divisive
    (C) overcome. . unattractive
    (D) extend. . satisfactory
    (E) resolve. . acceptable   *Answer: E.*

Sentence Completions are **arranged by difficulty**: the first ones will be easy and the last ones will be hard. These questions test students' ability to understand the structure and meaning of a sentence and their vocabulary. Thus, a difficult question may have a difficult sentence structure, difficult vocabulary, or both.

There will be **48 Passage-based Questions** split across the three sections. These will present a short passage on a particular topic followed by questions asking about what the passage says. Passages may be as short as one paragraph or as long as a full page. There will also be two sets of *double passages*, in which two passages on a similar topic are presented, followed by questions discussing each passage individually or the relationship between the two. One double passage will contain short 10- to 15-line passages, while the other will contain longer 30- to 50-line passages.

The exact distribution of questions to passages will vary, but they're usually distributed something like this:

Passage type	Length	Questions
2 mini passages	1 paragraph each	2 questions each
1 double mini passage	1 paragraph each, 2 paragraphs total	4 questions total
2 medium passages	1 to 1.5 columns each	5 to 10 questions each
1 long passage	1.5 to 2 columns	12 questions
1 long double passage	1 column each, 2 columns total	13 questions

Unlike the rest of the SAT, passage questions aren't ordered by difficulty. Instead, questions ask about details **in the order in which they appear in the passage** (e.g. questions about paragraph 1, then questions about paragraph 2, etc.)

---

[*] Tied with Math and Writing.

The passages used for the SAT will be drawn from one of four content areas: **Literary Fiction, Humanities, Social Studies,** and **Natural Science.** The distribution of these content areas will vary from test to test. Note that all fiction passages will be *prose* fiction: no drama and no poetry. Passages will be fairly modern. Every once in a while there's a doozy from the 19th century that has some weird crazy language in it. But most of the passages use modern, broadly accessible language.

TIMING

Because each section is split between different types of questions, pacing yourself can be tough. Here are three guidelines to timing on an SAT Critical Reading section.

1. **For Sentence Completions, subtract 2 from the number of questions in the section to get the number of minutes to take.**
   - ○ Take 6 min for the 8-question section.
   - ○ Take 4 min for the 6-question section.
   - ○ Take 3 min for the 5-question section.

2. **Take 1-4 minutes to read each passage, depending on its length. <u>Do not spend more than 4 minutes.</u> After 4 minutes, STOP and go to the questions.**
   - ○ Take 1 min to read a 1-paragraph passage.
   - ○ Take 2 min to read a 1-column passage.
   - ○ Take 3 min to read a 1.5-column passage.
   - ○ Take 4 min to read a 2-column passage.

3. **For each passage, take as many minutes to do the *entire* passage (reading and answering the questions) as there are questions.**
   - ○ For example, for a medium passage with 8 questions, take 8 minutes total (3 min reading the passage, 5 min answering the questions).

If you run out of time in any of these parts, you can move on to the next part of the section. For example, say you are doing an 8-question Sentence Completion section. If after 6 minutes you are only on question 6, you should skip questions 7 and 8 and move on to the first passage. If you have time at the end of the section, you can go back and try the questions you skipped.

Here's an example of how the above timing would work on three sections of a full test:

Section 4		Section 7		Section 8	
8 sentence completions	6 minutes	5 sentence completions	3 minutes	6 sentence completions	4 minutes
4-Q double mini passage	4 minutes *1 min reading,* *3 min answering*	2-Q mini passage	2 minutes	13-Q long passage	13 minutes *4 min reading,* *9 min answering*
		2-Q mini passage	2 minutes		
12-Q double long passage	12 minutes *4 min reading* *8 min answering*	6-Q medium passage	6 minutes *2 min reading* *4 min answering*		
		9-Q medium passage	9 minutes *3 min reading,* *6 min answering*		
24 Questions	**22 min (3 min extra available)**	**24 Questions**	**22 min (3 min extra available)**	**19 Questions**	**17 min (2 min extra available)**

Remember: **these are guidelines not rules**. This timing system has a built-in cushion—notice that for all the sections above, the time spent on the questions doesn't quite add up to the time allowed. That means that if you follow these timing rules, you will wind up with extra time at the end. That's good! That means you can use that extra time to go back and check your work. Or you can go a bit more slowly without worrying about running out of time.

But don't deviate from this plan too much. If you're spending 8 minutes reading a passage before answering any questions, you need to move along more quickly.

GENERAL STRATEGIES

We'll get into details of particular strategies in the following chapters, but all our strategies overlap in similar ways, so it's good to look at the big picture.

One of the most important thing to keep in mind about the Critical Reading section is this:

You do not need any outside knowledge to do the questions.

Other than knowledge of the English language, that is. Students will not be tested on specific content of literary history, nor of any historical events or scientific principles discussed in the passages. You do not need to be a historian or a scientist.

The natural consequence of this is:

All the information you need is given to you on the test.

Either in the sentence or the passage, everything you need is on the page. You just need to be able to read and understand what you've read. When we say this is a test of reading, we mean exactly that: *can you read?* Nothing more.

All of our strategies flow from this fact. There are two components to our Critical Reading strategies.

1. Anticipation

As we said, all the information you need to answer the question is given to you on the page. In Sentence Completions, clues in the sentence tell you the meaning of word that goes in the blank. In Passages, the question will usually give you a line reference and tell you exactly which part of the passage contains the answer. That means you can read the sentence or go back to the passage and **anticipate** what the answer will be.

An important part of anticipation is to **ignore the answer choices**. Wrong answers are full of distractions and misleading information that can affect the way you read the passage or sentence. We want to base our anticipation *only* on the material on the page, not the choices.

You won't be able to predict *exactly* what the answer choice will be. Instead, you're determining what the *meaning* of the answer choice will be. On a Sentence Completion, you might anticipate that the word in the blank means "hard working" but "hard working" probably won't be an answer choice. Instead you might see *studious* or *diligent* or *assiduous* or some other word that *means* "hard working". Don't worry about the answer choices yet. Get the meaning of the blank before you even *look at* the choices.

Similarly, on a passage question, follow the line reference back into the passage, and see what those lines say about the question. Try to *paraphrase* the lines in your own words. The right answer will rarely be an *exact* match for the anticipation. The anticipation gives you the *meaning* you're looking for. The right answer will have the same meaning as the anticipation, but will be worded differently.

2. Elimination

Once you have an anticipation, go to the choices and look for one that has the same meaning. Sometimes, you can spot it right away. Great, you're done!

But it often doesn't work out so easily. You may not be able to find a choice that matches your anticipation perfectly. But that's okay! You can still **eliminate** choices that are obviously wrong. Remember that four out of five choices are wrong—that's 80% of all the choices. It's easier to find a wrong choice than a right choice. Usually, there's at least one choice that you can tell is obviously wrong, even on the hardest questions.

On Sentence Completions, the problem is usually vocab. You know the word in the blank should mean "hard working" but there are a lot of words in the choices you don't know. You may not know all the vocab in the choices, but you probably know *some* of the vocab. You're not sure if *querulous* or *sedulous* means "hard working" but you know that *joyous* definitely doesn't, so you can eliminate it. Eliminate the words you know that definitely don't match.

On passages, you may have similar problems if the choices are phrased vaguely or awkwardly. Or if several choices seem similar to your anticipation. On difficult passages, you're also more likely to have a question you can't anticipate for at all. But there are still choices that are obviously wrong. Some choices are totally *random*—the choice talks about things the passage doesn't mention. Others are clearly *false*—they're explicitly contradicted by the passage. Even on the hardest questions, there's usually something you know. Seeing that a wrong choice is wrong is often simpler that understanding the nuances of the correct answer. It's easier to spot a wrong choice than a right choice—after all, 80% of the choices are wrong.

The most important part of elimination is to **write stuff down**. Don't do this in your head. Mark up the choices. Cross out words in a Sentence Completion choice that don't fit the blank. Cross out the words in a passage choice that make the choice wrong. **Don't rely on your memory. YOUR MEMORY IS FALLIBLE. WRITE THINGS DOWN.**

Working together

Almost every question on the Critical Reading section can be done with some combination of Anticipation and Elimination, but the exact ratio is flexible. If you have a good vocabulary, you'll be able to easily match your Anticipations on Sentence Completions to the right answer choice immediately. If you've got a poor vocabulary, you'll have more mystery words and have to do more eliminating. On a passage, you'll often do both. You'll anticipate easily, no choices perfectly match your anticipation, so you'll eliminate the ones that are obviously wrong.

The point is that both these strategies are working together for you. On any given question, the more you use one, the less you'll use the other. If one fails, look to the other. They complement each other into a harmonious unity of test-taking peace and perfection.

VOCABULARY

The Critical Reading section tests your ability to, well, read critically. This includes your ability to understand the meaning of a complex sentence, your ability to understand an argument, your ability to understand assumptions implicit within a text, your ability to make inferences and deduce the logical consequences of a position, and your vocabulary. Guess which of these skills is the easiest to improve?

In olden times, vocabulary used to be a bigger part of the SAT, but it still counts for a lot.[*] The Sentence Completions are obviously very vocabulary dependent, and they alone account for almost 30% of the section, potentially worth **150 points**.

Often, the only thing that makes a question hard is its vocabulary. Compare these two questions:

☞ **Dave was in a ------- mood; he was smiling and cheerful all day long.**

    (A) happy
    (B) angry
    (C) sad
    (D) smart
    (E) cold

☞ **Dave was in a ------- mood; he was smiling and cheerful all day long.**

    (A) sanguine
    (B) bilious
    (C) disconsolate
    (D) perspicacious
    (E) boreal

---

[*] Back in the day, there used to be Analogies, where you had to understand the relationship between two words. And before that, there were Antonyms, where you had to pick the word opposite in meaning from a given word.

Did you notice the difference?

Vocabulary is important on the Passages, as well. Vocabulary-in-Context questions and Tone questions are often blatantly vocab-dependent, but all questions and their choices may use hard words, and the right answer often hinges on a tricky word. Then there's the passage itself, which is also made up of words, words you'll have to know. Vocabulary is always an important part of reading—if you want to be able to read, you have to know words. For comparison, here's an example passage question.

> **The author's tone throughout the passage can best be described as**
>
> (A) **scholarly appreciation**
> (B) **objective criticism**
> (C) **scornful derision**
> (D) **celebratory exultation**
> (E) **contrite melancholy**

Because vocabulary is so important to so many questions, we at A-List have developed a foolproof rule to help you turn the hardest Reading questions into the easiest questions:

LEARN MORE WORDS

That is all.

Luckily, we've got a great way to do that: *the A-List Vocabulary Box*.

The Vocabulary Box

The 500 words used in the Vocab Box were selected based on a study to determine which words occur most frequently on the SAT. This isn't just a list of words we like or some vocab trivia game where we pull out the hardest words we can find. We only chose words that have appeared frequently on the SAT.

The words themselves are organized according to frequency. The words at the beginning appear the most frequently, so they are the most important to learn.

On the front of each card you'll find:

> **The Word itself**. We refer to these as "boxwords".
>
> The word's **part of speech** (noun, verb, or adjective).
>
> An easy-to-read **pronunciation guide**.
>
> The word's **number** in the box.

On the back you'll find:

> The **definition** of the word. Note that sometimes a boxword may have two different but related definitions.
>
> An **example sentence** showing the word in use.

Some, but not all, cards may also have:

> A **Category** or list of **Synonyms**: We have grouped boxwords that have related or overlapping meanings together. Note that members of a given category may not be exact synonyms, but simply have related meanings.
>
> **Word Alerts**: These notes give additional forms of the word, either by changing its part of speech or by adding prefixes or suffixes. They also give information about roots and relationships between boxwords.

> You don't have to memorize the number, but whenever we refer to a boxword in the text, we'll put the word's number in parentheses.

How to use the Box

It's easy to just say "learn more words" but it can be hard to actually get started and even harder to make the words stick. There are no right or wrong ways to learn the words. Actually, we take that back; there are definitely wrong ways to do it. But there are many different right ways.

Here's a basic outline of how to learn your words. Let's say today's assignment is to learn 10 words:

1. Read through all of that day's cards. Make sure you know how to pronounce the word. Read the definition and the sentence. Make sure you understand the definition. Check out any extra information about synonyms or alternate forms.

2. Quiz yourself. Look at the front of each card, and guess the definition. Make two piles: if you get the word right away put it in the "know" pile; if you don't know it or if you hesitate—even for a second—put it in the "don't know" pile.

3. Cycle through all the cards, then quiz yourself on the "don't know" cards. Repeat until they're all in the "know" pile.

4. Shuffle the cards and go through them one more time.

That's basically all there is to it. Here are a few guidelines to help you maximize your box use:

1. Start early, stick to a schedule

The hardest part is to <u>keep it up</u>. If you get in the habit of learning words early, you'll have no problem. If you fall behind, it will be that much harder to catch up later.

The most important thing to keep in mind is that this is a large, ongoing project. You cannot cram 500 boxwords at the last minute the night before the SAT. That's a lot. This is a major commitment, and you have to treat it seriously. This is a marathon, not a sprint. <u>If you fall behind, you will never catch up</u>.

BUT, if you manage your time, you'll fly through the box in no time.

- ☛ You can learn 10 words in 15-20 minutes. If you're quick it could take 10; if you're slow, 30.

- ☛ If you learn 10 words a day for 5 days a week, you'll learn 50 a week.

- ☛ If you learn 50 words a week, it will take 10 weeks—about two and a half months—to get through the whole box.

But what if you don't have 15-20 minutes a day to spare?

<u>**That's ridiculous**</u>. **Everyone can spare 15 minutes a day.** Do you know how much time you waste over the course of the day? The flashcards are portable: grab a handful and take them with you wherever you go. On your way to school, you could be studying words. Between classes, you could be studying words. Watching TV, during the commercials, you could be studying words. Better yet, put your vocab box in the bathroom. Everyone spends 15 minutes in the bathroom every morning. That's time you could spend studying words.

2. Write them down

Not everyone learns the same way, so you may find other methods more helpful. If you cycle through the flash cards and the words still don't stick, try **writing the words down**. Get a notebook, take today's cards and write down each card's information going across the page. The word, the definition, the sentence, the alternate forms.

Writing everything down will take longer and is more tedious, but the act of writing will cement the word more deeply in your head. And if you use the same notebook each time, by the end you'll have a nice convenient list you can use to review past words. Very helpful.

3. Note different word forms

Remember that when a boxword shows up on the test, it may not look exactly the same as it does on the cards: almost every word in the English can be altered to become another part of speech. Here are a few:

➤ *Deride* (**77**) means "to speak of with cruelty"   He *derided* me in his speech.

    Something *derisive* uses cruel words   His *derisive* speech hurt my feelings.

    Derision is the act of speaking cruelly   His speech was full of *derision* towards me.

➤ *Skeptical* (**3**) means "doubting"   Dave was *skeptical* about the effectiveness of the pills.

    A *skeptic* is a person who is skeptical   Dave is a *skeptic* about new medications.

    Skepticism is a skeptical attitude   Dave responded to your claims with *skepticism*.

➤ *Temper* (**35**) means "to soften or moderate"   Please *temper* your emotions: stop shouting.

    Temperance is "moderation or self-control"   The monk practiced *temperance* of his desires.

    Temperate means "soft or moderate"   The climate here is *temperate* and pleasant.

Often the card itself will list alternate forms, but not every form is on every card, so you'll have to figure out some of these forms on your own. If you see a word that *really* looks like a boxword, there's a good chance they're related.

4. Notice roots and prefixes

One way to help get the meanings of these words to stick is to look at the *origins* of the words. In every language, words come from other words. Almost every word in English comes from older words that have been broken up, mangled, expanded or rearranged in different ways. So a lot of different words are made up of the same pieces. When they're made up of the same pieces, we can start to notice their relationships.

The little word-bits that form the core of the meaning of a word are called *roots*. Sometimes, you'll be able to see the meaning of a word from its roots—you can literally see how the word is a combination of other words. For example, *entrench* (**355**) means "to fix firmly and securely". It literally means to put *in* a *trench*. You can see the meaning right there in the word itself.

Other times, it may not be immediately obvious, but if you learn to recognize common roots, you'll be able to figure out meanings of words you haven't seen before, and you'll be able to remember the meanings of words better. You'll remember a word's meaning better if you understand *why* that's what it means.

Here are some examples of negative prefixes:

➤ a-/an-   ➤ in-/im-/il-/ir-
➤ anti-   ➤ mis-
➤ de-   ➤ non-
➤ dis-   ➤ un-

Here are some examples of roots that appear in multiple words:

-chron- means "time".   A <u>chron</u>ology is a time-line.

    <u>Chron</u>ological order is when things are ordered in time.

    <u>Chron</u>ic (**375**) means "continuing" or "happening all the time".

-verb- means "word"   <u>Verb</u>al means having to do with words or speech.

    A pro<u>verb</u> is a common saying, an expression made up of words.

    <u>Verb</u>ose (**412**) means "using lots of words".

-cred- means "believe"   <u>Cred</u>ible (**39**) means "believable".

    <u>Cred</u>ulous means "tending to believe".

These roots are often changed by adding different **prefixes** to them. Prefixes are little bits that come at the beginning of the word that determine the direction or flavor of the root. Here are a few examples:

in- means "not"   <u>In</u>credible means "unbelievable".

    <u>In</u>credulous (**144**) means "not believing, skeptical".

a- or *an-* means "without"   <u>A</u>pathetic (**28**) means "lacking interest or emotion".

    <u>An</u>archy means "chaos, lacking government".

    <u>Ana</u>chronistic (**170**) means "in the wrong time".

eu- (pronounced like "you") means "good"	<u>Eu</u>logy (**303**) is a speech praising someone ("good words").
	<u>Eu</u>phonious means "pleasant sounding" or "harmonious".
	<u>Eu</u>phemism (**231**) is a clean (or good) phrase used to describe something dirty. Like "use the restroom" instead of, well, you know…
circum- means "around"	<u>Circum</u>ference is the path *around* a circle.
	<u>Circum</u>vent (**411**) means to get *around* something, or to avoid.
	<u>Circum</u>spect (**219**) means cautious. "Spect" means "look", so this literally means "look around" (like you're checking for danger).

Knowing a foreign language can help you here.[*] French, Spanish, and Latin all share a lot of the same roots as English, so your knowledge of those languages can help you pick up on meanings. Observe:

Spanish	French	Meaning	Boxword
fácil	facile	"easy"	<u>facil</u>itate (**490**) = to make easy
flor	fleur	"flower"	<u>flor</u>id (**475**) = elaborately decorated, flowery
bueno	bon	"good"	<u>bene</u>volent (**99**) = tending to be good

Some of you are freaking out now, because some of you are even worse at Spanish than you are at English. "What, it's not enough that I'm bad at Reading, I've got to study *Latin* now? Great! I'm doomed!"

Don't freak out. You don't *need* to know all this stuff about roots and prefixes. It *can* help you remember meanings if you see the connections between words. You could trace connections and origins of *every* word in the language—that's what people who write dictionaries do. But you're not going to spot them all, and you get no extra points for knowing that "eloquent" and "circumlocution" share a root.

Just learn the words, any way you can.

5. Use mnemonic devices

Mnemonic[†] devices are memory tricks you can play to help connect a word and its meaning in your head. People remember things more easily when they have **concrete pictures** to go with them.

- *Undermine* (**6**) means to "weaken". Imagine if you dig a <u>mine</u> <u>under</u> a house; you will weaken the foundation.
- *Gregarious* (**404**) means "sociable". Imagine two people, <u>Greg</u> and <u>Gary</u>, who are the life of the party and are best friends with everyone.
- *Sagacious* (**393**) means "wise". Imagine a very wise, very old monk, living on the top of a tall mountain. He is so old that his skin is beginning to <u>sag</u> off of his face.

Stupid? Perhaps. But the stupider you make them, the easier they'll be to remember. It's always the really annoying jingles that get stuck in your head for days.

6. Review!

It's not enough to learn this week's words just so you'll do well on this week's quiz. (Yes, there will be quizzes.) The point is to remember them *when you take the SAT*. So as you work your way through the box, you should periodically review the words you've already learned. Just grab some random cards from a previous week's haul, and see if you still remember them. If you don't, learn them again.

---

[*] Well, not *any* language. Just languages related to English. Knowing Japanese or Finnish or Ojibwe probably won't help much.

[†] Pronounced "Neh-MON-ic". Weirdly, the first "m" is silent. This word comes from a Greek root that means "memory"; the same root appears in *amnesia* which means "lack of memory".

By the way, you do really need to know these words. Not just to do well on the SAT, but to do well at life. These are words in the English language that you will encounter for the rest of your life. Without good command of the language, you may be doomed to a *meager* (**424**) salary at a *mediocre* (**87**) job.

Beyond the Box

Mystery words

The Box is an essential source of words that you'll need for the SAT. But it isn't a complete source. There are other words in the language and there is a 99.99% chance that you will see words you don't know on the test.* We call those words "Mystery words" When you do encounter mystery words, there are a few things to keep in mind:

1. Don't lie to yourself.

Don't pretend you know what it means. If you don't know it, you don't know it. Put a **question mark** next to it. This is a placeholder: "I'm not sure what this word means, so I'll deal with the words I know first and get back to it."

2. Don't eliminate them.

Some kids refuse to choose words they don't know; they'll pick words they *know are wrong* just because they're comfortable with them. You can only eliminate the words you know, not the words you don't.

Deal with the words you know first. If the right answer is a word you know, great, you're done! Move on to the next question. If you eliminate all the words you know, then you'll have to deal with the mysteries.

3. Guessing

Eventually, you're going to find yourself in a situation where you'll have to guess a word you don't know. Remember: if you can eliminate even just one choice, you have to put an answer down. But how will you know which one to guess? Here are some tips.

Look for roots
As discussed above, often you can figure out a word's meaning but looking at its parts. See if any of those words you don't know look like words you do know. Even if you can't figure out exactly what it means, you might still be able to tell the character of a word. For example, if it starts with "eu-", you know it will probably mean something *good*, even though you won't necessarily know in what way it's good.

Beware of false roots
A lot of the time roots can help you figure out meanings, but sometimes guessing roots can lead you astray. Here are a few examples of words that may not mean what you think:[†]

- *Inflammable* looks like it means "not flammable". But actually, it means "flammable".

- *Indifferent* (**10**) looks like it means "not different". But actually, it means "impartial".

- *Judicious* (**353**) looks like it has to do with a courtroom. But it actually means "prudent".

- *Bombastic* (**155**) looks like it has something to do with explosions. But it actually means "using arrogant or pompous speech".

- The prefix *con-* looks like it means "negative" (as in "pros and cons"). But it often means "with", as in *concord* (**207**). (Note that "con" also means "with" in Spanish.)

---

* We will admit there is a 0.01% chance that there is someone reading this whose vocab is so good that he or she will know every word on the test. If that person is you, why are you reading this? Go back to the Math chapters.

† Even though these words don't mean what you think they do, their origins still make sense. *Inflammable* comes from *enflame*, which means "to catch fire". *Indifferent* is how you feel if it "makes no difference" to you. Being *judicious* is showing good "judgment". *Bombastic* comes from a French word meaning "cotton wadding"…okay, that one doesn't make much sense.

Also note that words you do know might have more than one meaning or use. For example, *exploit* (**108**) can mean "to selfishly take advantage", but it doesn't have to be bad. It can also simply mean "to use advantageously" without a negative connotation.

Be advised that the folks who write the questions know which words kids get confused by, and they will use that against you. In fact, you'll sometimes see a **Fool's Gold** choice on Reading questions. Just like in Math, there'll be a choice that's very tempting but wrong, because a word doesn't mean what everyone thinks it means. This is why we have Rule 1 above: *Don't lie to yourself.* [*]

If all else fails, guess the hardest word.
Because the test makers know that kids are afraid of guessing mystery words, a hard word is more likely to be right than an easy word, especially on a hard question. So if you've got three choices left and you have no idea what any of them mean, don't waste time: just pick the word that looks scariest, and move on.

Adding to the box

As you go through drills and practice tests, you'll encounter some hard words that aren't in the box. As you do the drills, treat them like mysteries and guess as needed. But later, you'll go over those questions and find out what they mean. Even though they're not in the box, *you could be learning those words too.*

There are two good places you can keep track of those words: you can write them in the "Vocabulary Log" on the very last page of this book. Or you can make your own flash cards: the back of the Vocab Box is filled with blank cards that you can fill with any additional words you find.

And of course, there are all sorts of other places to learn words. [†] You may have gotten other vocabulary books in school. There are vocabulary resource and word-a-day features on the Internet. Crossword puzzles are full of good hard words. You could even just read things. Books, for example. Or even newspapers. After all, it is possible that you can improve your reading skills by reading more.

---

[*] Of course, *these* words listed above are boxwords, so you'll learn their meanings and you won't fall for these traps. The more words you actually *learn*, the less often you'll have to guess.

[†] We encourage you to use other sources to supplement your vocabulary, but don't use other sources *instead* of the Vocab Box. Remember that the Box contains words *that frequently appear on the SAT*, so these words should be your number-one priority. If you learn what "epizootic" means, that's great, but you probably won't see it on the test, and it's much more important that you know what "indifferent" means.

SENTENCE COMPLETIONS

Sentence Completions test two things: your ability to understand the structure of a sentence and your vocabulary. A hard Sentence Completion is hard because it has a complicated structure, it has hard vocab, or both. In fact, sometimes the ONLY thing that makes a Sentence Completion question hard is that it has hard vocabulary.

Sooo.... (can you guess where we're going with this?)

If you learn more words, you will do better on the Sentence Completions.

Sentence Completions sound simple: just pick which word goes in the blank. What could be easier? However, a lot of people have trouble with them because they don't really understand the point of this section.

Many students use the following method on Sentence Completions:

1. Read the sentence with the blank.

2. Read the sentence with choice (A) in the blank and see if it sounds okay.

3. Read the sentence with choice (B) in the blank and see if it sounds okay.

4. Read the sentence with choice (A) again, cause I think that sounded more okay then (B)?

5. Read the sentence with choice (B) again, yeah I think (A) is better than (B), or wait, no, (B) is better. (B)? Yeah, (B) is better than (A).

6. Read the sentence with choice (C) and see if...

STOP THAT! Stop that. *Stop.* Right now. Promise me you'll never do that again.

This method is obviously moronic. First of all, you're reading the sentence so many times it's going to take you half an hour to do one question. Secondly, you're not using any basis for judging whether a choice is correct other than whether it "sounds okay". Don't do that. We're not writing poetry here, Shakespeare. This is a reasoning test.

Let's say that again: this is a *reasoning* test. Sentence Completions aren't creative-writing questions. You don't have to be artsy or literary to do well on them. They are logic puzzles. The word that goes in the blank isn't random. It isn't just a word that the big bad SAT people chose because they like it and they're trying to hurt me and *I* could think of a word that could go there that'd be much better than any of these choices and it's just *not fair!*

Calm down. In every question, there is something *in the sentence* that tells you which choice *must* go in the blank. Let's say that again: the answer to the question is *in the sentence.* So instead of spending all our time looking at the answer choices, let's spend our time looking at the sentence. This is our strategy, and it's called *anticipation*.

I. YOUR STRATEGY: ANTICIPATION

As we just said, the answer to every Sentence Completion question is *in the sentence.* You don't have to know anything about the sentence beforehand[*]—you can figure out what's supposed to go in the blank before you look at the choices.

You're never going to see a sentence like this:

➢ **John is a ------- .**

---

[*] Except vocab.

What the—? John could be anything! Is he a scientist? A Sagittarius? A Presbyterian? A house cat? Who is John and just what the heck is he trying to pull?!? This question isn't fair because we don't know anything about John. We could put *literally any noun* in the blank and the sentence would make sense.

On the other hand, you might get a sentence like this:

> ✎ **John is a ------- ; he always sees things in a negative light.**

Aha! Now we know something about John—that he's negative. We *know* the word in the blank must reflect that. So the word in the blank must mean "a negative person".

That's **anticipation**. Instead of working backwards from the choices, we try to figure out what goes in the blank based on what we know from the sentence and **anticipate** what the meaning of the word in the blank will be. In this sentence, we know that our answer must be a word that means "negative person".

So now that we've anticipated, let's look at some answer choices:

> ✎ **John is a ------- ; he always sees things in a negative light.**
>
> **(A) biologist (B) romantic (C) grocer**
> **(D) fanatic (E) pessimist**

Oh no! "Negative person" isn't a choice. Did I mess up?

No, you're fine. Obviously "negative person" isn't *literally* going to be the answer. It's two words! When we anticipate, we're not trying to actually *guess* what the answer will be; we're trying to figure out the *meaning* of the answer. One of these words will *mean* "negative person".

So let's go through the choices. If a choice means "negative person", we'll put a "✓" by it. If it doesn't, we'll put an "✗" by it. If we're not sure, we'll put a "?" by it.

> ✗   (A)   a **biologist** is a scientist who studies biology. This is totally random. It's gone.
> ✗   (B)   a **romantic** is, uh, like, someone who's romantic. No.
> ✗   (C)   a **grocer** is a guy who runs a grocery store. Like, a guy who sells fruit. This is more random than "biologist" was.
> ✗   (D)   a **fanatic** is someone who's overly enthusiastic about something. No, no, no.
> ✓   (E)   a **pessimist** is someone who's always negative. That's our answer!

Easy? Very easy. That's how we do Sentence Completions, and we're going to do pretty much exactly the same thing on every question.

Let's try another and outline the steps more rigorously:

> ✎ **Because he always works twice as hard as everyone else, John is considered the most ------- student in class.**
>
> **(A) intelligent (B) beautiful (C) diligent**
> **(D) wealthy (E) generous**

1. Ignore the answer choices

DO NOT LOOK AT THE CHOICES. Cover them up. Pretend they aren't there. Seriously. Looking at the choices will only mess you up. In fact, let's get rid of them. Here's the question:

> ✎ **Because he always works twice as hard as everyone else, John is considered the most ------- student in class.**

Much better.

2. Look for clues

Sometimes, it helps to split the sentence into parts. This sentence has two:

> 1. **Because he always works twice as hard as everyone else,**
>
> 2. **John is considered the most ------- student in class.**

In our sentence, the blank is in the second part of the sentence. So we'll look to the first part to find out what goes in the blank.

Now, there are two types of words that interest us here:

Connectors are words that connect the parts of the sentence. They tell us whether the two parts are saying the same thing or different things. Here are some examples of connectors:

Similarity (parts are the same)			Contrast (parts are different)		
And	Because	Furthermore	But	Although	On the contrary
Also	Therefore	; [semicolon]	However	Even though	In contrast
Since	Moreover	: [colon]	Yet	Nevertheless	While

Note that the connector does not have to literally come between the two parts. Here, the connector is "because"; that means that the first part of the sentence will be saying the *same* thing as the second part.

Clues are words that tell us the *meaning* of the sentence. What does the first half say? What do we know about John? We know he "works hard".

3. Anticipate!

Put two and two together:

- ☞ The first half says John "works hard"

- ☞ The second half will say the same thing as the second half

- ☞ So the word in the blank must mean "*hard working*". That's our anticipation.

4. Match your anticipation to the answer choice.

Which word means "hard working"? (Hint: it's boxword #**164**…)

- ✗ (A) intelligent ← Don't be fooled. It's a trap!
- ✗ (B) beautiful
- ✓ **(C) diligent**
- ✗ (D) wealthy
- ✗ (E) generous

5. Fill in the corresponding bubble on your answer sheet.

Ⓐ Ⓑ ● Ⓓ Ⓔ   Otherwise it doesn't count.

6. Raise your arms triumphantly and shout, "I AM THE GREATEST!"

You've earned it.

II. ANTICIPATION

It's going to take some getting used to before you start anticipating regularly; it's *really* tempting to look at the answer choices right away, so let's practice some more. We'll go through some problems together—without choices—and just work on anticipating.

➤ **John thought his salary was -------, but it was actually twice as much as that of any other employee.**

Once again, there are two parts to the sentence.

1. John thought his salary was -------,

2. but it was actually twice as much as that of any other employee.

This time the connector is "but". That's a *contrast* connector. That means that the first part of the sentence will be saying the opposite of the second part.

Okay, so what does the second part say? That John had a *big* salary. Therefore, the first part should say he had a *small* salary. So that's our anticipation for the blank: **small**.

Remember: we're not trying to *guess* the word in the blank; we're trying to figure out the *meaning* of the word in the blank. So don't wrack your brain trying to come up with a fancy word for "small". Just use "small".

In fact, it's often best to use *words from the sentence itself* as your anticipation. Observe:

➤ **If a child experiences a ------- at a young age, that ordeal can often negatively affect the child's development in ways that can manifest themselves later in life.**

Whoa! Man, that's a long sentence. But wait—there's one key word in this sentence that will directly give us our anticipation. The blank describes something the child experienced, so ask yourself: *what did the child experience?*

Can you see it? We'll give you a hint:

➤ If a child experiences a ------- at a young age, **that ordeal** can often negatively affect the child's development in ways that can manifest themselves later in life.

That ordeal? Which ordeal? Ah! The one that the child experienced at a young age! That's exactly what the blank is going to mean: an *ordeal*. We don't even have to look at all that other junk!

Again, the answer isn't literally going to *be* "ordeal". It's going to be a word that *means* "ordeal".

Here's a tougher one:

➤ **As the band's fame grew, so did John's indulgent lifestyle, with simple excess soon turning into outright ------- .**

Hmmm. The word in the blank describes John's lifestyle. So. What else do we know about John's lifestyle? Well, we know it's *indulgent* and shows *simple excess*. Okay, but should the blank be a word *like* that or *unlike* that? Is it *similar* or *different*?

It's both. We want a word that's similar to our clues, but *stronger*. This sentence shows a *difference of degree*. The key here is that his indulgence *grew*. So his lifestyle went from having *a little excess* to having *a lot of excess*. So that's our anticipation: *a lot of excess*. It's okay if our anticipation isn't one word or is awkwardly phrased. All that matters is that we get across the *meaning* of the blank.

ANTICIPATION DRILL

*Okay, try these out on your own. You still get no answer choices; just write your anticipation in the space on the right. You don't have to get the exact word, just figure out the **meaning** of the word in the blank.*

1. The Pekingese is a ------- breed of dog, in that it is fiercely loyal to and protective of its home.

   ANTICIPATION:

2. Lindsay disliked her English class more than any other class, but it was -------, so she was required to attend.

   ANTICIPATION:

3. Many animals have heightened ------- senses; in fact, some even rely on their noses more than their eyes when trying to perceive their environment.

   ANTICIPATION:

4. Lisa spent the last four years developing medical machines that are so small they are virtually -------, unable to be seen with the naked eye.

   ANTICIPATION:

5. George Washington was a great military commander with the ability to ------- his soldiers, giving them great motivation and courage.

   ANTICIPATION:

6. While some students appreciated the historical qualities of the old school, others found the facilities too ------- to be useful.

   ANTICIPATION:

7. Brett has a ------- role in the company: he has an impressive-sounding title, but no real power.

   ANTICIPATION:

8. The salesman promised us that this software would revolutionize our office and increase efficiency, but it has hardly been the ------- we had anticipated.

   ANTICIPATION:

9. Although a skilled technician, Anna was confused by the ------- used by the staff at her new job; she could perform the procedures, but she did not understand her coworkers' specialized language.

   ANTICIPATION:

10. Robertson was surprised and relieved that his new play was well received by the same critics who had ------- his last work.

    ANTICIPATION:

III. ELIMINATION

Okay, we've got the hang of anticipation now (hopefully). So let's talk about how to deal with answer choices. It's simple. All you have to do is go through the choices and see which one matches your anticipation. Let's try it on one of the questions we've already seen.

> ⟩ **John thought his salary was -------, but it was actually**
> **twice as much as that of any other employee.**
>
> **(A) extravagant**
> **(B) sinister**
> **(C) taxable**
> **(D) paltry**
> **(E) cynical**

Earlier we said our anticipation here is "*small*". So let's go to the choices and see which means "small".

✗ (A) **extravagant**	Hey, that's boxword #76! It means "excessive". That's not "small". It's gone.
✗ (B) **sinister**	That means "threatening danger" or "evil". What the? No. It's gone.
✗ (C) **taxable**	Aha! That's a trap! If we put "taxable" back into the sentence it kinda sounds okay. We're talking about money and money is taxable, right? But we want a word that means "small". This does not. It means "able to be taxed." It's gone.
? (D) **paltry**	Hmm. I'm not sure what that means. We'll come back to this one.
✗ (E) **cynical**	Hey, that's boxword #13! That means "the belief that people are selfish".* That's not "small". It's gone.

So we eliminated everything except for (D), which we didn't know. So (D) must be the answer! It's the only one left! Sure enough, "paltry" means "insultingly small". A perfect fit.

There are a few things we want to emphasize about dealing with answer choices.

1. ✓, ✗, ?

Notice that here and earlier, we wrote a "✓" next to choices that match our anticipation, an "✗" next to those that don't, and a "?" next to words we don't know.

It's good to keep track of the choices. One of the keys to Sentence Completions is working quickly; the faster you get through these, the more time you have for the long passages. So it's important that we eliminate quickly. Don't hesitate; eliminate. Writing these little symbols down can immeasurably help you keep track of everything.

The rules to remember are:

1.	A ✓ beats an ✗	I hope I don't have to explain this.
2.	A ✓ beats a ?	I'll take a choice that *I know* works over a choice I'm not sure about.
3.	A ? beats an ✗	I'll take a choice I'm not sure about over a choice that *I know is wrong*.

2. Don't eliminate the mystery choice

This is the most important part of the "✓ ✗ ?" stuff—if you don't know the word, don't eliminate it. Just put a "?" by it and move on. Obviously, we wish there were no mystery words. That's why we give you so much vocabulary—it would be great if we knew every word on the test.

---

* Fun word fact: The words "cynical" and "cynicism" come from an ancient Greek philosophical sect (okay, cult) called the Cynics who weren't cynical at all (in the modern sense of the word). The word means "doglike", named after the Diogenes of Sinope, a famous member of the group who lived life like a dog. He rejected excessive wealth and lived in a dirty tub. Some accounts describe him urinating and, uh, enjoying himself in public, as well as openly barking like a dog. Pretty much all ancient Greeks were crazy.

But guess what? That's not gonna happen. No matter how much vocabulary you study, there's a good chance that there'll be some words on the test you don't know. And we'll have to deal with them. We call those words "mystery words". When you do encounter mystery words, there are a few things to keep in mind:

Don't lie to yourself. Don't pretend you know what it means. If you don't know it, you don't know it. Put a question mark next to it. This is a placeholder: "I'm not sure what this word means, so I'll deal with the words I know first and get back to it."

Don't eliminate them. A lot of kids are afraid of words they don't know. So they find themselves picking words that *they know are wrong* simply because they don't want to choose the word they don't know. Don't do that.

The best way to deal with these words is to not deal with them. Deal with the words you know first. Put them aside with a "?" and move on to the other choices. One of three things will happen:

- You'll find a better choice, one that you know is right. Pick it and move on to the next question.

- You'll eliminate every other choice except the mystery. So the mystery word has to be the answer.

- You'll eliminate some choices and be left with more than one mystery word. If this happens…

3. Guess!

If you eliminate some choices and you're still left with more than one mystery word, you'll have to guess one. Remember: if you can eliminate even just one choice, you have to put an answer down. But it's *really hard* to guess a word you don't know. How will you know which one to guess? Here are some tips.

Good word/ Bad word
Sometimes you may not know what a word means but you can tell if it means something positive or negative. For example, words that start with *in-* or *un-* or *dis-* are usually negative.[*]

Look for roots
Often you can figure out a word's meaning but looking at its parts. See if any of those words you don't know look like words you do know. Even if you can't figure out exactly what it means, you might still be able to tell the character of a word. For example, if it starts with *bene-*, like *benefit,* you know it will probably mean something *good*, even though you won't necessarily know in what way it's good.

But be careful. A lot of the time roots can help you figure out meanings, but sometimes guessing roots can lead you astray. Be advised that the folks who write the questions know which words kids get confused by, and they will use that against you. In fact, you'll sometimes see a **Fool's Gold** choice on Reading questions. Just like in Math, there may be a choice that's very tempting but it's wrong because a word doesn't mean what everyone thinks it means.

If all else fails, guess the hardest word.
A helpful guide to guessing mystery choices is to *guess the hardest word.* The people who make the test *know* that kids are afraid of the hard words. Therefore, they make the hard words the right answer as often as they can. So if you're guessing between two or more mystery words—especially if it's a later, harder question—guess the hardest word; it's more likely to be right.[†] So if you've got three choices left and you have no idea what any of them mean, don't waste time: just pick the word that looks scariest, and move on.

---

[*]   But not always, of course, as in *incredible* or *unflappable* or *disinfect.*

[†]   It's important to note that this is not a foolproof rule—this is a *guideline* to help you *guess.* First of all, it's subjective to say which word is the "hardest". Secondly, remember that you are still guessing here. You might guess wrong. That's okay. Since you get so many more points for a right than you lose for a wrong, it's totally worth your while to guess. This is just a way to help you make a decision. Third, the hardest word won't *always* be right. If that were true, we'd tell you to jump to the hardest word right away and forget about all this anticipation claptrap.

*You may recognize these questions. You had better; you just did them. These are the same questions you anticipated for earlier, but now you've got answer choices. **Write ✓, ✗, or ? in the line before each choice.***

1. The Pekingese is a ------- breed of dog, in that it is fiercely loyal to and protective of its home.

    ___ (A) miniature
    ___ (B) territorial
    ___ (C) belligerent
    ___ (D) jovial
    ___ (E) miserable

2. Lindsay disliked her English class more than any other class, but it was -------, so she was required to attend.

    ___ (A) pedantic
    ___ (B) difficult
    ___ (C) mandatory
    ___ (D) transient
    ___ (E) lengthy

3. Many animals have heightened ------- senses; in fact, some even rely on their noses more than their eyes when trying to perceive their environment.

    ___ (A) alimentary
    ___ (B) predatory
    ___ (C) carnivorous
    ___ (D) optic
    ___ (E) olfactory

4. Lisa spent the last four years developing medical machines that are so small they are virtually -------, unable to be seen with the naked eye.

    ___ (A) incorrigible
    ___ (B) bogus
    ___ (C) indestructible
    ___ (D) perfect
    ___ (E) imperceptible

5. George Washington was a great military commander with the ability to ------- his soldiers, giving them great motivation and courage.

    ___ (A) galvanize
    ___ (B) taunt
    ___ (C) insinuate
    ___ (D) organize
    ___ (E) mollify

6. While some students appreciated the historical qualities of the old school, others found the facilities too ------- to be useful.

    ___ (A) obvious
    ___ (B) enterprising
    ___ (C) nebulous
    ___ (D) antiquated
    ___ (E) contrived

7. Brett has ------- role in the company: he has an impressive-sounding title, but no real power.

    ___ (A) a pivotal
    ___ (B) an economic
    ___ (C) a dominant
    ___ (D) a nominal
    ___ (E) an administrative

8. The salesman promised us that this software would revolutionize our office and increase efficiency, but it has hardly been the ------- we had anticipated.

    ___ (A) vituperation
    ___ (B) boon
    ___ (C) embellishment
    ___ (D) refutation
    ___ (E) catastrophe

9. Although a skilled technician, Anna was confused by the ------- used by the staff at her new job; she could perform the procedures, but she did not understand her coworkers' specialized language.

    ___ (A) allegories
    ___ (B) jargon
    ___ (C) curriculum
    ___ (D) equipment
    ___ (E) techniques

10. Robertson was surprised and relieved that his new play was well received by the same critics who had ------- his last work.

    ___ (A) expurgated
    ___ (B) espoused
    ___ (C) lauded
    ___ (D) lambasted
    ___ (E) demystified

IV. HOLY #*@%! TWO BLANKS?!?

Jeez, calm down. Don't be a drama queen.

Yes, sometimes the sentence will have two blanks. In fact, this will happen quite a lot; about half the questions will be two-blankers. But don't worry: our strategy is the same, with some slight variations. There are three different ways to handle two-blank questions:

1. Double Anticipation

Sometimes, a two-blank question is just like two one-blank questions stuck together: you can anticipate each blank separately:

☛ **John's temperament has changed recently; he has become ------- instead of quiet and ------- instead of gloomy.**

  (A) talkative . . skeptical
  (B) stingy . . friendly
  (C) timid . . imperious
  (D) garrulous . . sanguine
  (E) brusque . . provincial

Here, you can anticipate for each of these blanks individually. The first blank will mean *not quiet* and the second blank will mean *not gloomy*. Only (D) matches both—**garrulous (469)** and **sanguine (281)**.[*] Don't know those words? *Brusque* (**453**) and *provincial* (**102**) are also boxwords. Easy! Don't waste our time.

2. Divide and Conquer

Sometimes, one of the blanks will be really tricky to anticipate—there aren't a lot of clues or it's just a weird word or something. BUT, the other blank *is* easy to anticipate for. So focus on the stuff you can deal with: anticipate for the easy blank and eliminate anything that doesn't match. Let's demonstrate:

☛ **Although John is ------- for his cruelty, he can actually be quite ------- and compassionate to those he cares about.**

  (A) legendary . . meticulous
  (B) celebrated . . benevolent
  (C) infamous . . magnanimous
  (D) notorious . . witty
  (E) acknowledged . . duplicitous

Hmmm… that first blank is tricky. Something like "known" would work, but just about all of the choices would fit there. Okay, we can eliminate (B): he wouldn't be *celebrated* for cruelty—we want either a bad word or a neutral word. But we've still got 4 choices. Whatever shall we do?

Aha! But look at the second blank. That one's easy! Our anticipation could be "*compassionate*" or "*not cruel*". Only (B) and (C) work—and we already eliminated (B). Choice (E) "duplicitous" might be a mystery word for you, but since (C) works well, we'll pick the check over the question mark.

So even though the first blank had us stuck, the second blank was a snap.

---

[*] Fun word fact: sanguine means "cheerful" but its root means "blood". So how did *bloody* come to mean *cheerful*? It goes back to the Middle Ages, when doctors believed the human body contained four fluids called "humors". Having too much of a humor would affect your personality: excess blood made you cheerful, yellow bile (*choler*) made you angry, black bile (*melancholia*) made you sad, and phlegm made you sluggish. None of this is true, of course—they also believed in dragons. But it's where we get the words *sanguine, choleric, melancholy,* and *phlegmatic*.

One of these blanks is easier to anticipate for than the other. Anticipate for the easy blank, and go to the choices to eliminate. Then figure out which works best for the harder blank.

> The ------- included in the new edition of Dr. Kazlov's book not only failed to improve upon the original text, but it seemed to completely ------ his original theory.

ANTICIPATION 1: _____

ANTICIPATION 2: _____

___ (A) addendum . . invalidate ___
___ (B) errata . . corroborate ___
___ (C) masthead . . alleviate ___
___ (D) appendix . . substantiate ___
___ (E) epilogue . . bolster ___

3. Relationship Questions

Take a look at this guy:

> John may seem ------- in public, but his close friends think he's actually quite ------- .

(A) witty . . amusing
(B) scornful . . hostile
(C) elusive . . loyal
(D) erratic . . unpredictable
(E) reserved . . boisterous

What the—? We don't know anything about John here! Didn't we say before that they never ask us questions like this? This is %#$^ing *$#@#!!!

Ah, it may appear that we don't know anything, but we know more than you think. This sentence seems clueless, in that we don't have any specific clues about the blanks themselves.

However, we do have one clue: the connector "but". That's a contrast connector. So while it's true that anything could go into either of the blanks *individually*, there is a definite *relationship* between the blanks. We do know that whatever goes in the second blank has to be the ***opposite*** of the first blank. So …

> If the first blank is "*happy*", the second blank will be "***unhappy***".

> If the first blank is "*talkative*", the second blank will be "***not talkative***".

> If the first blank is "*honest*", the second blank will be "*dishonest*".

> Et cetera.

So all we have to do is go to the answer choices and find a pair of **opposites**. Let's see what we have:

(A) witty . . amusing	✗ Similar!	*Witty* means "amusing".
(B) scornful . . hostile	✗ Similar!	*Scorn* (**61**) means "intense hatred or disrespect".
(C) elusive . . loyal	✗ Unrelated!	*Elusive* (**84**) means "tending to escape".
(D) erratic . . unpredictable	✗ Similar!	*Erratic* (**168**) means "irregular"
(E) reserved . . boisterous	✓ *Opposites!*	*Boisterous* (**390**) means "noisy". *Reserved* means "quiet"

Note that "opposites" is just one example of a relationship between blanks; the relationship might be more subtle or nuanced. It could be a *similarity*, a *causal* relationship, a difference of *degree*, or any number of other relationships. If you can't quite tell what the relationship should be, start by asking whether the words should be similar or different, eliminate some choices, then refine your relationship based on the remaining available choices.

TRY ONE:

*Anticipate the relationship between the blanks in the sentence,
Then identify the relationships between the words in the choices
and see which one matches our anticipation.*

➣ **Already the most ------- boy in class, Jeffrey became
even more ------- during our sophomore year.**

RELATIONSHIP: _____

                                          RELATIONSHIP:

___ (A) talented . . defiant   _____

___ (B) studious . . assiduous   _____

___ (C) indigent . . affluent   _____

___ (D) dangerous . . sagacious _____

___ (E) contentious . . affable   _____

SENTENCE COMPLETION SUMMARY

1. Anticipate

- **Ignore the answer choices.** Focus on the sentence alone.

- Read the sentence to figure out the **meaning** of the word in the blank.

- Look for **clue words** that tell you what the sentence is about. Look for **connectors** that tell you about the relationship between parts of the sentence.

- If you can't come up with a specific anticipation, start by figuring out if the blank is a **good word** or a **bad word**.

2. Eliminate

- Once you have an anticipation, ignore the sentence and focus on the answer choices. Find one that **means the same thing** as the word you anticipated.

  - If the choice matches your anticipation, put a check (✓) by the choice.

  - If the choice doesn't match, put an ✖ by the choice **and eliminate it.**

  - If you **don't know what the word means** put a question mark (?) by the choice.

- **Don't eliminate mystery choices.** If you don't know what it means, leave it and come back later

- If you're not sure whether a choice works, don't eliminate it. Start by eliminating the choices that **definitely don't match** your anticipation, then come back to what's left. Remember: 80% of the choices are wrong. Finding a wrong answer is easier than finding the right one.

3. Guessing

- If you get down to two or three mystery choices and can't decide, **guess one.** Don't leave it blank.

- See if you can guess the meaning of the words based on their **roots.** See if they look similar to any words you do know.

- When in doubt, **guess the hardest word**. Hard words are more likely to be right than easy words.

4. Two blanks

- Sometimes two-blank questions are just like two one-blank questions stuck together. **Anticipate separately** for each blank.

- **Divide and Conquer**: Sometimes one blank is really hard to anticipate for, but the other one is really easy. **Anticipate for the easy blank** and eliminate what doesn't work.

- For **Relationship Questions**, you can't anticipate for the blanks directly, but you can figure out the relationship between the blanks.

SENTENCE COMPLETIONS EXERCISES

Circle the clues, write your anticipation in the space provided, write ✓, ✗, or ? in the line before or after each choice, and choose your answer.

Easy Exercise

1. Older women are especially at risk for osteo-porosis, a disease that causes bones to be ------- and break easily.

ANTICIPATION: _____

___ (A) brittle
___ (B) noxious
___ (C) critical
___ (D) neutral
___ (E) cloying

2. Unhappy that his article had unintentionally insulted some of the community, Dave tried to ------- the people he had ------- by publishing an apology in the next day's paper.

ANTICIPATION 1: _____

ANTICIPATION 2: _____

___ (A) forgive . . angered   ___
___ (B) provoke . . described   ___
___ (C) reward . . complimented ___
___ (D) appease . . offended   ___
___ (E) demean . . approached   ___

3. With its high vaulted ceilings and giant rose windows, the church ------- a sense of awe and wonder in the worshippers.

ANTICIPATION: _____

___ (A) squanders
___ (B) eludes
___ (C) avoids
___ (D) bludgeons
___ (E) evokes

4. The city parks department is ------- to ------- the population of street trees so that no single species dominates the neighborhood.

ANTICIPATION 1: _____

ANTICIPATION 2: _____

___ (A) attempting . . consume   ___
___ (B) striving . . diversify   ___
___ (C) helping . . fertilize   ___
___ (D) deciding . . engage   ___
___ (E) waiting . . promote   ___

5. The members of this political party have a ------- of thought that causes them to always come to an immediate agreement on every tough issue.

ANTICIPATION: _____

___ (A) freedom
___ (B) severity
___ (C) conformity
___ (D) discrepancy
___ (E) presentation

Medium Exercise

1. In order to avoid detection by her teacher, Jane ------- placed the note under her foot and slid it over to her friend.

ANTICIPATION: _____

(A) sporadically
(B) voraciously
(C) tacitly
(D) surreptitiously
(E) laboriously

2. Dr. Hugh dismissed all arguments against his new hypothesis as ------- in light of ------- evidence supporting his theory.

ANTICIPATION 1: _____

ANTICIPATION 2: _____

___ (A) valid . . spurious   ___
___ (B) inconsequential . . incontrovertible ___
___ (C) provoking . . blatant   ___
___ (D) fastidious . . intriguing   ___
___ (E) incongruous . . meager   ___

3. The politician's tendency to ------- cast doubt upon the ------- of his campaign promises.

ANTICIPATION 1: _____

ANTICIPATION 2: _____

___ (A) alleviate . . legitimacy   ___
___ (B) jeer . . pretentiousness   ___
___ (C) prevaricate . . veracity   ___
___ (D) insinuate . . probability   ___
___ (E) rebuke . . wantonness   ___

4. Because there is such a ------- of workers who know how to run this equipment, those who are qualified often charge exorbitant fees.

ANTICIPATION: _____

___ (A) regimen
___ (B) glut
___ (C) swarm
___ (D) promotion
___ (E) dearth

5. The ------- curtain that surrounded Sebastian's hospital bed prevented him from seeing any of the patients next to him.

ANTICIPATION: _____

___ (A) transparent
___ (B) putative
___ (C) injurious
___ (D) rakish
___ (E) opaque

Hard Exercise

1. The ------- and abrasive chemicals in the cleanser irritated the skin on Jennifer's hands.

ANTICIPATION: _____

___ (A) caustic
___ (B) iterative
___ (C) mystic
___ (D) intrepid
___ (E) scintillating

2. Some people believe that art schools cannot truly teach artistic ability; they can only ------- the ------- skills that their students already possess.

ANTICIPATION 1: _____

ANTICIPATION 2: _____

___ (A) refine . . innate ___
___ (B) impart . . derivative ___
___ (C) instill . . pernicious ___
___ (D) recreate . . intrinsic ___
___ (E) mimic . . professional ___

3. Aesop's fables are intended to be -------; they are primarily meant to provide moral instruction rather than simply to entertain.

ANTICIPATION: _____

___ (A) lyrical
___ (B) aesthetic
___ (C) fortuitous
___ (D) didactic
___ (E) incorrigible

4. Despite his terrible performance this year, Peterson has been ------- criticism since he had such a ------- impact on winning the championship last year.

ANTICIPATION 1: _____

ANTICIPATION 2: _____

___ (A) adept at . .beneficial ___
___ (B) enamored with . .frank ___
___ (C) conducive to. . truculent ___
___ (D) immune to . .negligible ___
___ (E) impervious to . .prodigious ___

5. Gerry's novels are filled with ------- allusions to obscure texts that only the most well-read specialists would recognize.

ANTICIPATION: _____

___ (A) ornate
___ (B) recondite
___ (C) pecuniary
___ (D) disparaging
___ (E) meretricious

READING PASSAGES

eading passages are one of the most hated parts of the SAT because nobody likes to read. Ugh… so many words… it's not fair. Well, suck it up. We're going to have to do some reading. If the hardest thing you do on this test is read, you'll do fine.

However, the thing about these passages is that they involve *so much* less thought than most people realize. The point of this section is to understand something you just read. Sometimes this is *really easy* and *really dumb*. It's literally a question of whether you read the passage. Not whether you understand it, not whether you know where to find a thesis, not whether you know what a thesis is, not whether you caught the nuances of the author's biting satire on the bourgeoisie—no: *can you read English*? That is all.

Here's your passage:

And here's your question:

Passage 1

I like cats.

End of passage.

1. Which of the following statements would the author most likely agree with?

    (A) The U. S. government must dedicate more time and resources to preserving its native wildlife.
    (B) Pet ownership has therapeutic effects on people recovering from traumatic events.
    (C) Feline social interaction is as complex as human social interaction.
    (D) I like cats.
    (E) Cats are dangerous creatures that are a threat to modern society.

It's a tough one, I know. Do you need extra time?

Obviously this is a joke, but it's not *that* much of a joke. You'd be astounded by how much of this section can be done with little more than knowing *what* the passage says. Not any fancy interpretations: literally "what does it say?"

Before we get into specifics, here are three "don'ts" to remember for the reading passages:

1. Don't enjoy yourself.

None of the passages will be fun. You will not like them. They will be on subjects you don't care about. They will not be things you will want to read on the beach in your leisure time. Get used to it.

2. Don't know anything.

Just because the passage is about particle physics doesn't mean you have to know anything about particle physics. This is a *reading* test. You're being tested on *what you just read*. Just like on the Sentence Completions, everything you need to answer the questions is *in the passage*, written on the page itself. In fact, it's actually counterproductive to know anything about the topic, because you may be tempted to use your existing knowledge or beliefs to help you answer the question. Don't do that. No one cares what *you* think about the topic. We only care what the *author* thinks about the topic.

3. Don't remember anything.

You don't have to memorize the passage. It's all on the page and it's going to stay on the page. If you can't remember what the author said in line 35, *go back to line 35 and check*! It's right there! Don't waste a lot of time trying to memorize all the details of the passage; just get a sense of what it's about and move on to the questions. This brings us to our first strategy: ***Main Ideas.***

I. READING THE PASSAGE: MAIN IDEAS

One of the biggest problems kids have with the passages is that reading them takes a loooong time. Kids try to memorize every point and understand every subtle detail and convoluted sentence in the passage. That's bad. It's a waste of time—it takes forever and it doesn't actually help you.

Instead, read the passage quickly and just get the **Main Ideas**. Every paragraph is nothing more than a collection of sentences that have some common theme. That common theme is the Main Idea of the paragraph. It's the answer to this question:

What's it about?

That's it. For each paragraph, just get a sense of the topic of that paragraph. Paraphrase the idea into a short phrase. It doesn't have quote the passage or even be a complete sentence. It's a note to yourself about what the paragraph is about.

Here are a few tips on finding Main Ideas:

> The content of the passages will fall into one of these four categories:
>
> ➤ Fiction
> ➤ Humanities
> ➤ Social Science
> ➤ Natural Science

Skim the details

Don't worry about all the piddly little details. We don't care about *every* idea, just the *Main* Idea. All those details are confusing and unnecessary.

The goal here is to **spend less time reading the passage** so you can spend more time on the questions, since the questions are the things that actually matter. Therefore, when you read the passage, you just want to get a sense of what it's about. We'll worry about the details later.

You may be asking yourself, "But wait, don't I need those details?" Surprisingly, no. For two reasons:

1. The questions might never ask you about the details.

Why would you spend five minutes trying to understand a sentence *that they never ask you about!* That's five minutes you wasted and won't get back. Yes, you'll need *some* of the details to answer the questions. But *every* passage has *huge* chunks of information that never show up in the questions. And when you're reading the passage, you don't know which details are important and which ones aren't.

2. If a question *does* ask you about details, you can go back and check.

If they do ask you about line 35, well, *go back to line 35 and see what it says!* Most questions about details come with *specific line references*, so you know exactly where to go to find the answer. So even if a detail *is* important to a question, you don't have to worry about it while you're reading the passage. Worry about it when they ask you about it, not before.

Not all questions are about specific lines; some are about entire paragraphs or the passage as a whole. But if that's the case, *you can use your Main Idea to answer the question.*

Skip hard sentences

Passages will *often* contain difficult writing. Sentences can be long, intricate, or convoluted. They may use subtle or confusing metaphors. The vocabulary can be difficult. With Main Ideas, if you encounter a sentence you don't immediately understand, **skip it**. You don't need to understand every single sentence to understand the paragraph. If the details of that sentence are important, you can deal with them if and when the question asks you about them.

Check the first and last sentence

The difficulty of finding the Main Idea for a paragraph can vary depending on the particular passage. Sometimes it's really obvious, sometimes not so much. If you're having trouble, **check the first and last sentence of the paragraph**. That's often the introduction to the topic and the conclusion to the topic, so that will help you find the theme of the paragraph.

This is a guideline, not a rule. The Main Idea is often in the first and last sentence, but not always. If the main idea *isn't* there, but that's all you've read, you'll be confused, you'll have to backtrack, and it'll be a mess. So you should read the whole paragraph. But if you're having trouble finding the Main Idea, the first and last sentences are a good place to look.

Look for transitional language

By "transitional language" we mean all the words that connect clauses and sentences to each other, words like *but, however, furthermore*, etc. Words like this can signal a shift in the topic, which often affects the overall point of the sentence or paragraph.

For example, here is the first beginning of a paragraph:

> ✎ **David, you have been a wonderful boyfriend for several years now. You have been kind and caring towards me, and you're always a lot of fun to be with.**

Aww, thanks honey! I love you, too. It's nice to know I'm apprecia—oh, I'm sorry, you weren't finished?

> ✎ **David, you have been a wonderful boyfriend for several years now. You have been kind and caring towards me, and you're always a lot of fun to be with. <u>However,</u>**

Uh oh…

> ✎ **David, you have been a wonderful boyfriend for several years now. You have been kind and caring towards me, and you're always a lot of fun to be with. <u>However,</u> I've met someone else and I'm going to have to break up with you.**

Now, if you were to ask David what the Main Idea of this paragraph was, which part of it do you think he's going to focus on? Would he say "this is my girlfriend talking about how great I am"? *No!* He'd say "this is what she said when she dumped me." That "however" was a big warning sign that the paragraph was about to be transformed into a whole new set of ideas. So if you see transitional words like this, **circle them.** They can be important clues about the author's ultimate point.

Write your Main Ideas down

Once you find a Main Idea: **write it down in the margin**. You'll need it later. If you do this for every paragraph, you'll wind up with a nice little outline of the passage. This can help you later if you're trying to look for a particular detail in the passage. The Main Ideas in the margin become like the table of contents for a book telling you exactly where to go.

Ultimately, you don't really have to write out all your Main Ideas, because doing so does take up valuable time. But when you first start trying to get Main Ideas, you might struggle with it. It takes some time to get good at it, and writing everything down helps. The more practice tests you do, the easier it will become.

Don't spend too much time on this

Remember that the point of this is to *spend less time reading the passage*. Don't spend a lot of time trying to get your Main Idea absolutely perfect. Don't struggle with the precise wording or try to capture all the nuances of the paragraph. This is supposed to be quick and dirty.

> ✎ You Main Ideas should be short—don't even use complete sentences. Something like "author likes cats" or "cats are cute and smart" or "dogs = not as good".

> ✎ If a paragraph is so dense and confusing that you can't figure out the Main Idea at all, just skip it. Move on. Maybe make your Main Idea some sort of vague placeholder ("something about cats").

> ✎ If single paragraph has several different ideas in it, you can split up the paragraph and give two Main Ideas. Maybe the first half of the paragraph is about one thing and the second half is about something else. That's fine.

> ✎ If it's a fiction passage that has long stretches of dialogue, each line of speech will be its own paragraph. Here, you can split the dialogue arbitrarily to assign Main Ideas. In the first 10 lines they're arguing about where to eat; in the second 10 lines they're trying to find the restaurant; etc.

> ✎ If you're having trouble finding Main Ideas, **move on to the questions.** You can actually learn a lot about the passage as you do the questions. And you can always go back to the passage to fill in the gaps as necessary.

MAIN IDEA DRILL

Read the following passage and write the main idea for each paragraph in the space on the right

The following passage is about the American astronomer Henrietta Leavitt (1868–1921).

One of the most important discoveries in the history of astronomy was made by a computer in 1908. This may sound like an anachronism; computing machines of the early twentieth century, predecessors of our modern PC's, were nowhere near advanced enough to be making discoveries. However, this "computer" was not a machine at all, but a woman named Henrietta Swan Leavitt.

MAIN IDEA:

Throughout the nineteenth century, as optic technology burgeoned, academic institutions built larger and larger telescopes that could peer farther and farther into the night sky. With the invention of photography, observatories could now produce records of the images their telescopes captured. This meant the astronomers could leave the tedious work of data collection to low-paid workers without wasting valuable telescope time. These workers were called "computers", women who would compute the data in the photographs for 25 cents an hour.

MAIN IDEA:

Henrietta Leavitt was one such computer. Having graduated from Radcliffe College in 1892, she developed an interest in astronomy. The opportunities open to women in the scientific world being few and far between, she joined the photographic photometry department at the Harvard College Observatory as a computer. Her particular task was to search for "variables", stars whose brightness would vary over regular intervals, like a flashing street light. This sort of work resonated with her meticulous disposition, and she catalogued thousands of variables at an incredible rate.

MAIN IDEA:

While examining a group of variables within one of the Magellanic Clouds*, she noticed that the magnitude of the variables was directly proportional to the period of their pulsation. The brighter the star, the slower it flashed. This discovery was groundbreaking. For centuries, one of the chief mysteries of the universe was its size. Astronomers had no way of determining the distance to the stars. Brightness could be used as a guide, since objects are brighter when they are close and dimmer when they are far away. Brightness alone, however, can be deceptive without a frame of reference. To the casual observer, Venus seems about as bright as the North Star. But Venus is a planet, and is therefore much dimmer than any star. It only seems brighter because it is much, much closer to us. With Leavitt's discovery of the period-luminosity relationship, there was now a way to determine the *true* brightness of stars, not just the apparent brightness. While there were still a number of questions to be answered before actual distances could be determined, Leavitt's discovery was fundamental to the eventual calculation of the size of the universe.

MAIN IDEA:

Line 5

10

15

20

25

30

35

40

45

GO TO THE NEXT PAGE

_____
* The Magellanic Clouds are two galaxies visible from Earth.

Leavitt never produced any other important work. She only worked sporadically, since she was plagued by poor health for most of her life. The most obvious factors working against her were her position and her sex. As a computer, she had no auton-
50   omy and could only work on what she was assigned, and as a woman, she had no chance for advancement. The tide of women's rights had begun to turn—Harvard would award a PhD in astronomy to a woman for the first time in 1925—but these changes came too late for Leavitt, who died of cancer in 1921.
55   However, the importance of her discovery did not go unnoticed by the scientific community. Later astronomers such as Hubble and Hertzsprung acknowledged how indebted their work was to her discovery, and she was even nominated for a Nobel Prize five years after her death. Yet outside of academia, she remains
60   little more than a footnote of history.

MAIN IDEA:

II. ANSWERING THE QUESTIONS

There's often more than one way to do a Passage question. Sometimes it's easier to get the answer directly from the passage, sometimes it's easier to eliminate from the answer choices, and sometimes you'll want to do both. Here we'll outline a number of different strategies for tackling all types of passage questions.

1. Go Back to the @#&*%$! Passage!!

We told you not to worry about the details when reading the passage. Now that you're actually asked about the details, you can worry about them. Luckily, you don't have to rely on what you remember about the passage. *This is an open-book test. You can look it up.*

Most questions will give specific line references in the question itself. Once you read the question, before you do anything else, **go back to the passage and check the line reference.** If they ask you a question about line 35, go back to line 35 and see what it says, *before you even look at the choices.*

Don't just read the literal line mentioned in the question: **read the whole sentence that includes that line.** Most sentences stretch over a couple of lines, and you'll need the full sentence to understand the context.

The effectiveness of this technique is a testament to how little they're asking of you on this test. The grand majority of questions will give you specific line references. Not only are all the answers literally written on the page, but *they even tell you where the answers are!*

> Unlike the rest of the SAT, passage questions aren't ordered by difficulty. Instead, they're ordered roughly "chronologically", with questions asking about details in the order they appear in the passage (e.g. questions about paragraph 1, then questions about paragraph 2, etc.)

Okay, we've gone back to the passage and read the sentence. Now what?

2. Anticipate

Ah, Anticipation. Our old friend shows up again here. The concept we saw in Sentence Completions is just as valid here: **all the information you need to answer the question is in the passage.** That's why we look in the passage, not in the choices, for our answers.

Read the question, follow the line reference back into the passage, and see what those lines say about the question. That's your anticipation. Then look at the choices and see which one matches your anticipation.

When you go back to the paragraph, think about what the lines say and what they mean. Try to **paraphrase** the lines in your own words. The right answer will rarely be an *exact* match for your anticipation. Just like in the Sentence Completions, your anticipation gives you the *meaning* you're looking for. The right answer will have the same meaning as your anticipation, but will be worded differently.

Keep in mind that the line reference might not tell you exactly where the answer is; it might just point you to the ballpark. If you don't find the answer in the line you're given, **check one sentence before or after the line reference** to get a fuller context.

We did a study of real SAT passages to answer the question: *where in the passage can the answer be found?* In **74%** of the questions, the answer was in the sentence itself, one sentence before, or one after.

Location	Frequency
Answer is **in the sentence given** by the line reference	60%
Answer is in **the sentence before** the line reference	7%
Answer is in **the sentence after** the line reference	7%
Answer requires a **main idea**, either of the passage or paragraph(s)	21%
Answer is **somewhere else** in the passage	5%

Let's look at a sample question from the Henrietta Leavitt passage:

1. **The author mentions Hubble and Hertzsprung (lines 56-57) in order to emphasize**

   (A) the recognition she got from the general public
   (B) the extent to which astronomy was dominated by men
   (C) her dependence on the work of earlier scientists
   (D) the fame associated with winning the Nobel Prize
   (E) the esteem other scientists had for her work

First, we'll ignore the answer choices and just focus on the question:

1. **The author mentions Hubble and Hertzsprung (lines 56-57) in order to emphasize**

The question asks about lines 56-57, so let's see what those lines say. Remember to read the whole sentence, not just the lines mentioned. We'll reproduce that sentence here:

> *Later astronomers such as Hubble and Hertzsprung acknowledged how indebted their work was to her discovery, and she was even nominated for a Nobel Prize five years after her death.*

What does this sentence say about Hubble and Hertzsprung? You don't have to use the exact words in the sentence—just paraphrase. It says that **they thought her work was important**.

Great. Now let's go to the choices and see which one sounds closest to our anticipation. Remember: the choice won't *exactly* match our anticipation. We just want a choice that has the same *meaning* as our anticipation.[*]

   (A) ✗ the recognition she got from ~~the general public~~
   Hubble and Hertzsprung are astronomers, not "the general public".

   (B) ✗ the extent to which astronomy was ~~dominated by men~~
   This has nothing to do with our sentence.[†]

   (C) ✗ her dependence on the work of ~~earlier scientists~~
   Hubble and Hertzsprung were *later* scientists, not earlier.

   (D) ✗ the fame associated with ~~winning~~ the Nobel Prize
   It doesn't say she won, just that she was nominated.

   (E) ✓ the esteem other scientists had for her work
   Perfect! Hubble and Hertzsprung were "astronomers", so they were "other scientists". And they thought her work was important, so they had "esteem for her work."

Notice that we can pinpoint very specific reasons why each of the wrong answers is wrong. When you find something in an answer choice that makes the choice obviously wrong, you should **literally cross those words out**. This may seem silly, but just like circling the question on math problems, the act of writing on a choice can help you focus your thoughts and be more certain of your elimination.

Let's try another one:

2. **The "invention of photography" (line 11) was important to astronomers because it**

   (A) allowed them to see farther into the night sky
   (B) made data collection easier
   (C) gave them more leisure time
   (D) provided opportunities for women
   (E) contributed to the development of computing technology

---

[*] This is *exactly* like what we did on Sentence Completions: we anticipate a word (like "hard-working"), then we pick the choice that *means* the same thing as our word (like "diligent"). The only difference is that here we're anticipating full sentences instead of single words.

[†] We don't even know whether Hubble and Hertzsprung were men. (They were, but the passage doesn't tell us that.)

Let's go back to line 11 and see what that sentence says:

With the invention of photography, observatories could now produce records of the images their telescopes captured.

Okay. Astronomers could produce records of the images. But that doesn't match *any* of the choices; none of them talk about producing records. Let's keep reading to the **sentence after** the line reference:

This meant the astronomers could leave the tedious work of data collection to low-paid workers without wasting valuable telescope time.

So having records meant **they could hire other people to do data collection**. That's our anticipation.

Now we see which choice best matches it. Again, the right answer won't be *exactly* what we anticipated. Let's see which ones come close:

(A) × allowed them ~~to see farther~~ into the night sky
There's nothing about how far they can see.

(B) ✓ made data collection easier
Okay, it did mention data collection.

(C) ✓ gave them more leisure time
Okay, it did mention freeing up time.

(D) × provided ~~opportunities for women~~
Women are not mentioned here.

(E) × contributed to the development of ~~computing technology~~
Computing technology is not mentioned here.

This time, we had two choices that sound good, (B) and (C). What should we do?

First of all, **eliminate the choices that are definitely wrong**. We're down to two choices, so even if we have no idea what else to do, we could guess one. There's no way we're leaving this blank now.

So which is better? What's the difference between these two choices? Are there any words here that don't fit what the sentence says?

Let's focus on choice (C): it "gave them more leisure time". That sounds plausible. If the scientists have other people to do the work, won't they have more time to themselves?

Well, maybe, but what is *leisure* time? "Leisure time" means free time, time to relax, vacation time. Are the astronomers going to the beach? Playing a few holes at the golf course? Do they have an all-astronomer softball league? All the passage says is that *they don't have to collect data anymore*; it doesn't say what they do with their extra time. That one word, "leisure", makes the whole choice wrong. That leaves us with **choice (B): it made data collection easier**. That's it!

The key is to eliminate choices **quickly**. If you're not sure whether a choice works, just skip it and check the next one. If you're having trouble, just try to get it down to two choices and see which one is better. Go through the choices in several waves: first get rid of the choices that are obviously wrong, then go back to what's left and look for nuances.

TRY ONE:

3. The author refers to Leavitt as "a footnote of history" (line 60) because

(A) despite early promise, she never made any important scientific contributions
(B) she made an important step in the advancement of women's rights
(C) she is still unknown to those outside her field
(D) her work has been overshadowed by the actual calculation of the size of the universe
(E) her work was not as important as that of Hubble

Use your Main Ideas

The questions we've seen so far have all been about single lines or sentences. But sometimes a question will ask you about a whole paragraph, or a large chunk of text that includes several sentences. In that case, we can use the Main Ideas to answer the question.

For example:

4. The third paragraph (lines 17-26) chiefly serves to

    (A) discuss opportunities available to women in astronomy
    (B) describe the daily activities of a typical computer
    (C) explain Leavitt's discovery of the period-luminosity relationship
    (D) provide biographical background on the subject
    (E) examine the role of technology in the observatory

Here, the question is asking about the entire third paragraph. That's 10 lines, which are made up of 5 sentences. Ugh. We still want to anticipate, but that's a lot of text to go back, read, and paraphrase. If only we had a summary of this paragraph…

Wait, we do! We already got the **Main Idea** of each paragraph. We can just use our Main Idea as our anticipation.

Your Main Idea for paragraph 3 may have differed from ours, but it should be something like "**How Leavitt became a computer**" or "**background about Leavitt**". Let's look at our choices:

    (A) ✕ discuss ~~opportunities available to women~~ in astronomy
        Too broad. The paragraph is about Leavitt, not women in general.

    (B) ✕ describe the daily activities of ~~a typical computer~~
        It's about Leavitt specifically, not the "typical" computer.

    (C) ✕ explain Leavitt's discovery of the ~~period-luminosity relationship~~
        The period-luminosity relationship isn't mentioned until the next paragraph.

    (D) ✓ provide biographical background on the subject
        Perfect! She went to Radcliffe, she got a job at Harvard, and she became a computer.

    (E) ✕ examine the role of ~~technology~~ in the observatory
        No technology is mentioned in this paragraph. That was in paragraph 2.

Choice (D) is our answer.

No matter what, once we read the question we'll go back to the passage to see what it says. But what we do when we get there depends on the question.

    ☛ If the question asks about a **single line or sentence**, we'll read the line and get an **anticipation**.

    ☛ If the question asks about a **paragraph or chunk of text**, we'll use our **main idea** as our anticipation.

But sometimes passages are hard to understand. What if we can't figure out what the passage says? That's were the third strategy comes in…

3. Eliminate Nonsense

When you anticipate successfully, you can often jump right to the correct answer. But it's not always that easy. Sometimes when you go back to the passage, you can't get an anticipation. Maybe you don't understand what the line says. Maybe you understand the line, but you don't understand what it has to do with the question.

That's okay. There's still *a lot* we can do even if we don't understand what the passage says. All reading passages are loaded with nonsense choices—choices that are obviously wrong. If we can **eliminate the nonsense** and guess from what's left, we can greatly increase our odds of getting the question. If we can get each tough question down to two choices, we'll get half of them right.

There are three main ways that a choice can be wrong:

1. Random	The choice talks about things that the passage doesn't even mention. You'd be *astounded* to learn how often this happens. (See the question about cats on the first page for an example. All four wrong choices were random.)
2. False	The choice is explicitly contradicted by the passage.
3. Irrelevant	The choice is something the author *says*, but it doesn't actually *answer the question*.

Here are some tips to keep in mind:

- As before, you should **literally cross out** the words that make a choice wrong. This will greatly help you keep track of what you're doing.

- We're not looking for the right choice, **we're looking for wrong choices**. If you're not sure whether a choice fits, just leave it in. Just ask whether the choice is Random, False, or Irrelevant. If you can't find a specific reason to eliminate it, leave it in for now. On every question, four out of five choices are wrong. So if we think a choice is wrong, there's an 80% chance we're right.

- Again, the key here is to **work quickly**. Don't spend too much time agonizing over every choice. Go through the choices, get rid of the ones that are *obviously* wrong, and see what you have left.

- Once you get down to two or three choices, you can go back to the passage again to see which is better. If you really can't decide which is better, **guess one**.

Let's look at an example:

5. **Lines 19-22 ("The opportunities…computer") suggest that**

    (A) Leavitt was unhappy with her position at the observatory
    (B) women had fewer opportunities in astronomy than in other sciences
    (C) only men were allowed to work at Harvard College Observatory
    (D) being a computer was one of the only positions available to Leavitt
    (E) Leavitt was particularly skilled at searching for variables

It asks about 19-22, so let's go back:

> *The opportunities open to women in the scientific world being few and far between, she joined the photographic photometry department at the Harvard College Observatory as a computer.*

That's a bit of a complicated sentence, and it may be tough to come up with an anticipation here. Let's do this one by *Eliminating Nonsense* instead.

(A) × Leavitt was ~~unhappy~~ with her position at the observatory
Random. It doesn't talk about her happiness. If anything, it's more likely that she liked it, because the work "resonated with her meticulous disposition".

(B) × women had fewer opportunities in astronomy ~~than in other sciences~~
Random! Nowhere does the passage compare astronomy to other sciences. If anything, the first part of this line implies that the situation was *the same* across "the scientific world". A lot people pick this choice because it looks pretty good at first, until you get to the last four words. Please: don't be one of those people too lazy to be bothered to read the last four words of a choice.

(C) × ~~only men were allowed to work~~ at Harvard College Observatory
False! Henrietta Leavitt *did* get a job at the Observatory! In the photographic photometry department! So women *could* work there.

(D) ✓ being a computer was one of the only positions available to Leavitt
Bingo. "Opportunities" were "few", so she became a computer. That means that being a computer was an opportunity that was available to her.

(E) × Leavitt was particularly skilled at ~~searching for variables~~
Irrelevant. This choice is true—the passage says so explicitly. But it doesn't say that until lines 24-26! This question specifically asks what lines 19-22 suggest, and these lines say nothing about Leavitt's skill at finding variables.

Note here that you don't have to understand why (D) is right because it's easy to see why all the other four choices are wrong.

Let's look at a harder example:

6. It can be inferred that the "anachronism" mentioned in line 3 results from the fact that

(A) a common word is being used in a different sense
(B) predecessors of modern PC's were unavailable in 1908
(C) Harvard had access to more advanced technology than other institutions
(D) computer science advanced at a greater rate than astronomy
(E) women were excluded from fields in which they thrive today

As always, let's start by going back to the passage. Let's start with line 3:

*This may sound like an **anachronism**;*

We can already see we'll have to go one sentence earlier to see what "this" refers to. Let's start with line 1:

*One of the most important discoveries in the history of astronomy was made by a computer in 1908. This may sound like an **anachronism**; computing machines of the early twentieth century, predecessors of our modern PC's, were nowhere near advanced enough to be making discoveries.*

Hmm. I still don't know what that means. Let's do it by *Eliminating Nonsense.* We'll look through the choices and eliminate anything that's *Random, False,* or *Irrelevant.*

(A) a common word is being used in a different sense
Not sure what this means. We'll leave it in.

(B) predecessors of modern PC's were unavailable in 1908
Not sure what this means either. We'll leave this in, too.

(C) ✗ ~~Harvard~~ had access to more advanced technology than ~~other institutions~~
Random! The passage doesn't mention Harvard until line 21, and it doesn't compare it to any other institutions.

(D) ✗ computer science advanced at a ~~greater rate than astronomy~~
False! The passage doesn't actually say anything about the rate of advancement for either computer science or astronomy. But it strongly implies that this is *backwards*: in 1908 astronomy was pretty advanced and computing machines "were nowhere near advanced".

(E) ✗ ~~women were excluded~~ from fields in which they thrive today
Random! We haven't mentioned women at all yet.

Great! We're down to two choices now, (A) and (B). If we can't figure anything else out, we can guess.

Let's take a closer look at our two remaining choices. Choice (A) is totally confusing, so let's pick apart choice (B). It says "*predecessors* of modern PC's were unavailable." "Predecessor" means "precursor" or "ancestor". So "predecessors of modern PC's" are the devices that came before our modern PC's. But the computing machines available in 1908 *were* the predecessors of modern PC's. It says so right in lines 3-4. It's the *modern* PC's were unavailable, not their predecessors. So choice (B) is *false*. **Choice (A) is our answer**.

Even though we still don't understand what choice (A), the correct answer, means, we can still get the question right.

Let's go back to what we know. The question asks how to explain the anachronism in line 3.[*] Lines 1-5 say that a computer made a discovery in 1908, but computers as we know them weren't around in 1908. That *is* the anachronism, but it doesn't *explain* the anachronism. If computers weren't around, how is it possible that one made a discovery? Let's keep reading one more line:

> *However, this "computer" was not a machine at all, but a woman named Henrietta Swan Leavitt.*

Aha! It seemed like an anachronism because we thought the word "computer" meant a machine like a laptop. But it really means a *person*. So in this sentence the word "computer" doesn't mean what it usually means. That's **choice (A) a common word is being used in a different sense**.

This was a tough question, and you may have some trouble understanding why (A) is right. But that's not the point. The point here is that *even on hard questions*, there are *a lot* of choices that you can easily eliminate. If you get narrow every hard question down to two choices, the odds are in your favor—you can get half of them right just by guessing.

---

[*] It helps to know what "anachronism" means. Luckily, it's boxword **170**, so we know it means "something in the wrong time period". Of course, you may be able to see that from the context as well.

III. QUESTION TYPES

Let's take a closer look at the different types of questions you'll see with the passages.

1. Explicit Questions

These are the questions that ask you **what the passage literally says**. We've already established that most passage questions give you specific line references, so all you have to do is go back, anticipate the answer, then match your anticipation to the choices.

It's important to see that every answer you put to explicit questions must be grounded in the passage. Don't pick a choice unless you can show us *exactly* where in the passage it says that. Don't just say, "Well, somewhere in the middle the author kinda says something about how cats are good." Say, "*Look*: in line 23 he says QUOTE 'I like cats.'"

Most explicit questions can be done by anticipating, and we've already seen some examples:

2. The "invention of photography" (line 11) was important to astronomers because it

   (A) allowed them to see farther into the night sky
   (B) made data collection easier
   (C) gave them more leisure time
   (D) provided opportunities for women
   (E) contributed to the development of computing technology

These questions may vary in difficulty. "Explicit" doesn't necessarily mean "easy", just that the answer is written in the text of the passage.

Take a look at this one:

7. **In lines 46-54 ("Leavitt never...in 1921"), all of the following are given as reasons that Leavitt did not produce more work EXCEPT**

   (A) her deteriorating health kept her from her work
   (B) she did not have the same opportunities for advancement that men had
   (C) she did not have the freedom to choose her tasks
   (D) the academic community did not realize the importance of her achievements
   (E) she died before she could achieve greater power

Here, the question tells us that four of the choices are *given* in the passage, and one isn't. So let's go back to the passage and read lines 46-54. As we see the answer choices in the text, we'll eliminate them:

> *Leavitt never produced any other important work. She only worked sporadically, since **she was plagued by poor health** [eliminate (A)] for most of her life. The most obvious factors working against her were her position and her sex. As a computer, **she had no autonomy and could only work on what she was assigned** [eliminate (C)] and as a woman, **she had no chance for advancement** [eliminate (B)]. The tide of women's rights had begun to turn— Harvard would award a PhD in astronomy to a woman for the first time in 1925—but **these changes came too late for Leavitt, who died of cancer in 1921** [eliminate (E)].*

Choice (D) is the only one not mentioned in these lines.

2. Vocab-in-context Questions

Vocabulary isn't just for Sentence Completions: it's important in the passages, too. Sometimes they'll ask you the meaning of a specific use of a specific word in the passage. These questions are really a sub-category of explicit questions and they can be done exactly the same way: go back to the passage and see how the word is used.

On these questions, it's *doubly* important to go back and anticipate. Usually, the word they're asking you about is being used in a strange way—that is, it *doesn't* have its usual meaning. Don't just go by what you think the word means; go back and look at what it means in the sentence. Treat it like a Sentence Completion, with the word in question as the blank.

Let's try one:

8.   **In context, the word "resonated" (line 24) most nearly means**

   (A) vibrated
   (B) agreed
   (C) sympathized
   (D) enhanced
   (E) rejoiced

Don't just try to define "resonate"; we have to look at its meaning *in the context of the sentence*. So let's go back to line 24, but we'll treat the word "resonate" like a blank in a sentence completion. (We'll start with the sentence before to remind you of the context.)

> *Her particular task was to search for "variables", stars whose brightness would vary over regular intervals, like a flashing street light. This sort of work --------- with her meticulous disposition, and she catalogued thousands of variables at an incredible rate.*

Can you anticipate the meaning of the word in the blank?[*] The second part of the second sentence says that she was good at her job. So by nature she was well suited to this kind of work. So the work **suited** or **fit** or **worked well with** her disposition. As with Sentence Completions, we're just trying to figure out the *meaning* of the word in the blank, so any of these is a fine anticipation.

Now we'll go back the choices. Do any of our choices mean something like *suited, fit,* or *worked well with*? **Choice (B), agreed,** works nicely.

Note that choice (A), vibrated, is what "resonated" literally means most of the time. However, that's not how the word is being used *in this context*. Seriously, it vibrated with her disposition? What the #@& does that mean? That's why it's important to go back to the passage and anticipate on every vocab-in-context question.

---

[*] It helps if you know what "meticulous" means. Thankfully, "meticulous" is boxword **92**, so we're good.

3. Interpretive Questions

These are questions about things the author doesn't *literally* say. Rather, it's about the author's purpose or beliefs or the strategies he or she uses in laying out the argument. But even though the answer isn't literally on the page, it's still *based on* what's in the passage.

There are several different types of inferred questions:

A. Main Idea Questions

Often, questions will literally just be looking for the Main Ideas. We've already seen an example of that:

4. The third paragraph (lines 17-26) chiefly serves to

    (A) discuss opportunities available to women in astronomy
    (B) describe the daily activities of a typical computer
    (C) explain Leavitt's discovery of the period-luminosity relationship
    (D) provide biographical background on the subject
    (E) examine the role of technology in the observatory

Sometimes, a question may ask for the Main Idea **of the entire passage**. Take a look at this:

9. **The primary purpose of the passage is to**

    (A) identify factors that led to the development of modern computers
    (B) show how technology contributed to Leavitt's work
    (C) detail how astronomers calculated the size of the universe
    (D) discuss women's rights in the early twentieth century
    (E) describe a scientist who made an important discovery

This question asks about the purpose of the whole passage, so let's find the main idea of the whole passage:

> ➤ **What's the passage about?**
>
> It's about this woman, Leavitt.
>
> ➤ **What does it say about her?**
>
> She's a scientist and she figured out some important stuff.
>
> ➤ **What stuff?**
>
> I dunno. Uhh... something about stars?

> Whenever a question asks about the **purpose** of the passage or of a particular paragraph, it's really just asking for the **Main Idea**.

Good enough. We don't care about the specifics of the discovery unless they ask us about it. So we'll just say the main idea is

> **Henrietta Leavitt figured out some important stuff about stars.**

Perfect. Let's look at our choices:

(A) ✗ identify factors that led to the ~~development of modern computers~~
Random. It's not about laptops. No one cares about modern computers.

(B) ✗ show ~~how technology contributed~~ to Leavitt's work
It mentions how photography (i.e. technology) contributed to astronomy in paragraph 2, but is that the purpose *of the passage*? No, that's just one bit in one paragraph. Yes, Leavitt used technology, but this is too specific. The passage is about a lot more than just the technology she used.

(C) ✗ ~~detail~~ how astronomers ~~calculated the size of the universe~~
No, no, no. Again, the passage does mention that Leavitt's discovery was "fundamental to the eventual calculation of the size of the universe" (lines 44-45), but that's the only mention of it. It doesn't say how it was calculated, or even who did it. It certainly doesn't provide any "details" about it.

(D) ✗ discuss women's rights in the early twentieth century

No. True, the last paragraph does say that Leavitt had fewer opportunities because she was a woman. But the passage isn't about women's rights throughout the twentieth century. It's about this one woman and how she was a good scientist. The passage isn't about women's rights in general—it's about Leavitt in particular.

(E) ✓ describe a scientist who made an important discovery

Does it describe a scientist? Yes! Henrietta Leavitt! Did she make a discovery? Yes! That thing about the stars, variables or whatever they're called. Perfect. **Choice (E)** is our answer.

> **PLEASE NOTE:** The right answer here doesn't mention Leavitt herself by name; it just mentions a vague "scientist" and a vague "discovery". This is a common trick the test likes to pull. Students generally prefer to pick a choice that mentions something specific they saw in the passage, like choice (B). Don't be fooled. The fact that a choice was mentioned in the passage isn't necessarily enough to make it right. It also has to answer the question.

B. Inferential Questions

These questions ask about things that aren't literally said, but can be *inferred* from what is said.

We've already seen two examples of Inferential Questions:

5. Lines 19-22 ("The opportunities...computer") suggest that

   (A) Leavitt was unhappy with her position at the observatory
   (B) women had fewer opportunities in astronomy than in other sciences
   (C) only men were allowed to work at Harvard College Observatory
   (D) being a computer was one of the only positions available to Leavitt
   (E) Leavitt was particularly skilled at searching for variables

6. It can be inferred that the "anachronism" mentioned in line 3 results from the fact that

   (A) a common word is being used in a different sense
   (B) predecessors of modern PC's were unavailable in 1908
   (C) Harvard had access to more advanced technology than other institutions
   (D) computer science advanced at a greater rate than astronomy
   (E) women were excluded from fields in which they thrive today

In each of these questions, the answer isn't literally said in the passage. But the answer is a *conclusion* that we can reasonably draw from what is in the passage. Because the answer isn't literally stated in the passage, inferred questions are often more likely to be solved by elimination than by anticipation.

> Words like *suggest*, *imply*, and *inferred* are signs that you're dealing with an inferential question.

C. Strategy Questions

Most questions ask about the *content* of the passage: what happened, who did what, what does the author say? Some questions, however, ask about the *form* of the passage, about the author's *rhetorical strategies*. That is, why does the author or narrator write what he writes? We've seen an easy example of this:

1. The author mentions Hubble and Hertzsprung (lines 56-57) in order to emphasize

   (A) the recognition she got from the general public
   (B) the extent to which astronomy was dominated by men
   (C) her dependence on the work of earlier scientists
   (D) the fame associated with winning the Nobel Prize
   (E) the esteem other scientists had for her work

The form of the question makes this a Strategy Question—it asks *why* the author mentions Hubble and Hertzsprung. But we easily did this question by anticipating, so it was very similar to an explicit question.

However, Strategy Questions can be much harder:

10. **The discussion of Venus in lines 36-39 is intended as**

    (A) a counterexample that disproves Leavitt's theory
    (B) an example of the period-luminosity relationship
    (C) an analogy that illustrates an astronomical phenomenon
    (D) a question that astronomers could not answer
    (E) a demonstration of a discovery made by new technology

This question is asking what the *role* of the discussion of Venus is. Why does he talk about Venus? What is the author trying to accomplish with these lines? We'll start by going back to the passage. Lines 36-39:

> *To the casual observer, Venus seems about as bright as the North Star. But Venus is a planet, and is therefore much dimmer than any star. It only seems brighter because it is much, much closer to us.*

It's tough to anticipate based purely on that quote. So let's just go through the choices and see which choices *could describe* that quote.

(A) × a ~~counterexample that disproves~~ Leavitt's theory
   False. Leavitt's theory was about how stars flash (line 30). The brightness of Venus does not disprove that. The author believes Leavitt's theory is true.

(B) an example of the period-luminosity relationship
   Hmm. This seems plausible. The paragraph is about that luminosity thingy. We'll leave it in.

(C) an analogy that illustrates an astronomical phenomenon
   This is kind of vague, but it might work. It's certainly about astronomical stuff. We'll leave it in.

(D) × a ~~question~~ that astronomers ~~could not answer~~
   Random. What question? How bright Venus is? Is that a question astronomers couldn't answer?

(E) × a demonstration of a ~~discovery made by new technology~~
   Random. Venus was not discovered using new technology.

Great! We're down to two choices, (B) and (C). Worst-case scenario, we'll guess one. Let's take a closer look at these guys.

Choice (B) mentions the "period-luminosity relationship"—that's the fancy name for Leavitt's discovery. *What was* her discovery? Line 30: "The brighter the star, the slower it flashed." Is Venus an example of a flashing star? **No!** It doesn't flash, and it's not a star—it's a planet! It says so in line 37. So the Venus discussion *can't possibly* be an example of this relationship. **Our answer must be choice (C).**

It's easy to be afraid of a choice like (C) because it sounds so *broad*. "An astronomical phenomenon." What is that? Choice (B) is more tempting because it's *specific*. It mentions that "period" thingy, and we know the paragraph is about that period thingy.

But that's backwards. Like we saw with the Main Idea question above, the *correct* answer is the broad and vague, while a *wrong* choice specifically mentions something in the passage. In fact, when a choice does have specific details, it's easier to show that choice to be wrong.

So why is (C) right? Lines 36-39 say that Venus looks brighter than the North Star, not because it *is* brighter, but because it's closer to us. Go a few lines earlier:

> *Astronomers had no way of determining the distance to the stars. Brightness could be used as a guide, since objects are brighter when they are close and dimmer when they are far away.*
> **Brightness alone, however, can be deceptive without a frame of reference.**

So the Venus discussion is intended to explain *why* brightness alone is not a reliable way to determine the distance to the stars. That's the "astronomical phenomenon" that Venus illustrates. This is the same thing as the difference between "true brightness" and "apparent brightness" mentioned in lines 41-42.

Once again, even on a very hard question, we could easily eliminate and narrow it down to two choices.

D. Tone Questions

We saw with Strategy questions that you may be asked about the form of the passage instead of the content. Similarly, Tone questions ask you about the emotional character of the text. How does the author or narrator *feel* about a particular subject, and what feeling is conveyed in the language? It's the difference between saying "Cats are popular" and "I adore cats!"

Tone questions are somewhat infrequent, but they can often throw you for a loop. Let's look at one:

> Some passages are **informative**, giving you facts of a situation, while others are **persuasive**, arguing for a particular position or opinion.

11. The author's tone throughout the passage can best be described as

    (A) scholarly appreciation
    (B) objective criticism
    (C) scornful derision
    (D) celebratory exultation
    (E) contrite melancholy

To help you determine the tone of a passage, we here at A-List have spent millions of dollars in research using the most advanced computer analytic technology to develop the *A-List Passage Tone Scale*™:

Let's take a minute to explain this complicated terminology:

 means the author **likes** the subject. This could mean he's arguing *in favor of* something, that he's saying someone is a good person, or just telling a happy anecdote.

 means the author **does not like** the subject. This could mean he's arguing *against* something, that he's giving a warning about something, or that he's telling a sad or angry anecdote.

 means the author **does not have an opinion** about the subject. This means the author is *just presenting the facts* without saying if they're good or bad. Think of this author as a *historian* or a *scientist*. Imagine that he has little glasses and a pipe.[*]

So where does the author of the Leavitt passage fall in this spectrum? Generally, he's a *historian*. Most of the passage simply *gives the facts* of her life and discovery. She grew up here, worked there, discovered this, and died.

> **Objective** (boxword 7) means "unbiased"; it's an important word to know for tone questions.

At the same time, he seems to *like* Henrietta Leavitt. He thinks she's a good scientist. He does say that she made "One of the most important discoveries in the history of astronomy" (lines 1–2). So that's good. We can certainly agree that he doesn't say *bad* things about her.

The tone should be somewhere between ☺ and ☺. Each choice has two words, so we'll rate both of them:

(A) scholarly appreciation	☺/☺	✓ That looks perfect.
(B) objective (**7**) criticism	☺/☹	✗ "objective" fits, but there's no "criticism".
(C) scornful (**61**) derision (**77**)	☹/☹	✗ Too angry.
(D) celebratory exultation (**402**)	☺/☺	✗ Way too happy.
(E) contrite (**435**) melancholy (**50**)	☹/☹	✗ Too sad.

Note that tone questions often have some tough vocab in the choices. <u>Know your box.</u>

Of course, tone questions can also be more complicated than this. The passage in question may have a nuanced tone that doesn't fit well into this scale. Or there may be more than one choice that matches the smiley faces you want. But at the very least this is a good place to start. Use it to eliminate some choices and see what's left.

---

[*] Despite our vast technology budget, it's very difficult to draw a little pipe. You'll have to use your imagination.

Read the passage and anticipate for the questions. You get no answer choices. Deal with it. Just look up the line references, see what the passage says, and try to answer the question in your own words.

"Form ever follows function," the American architect Louis Sullivan decreed in 1896. Sullivan's motto offered a new way of approaching design problems, becoming the
Line guiding principle for modernist movement in architecture for
5 nearly a century. Up until this point, architecture throughout Europe and the United States had been dominated by Neoclassicism, a revival of Greek and Roman architectural styles. But as the twentieth century ushered in industrial innovations, designers sought to shake off conventions of the
10 past and embrace a new aesthetic. In this era of growing cities and new production methods, buildings with fluted columns and gilded angels suddenly seemed old fashioned and out of touch. Modernists rejected these established styles, believing that the shape and substance of buildings should be dictated
15 only by their purpose, not unnecessary adornment. The results of this philosophy were radical: details were pared down, and buildings took on a sleek, simple, almost naked quality. The ornate stone buildings of the past were replaced with minimalist structures made from plate glass and steel.
20 One striking example of modernist architecture is the Guggenheim Museum, designed by Frank Lloyd Wright. The Guggenheim derives its visual appeal from its unusual shape, a simple spiral that gradually widens as it rises, standing in stark contrast to its rectilinear neighbors. This shape was
25 inspired by the building's primary purpose of exhibiting artworks. Visitors enter the gallery at the ground level and slowly ascend the ramp, viewing pieces that are displayed on the periphery of the spiral, as light floods the center through a glass ceiling. In this way, visitors enjoy a traffic-free,
30 continuous experience through the exhibition. By addressing function first, Wright was able to create a visually striking design that is also a work of art in its own right.
The modernist viewpoint was not confined to architecture, but was also adopted in the larger world of industrial and
35 graphic design. Furniture designers, for example, rejected the traditional idea of a piece's value being defined by the quality of workmanship. Modernist furniture like the Eames lounge chair emphasized simplicity and accessibility. Designed by Charles and Ray Eames, the chair was made of three shell-
40 shaped pieces fitted with leather cushions that could be easily disassembled for shipping. By separating the pieces of the chair, the design offered greater flexibility in reclining, but remained uncluttered and sophisticated. Likewise, poster designers in Switzerland developed Helvetica, a new typeface
45 that epitomized the minimalism of modernist design by presenting stark, unadorned letters. Since the purpose of any text should be to convey information, Helvetica's simple letter shapes offered no curlicues or flourishes that might distract from the content of printed words.
50 Although modernism gave way to some of the most iconic designs of the twentieth century, other designers argued that whimsical elements can also contribute to an object's appeal. These dissenters felt that too strict an adherence to the "form follows function" mentality results in stifling uniformity and
55 aesthetic boredom. After decades of impassive simplicity, they rediscovered the expressive power of decorative elements: architectural details, vibrant upholstery, or quirky fonts.

1. The reference to "fluted columns and gilded angels" in line 11–12 is given in order to

_____

_____

_____

2. Lines 13-15 ("Modernists... adornment") suggest that modernist buildings

_____

_____

_____

3. The passage states that the purpose of the "unusual shape" (line 22) of the Guggenheim is to

_____

_____

_____

4. The passage suggests that, compared to the Guggenheim, the "neighbors" mentioned in line 24

_____

_____

_____

5. Lines 38–43 ("Designed ... sophisticated") serve primarily to

_____

_____

_____

6. Which of the following most closely describes the views of the "designers" mentioned in line 51?

_____

_____

_____

7. The list in line 57 ("architectural... fonts") is intended to give examples of

_____

_____

_____

Here are the same passage and questions, but with answer choices. **Use your anticipations from the last drill** *and match them to the* *choices.* **Explain your reasoning** *by writing in the line below the choice, or by crossing out words that make the choice wrong.*

"Form ever follows function," the American architect Louis Sullivan decreed in 1896. Sullivan's motto offered a new way of approaching design problems, becoming the guiding principle for modernist movement in architecture for nearly a century. Up until this point, architecture throughout Europe and the United States had been dominated by Neoclassicism, a revival of Greek and Roman architectural styles. But as the twentieth century ushered in industrial innovations, designers sought to shake off conventions of the past and embrace a new aesthetic. In this era of growing cities and new production methods, buildings with fluted columns and gilded angels suddenly seemed old fashioned and out of touch. Modernists rejected these established styles, believing that the shape and substance of buildings should be dictated only by their purpose, not unnecessary adornment. The results of this philosophy were radical: details were pared down, and buildings took on a sleek, simple, almost naked quality. The ornate stone buildings of the past were replaced with minimalist structures made from plate glass and steel.

One striking example of modernist architecture is the Guggenheim Museum, designed by Frank Lloyd Wright. The Guggenheim derives its visual appeal from its unusual shape: a simple spiral that gradually widens as it rises, standing in stark contrast to its rectilinear neighbors. This shape was inspired by the building's primary purpose of exhibiting artworks. Visitors enter the gallery at the ground level and slowly ascend the ramp, viewing pieces that are displayed on the periphery of the spiral, as light floods the center through a glass ceiling. In this way, visitors enjoy a traffic-free, continuous experience through the exhibition. By addressing function first, Wright was able to create a visually striking design that is also a work of art in its own right.

The modernist viewpoint was not confined to architecture, but was also adopted in the larger world of industrial and graphic design. Furniture designers, for example, rejected the traditional idea of a piece's value being defined by the quality of workmanship. Modernist furniture like the Eames lounge chair emphasized simplicity and accessibility. Designed by Charles and Ray Eames, the chair was made of three shell-shaped pieces fitted with leather cushions that could be easily disassembled for shipping. By separating the pieces of the chair, the design offered greater flexibility in reclining, but remained uncluttered and sophisticated. Likewise, poster designers in Switzerland developed Helvetica, a new typeface that epitomized the minimalism of modernist design by presenting stark, unadorned letters. Since the purpose of any text should be to convey information, Helvetica's simple letter shapes offered no curlicues or flourishes that might distract from the content of printed words.

Although modernism gave way to some of the most iconic designs of the twentieth century, other designers argued that whimsical elements can also contribute to an object's appeal. These dissenters felt that too strict an adherence to the "form follows function" mentality results in stifling uniformity and aesthetic boredom. After decades of impassive simplicity, they rediscovered the expressive power of decorative elements: architectural details, vibrant upholstery, or quirky fonts.

1. The reference to "fluted columns and gilded angels" in line 11–12 is given in order to

   (A) describe some typical elements of modernist architecture
   _____

   (B) bemoan the decline of artistic quality due to industrial growth
   _____

   (C) give examples of stylistic elements that came to be seen as antiquated
   _____

   (D) compare ancient Greek and Roman buildings with those of the twentieth century
   _____

   (E) advocate for the renovation of dilapidated old structures
   _____

2. Lines 13-15 ("Modernists... adornment") suggest that modernist buildings

   (A) intentionally lacked excessive ornamentation
   _____

   (B) used aesthetics based on Greek and Roman styles
   _____

   (C) were constructed using innovative technology
   _____

   (D) avoided materials like glass and steel
   _____

   (E) were harshly received by older critics
   _____

3. The passage states that the purpose of the "unusual shape" (line 22) of the Guggenheim is to

   (A) exploit new construction materials
   _____

   (B) distinguish it from older museums
   _____

   (C) mock the simplicity of earlier aesthetics
   _____

   (D) demonstrate Wright's artistic virtuosity
   _____

   (E) enhance the building's intended use
   _____

GO TO THE NEXT PAGE

4. The passage suggests that, compared to the Guggenheim, the "neighbors" mentioned in line 24

(A) are significantly different in appearance

(B) do not properly communicate their function

(C) are more difficult to walk through

(D) display their artworks less effectively

(E) are not as visually appealing

5. Lines 38–43 ("Designed ... sophisticated") serve primarily to

(A) demonstrate the expense and effort required to produce a high-quality chair

(B) show the difficulties of applying modernist principles to other fields

(C) argue that architecture and furniture design both rely on outdated ideas

(D) elaborate on the convenience and innovation of a particular design

(E) criticize the Eames chair for its poor quality workmanship

6. Which of the following most closely describes the views of the "designers" mentioned in line 51?

(A) A building's shape should be dictated by its function.

(B) Excessive focus on an object's purpose can lead to monotonous designs.

(C) Technological innovation has made artistic qualities unnecessary.

(D) Modernism allows museums to be works of art in their own right.

(E) Industrial materials like plate-glass and steel provide sleek, elegant construction.

7. The list in line 57 ("architectural... fonts") is intended to give examples of

(A) embellishments that modernists valued for their expressive power

(B) industrial innovations developed in the twentieth century

(C) features whose presence helps designers emphasize an object's function

(D) architectural elements that Sullivan sought to eliminate

(E) details that critics of modernism have come to appreciate

IV. OTHER TYPES OF PASSAGES

Mini Passages

These are about one paragraph long and each has two or three questions attached. These work exactly the same as the bigger passages, just with fewer questions. So don't worry too much about them.

Double Passages

There will be two double passages per test: one with two long passages, one with two mini passages. Here, you'll see two passages on a similar topic followed by questions on both of them.

Because they give you both passages upfront, you may be tempted to read both passages before you start the questions. Do NOT do that.

The questions about the double passage are roughly ordered like this:

1. Questions about Passage 1

2. Questions about Passage 2

3. Questions about both Passages (how they're the same or different, etc.)

If you read both passages upfront, you'll read Passage 1, then Passage 2, then try to answer questions on 1—but you just read 2, so you get them mixed up in your head. And we promise you: the wrong answers on these questions are banking on that. There'll be questions about Passage 1 that have choices describing Passage 2. It's very easy to get them mixed up.

Instead, do this:

1. **Read Passage 1.** Just like you would with any other passage.

2. **Answer the questions about Passage 1.** The first few will be *only* about Passage 1. That way, when you're doing the questions about Passage 1, it's still fresh in your mind. Plus, you haven't even *looked* at 2 yet, so you're not confused about which is which. As soon as you get to a question about something you haven't read yet...

3. **Go back and read Passage 2.** Just like you would with any other passage.

4. **Answer the rest of the questions.** There will be some *only* about 2, then some about *both* of them together.

Here are a few tips to keep in mind:

- Questions about Passage 1 are *usually* first, but there may be some questions on both passages first. But it's easy to tell which passage a question is asking about—just look at the line references in the question.

- As you read Passage 2, think about what you read in Passage 1. Think about how they agree and how they disagree. You *know* you'll be asked questions that directly compare and contrast the passages, so you might as well start thinking about it now. Questions that ask about both passages often rely on the Main Ideas of the passages, so make sure to look for them.

- Often, it's pretty easy to see that difference between the passages. It can sometimes be boiled down to a simple disagreement: Passage 1 thinks X is good, Passage 2 thinks X is bad. But don't assume it will be that easy. The connection between them can sometimes be more subtle.

- Mini double passages are often very heavy on questions about both passages, as well as Main Ideas, so be sure to look out for them. But this also means that there are few questions about one passage only, so you don't have to follow the reading strategy given above. Read both small passages and go to the questions.

Let's look at a sample double passage so we can see some examples of **Questions about Both Passages**:

Questions 12-15 refer to the following passages

Passage 1

There is unquestionably a great deal of stupidity, incoherence, and bile on the Internet, feelings that can be deleterious to actual constructive communication. Granted, this is not a new phenomenon—people have been angry and inarticulate since the dawn of civilization. But the anonymity of the Internet makes it easier for that unpleasant side to be unleashed. In the real world, social interactions are governed by rules that prevent people from acting inappropriately, for fear of embarrassment or opprobrium. But people can wander online freely without anyone knowing anything about them. This gives them a total freedom of expression that allows them to write whatever is on their minds, no matter how ugly, without fear of repercussion.

Line 5

10

Passage 2

Some people list the growth of the online news as a contributing cause of the current wave of sensationalism in journalism, in which objective reporting and civil debate have been replaced by shouting, name-calling, and irresponsible rumor-mongering. But while the Internet certainly does its share of those things, it also has become an important antidote to 24-hour news stations. Despite the vast number of available channels, television news is still controlled by a small number of corporations. But because anyone with a computer can start a web page, the Internet encourages "citizen journalism". Whereas in the past the public was forced to blindly accept media accounts of news stories, now anyone can start a website to fact-check, challenge, and expose fraudulent politicians or lazy journalism.

15

20

25

MAIN IDEAS FOR PASSAGES:

Passage 1: _____

Passage 2: _____

12. Which of the following best describes the relationship between the two passages?

   (A) Passage 1 discusses a negative aspect of the Internet, while Passage 2 focuses on a positive effect.
   (B) Passage 1 praises television news channels, while Passage 2 denounces them.
   (C) Passage 1 argues that the public is objective and civil, while Passage 2 says they are irresponsible.
   (D) Passage 1 traces the causes of sensationalism in journalism, while Passage 2 discusses its consequences.
   (E) Passage 1 condemns the Internet as a whole, while Passage 2 claims that only online news is irresponsible.

13. Unlike Passage 1, Passage 2 is primarily concerned with

   (A) the effect of the Internet on people's behavior
   (B) the relationship between the Internet and other media
   (C) different ways that websites attract new readers
   (D) the technology that allows anyone to start a website
   (E) social rules that govern objective journalism

14. The authors of both passages agree that

   (A) 24-hour news channels contribute to sensationalism in journalism
   (B) social interactions in the real world are more repressive than social interactions online.
   (C) online news sites can make constructive contributions to society
   (D) some websites contain material that is excessively unpleasant or hostile
   (E) the Internet makes people incoherent and belligerent

15. The author of Passage 2 would likely argue that the "freedom of expression" mentioned in line 11 of Passage 1 is

   (A) undermined by people who practice citizen journalism
   (B) nonexistent when Internet users reveal their identities
   (C) the phenomenon that allows the public to challenge claims by the media
   (D) the main reason people become more irrational and belligerent
   (E) more noticeable on television news stations that on websites

First let's get the Main Ideas of the two passages.[*] Yours may vary, but remember to *keep them short:*

> **Passage 1:** Internet is ugly (because of anonymity).
>
> **Passage 2:** Internet can be good (by encouraging citizen journalism).

Now let's take a look at question 12 together:

12. Which of the following best describes the relationship between the two passages?

Notice that each choice here contains two statements—the first about Passage 1 and the second about Passage 2. Much like a two-blank Sentence Completion question, we can eliminate choices one passage at a time. Let's go through and *only read the first half of each choice*. If the first half doesn't accurately describe Passage 1, we'll eliminate it.

> **(A)** ✓ **Passage 1 discusses a negative aspect of the Internet,**
> Sure. Passage 1 definitely discusses "stupidity, incoherence, and bile on the Internet" (lines 1-2).
>
> **(B)** ✗ **Passage 1 praises ~~television news channels,~~**
> *Random*. Passage 1 doesn't mention television news channels at all.
>
> **(C)** ✗ **Passage 1 argues that the public is ~~objective and civil,~~**
> *False*. It says "people have been angry and inarticulate since the dawn of civilization" (lines 4-5).
>
> **(D)** ✗ **Passage 1 traces the causes of sensationalism in ~~journalism,~~**
> *Random*. Passage 1 doesn't mention journalism at all.
>
> **(E)** ✓ **Passage 1 condemns the Internet as a whole,**
> Sure. Lines 1-3 list "stupidity" and other "deleterious" things, and the passage only refers to "the Internet", not to any specific parts of the Internet.

Great! Right away, we eliminated three choices without even looking at Passage 2!

Now we'll just read the second half of each choice and see which accurately describe Passage 2. Remember: we already eliminated three choices, so we'll only check the remaining ones, (A) and (E):

> **(A)** ✓ **... while Passage 2 focuses on a positive effect.**
> Sure. Passage 2 says websites can "expose fraudulent politicians or lazy journalism" (lines 27-28).
>
> **(E)** ✗ **... while Passage 2 claims only online news is ~~irresponsible.~~**
> *False*. Passage 2 *likes* online news. It's "an important antidote to the 24-hour cable news stations" (line 20).

So **choice (A)** is our answer.

As we've seen before on many different types of questions, if we eliminate *systematically*, we can do the question *quickly*. And even if we aren't sure of the right answer, we can easily eliminate some wrong answers.

Try the rest of the questions on your own. Remember to keep track of which passage is which.

---

[*] Note that there are a ton of boxwords in the passages. Line 2: incoherence (**101** – coherent); line 3: deleterious (**380**); line 5: inarticulate (**65** – articulate); line 16: objective (**7**).

READING PASSAGE FLOW CHART

Here's a quick outline of what you should be doing on pretty much every passage question.

The Passage

- Read quickly and get the **Main Ideas** of the passage, paragraph by paragraph.
- To find the main idea, just ask yourself: **what's it about?**
- If you're not sure what the main idea is, check the **first and last sentences** of the paragraph.
- Don't spend too much time. Don't overanalyze. If you're not sure, move on.

The Question

- Read the question, **ignore the choices**.
- *Is the question about a large chunk of text or a specific line or sentence?*
  - Chunk: get the **Main Idea** of the chunk.
  - Line: go back to the line reference and read **the whole sentence**.
- *Can you answer the question with what you just learned?*
  - Yes: that's your **anticipation**. Go to the choices.
  - No: read the **sentence before** and/or the **sentence after** to understand the context.
- *Now can you answer the question?*
  - Yes: that's your **anticipation**. Go to the choices.
  - No: go to **elimination**.

The Choices

Anticipation

- *How many choices match your anticipation?*
  - None: Your anticipation wasn't good enough. Go back to the passage and try again, or go to elimination.
  - One: **That's your answer! Pick it!**
  - Two or three:
    - **Eliminate** the ones that fail.
    - Ask yourself: what's the difference between the choices?
    - Go back and check the line again to see which is better.
    - If you can't decide, **guess one**.
  - Four or Five: Go to Elimination.

Elimination

- Go through the choices looking for wrong answers.
  - Don't look for the right answer, **look for the wrong answers**.
  - **Work quickly.** If you can't eliminate a choice, skip it and come back to it later
  - As you eliminate, **cross out** the words that make a choice wrong.
- Eliminate for three reasons:
  1. Is the choice *mentioned* in the passage? If not, it's **random**.
  2. Is the choice *true* according to the passage? If not, it's **false**.
  3. Does the choice *answer the question*? If not, it's **irrelevant**.
- After you eliminate, *how many choices do you have left?*
  - None: Run through them again. Don't eliminate choices you don't understand.
  - One: **That's your answer! Pick it!**
  - Two or three:
    - **Eliminate** the ones that fail.
    - Ask yourself: what's the difference between the choices?
    - Go back and check the line again to see which is better.
    - If you can't decide, **guess one**.
  - Four or Five:
    - You didn't eliminate enough. Run through them again and look more closely.
    - If you really can't eliminate anything else, move on to the next question.

READING PASSAGE SUMMARY

1. The Passage

- Read quickly and get the **Main Ideas** of the passage, paragraph by paragraph.
- To find the main idea, just ask yourself: **what's it about?**
- If you can't find the main idea, read the **first and last sentences** of the paragraph.
- Don't spend too much time. Don't overanalyze. If you're not sure, **move on.**

2. The Question

- Read the question, **ignore the choices.**
- When there's a line reference, **go back to the passage** and read the line.
- **Read the whole sentence**, not just the line referred to.
- If that line is unclear, read **the sentence before or the sentence after.**
- Try to answer the question with what you just learned. That's your **anticipation.**
- If you can't anticipate, go to the choices to **eliminate.**

3. The Choices

- If you find a choice that matches your anticipation, pick it.
- If you don't find a match or if you don't have an anticipation, don't look for right choice, **look for wrong choices.** 80% of the choices are wrong. You can eliminate wildly wrong choices even if you don't understand the passage or question.
- **Work quickly.** If you're not sure about a choice, skip it and come back later.
- Eliminate choices that are **random, false,** or **irrelevant.**
- As you eliminate, **cross out** words that make a choice wrong.
- If you get down to two or three choices and can't decide, **guess one.**

4. Other types

- **Vocab-in-context questions** are similar to sentence completions. Treat the word in question as a blank and anticipate its meaning. Use the context of the sentence and the meaning of the word itself as clues.
- **Tone questions** often come down to *positive, negative,* or *neutral.*
- For **double passages**, do the passages separately. Read the passage 1 and do the questions about passage 2. Then read passage 2 and do the questions about passage 2. Then do the questions about both of them.

*Now you're ready to do the following passages. For each passage, **write the main ideas** for the passage and/or for individual paragraphs within the passage. For each question, anticipate whenever possible, and **write your anticipation** in the space provided.*

Questions 1-2 refer to the following passage.

It is difficult for modern eyes to see why Manet's *Olympia* was so scandalous in 1863. It simply depicts a reclining nude. Hadn't artists been painting nudes for centuries? A museum-
Line goer today might walk past it without looking twice. Two
5 factors contributed to the outrage. The nude, traditionally an ideal of perfect beauty, was here a prostitute, staring at the viewer with cold, accusatory eyes. Furthermore, it was painted in a deliberately flat style that flouted the conventions of artistic representation. These elements seem tame by today's
10 standards, in which provocation is ubiquitous in art, and con- ventions of representation have been all but flouted out of existence. It was *Olympia*, however, that opened the modernist floodgates for taboo.

MAIN IDEA:

_____

1. The attitude of the "museumgoer" (line 3-4) towards *Olympia* could best be described as

ANTICIPATION: _____

    (A) offended
    (B) contemplative
    (C) resentful
    (D) indifferent
    (E) enthralled

2. In lines 9-12 ("These elements ... existence"), the author suggests that, compared to people in Manet's time, people today

ANTICIPATION: _____

    (A) prefer art that is more conventional
    (B) are less concerned with moral values
    (C) have a different idea of what is offensive
    (D) have less stringent obscenity laws
    (E) are less offended by nudity in art

Questions 3-4 refer to the following passage.

Nature seems (the more we look into it) to be made up of antipathies: without something to hate, we lose the very source of our thought and action. There is a secret affinity, a
Line hankering after evil in the human mind, which takes a perverse
5 but fortunate delight in mischief, because it is a never-failing source of satisfaction. Do we not see this principle at work everywhere? Animals torment and worry one another without mercy; children kill flies for sport; a whole town runs to be present at a fire, and the spectator by no means exults to see it
10 extinguished.

MAIN IDEA:

_____

3. The primary purpose of the passage is to

ANTICIPATION: _____

    (A) denounce a type of behavior
    (B) advocate a view of nature
    (C) promote a legal strategy
    (D) explain a biological phenomenon
    (E) investigate the history of a concept

4. In lines 9-10, the author suggests that "the spectator"

ANTICIPATION: _____

    (A) started the fire out of hatred
    (B) feels guilty about enjoying the fire
    (C) is trying to extinguish the fire
    (D) sympathizes with the fire's victims
    (E) takes pleasure in watching destruction

GO TO THE NEXT PAGE

Questions 5-11 refer to the following passage.

The following passage is from a Japanese novel written in 1906. The narrator has left Tokyo to become a math teacher in a small town. In this passage, it is his first day of class in his new school.

I had been to the school the previous day, so I had a good idea of how to get there, and after turning a few corners I came to the front gate. On my way to the school, I met a
Line number of the students in cotton drill uniforms coming
5 through this gate. Some of them were taller than I and looked much stronger. When I thought of teaching these people, I suddenly felt an odd sort of uneasiness. When I arrived, my card was taken to the principal, and I was quickly ushered to his room. With a scant mustache, dark skin, and big eyes, the
10 principal looked a bit like a badger. He studiously assumed an air of superiority, and, saying he would like me to do my best, handed me a certificate of appointment stamped with a big, official seal. He said he would introduce me to all my fellow teachers, and I was to present the certificate to each one of
15 them. What a bother! It would be far better to post it up in the teachers' room instead of going through such a monkey process.

The other teachers would not arrive until the first bugle was sounded, and there was still plenty of time. The principal
20 looked at his watch and said that he would acquaint me with the school soon enough, but now he would discuss general matters with me. With that, he started a long lecture on the spirit of education. For a while I listened to him with my mind half somewhere else, but about halfway through his lecture, I
25 began to realize that I would soon be in a bad fix. I could not do, by any means, all he expected of me. He expected that besides teaching technical knowledge, I had to make myself an example to the students, to become an object of admiration for the whole school and to exert my moral influence in order
30 to become a real educator, or something ridiculously high-sounding. No man with such admirable qualities would come to this faraway place for only 40 yen* a month! Like most people, if I get angry, I'm likely to get into a fight. According to what the principal said, however, I could hardly open my
35 mouth or even take a stroll around the place. If they wanted me to fill such an onerous post, they should have told me all that before. I hate lying, so I would have to face up to the fact that I had been cheated and get out of this mess like a man, there and then.
40 "I cannot do everything you want me to," I told the principal. "I therefore return this appointment."

I shoved back the certificate. The principal blinked his badger-like eyes and stared at me. Then he said, "I am only talking about my ideal for you. I know well that you cannot do
45 it all, so don't worry," and he laughed. If he knew it so well already, why on earth did he scare me with that big speech?

Meanwhile, the bugle sounded. The teachers would be ready now, the principal said, and I followed him to the teachers' room. In a spacious rectangular room, they sat each
50 before a table lined along the walls. When I entered the room, they all turned and stared at me in unison, as if my face were a show. Then, as per instructions, I introduced myself and showed the certificate to each one of them. Most of them stood and made a slight bow of acknowledgment. But some of

55 the more painfully polite ones actually took the certificate, read it, and respectfully returned it to me. It was all like a cheap performance at a play! When I came to the fifteenth, the gym teacher, I got impatient at repeating the same old thing over and over. They each had to do it only once, but I had to
60 do it fifteen times. They ought to have some sympathy.

* the currency of Japan.

MAIN IDEAS:

Paragraph 1: _____

Paragraph 2: _____

Paragraph 3-4: _____

Paragraph 5: _____

5. Lines 6-7 ("When I...uneasiness") suggest that narrator is worried about

ANTICIPATION: _____

(A) making a good first impression with the students
(B) teaching children that are academically advanced
(C) living up to the principal's expectations
(D) overseeing physically imposing students
(E) being introduced to the other teachers

6. The narrator believes he is "in a bad fix" (line 25) because he

ANTICIPATION: _____

(A) must present his certificate of appointment to the other teachers
(B) does not possess any admirable moral qualities
(C) is unqualified to teach the technical knowledge required for his class
(D) has lied about his qualifications for the position
(E) thinks the demands of his position are incompatible with his lifestyle

GO TO THE NEXT PAGE

7. It can be inferred from lines 31-32 ("No man…month") that the narrator believes

ANTICIPATION: _____

    (A) the principal is paid more than the other teachers at the school
    (B) schools in large cities do not value moral influence as much as schools in small towns do
    (C) his compensation is not appropriate for the principal's expectations
    (D) most admirable people cannot afford the cost of the trip to this school
    (E) it is impossible for anyone to meet the principal's moral expectations

8. In lines 42-45, the principal reacts to the narrator with

ANTICIPATION: _____

    (A) disappointment and shame
    (B) anger and resentment
    (C) elation and mirth
    (D) disbelief and remorse
    (E) perplexity and amusement

9. The narrator apparently believes that the "polite ones" (line 55) are

ANTICIPATION: _____

    (A) overly concerned about the narrator's qualifications
    (B) not actually interested in what the certificate says
    (C) not adequately prepared for the performance
    (D) demanding about following tradition
    (E) courteous in accepting the new teacher

10. The reference to "a cheap performance at a play" (line 57) serves to emphasize the

ANTICIPATION: _____

    (A) importance of ceremony in Japanese culture
    (B) unjustly low salary the narrator receives
    (C) narrator's lack of moral qualities
    (D) artificiality of the situation
    (E) teachers' need for better theatrical training

11. The narrator's tone in lines 47-60 is best described as

ANTICIPATION: _____

    (A) querulous
    (B) skeptical
    (C) solemn
    (D) objective
    (E) apathetic

GO TO THE NEXT PAGE

Questions 12–24 are based on the following passages.

The following passages discuss the decrease in the number of different languages spoken around the world. Passage 1 is from an article about language death. Passage 2 is from a book about linguistic fieldwork written by a British linguist.

Passage 1

On October 7, 1992, Tevfik Esenc died peacefully in his sleep at the age of 88, and with him died an entire language. His gravestone memorializes him as "the last person able to
Line speak the language they called Ubykh". Imagine if this were to
5 happen to your language, if all the vocabulary, the sounds and poetry, the intricate grammars of English simply died quietly overnight. The phenomenon is called language death and unfortunately it is all too common. Some sociolinguists estimate that a language dies every two weeks. This means that, of the 6,000
10 languages that are currently spoken throughout the world, half will be extinct within a century.

How does this happen? When people hear the term "language death", they often think of "dead languages", imagining lost civilizations, and ruins filled with broken stone pillars.
15 True, there are thousands of ancient languages no longer in use, but most didn't simply vanish—they evolved into other languages over the course of hundreds of years. Latin didn't "die"; it turned into French, Italian, and other Romance languages. Language death, however, is a different phenomenon. It's
20 happening now and it happens suddenly, sometimes over the course of just a few generations. Furthermore, the death of a language does not even require the death of the culture that speaks it. A language dies from disuse, when another language becomes dominant in the area, and the speakers of the
25 indigenous language shift to the dominant language. The Ubykh language may be dead, but the Ubykh people live on, their native language having been supplanted by Turkish.

But even though the community survives the death of its language, the culture nonetheless suffers. Every language is a
30 repository of its people's history. Not only the traditional myths and stories, but the very words themselves are the heritage of the people, their bloodline and connection to the past. Without a language of its own, a community is robbed of its identity, particularly if the native language has been supplanted by that
35 of an oppressor.

One way to preserve a dying language is through documentation. At a minimum, it ensures that future generations can continue to study its sounds and structures. Occasionally, documentation can even allow a dead language to be resurrected.
40 Hebrew had fallen out of everyday use around the time of the late Roman Empire, kept alive only by religious scholars. A revival in the nineteenth century brought it back, and it is now spoken by 15 million people worldwide, over 1500 years after its original displacement. Several studies of Ubykh were pub-
45 lished before the death of poor Tevfik. Perhaps it too will be revived in a few hundred years.

Passage 2

Language death, more often than not, is more like language suicide: when parents stop teaching their native tongue to their children in infancy, children will not be fluent
50 speakers. They will identify with the language they learned, which they will in turn pass on to their children. While many people bemoan this loss of the diversity of speech, it is important to note that only the speakers can decide what they pass to the next generation; we cannot force other cultures to
55 save their own languages.

When a community abandons its language, there is often good reason to do so—sometimes it even can mean the difference between life and death. In areas of extreme poverty, speaking the dominant language can mean better economic
60 opportunities, a greater income, or a better life. In imperialist colonies or war-torn regions, a group in power will sometimes prohibit the use of indigenous languages, sometimes even under penalty of death. It is easy for cozy scholars to lament the loss of curious phonetic systems, but if faced with the
65 choice between your language and your life, you will not take long to deliberate.

Even when members of a community aren't in actual physical danger, field linguists working to save dying languages often have encountered resistance, even animosity
70 from the indigenous people. Some cultures have strong feelings of ownership towards their languages and are unwilling to share them with outsiders. Some feel that the act of documenting or recording a language deprives it of its spirit. Some communities are interested in saving their
75 languages, but distrust European linguists, who resemble speakers of the dominant language more closely than they do members of the community.

Efforts to revive dying languages can be successful, but the spark for revitalization must originate internally. Welsh*
80 was once on the verge of vanishing, but a resurgence of interest in the late twentieth century helped revive it, and it now enjoys equal footing with English in the Welsh government. The key to its success was the support and enthusiasm of *the people*, who see their language as the heart
85 of their culture. It is vital for linguists to approach a dying language not like a physicist, but like a physician. A language is not a cold object of study but an element of a culture made up of living people. It is their interests and their safety that must be taken into account before we worry about their tenses
90 and conjugations.

* Welsh is the language of Wales, a nation in the United Kingdom.

MAIN IDEAS FOR FULL PASSAGES:

Passage 1: _____

Passage 2: _____

GO TO THE NEXT PAGE

MAIN IDEAS, Passage 1:

Paragraph 1: _____

Paragraph 2: _____

Paragraph 3: _____

Paragraph 4: _____

MAIN IDEAS, Passage 2:

Paragraph 1: _____

Paragraph 2: _____

Paragraph 3: _____

Paragraph 4: _____

12. Which of the following best describes the relationship between the two passages?

ANTICIPATION: _____

   (A) Passage 1 identifies the benefits of a situation while Passage 2 identifies its drawbacks.
   (B) Passage 1 outlines a problem while Passage 2 describes obstacles to its resolution.
   (C) Passage 1 argues against the policies recommended by Passage 2.
   (D) Passage 1 catalogs ancient phenomena that Passage 2 applies to the modern day.
   (E) Passage 1 espouses political beliefs that are denounced by Passage 2.

13. The author of Passage 1 mentions "stone pillars" (line 14) primarily in order to

ANTICIPATION: _____

   (A) describe the devastation language death causes
   (B) demonstrate the rapidity of language death
   (C) evoke something archaic and inactive
   (D) connect language to a cultural past
   (E) show how linguists are unfeeling toward their subjects

14. It can be inferred from lines 23-27 "a language…Turkish" that the Ubykh people

ANTICIPATION: _____

   (A) spoke a language that evolved from Turkish
   (B) do not have a connection to their cultural past
   (C) were oppressed and exploited by the Turkish people
   (D) suffer because of the death of their language
   (E) live in an area with many Turkish speakers

15. Lines 28-35 ("But even…an oppressor") serve primarily to

ANTICIPATION: _____

   (A) show why conservation of languages is important
   (B) explain the causes of language death
   (C) catalog success stories of language resurrection
   (D) give examples of traditions worth preserving
   (E) illustrate the link between words and myths

16. The tone of lines 45-46 ("Perhaps it…years") can best be described as

ANTICIPATION: _____

   (A) wistful
   (B) choleric
   (C) pretentious
   (D) ebullient
   (E) ominous

17. The author of Passage 2 uses the term "language suicide" (lines 48) primarily to emphasize

ANTICIPATION: _____

   (A) the suddenness with which language death occurs
   (B) that children's health and safety are at risk
   (C) the hopelessness of trying to save a dying language
   (D) that language death is often self-inflicted
   (E) the tragic nature of language death

18. In line 63, the word "cozy" serves to

ANTICIPATION: _____

   (A) praise the warmth and caring attitude of linguists
   (B) condemn the scholars' role in oppressing endangered cultures
   (C) affirm the satisfaction of helping a dying language
   (D) highlight scholars' distance from the reality of the communities
   (E) encourage interest in preserving ancient languages

GO TO THE NEXT PAGE

19. In Passage 2, it can be inferred that the members of the "communities" mentioned in line 74

ANTICIPATION: _____

  (A) face physical dangers that prevent them from saving their language
  (B) differ physically from those who speak the dominant language
  (C) lack a sense of heritage and identity necessary to save their language
  (D) think European linguists will be more interested in the dominant language
  (E) have successfully saved their language without the help of European linguists

20. In line 82 "enjoys" most nearly means

ANTICIPATION: _____

  (A) apprehends
  (B) tolerates
  (C) disdains
  (D) desires
  (E) retains

21. The difference between being a "physicist" and being a "physician" (lines 86) is best described as the distinction between

ANTICIPATION: _____

  (A) precision and approximation
  (B) a professional and a dilettante
  (C) objectivity and compassion
  (D) dominance and subservience
  (E) alienation and merriment

22. The author of Passage 2 would most likely respond to lines 36-38 of Passage 1 ("One way...structures") by

ANTICIPATION: _____

  (A) mocking the futility of trying to save endangered languages
  (B) claiming that the sounds of a language are not as important as its stories and myths.
  (C) illustrating the difficulty of accurately transcribing a dead language
  (D) arguing that the community must consent to documentation of its language
  (E) restating the benefits of children being fluent in the dominant language

23. Unlike the author of Passage 2, the author of Passage 1 supports his argument by

ANTICIPATION: _____

  (A) recounting personal experiences
  (B) providing statistics to substantiate a claim
  (C) refuting statements posed by opponents
  (D) citing specific cases as models of success
  (E) deferring to scientific authorities

24. Both authors would agree that

ANTICIPATION: _____

  (A) language death does not require the death of the culture
  (B) linguists should never interfere with other cultures
  (C) linguists should remain objective towards the languages they study
  (D) it is possible to resurrect ancient languages
  (E) war and poverty are the main causes of language death

STOP

Appendices

APPENDIX A: MATH DRILLS

PLUG IN DRILL

1. If $a + 3b = 10$, what is the value of $2a + 6b = ?$

   (A) 12
   (B) 15
   (C) 20
   (D) 30
   (E) 40

2. The number x is 3 less than 2 times the number y. Which of the following expressions gives y in terms of x?

   (A) $2x - 3$

   (B) $3x + 2$

   (C) $\dfrac{x-2}{3}$

   (D) $\dfrac{x+3}{2}$

   (E) $\dfrac{x-3}{2}$

3. If $x = 3t - 1$ and $y = t + 4$, what is x in terms of y?

   (A) $y + 3$
   (B) $y - 4$
   (C) $3y + 3$
   (D) $3y - 5$
   (E) $3y - 13$

A	B

Note: Figure not drawn to scale.

4. The length of rectangle B is double that of rectangle A, and the width of rectangle B is half that of rectangle A. If rectangle A is a square, what is the ratio of the perimeter of A to the perimeter of B?

   (A) 1:1
   (B) 1:2
   (C) 1:4
   (D) 2:3
   (E) 4:5

5. Three people are eating a box of cookies. Caroline ate half the number of cookies that Sherwyn did, and Sherwyn ate 4 times as many as Laura. What fraction of the cookies did Sherwyn eat?

Grid in your answer:

6. If $z = x - 3$ and $z = y + 5$, which of the following *must* be true?

(A) $x > y$
(B) $x < y$
(C) $x = y$
(D) $z < 0$
(E) $z > 0$

---

7. A certain two-digit number, n, has a units digit that is three times the tens digit. Which of the following *must* be true?

(A) $n > 20$
(B) $n < 40$
(C) n is odd
(D) n is even
(E) n is a multiple of 3

---

8. Sujit has only white shirts and red shirts. He has four times as many white shirts as red shirts. What percent of his shirts are red?

(A) 20%
(B) 25%
(C) 40%
(D) 75%
(E) 80%

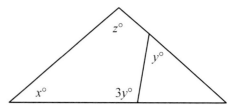

Note: Figure not drawn to scale.

9. In the figure above, what is z in terms of x and y?

(A) $3y + x$
(B) $4y - x$
(C) $180 - 2y - x$
(D) $180 - 3y - x$
(E) $180 - 4y + x$

---

10. Veerle is selling waffles for x dollars each. If her expenses totaled y dollars, which of the following expressions represents the number of waffles she must sell in order to make a profit of \$100? (Profit equals total sales minus expenses.)

(A) $\dfrac{100 + y}{x}$

(B) $\dfrac{100 - y}{x}$

(C) $\dfrac{100 + x}{y}$

(D) $100x - y$

(E) $100 - xy$

BACKSOLVE DRILL

1. If $18 - (xy)^2 = 2$, which of the following could be the value of xy?

   (A) −4
   (B) 3
   (C) 9
   (D) 16
   (E) 20

2. The number of koalas, k, in a certain colony can be predicted according to the function $k(t) = 3125 \times 2^{2t}$, where t represents the number of minutes after the start of the observation. After how many minutes will the population reach 50,000 koalas?

   (A) 0
   (B) 1
   (C) 2
   (D) 3
   (E) 4

3. The length of a certain rectangular box is twice the width, and the width of the box is twice the height. If the volume of the box is 64 cubic inches, what is its height, in inches?

   (A) 2
   (B) 4
   (C) 6
   (D) 8
   (E) 10

4. Emily's Bakery made some pies for a party. Half of the pies were blueberry, one third were raspberry, and the remaining 21 were pecan. How many total pies did the bakery make for the party?

   (A) 42
   (B) 63
   (C) 72
   (D) 108
   (E) 126

5. Each term of a certain sequence is formed by adding a positive integer, c, to the term immediately before it. The first term in the sequence is negative and the second term is positive. If the sixth term is 28, what is the value of c?

   (A) 3
   (B) 4
   (C) 5
   (D) 6
   (E) 7

6. If $x^2 - 6x \le -8$, which of the following is a possible value of x?

    (A) −7
    (B) −5
    (C) −3
    (D) 0
    (E) 3

7. If the measures of the angles of a triangle are in a 1:3:5 ratio, what is the measure of the largest angle?

    (A) 20°
    (B) 40°
    (C) 60°
    (D) 80°
    (E) 100°

8. One number is 5 less than half of another number. If the sum of the two numbers is 34, what is the greater of the two numbers?

    (A) 8
    (B) 13
    (C) 24
    (D) 26
    (E) 39

9. Of the 68 students in tenth grade, 31 students take Dutch, 45 students take Polish, and 5 students take neither language. How many students take both Polish and Dutch?

    (A) 8
    (B) 11
    (C) 13
    (D) 18
    (E) 23

10. There are three integers, x, y, and z, such that $x < y < z$. The median of the three numbers is equal to three times their average (arithmetic mean). If $z = 10$, what is the least possible value of y?

    (A) −10
    (B) −9
    (C) −3
    (D) 3
    (E) 9

_____ **1.** $\dfrac{7}{2} + \dfrac{5}{6} =$

_____ **4.** $\dfrac{4}{5} \div \dfrac{3}{10} =$

_____ **2.** $\dfrac{13}{8} - \dfrac{2}{3} =$

_____ **5.** $\dfrac{1}{2}\left(\dfrac{8}{9} + \dfrac{11}{18}\right) =$

_____ **3.** $\dfrac{3}{4} \times \dfrac{2}{3} =$

_____ **6.** $\dfrac{1}{3} \times \dfrac{5}{8} \times \dfrac{9}{7} =$

_____ 7. $\dfrac{\dfrac{2}{3}+\dfrac{3}{5}}{\dfrac{1}{3}}$ =

_____ 9. Elle is trying to plan her monthly budget. She plans to use one fourth of her income on rent, one fourth on shoes, one sixth on hair products, and the rest on food. What fraction of her income is left to spend on food?

_____ 8. Bruiser is planning his budget. Daddy Woods gives him an allowance of $200 a month. If he spends one half of his allowance on candy, one quarter on ice cream, and one fifth on dental care, what fraction of his allowance did he spend?

_____ 10. Sweetie and Cutie are making horse treats for the annual pony show. They have a recipe that calls for: $1\dfrac{1}{2}$ cups of oats, $\dfrac{3}{4}$ cup of apples, $2\dfrac{1}{4}$ cups of hay, and $\dfrac{1}{2}$ cup of carrots. After mixing all the ingredients together, carrots make up what fraction of the mix?

RATIO DRILL

_____ 1. In Jackson Middle School's 8th grade class, there are 24 boys and 16 girls. What is the ratio of boys to girls in the class? (Remember to simplify!)

_____ 2. A certain recipe for apple pie calls for 3 cups of crust for every 5 cups of filling. If you use 12 cups of crust, how many cups of filling do you need?

_____ 3. For every 4 hot dogs he eats, Fat Sal drinks 5 Big Sip soda pops. If Fat Sal ate 20 hot dogs on Tuesday, how many sodas did he drink?

_____ 4. At Pablo's Perfect Petting Zoo, Pablo keeps llamas and goats. There are 3 llamas for every 4 goats. If there are 28 animals, how many llamas does Pablo have?

_____ 5. Bob's Bookstore stocks books and magazines in a 5 to 3 ratio. If this week Bob stocked 40 total items, how many magazines did he stock?

_____ 6. If x is directly proportional to y and $x = 6$ when $y = 9$, what is x when $y = 24$?

_____ 7. Terry's truck has a 20-gallon gas tank. On a full tank, Terry can drive 375 miles. How many tankfuls of gas would Terry need to drive from Boston to Seattle (3000 miles)?

_____ 8. 20% of the employees at a company are single, childless, and lonely. Of the rest, half are married with children, and half are married without children. What is the ratio of employees with children to employees without children?

_____ 9. Steve's Grocery Delivery Truck delivers groceries to Sam's Little Grocery Store, and each shipment contains meat, dairy, and produce in a 1:5:10 ratio by weight. If this week's delivery weighs 480 pounds, how many pounds of dairy does it contain?

_____ 10. A certain type of cotton gin working at a constant rate will separate 3 bushels of cotton in 2 hours. If 3 of these cotton gins work simultaneously, how long, in hours, will it take them to separate 36 bushels of cotton?

_____ **1.** What is 60 percent of 45?

_____ **2.** 15 is 20% of what number?

_____ **3.** 45 is what percent of 75?

_____ **4.** 16 is 5% of what number?

_____ **5.** 69 is 23% of what number?

_____ **6.** What is 50% of 15% of 240?

_____ **7.** What is $\frac{1}{2}$ percent of 160?

_____ **8.** Holden goes out to dinner at Salinger's Saloon, and his bill is $36 without a tip. What will his total cost in dollars be if he pays his bill with a 15% tip?

_____ **9.** Timmy earns a 5% commission on every vehicle he sells at Lenny's Lemon Lot. On Friday, he sold a car for $450, a truck for $1,300 and a scooter for $200. How much money in dollars did Timmy earn in commissions on Friday?

_____ **10.** In February, Rosie's Flower shop sold 300 bouquets of roses for $40 each, 250 bunches of tulips for $30 each, and 44 wedding centerpieces at $125 each. In March, Rosie advertised a special St. Patty's Day clover arrangement, and the shop made a total of $30,000 in sales. What was the percent increase in her sales from February to March?

EXPONENT DRILL

Simplify the following expressions:

_____ 1. $\left(4x^2\right)\left(2x^3\right) =$

_____ 2. $\dfrac{12x^4}{3x^2} =$

_____ 3. $\left(3x^2\right)^3 =$

_____ 4. $\dfrac{15x^{10}}{5x^5x^2} =$

_____ 5. $\left(5x^2\right)\left(x^{-4}\right) =$

_____ 6. $\left(9x^4\right)^{\frac{1}{2}} =$

_____ 7. $\left(2^x\right)\left(8^{2x}\right) =$

_____ 8. $\left(2x^2\right)^3 + 3x\left(2x^5\right) =$

_____ 9. $\left(\dfrac{\left(5x\right)\left(5x^3\right)}{x^2}\right)^{\frac{1}{2}} =$

_____ 10. $\dfrac{10x^2\left(\dfrac{4x^5}{2x^3} + 6x^2\right)}{4x^3} =$

_____ 1. There are five numbers whose average is 16. The average of three of the numbers is 10. What is the average of the remaining two numbers?

_____ 2. A certain block on 105th Street has 8 buildings with an average height of 62 feet. After a new building is constructed on a formerly empty lot, the average height of all 9 buildings is now 74 feet. What is the height, in feet, of the new building?

_____ 3. The average of 5, 13, and x is 15. What is the average of 10, 26, and $2x$?

_____ 4. What is the least of six consecutive even integers whose median is 29?

_____ 5. Jenny has six weeks to read a 1200-page book for a book report. She reads an average of 150 pages per week for the first four weeks. How many pages per week must Jenny read over the last two weeks in order to finish the book?

Questions 6-10 use the following information:

Number of students	Grade
7	70
5	100
4	90
2	80
1	50
1	60

The table above shows the grades for 20 students who took Monday's geography test in Ms. Frizzle's class. The test was scored on a range from 0 to 100.

_____ 6. What was the mode of the scores on the test?

_____ 7. What was the average (arithmetic mean) score on the test?

_____ 8. What was the median score on the test?

_____ 9. Five students were absent on the day of the test so their grades were not included in the table. When they took the test on Tuesday, they each received a score of 100. What is the new average score for all 25 students in the class?

_____ 10. What is the new median score for all 25 students in the class?

ONE-VARIABLE ALGEBRA DRILL

Solve the following equations for <u>all</u> possible solutions.

_____ **1.** $5x + 3 = 18$

_____ **2.** $4x - 55 + 3x = 2x$

_____ **3.** $13 - 3z = 15z + 4$

_____ **4.** $\dfrac{5}{x} = \dfrac{2}{3}$

_____ **5.** $x + 4 > \dfrac{x}{5}$

_____ **6.** $(p + 4)^2 = 36$ and $p > 0$

_____ **7.** $x^2 - x = 0$

_____ **8.** $\dfrac{r}{8} = \dfrac{2}{r}$

_____ **9.** $\sqrt{x + 4} = 9$

_____ **10.** $\dfrac{2(q + 8.5)}{9} = \dfrac{5q + 5}{10}$

_____ **1.** If $y = 5x + 6$, then what is x in terms of y ?

_____ **2.** If $\dfrac{m-15}{4} = n + 3$, then what is m in terms of n ?

_____ **3.** If $z = 10 + 2x$ and $z = x - 5$, then $z = ?$

_____ **4.** If $x = 5t + 13$ and $y = 2 - t$, then what is x in terms of y ?

_____ **5.** If $t = 4u - 24$ and $3v - t = 16$, then what is u in terms of v?

_____ **6.** If $j = k + 1$, $k + 2 = m$, and $m - 5 = n$, then what is j in terms of n?

_____ **7.** If $2x + 3y = 31$ and $x - 2y = 5$, then what is the value of y?

_____ **8.** If $3a + b = 12$ and $\dfrac{2a + 2b}{3} = 12$, then what are the values of a and b?

_____ **9.** If $z = 3x^2$ and $x = y + 5$, then what is z in terms of y?

_____ **10.** If $a = bc$, $d = b - 5$, and $c = d - 3$, then what is a in terms of d?

90

SOLVE DIRECTLY FOR EXPRESSIONS

64 ___ **1.** If $3x - 10 = 32$, then $6x - 20 = ?$

$2 \, (3x - 10 = 32)$

$\dfrac{32 \times 2}{64}$

$6x - 20 = 64$

23 ___ **2.** If $2x + 5y = 11$ and $3x - 2y = 12$, what is the value of $5x + 3y$?

$5x + 3y = \dfrac{\overset{11}{+12}}{23}$

$$a + b = 9$$
$$b + c = 22$$
$$a + c = 17$$

24 ___ **3.** Given the equations above, what is the value of the sum of a, b, and c?

$a =$
$b =$
$c =$

$a + b + b + c + a + c = 48$

$\dfrac{2a + 2b + 2c = 48}{2} = 24$

−278−

$\dfrac{2}{}$ | $\dfrac{2}{}$

404 ___ **4.** If $x^2 + y^2 = 36$ and $xy = 5$, what is the value of $(x + y)^2$?

$(x+y)^2 = (x+y)(x+y)$

$x^2 + 2xy + y^2 = 36 + 10 = 46$

$x^2 + y^2 = 36$

$xy = 5 \cdot 2$

18 ___ **5.** If $(3x - 3)(3x + 3) = 9$, what is the value of $9x^2$?

$3x(3x + 3) - 3(3x + 3) = 9$

$9x^2 + 9x - 9x - 9 = 9$

$9x^2 - 9 = 9$
$\dfrac{+9 \quad +9}{18}$

$9x^2 = 18$

$3x \quad -3$

$3x$ | $9x^2$ | $3x-3$
3 | $9x$ | -9

16

6. If $(x + y)(x - y) = 4$, what is the value of $(2x + 2y)(2x - 2y)$?

$$x^2 - y^2 = 4$$
$$2x^2 - 2y^2 = 4x^2 - 4y^2$$
$$4(x^2 - y^2) =$$
$$4(4) = 16$$

4

7. If $\dfrac{x^2 y}{2x} = 2$ and $x \neq 0$, what is the value of xy ?

$$\frac{x^2 y}{2x} \qquad \frac{x \cdot \cancel{x} \cdot y}{2 \cdot \cancel{x}}$$

$$\frac{xy}{\cancel{(2)2}} = 2(2) \qquad xy = 4$$

8. If $a^2 + b^2 = c + 5$, $ab = c - 5$, and $c > 0$, what is $(a + b)^2$ in terms of c ?

$$(a+b)^2 = a^2 + b^2 + 2ab$$

9. If $\dfrac{a + 2b}{b} = \dfrac{8}{3}$ and $b \neq 0$, what is the value of $\dfrac{a}{b}$?

$$(2b)\frac{a + 2b}{b} = \frac{8}{3}(2b) \qquad \frac{a + 2 \cdot b}{b}$$

$$\frac{a}{b} = \frac{16b}{3} = 8b$$

10. If $b = a + 3c$ and $a + 2b + 3c = 12$, $b = $?

$$b = a + 3c$$
$$a + 2b + 3c = 12$$

$$a + 2(a + 3c) + 3c = 12$$
$$a + 2a + 6c + 3c = 12$$
$$\frac{3a + 9c = 12}{3}$$
$$\boxed{a + 3c = 4}$$

(handwritten, circled in pink at top) 100

35° *(handwritten)*

(handwritten work)
```
 18010
-145
  35
```

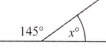

_____ 1. What is the value of x?

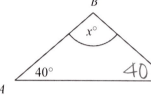

100° *(handwritten)*

(handwritten work)
```
40+40 = 80
100+80 = 180
```

_____ 2. In the figure above, AB = BC. What is the value of x?

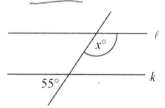

125° *(handwritten)*

(handwritten work)
```
 17
 18010
 - 55
 125
```

_____ 3. In the figure above, lines ℓ and k are parallel. What is the value of x?

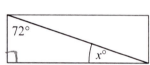

18° *(handwritten)*

(handwritten work)
```
 90      17
+72     18010
162    -162
         18
```

_____ 4. The figure above shows a rectangle. What is the value of x?

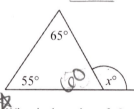

120° *(handwritten)*

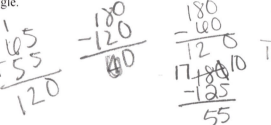

(handwritten work)
```
  65      180        180           55
 +55     -120        -60           55
 120       40        120           65
                  17 18010        125
                   -125
                    55
```

⊛ 5. What is the value of x?

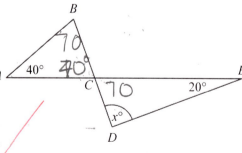

90° *(handwritten)*

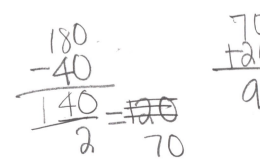

(handwritten work)
```
 180        70
 -40       +20
 140        90
  2 = 70
```

_____ 6. In the figure above, AB = AC. What is the value of x?

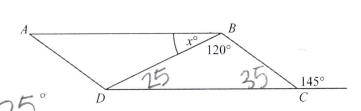

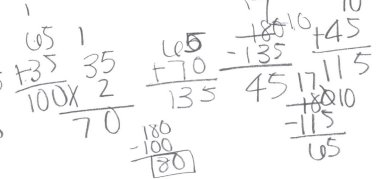

25° _____ **7.** In the figure above, *ABCD* is a parallelogram. What is the value of *x*?

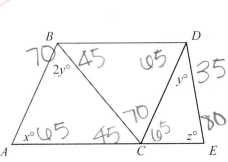

$$\begin{array}{r} 65 \\ +35 \\ \hline 100 \end{array} \times 2 \quad 35 \quad \begin{array}{r} 65 \\ +70 \\ \hline 135 \end{array}$$

$$\begin{array}{r} {}^{1}70 \\ -100 \\ \hline 80 \end{array}$$

$$\begin{array}{r} {}^{7}\cancel{8}10 \\ -135 \\ \hline 45 \end{array} \quad \begin{array}{r} 70 \\ +45 \\ \hline 115 \end{array}$$

$$\begin{array}{r} {}^{1}7 \\ \cancel{8}\cancel{8}10 \\ -115 \\ \hline 65 \end{array}$$

80° _____ **8.** In the figure above, *AB* ∥ *CD* and *BD* ∥ *AE*. If *x* = 65 and *y* = 35, what is the value of *z*?

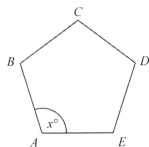

$$(5-2)180$$
$$3 \times 180 = \frac{540}{5}$$

$$5\overline{\smash{)}540} \quad \begin{array}{r}108\end{array}$$
$$-5 \\ 40$$

108° _____ **9.** In the figure above, *ABCDE* is a regular pentagon. What is the value of *x*?

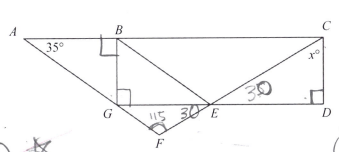

$$\begin{array}{r} 90 \\ +35 \\ \hline 125 \end{array} \quad \begin{array}{r} {}^{1}7\cancel{8}\cancel{8}10 \\ -125 \\ \hline 55 \end{array}$$

$$\begin{array}{r} 90 \\ +30 \\ \hline 120 \end{array} \quad \begin{array}{r} 55 \\ +90 \\ \hline 145 \end{array} \quad \begin{array}{r} {}^{1}7\cancel{8}\cancel{8}10 \\ -115 \\ \hline 65 \end{array}$$

$$\begin{array}{r} {}^{1}7 \\ \cancel{8}\cancel{8}10 \\ -145 \\ \hline 35 \end{array}$$

$$\begin{array}{r} 180 \\ -120 \\ \hline 60 \end{array}$$

$$\frac{65}{2}$$

$$2\overline{\smash{)}65}$$

60 ⊗ _____ **10.** In the figure above, *BCDG* is a rectangle and *AF* ∥ *BE*. If *C* and *F* lie on a straight line and ∠*GFE* = 115°, what is the value of *x*?

TRIANGLE DRILL

(handwritten, circled: 95)

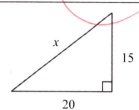

(handwritten: 3, 4, 5)
(handwritten: 15 20 25)

25 _____ 1. What is the value of x?

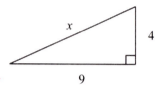

(handwritten right side:)
$$4^2 + 9^2 = C^2$$
$$16 + 81 = C^2$$
$$\frac{+81}{97} \qquad \sqrt{97} =$$

$\sqrt{97}$ _____ 2. What is the value of x?

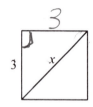

$3\sqrt{2}$ _____ 3. The figure above shows a square. What is the value of x?

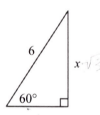

$3\sqrt{3}$ _____ 4. What is the value of x?

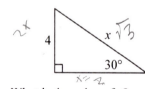

$2\sqrt{3}$ *(circled)* _____ 5. What is the value of x?

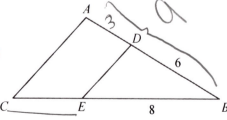

(handwritten:)
$$\frac{3}{x} = \frac{3}{4}$$
$$3 \times 4 = \frac{12}{3} = 4$$

4 _____ 6. In the figure above, $AC \parallel DE$. If $AB = 9$, what is the value of CE?

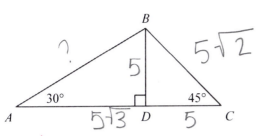

_**10**_   **7.** In the figure above, if $BC = 5\sqrt{2}$, what is the value of AB?

$x < \boxed{10}$

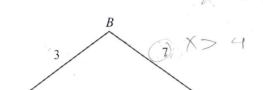

Note: Figure not drawn to scale.

7 $x > 4$

$\boxed{5,6}$ $7,8,9$

_**5, 6**_   **8.** In the figure above, BC is the largest side of the triangle. If $\triangle ABC$ is not isosceles, what is one possible value for the length of AC?

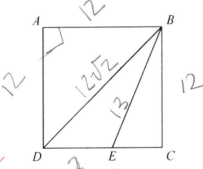

_**7**_   **9.** In the figure above, $ABCD$ is a square, $BD = 12\sqrt{2}$ and $BE = 13$. What is the length of DE?

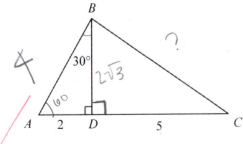 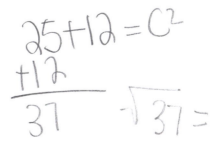

$25 + 12 = C^2$

$+12$

37 $\sqrt{37} =$

**$\sqrt{37}$**   **10.** What is the length of BC?

83

PERIMETER, AREA, VOLUME DRILL

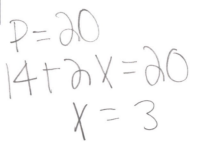

$P = 20$

$14 + 2x = 20$

$x = 3$

3

1. The rectangle shown above has a perimeter of 20. What is the value of x?

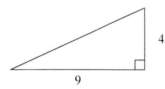

$10 + 12 = 22$

22

2. The rectangle shown above has an area of 30. What is the perimeter of the rectangle?

18

3. What is the area of the triangle shown above?

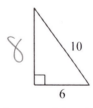

$36 + b^2 = 100$

$b^2 = \sqrt{64}$

$b = 8$

24

4. What is the area of the triangle shown above?

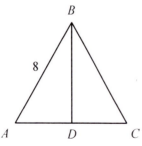

$a^2 + 16 = 64$

$a^2 = 48$

$a = 4\sqrt{3}$

16√3

5. In the figure above $\triangle ABC$ is equilateral and $BD \perp AC$. What is the area of $\triangle ABC$?

$A = \dfrac{bh}{2}$

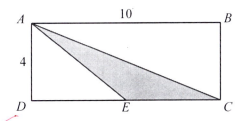

$$\frac{5(4)}{2} = 10$$

_10_ **6.** In the figure above, *ABCD* is a rectangle and *E* is the midpoint of *DC*. What is the area of the shaded region?

_63π_ **7.** What is the volume of a right circular cylinder with radius 3 and height 7?

$$V = \pi r^2 h$$
$$V = \pi 9(7)$$
$$V = 63\pi$$

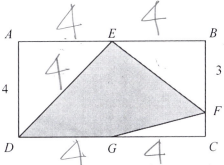

_8_ **8.** In the figure above, *ABCD* is a rectangle. *E* is the midpoint of *AB* and *G* is the midpoint of *DC*. If *AB* = 8, what is the area of the shaded region?

$$\frac{4(4)}{2} = 8$$

_630_ **9.** A rectangular box has dimensions of 3 centimeters by 5 centimeters by 7 centimeters. What is the surface area, in square centimeters, of the box?

$$15(7) = 105 \times 6 = 630$$

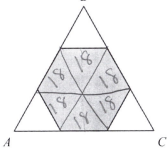

_108_ **10.** In the figure above, △*ABC* is an equilateral triangle with area 18 and the shaded region is a regular hexagon. What is the area of the shaded hexagon?

CIRCLE DRILL

9π

1. What is the area of a circle with radius 3?

$A = \pi r^2$
$A = (\pi) 3^2$

14π

2. What is the circumference of a circle with radius 7?

$C = \pi d$
$C = 7(2)\pi$

25π

3. What is the area of a circle with diameter 10?

$A = \pi 5^2$ $\dfrac{10}{2} = 5$

$A = 25\pi$

18π

4. What is the area of a semicircle with radius 6?

$A = \pi 6^2$
$A = 36\pi$

$\overline{2}\ \ A = 18\pi$

64π

5. What is the area of a circle with circumference of 16π?

$C = \pi d$

$d = \dfrac{16}{2}$ $r = 8$

$A = \pi 8^2$

12

12   12   12

12

360π

6. The figure above shows a circle inscribed within a square. If the square has a side of length 12, what is the area of the circle?

$r = 6$
$A = \pi r^2$
$A = 6^2 \pi$

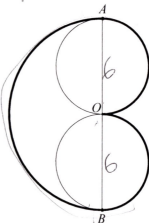

12π

7. The figure above is composed of two small circles and one large semicircle. *AB* is a diameter of the large circle, and *AO* and *OB* are diameters of the two small circles. If the radius of the large circle is 6, what is the total length of the darkened edge of the figure?

$C = \pi d$

$\dfrac{C = 12\pi}{2}$ $C = 6\pi + 6\pi$
12π

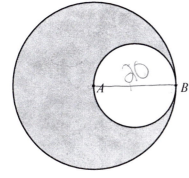

300π

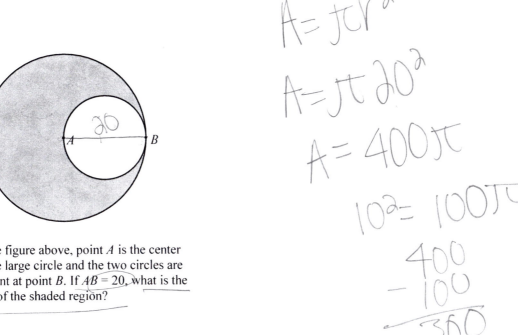

$A = \pi r^2$

$A = \pi \, 20^2$

$A = 400\pi$

$10^2 = 100\pi$

```
 400
-100
 300
```

_____ 8. In the figure above, point *A* is the center of the large circle and the two circles are tangent at point *B*. If *AB* = 20, what is the area of the shaded region?

3. 9. In circle *O* shown above, ∠*AOB* = 45° and the length of arc *ACB* = $\frac{3}{2}\pi$. What is the radius of the circle?

$\frac{3}{2}\pi$

$C = 2\pi r^2$

$\frac{45}{360} = \frac{3/2\pi = 1.5}{L}$

$C = 12/2 \, r = 6$

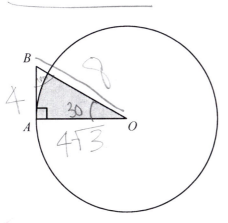

4π

10. In the figure above, ∠*BOA* = 30° and *OB* = 8. What is the area of the shaded region?

$\frac{30}{360} = \frac{x = 4\pi}{48\pi}$

A of circle = 48π

F(X) Drill

Questions 1 to 20 refer to the following functions:

Let $f(x) = 6x - 8$
Let $g(x) = x^2 - x$

_22_ **1.** $f(5) =$

$6(5) - 8$
$30 - 8 =$

_-26_ **2.** $f(-3) =$

$6(-3) - 8$
$-18 + 8 = -26$
8
20

_-6_ **3.** $f\left(\frac{1}{3}\right) =$

$6\left(\frac{1}{3}\right) - 8$
$18 - 8 = 10$

_12a-8_ **4.** $f(2a) =$

$6(2a) - 8$
$12a - 8$

_52_ **5.** If $f(3) = w$, what is the value of $f(w)$?

$w = 6(3) - 8$ $18 - 8 = \boxed{10}$
_a_ $10(6) - 8$ $60 - 8$

___ **6.** If $f(c) = 46$, what is the value of c?

_2_ **7.** If $2f(d) - 4 = 4$, what is the value of d?
$\frac{2}{2}$

$f(d) = 4$ $6d - 8 = 4$
$\underline{+8 \quad +8}$
$\frac{6d}{6} = \frac{12}{6}$ $d = 2$

_6_ **8.** If $f(z - 2) = 10$, what is the value of z?

~~$f(z-2) = 10$~~
$6(z-2) - 8 = 10$
$z = 6$

_56_ **9.** $g(8) =$

$8^2 - 8 =$

_12_ **10.** $g(-3) =$

$-3^2 - 3$

_-1/4_ **11.** $g\left(\frac{1}{2}\right) =$

$\frac{1}{2}^2 - \frac{1}{2}$

_4x⁴+2x²_ **12.** $g(-2x^2) =$
$\boxed{4X^4 + 2X^2}$

$(-2X^2)^2 - (-2X^2)$

_x²+7x+12_ **13.** $g(x+4) =$
$\boxed{X^2 + 7X + 12}$ $= 9$

$(X+4)^2 - (X+4) = 9$
$X^2 - X(X+4)$

_60_ **14.** $3g(5) =$

$3(X^2 - X)(5) = 60$

_0 or 1_ **15.** If $g(q) = 0$, what are the two possible values of q?

$X^2 - X = 0$

© A-List Services LLC

$z = 6$

64 _____ **16.** If $g(4) = v$, what is the value of $f(v)$?

$$x^2 - x(4) = (6x-8)v \qquad f(v)=$$

42 _____ **17.** If $f(-1) = k - 8$, what is the value of $g(k)$?

$$k-8=-14$$
$$k=-6$$

1 _____ **18.** If $g(3) = 4t$, what is the value of $f(t)$?

$$(x^2-x)(3) = 4t \qquad (t)=\frac{3}{2}$$

4.35 _____ **19.** If $f(2.5) = m$, what is the value of $\boxed{g(\sqrt{m})}$?

$$f(2.5)=m \qquad g(\sqrt{7}) \qquad (x+4)(x+4)=x^2+8x+16$$
$$=x^2+8x+16-x+4$$
$$x^2+7x-12$$

128 _____ **20.** If $g(-8) = f(-8) + s$, what is the value of s?

$$x^2 - x(8) = (6x-8)(-8)+s$$

$$x^2-1x(x+4)$$

$$x^3+4x^2-x^2-4x$$

289 –

GRAPHING DRILL

Questions 1 through 10 refer to the figure below:

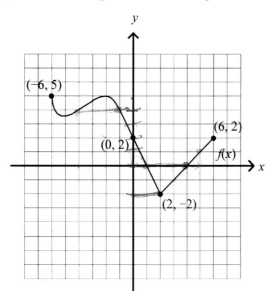

The function f graphed above is defined for
−6 < x < 6.

1. What is the value of f(−4)?

2. What is the value of f(5) + 7?

3. What is the value of 4f(3) − 2?

−4 ± 2 = −6

4. If f(b) = 5, what is one possible value of b?

5. If f(1) = k, what is the value of k?

1 < x < 4

6. For what values of x is f(x) negative?

7. For how many different values of x does f(x) = 4?

f(y)

8. If f(p) = f(4), which of the following could be p?

(A) −4
(B) 0
(C) 1
(D) 3
(E) 8

9. If g(x) = f(x − 2), what is the value of g(1)?

g(1) = f(1 − 2)

f(−1)

10. If h(x) = f(2x) + 3, what is the value of h(−2)?

h(−2) = f(2(−2)) + 3

Questions 11 through 20 refer to the figure below:

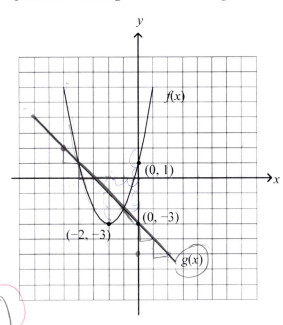

f(x)

(0, 1)

(0, −3)

(−2, −3)

g(x)

O

_____ **11.** What is the value of *f*(−3)?

8

_____ **12.** What is the value of *f*(1) + *g*(−5)?

6 + 2 = 8

2

_____ **13.** What is the value of *f*(−2) − *g*(2)?

−3 + (+5) = 2

0, −4

_____ **14.** If *f*(a) = 1, what could be the value of *a*?

_____ **15.** If *f*(−4) = −k, what is the value of *g*(k)?

_____ **16.** If *g*(0) = m, what is the value of *f*(m) + 6?

−1

_____ **17.** What is the slope of the graph of *g*(x)?

−1

_____ **18.** If *f*(r) = −3, what is the value of *g*(r)?

_____ **19.** What are all values of *x* between −7 and 2 for which *f*(x) ≤ *g*(x)?

−4 ≤ X ≤ 1

B

_____ **20.** Which of the following could be the equation of the graph of *f*(x)?

(A) $f(x) = -x^2 - 4x + 1$

(B) $f(x) = x^2 + 4x + 1$

(C) $f(x) = x^2 - 2x + 3$

(D) $f(x) = x^2 + 2x - 3$

(E) $f(x) = x^2 - 6x + 7$

APPENDIX B: WRITING DRILLS

VERB AGREEMENT DRILL

Circle the verb form that appropriately agrees with its subject.

1. Lynn, one of my best friends, **| is / are |** taking me to New Hampshire this weekend.

2. Despite the often unbearable heat, residents of Houston **| stay / stays |** in the city during the summer.

3. The staff of pastry chefs **| is / are |** working around the clock due to the holiday rush.

4. Pizza, originally introduced to the U.S. by Italian immigrants, **| has / have |** become a thoroughly American fast food.

5. For someone new to New York, the process of looking at apartments to rent **| is / are |** often daunting.

6. Nightmares about his student's performance on the national exam **| has / have |** plagued the tutor every night this week.

7. Each individual animal in the exhibit, including all the gulls, the seals, and the penguins, **| was / were |** prescribed a unique, specialized diet according to its particular needs.

8. Out of the cracks in the cobblestones **| grow / grows |** a tangle of weeds and wildflowers.

9. Ever since the movie was released, there **| has / have |** been many rumors about the co-stars' off-screen relationship.

10. Oprah Winfrey's business ventures, which include television shows, charities, a book club, and a magazine, **| has / have |** made her the most influential woman in the world.

PRONOUN AGREEMENT DRILL

Circle the pronoun that appropriately agrees with its antecedent.

1. Susan and Molly never enjoyed playing Scrabble until [**she** / **they**] started studying vocabulary.

2. If one speeds on the highway, [**you** / **one**] may get pulled over by the police.

3. Though [**it** / **they**] may not be very social, the house rabbit makes an excellent pet.

4. Reality television, which has given rise to a new type of celebrity, makes up a huge share of the market due to [**its** / **their**] relatively low production costs.

5. The coach informed his players that [**he** / **they**] would be retiring at the end of the season.

6. A huge number of zombies approached the school, but we were not intimidated; [**it was** / **they were**] clumsy, stupid, and easy to evade.

7. Representatives on the city-wide planning committee will need to get the support of [**his or her** / **their**] constituents in order to approve the construction of a new park.

8. Every teenage girl argues with [**her** / **their**] mother occasionally, but I used to fight with my mother every day.

9. Although [**it** / **they**] had already played for four hours, the ukulele band played four encores to thunderous applause at the end of its sold-out concert.

10. As recent graduates, we knew that the US debt crisis, though not as severe as that of other countries, would negatively impact [**their** / **our**] ability to get good jobs right out of college.

Circle the underlined phrase that makes a parallelism error, or "No error". If there is an error, write a correction of the underlined phrase below the sentence.

1. Neither the mayor <u>or</u> the governor <u>is</u> attending <u>the opening</u> <u>of</u> the new park. <u>No error</u>
                A   B   C   D   E

2. <u>Kenan's</u> study habits are far more <u>effective</u> <u>than</u> <u>his friend Kel</u>. <u>No error</u>
     A   B   C   D   E

3. The doctor <u>warned</u> the injured football player <u>to be</u> careful both on the field and <u>he should be careful off</u>
            A   B   C
   the field for <u>as long as</u> he is in physical therapy. <u>No error</u>
             D   E

4. Although <u>seemingly</u> simpler, the <u>orchestrations for jazz music</u> are just <u>as</u> technically challenging as
                A   B   C
   <u>classical music</u>. <u>No error</u>
      D   E

5. At his mother's <u>urging</u>, David not only cleaned both his room <u>and</u> his parents' room <u>but also</u> mowed
                 A   B   C
   the lawn, did his own laundry, and <u>went</u> to the store. <u>No error</u>
                              D   E

6. When practicing vinyasa yoga, a form derived <u>from ancient Indian tradition</u>, you should strive to
                                            A
   breathe deeply, <u>flow</u> between poses, and <u>contraction of</u> <u>your</u> muscles. <u>No error</u>
                  B   C   D   E

7. <u>According to</u> Maslow's hierarchy of needs, every human being <u>requires</u> air to breathe, food to <u>eat</u>, a
     A   B   C
   place to live, <u>and should have</u> water to drink. <u>No error</u>
                 D   E

8. <u>Although</u> originally pop stars, both Justin Timberlake <u>as well as</u> Mandy Moore <u>are</u> now more well
      A   B   C
   known for their movies than <u>for their music</u>. <u>No error</u>
                             D   E

9. <u>It is</u> much more satisfying to cook for <u>a group of</u> people than <u>cooking a meal for</u> <u>only one</u> person.
     A   B   C   D
   <u>No error</u>
     E

10. <u>Much bigger</u> than <u>Columbia's landing</u> in 1981, the crowd that <u>gathered</u> to witness the space shuttle
         A   B   C
    Atlantis' final landing marked the end of an era in <u>the nation's space program</u>. <u>No error</u>
                                                 D   E

VERB TENSE DRILL

Circle the verb form that is in the appropriate tense.

1. After Daniel left for college, his mother | **converts** / **converted** | his bedroom into a workout room.

2. Alexandra | **sees** / **saw** | all twenty-three of her cousins whenever she goes back home for her family reunion.

3. Charles Lindbergh was catapulted to international fame when he successfully | **flies** / **flew** | from New York to Paris in 1927, the first non-stop transatlantic flight in history.

4. I always pay my rent as soon as I | **received** / **receive** | the bill.

5. Every year there is a new trend in fantasy fiction: last year it was vampires, this year it is zombies, and next year it | **is** / **will be** | something else.

6. In 1291, the communities of Uri, Schwyz, and Nidwalden | **have allied** / **allied** | themselves to form the Old Swiss Confederacy, the precursor to modern Switzerland.

7. Despite growing up close to the beach, Marjorie had never | **swam** / **swum** | in the ocean until she went to Greece.

8. Although treatments and techniques in medicine | **evolved** / **have evolved** | a great deal over the last few centuries, the fundamental needs of patients for care and comfort remain the same.

9. When I was in high school I thought I knew everything, but I | **learned** / **have learned** | a lot since I started college last year.

10. Since 2005, when Lance Armstrong announced his initial retirement, he | **rode** / **has ridden** | in many bicycle races, including the 2009 Tour de France.

FRAGMENT DRILL

Determine whether each sentence is a complete sentence or a sentence fragment. If it is a fragment, write a corrected version below. If it is a complete sentence, circle the subject and verb of each independent clause.

1. On a trip to the mountains, Klaus and his daughters learning the basics of rock climbing.

2. "Spork", an example of a portmanteau, a blend of two words that are merged to form a new word.

3. Poems about war and conquest, which seem violent to today's reader, were considered romantic in the eighteenth century.

4. The five-year-old's playhouse, equipped with a kitchen, bathroom, and lounging area, which cost $10,000 to build.

5. Striving toward sustainable coexistence with the environment, permaculture, which is an approach to architectural and landscape design based on patterns that occur in nature.

6. Searching for the highest ratio of cookie dough to ice cream, Josie sampled every brand at the grocery store and determined that none of them had enough cookie dough.

7. The United States Flag Code lays out the official guidelines for the use of the American flag, many of which are routinely ignored; for example, prohibiting printing the American flag on clothing, bedding, or napkins.

8. The term "Siamese twins", popularized by the famous pair of conjoined twins, Chang and Eng Bunker, who traveled with the P. T. Barnum Circus in the late nineteenth century, but is now considered offensive.

9. His aunt, who was a physician herself and knew how difficult it was to see people in pain, warned him not to go into pediatrics if he couldn't bear to see children suffer.

10. A native of New York City, Theodore Roosevelt, who made his permanent home on Long Island at Sagamore Hill, which became known as the "Summer White House" during the seven summers he spent there as President.

RUN-ON DRILL

Identify which of the following sentences are run-ons. Circle the subject and verb of each independent clause, and circle the connection between the clauses (either the punctuation or the words used to connect the clauses). If it is a run-on, write a suggestion for how to fix it.

1. Travis told me about a new skate park on the east side of town, we should go there tomorrow.

2. Lucy's team had a substantial lead at halftime but wound up losing by just one point.

3. Veterinarians must be familiar with the anatomy of many different species, doctors only have to be familiar with that of humans.

4. People tend to think of democracy in monolithic terms, they are unaware that it can take many different forms.

5. Because his boss refused to listen to any of his ideas for improving the business, Manny decided to leave and start his own company.

6. Our family has a tradition of going camping every June to celebrate the beginning of summer vacation, but last year we had to cancel the trip because my father broke his leg.

7. Although Sophie often read Grimm's fairy tales as a child, she always found Greek myths much more compelling, she preferred the gods and goddesses to the witches and princesses.

8. During the Second Punic War, fought between the Roman Republic and Carthage, Hannibal marched his army, which notably included 37 war elephants, across the Alps; his shrewd war tactics eventually enabled him to defeat the Romans.

9. With the success of "The Wizard of Oz" in 1939, Judy Garland became a role model to little girls across America, however little was known of her troubles with drugs and alcohol.

10. Even though gold medal winner Thomas Hicks was given a strychnine injection during the 1904 Olympic marathon, he was not disqualified for doping, in fact, at the time this procedure was believed to be necessary in order to survive the demanding race.

APPENDIX C: READING DRILLS

SENTENCE COMPLETIONS DRILLS

Easy Drill

1. Federico has a deep ------- meat: he is a passionate carnivore.

ANTICIPATION: _____

___ (A) distrust of
___ (B) resentment of
___ (C) prejudice against
___ (D) fondness for
___ (E) phobia of

2. Yvette acts wild with her peers at school, but her behavior with her family at home is usually -------.

ANTICIPATION: _____

___ (A) tame
___ (B) rowdy
___ (C) mysterious
___ (D) plausible
___ (E) expedient

3. When the teacher complained that the students had not followed his instructions, they pointed out that his directions had been -------, or open to several different interpretations.

ANTICIPATION: _____

___ (A) enlightened
___ (B) ambiguous
___ (C) evident
___ (D) reserved
___ (E) vivid

4. Because there was constant ------- between Gwen and her twin, the sisters were sent to a mediator to ------- their disagreements.

ANTICIPATION 1: _____

ANTICIPATION 2: _____

___ (A) joy . . neglect
___ (B) rancor . . detect
___ (C) discord . . resolve
___ (D) appreciation . . belittle
___ (E) serenity . . prove

5. Although his literary career was a string of marvelous -------, Mark Twain's personal life was marked by a series of -------, including bankruptcy and his daughter's death in 1906.

ANTICIPATION 1: _____

ANTICIPATION 2: _____

___ (A) catastrophes . . novelties ___
___ (B) variations . . calamities ___
___ (C) miseries . . rigors ___
___ (D) successes . . excesses ___
___ (E) triumphs . . sorrows ___

Medium Drill

6. Laurence Olivier, famed for his realistic, unforced acting, delivered performances that were never ------- or --------.

ANTICIPATION 1: _____

ANTICIPATION 2: _____

___ (A) cynical .. generous ___
___ (B) artificial .. affected ___
___ (C) onerous .. confident ___
___ (D) conflicting .. impolite ___
___ (E) hasty .. ambivalent ___

7. The congressman argued that providing help for the jobless makes unemployed people ------- by reducing their motivation to find a job.

ANTICIPATION: _____

___ (A) exhausted
___ (B) complacent
___ (C) devout
___ (D) cheerful
___ (E) uncoordinated

8. Scientists have discovered that stem cells in the lab can ------- assemble into organ-like structures; the cells will suddenly grow into the form of new organs, without being provided with special signals or support.

ANTICIPATION: _____

___ (A) righteously
___ (B) guardedly
___ (C) chronically
___ (D) spontaneously
___ (E) diligently

9. The unruly crowd roared with approval at the play's toilet humor and slapstick comedy, but a more ------- audience might have been offended.

ANTICIPATION: _____

___ (A) fervent
___ (B) egotistical
___ (C) animated
___ (D) crass
___ (E) genteel

10. Historians once thought the reason the Aztecs of Tenochtitlan treated the Spanish explorer Hernando Cortés as an honored guest was that they believed him to be the ------- god Quetzalcoatl

ANTICIPATION: _____

___ (A) insignificant
___ (B) energetic
___ (C) weary
___ (D) revered
___ (E) argumentative

Hard Drill

11. To avoid seeming --------, Henry always strove to deal with his friends in a straightforward, honest way.

ANTICIPATION: _____

___ (A) candid
___ (B) futile
___ (C) amateurish
___ (D) peevish
___ (E) disingenuous

12. The -------- advantages of being at the top of the food chain are outweighed by one great disadvantage: being a big, fearsome predator means you have to satisfy -------- appetite.

ANTICIPATION 1: _____

ANTICIPATION 2: _____

___ (A) scant . . a petite   ___
___ (B) ignominious . . a digressive ___
___ (C) loquacious . . a colossal   ___
___ (D) blithe . . an abridged   ___
___ (E) innumerable . . a gargantuan ___

13. Judith Grace Warren's comportment was an ideal example of the prim, proper manners taught at Miss Porter's School for Girls: she was, in sum, the -------- of the school's teachings.

ANTICIPATION: _____

___ (A) abyss
___ (B) surety
___ (C) epitome
___ (D) stratagem
___ (E) juxtaposition

14. Nineteenth-century reports of grotesque acts of cannibalism among the people of the South Sea Islands have been ------- by modern anthropologists who argue that such tales were exaggerated because of ------- native tribespeople.

ANTICIPATION 1: _____

ANTICIPATION 2: _____

___ (A) overturned . . deference to   ___
___ (B) verified . . transgressions by ___
___ (C) challenged . . esteem for   ___
___ (D) disputed . . bigotry against   ___
___ (E) championed . . contempt for   ___

15. Because Sherwyn's behavior was ordinarily --------, everyone was shocked when his grievous -------- was discovered.

ANTICIPATION 1: _____

ANTICIPATION 2: _____

___ (A) unimpeachable . . altruism   ___
___ (B) irreproachable . . infraction ___
___ (C) divisive . . omission   ___
___ (D) dishonorable . . materialism ___
___ (E) inopportune . . conjecture   ___

Explicit Questions

The German filmmaker F.W. Murnau's silent film *The Last Laugh* may be less widely known today than his darkly expressionist *Nosferatu*, but it is arguably the
Line
more important film because of its technical accomplish-
5   ments. It was in this film that Murnau first experimented with the "unchained camera technique", in which the camera moved around during filming, mounted on a trolley, a crane, and even the cameraman's stomach. This allowed Murnau not only to tell the story from the literal
10 perspective of the protagonist but also to reflect his shifting mental state in the camera angles. This kind of camerawork was unheard of at a time when cameras were very bulky and very heavy. Despite the film's lackluster box-office performance, this innovation was
15 hugely influential with other directors at the time.

MAIN IDEA:

_____

1. According to the passage, one reason *The Last Laugh* was "arguably the more important film" (lines 3-4) was because of its

ANTICIPATION: _____

    (A) method of filming
    (B) musical score
    (C) dark lighting
    (D) complex protagonist
    (E) innovative script

2. The passage states that the "unchained camera technique" (line 6)

ANTICIPATION: _____

    (A) was the primary explanation for the box-office success of *The Last Laugh*
    (B) provided the director with new methods of expression
    (C) contributed to the uniquely dark mood of *Nosferatu*
    (D) allowed the main actor to deliver his lines in new ways.
    (E) was dismissed by other directors as too impractical

Vocab-in-context Questions

Allegiances during the Civil War were far more com-
plex than a simple dichotomy of North versus South. Some people from Northern states were sympathetic to
Line
and fought for the South, and vice versa. Letters from
5   soldiers in battle primarily reveal concerns not of loyalty to country or political ideals but of returning to their homes and providing for their families. Personal conflicts of duty and conscience were not unique to low-level soldiers. There is evidence that General Robert E.
10 Lee was an abolitionist at heart, supporting the Confederacy mostly out of loyalty to his native Virginia. President Lincoln himself openly mourned the death of Confederate brigadier general Benjamin Helm, his own brother-in-law.

MAIN IDEA:

_____

3. In line 3, "sympathetic to" most nearly means

ANTICIPATION: _____

    (A) supportive of
    (B) amorous toward
    (C) cordial with
    (D) aggressive to
    (E) consolatory for

4. In line 8, "unique" most nearly means

ANTICIPATION: _____

    (A) eccentric
    (B) bizarre
    (C) inexplicable
    (D) available
    (E) exclusive

Inferential Questions

The so-called "Spanish" flu of 1918 claimed more victims in a single year than the Black Death claimed in a century. However, as the disease raged, most were
Line unaware of the extent of the destruction. Countries
5 fighting in World War I suppressed news of the flu's devastation in order to protect morale. Spain, neutral during the war, was the lone country in Europe producing accurate coverage of the disease's toll, so it got the blame for the outbreak. In reality, scientists now
10 believe that the disease likely emerged near Fort Riley, Kansas, where it spread from U.S. military encampments to battlefields worldwide.

MAIN IDEA:

_____

5. The author would most likely agree with which of the following statements?

ANTICIPATION: _____

   (A) It is important for countries to provide honest assessments of public health issues.
   (B) Spain was the only nation to accurately report its war deaths.
   (C) During the Black Death most countries were not significantly affected by war.
   (D) The name of a disease does not necessarily reflect its actual origin.
   (E) The unsanitary conditions of the war allowed the flu to spread more rapidly.

6. It can be inferred from line 4-9 ("Countries… outbreak.") that some people

ANTICIPATION: _____

   (A) were unhappy with Spain's neutrality during the war
   (B) tried to prevent Spain from accurately reporting its death toll
   (C) were better able to immunize their citizens against the flu
   (D) lacked technology necessary to calculate the death toll of the disease
   (E) erroneously believed that Spain had higher flu casualties than the rest of Europe

Main Idea Questions

Given the multitude of wastes and toxins that permeate modern life, it is a moral imperative for all of us to live environmentally friendly lives. If we are not
Line attentive to the way we consume, we are in real danger
5 of using up precious resources, poisoning our air and water, and putting future generations at risk.

But what exactly does it mean to be environmentally friendly? Is it better to use paper towels that kill trees, or electric hand dryers that use electricity (which, in most
10 areas, means burning coal)? Is it worse to use light bulbs that draw a lot of power and must be replaced frequently, or long-lasting bulbs that contain deadly mercury?

MAIN IDEA:

_____

7. The primary purpose of the first paragraph is to

ANTICIPATION: _____

   (A) detail the damage that toxins can inflict on natural habitats
   (B) explain how best to live an environmentally friendly life.
   (C) convey the significance of the impact modern life has on environmental concerns
   (D) foretell the inescapable hazards that modernity will cause for future generations
   (E) chastise those who do not take appropriate steps toward conservation

8. The main idea of the second paragraph is

ANTICIPATION: _____

   (A) daily household decisions have a negligible impact on the environment
   (B) consuming excess energy is ultimately more detrimental than creating excess waste
   (C) determining the most environmentally ethical choice can be difficult
   (D) earlier warnings about the dangers of wastefulness were exaggerated
   (E) proposed solutions for environmental problems ignore the economic realities of modern life

Strategy Questions

The trend towards multiculturalism in the academy
has been a positive one. Multiculturalism is clearly
beneficial to fostering understanding and tolerance. But
Line multiculturalism is utterly irrelevant to scientific inquiry.
5 There's no such thing as "Western medicine" and
"alternative medicine"; there is medicine and there is
nonsense. It is important for me to respect your culture's
traditions and customs, but not if you're making claims
about medicine. When your culture claims that a certain
10 herb relieves headaches, that's an empirical question:
either it works or it doesn't. If it doesn't, then I'm not
taking the herb. If it works, then you should be able to
rigorously prove it. That's science: a formalized way to
distinguish truth from rubbish.

MAIN IDEA:

_____

9. The author uses quotation marks in lines 5-6 in order
    to

ANTICIPATION: _____

    (A) quote an authority on the topic
    (B) characterize terms as illegitimate
    (C) highlight a historical trend
    (D) emphasize an important distinction
    (E) identify expressions that are defined later

10. With respect to the rest of the passage, the first two
    sentences (The trend… tolerance.") serve as a

ANTICIPATION: _____

    (A) clarification of the scope of the author's
        argument
    (B) thesis statement for which evidence is later
        given
    (C) counterpoint that is refuted by the rest of the
        passage
    (D) personal anecdote that demonstrates the
        author's point
    (E) historical reference that gives background
        necessary to understand the topic

Tone Questions

One consequence of the sudden outpouring of
precious minerals in the West was an unusual confluence
of wealth and wildness. Take, for example, the city of
Line Leadville, Colorado, founded in 1877 after the discovery
5 of huge silver deposits nearby. It was the second most
populous city in Colorado and had a renowned opera
house that often hosted celebrities, including the writer
Oscar Wilde. Yet it was still very much a city of the
West. Wilde, who called Leadville "the richest city in the
10 world", spent one evening in a saloon where he reported
seeing "the only rational method of art criticism I have
ever come across. Over the piano was printed a notice:
'Please do not shoot the pianist. He is doing his best.'"

MAIN IDEA:

_____

11. The tone of the passage as a whole is

ANTICIPATION: _____

    (A) cautionary
    (B) nostalgic
    (C) exuberant
    (D) dispassionate
    (E) laudatory

12. Wilde's statement "the only … across" (lines 11-12)
    can best be described as

ANTICIPATION: _____

    (A) earnest
    (B) contemptuous
    (C) ironic
    (D) analytical
    (E) confounded

APPENDIX D: THE VOCABULARY BOX

These are the 500 words in *The A-List Vocabulary Box*. They represent the 500 words that appear most commonly on the SAT Critical Reading section, ordered by frequency of appearance. Learning these words is one of the best ways to gain points on the Reading section. Get to it!

1	DISMISS	51	LAMENT	101	COHERENT	151	RESIGNATION
2	INNOVATIVE	52	PRETENTIOUS	102	PROVINCIAL	152	MAGNANIMOUS
3	SKEPTICAL	53	PARTISAN	103	DEARTH	153	BELIE
4	PROFOUND	54	AUTONOMY	104	EPITOMIZE	154	EXACERBATE
5	ANECDOTE	55	AMBIGUOUS	105	FLOURISH	155	BOMBASTIC
6	UNDERMINE	56	PEDANTIC	106	ZEALOUS	156	ADROIT
7	OBJECTIVE	57	COMPLACENT	107	RECONCILE	157	INCONSEQUENTIAL
8	ADVOCATE	58	NOVEL	108	EXPLOIT	158	TRANQUIL
9	NOSTALGIA	59	REFUTE	109	SOMBER	159	LAVISH
10	INDIFFERENT	60	IDIOSYNCRATIC	110	DEBUNK	160	RESOLUTE
11	RESENT	61	SCORN	111	ADEPT	161	NONCHALANT
12	COMPROMISE	62	OBSOLETE	112	REPROACH	162	PLACID
13	CYNICAL	63	DISCREDIT	113	EXASPERATE	163	OPPORTUNE
14	AESTHETIC	64	INVOKE	114	REMINISCE	164	DILIGENT
15	AMBIVALENT	65	ARTICULATE	115	DIVERGENT	165	SUPPLANT
16	EVOKE	66	DENOUNCE	116	DESPAIR	166	MANDATE
17	DIMINISH	67	DEFER	117	CONDESCEND	167	PROLIFERATE
18	CONTEMPT	68	FUTILE	118	DEBILITATE	168	ERRATIC
19	DISDAIN	69	WHIMSICAL	119	CONCILIATE	169	INSOLENT
20	PRAGMATIC	70	INDUCE	120	INGENUOUS	170	ANACHRONISTIC
21	REVERE	71	ELOQUENT	121	COMMEND	171	GUILE
22	PROVOCATIVE	72	CONTEND	122	CONVOLUTED	172	EVASIVE
23	INDULGE	73	UNIFORM	123	VERSATILE	173	DISPOSITION
24	RHETORIC	74	BOLSTER	124	CANDID	174	PRECARIOUS
25	SCRUTINIZE	75	COMPETENT	125	CALLOUS	175	IMPETUOUS
26	FOSTER	76	EXTRAVAGANT	126	CONJECTURE	176	CONCISE
27	PLAUSIBLE	77	DERIDE	127	AFFLUENT	177	INHIBIT
28	INACCESSIBLE	78	EQUIVOCAL	128	TENACIOUS	178	WARY
29	UNDERSCORE	79	DISPASSIONATE	129	ESOTERIC	179	RECLUSIVE
30	AWE	80	LAUD	130	CAPRICIOUS	180	ACCORD
31	SUBSTANTIATE	81	SOLEMN	131	DUBIOUS	181	PERVASIVE
32	CONFORM	82	HOMOGENEOUS	132	SUCCINCT	182	ENCOMPASS
33	TRIVIAL	83	COLLABORATE	133	RESILIENT	183	HINDER
34	INDIGNATION	84	ELUSIVE	134	INCONGRUOUS	184	SMUG
35	TEMPER	85	NOTORIOUS	135	MANIFEST	185	CONCEDE
36	MUNDANE	86	ADMONISH	136	ANTAGONISTIC	186	FRIVOLOUS
37	VULNERABLE	87	MEDIOCRE	137	ALIENATE	187	EMULATE
38	APATHETIC	88	CONSENSUS	138	REITERATE	188	WISTFUL
39	CREDIBLE	89	ECCENTRIC	139	PRISTINE	189	INNATE
40	ARBITRARY	90	RETICENT	140	EMPIRICAL	190	EARNEST
41	INHERENT	91	ERADICATE	141	EMINENT	191	DUPLICITY
42	DISPARAGE	92	METICULOUS	142	SERENE	192	EXPEDITE
43	DISCERN	93	EMBELLISH	143	HAIL	193	OBFUSCATE
44	PROSPERITY	94	SUPPRESS	144	INCREDULOUS	194	PROSAIC
45	DIGRESS	95	ORTHODOX	145	CONFOUND	195	REVOKE
46	PERPETUAL	96	ASTUTE	146	APPREHENSIVE	196	RENOUNCE
47	ELITIST	97	ENIGMATIC	147	ENUMERATE	197	STEADFAST
48	ASSESS	98	BENIGN	148	PREVALENT	198	CACOPHONY
49	PARADOX	99	BENEVOLENT	149	OBLIVIOUS	199	THERAPEUTIC
50	MELANCHOLY	100	PROLIFIC	150	GRANDIOSE	200	CANTANKEROUS

201	QUELL	251	AMALGAM	301	ENCUMBRANCE	351	CONTRIVED
202	AUSTERE	252	PENCHANT	302	PAUCITY	352	INQUISITIVE
203	MOLLIFY	253	ARDOR	303	EULOGY	353	JUDICIOUS
204	DECRY	254	JADED	304	PRESCIENT	354	EUPHORIA
205	ALTRUISTIC	255	RELINQUISH	305	AUGMENT	355	ENTRENCH
206	CORROBORATE	256	PARAGON	306	AFFABLE	356	PATRONIZE
207	CONCORD	257	EXONERATE	307	ACCLAIM	357	ANIMOSITY
208	ILLUSORY	258	FLAGRANT	308	ALACRITY	358	CAMARADERIE
209	SUBDUE	259	DISSEMINATE	309	PRODIGIOUS	359	MUTABLE
210	SOLICITOUS	260	MITIGATE	310	PALLIATIVE	360	CONSTRAIN
211	ECLECTIC	261	CONSCIENTIOUS	311	NEFARIOUS	361	SURREPTITIOUS
212	EBULLIENT	262	AMIABLE	312	ASCETIC	362	CUNNING
213	CENSURE	263	BELITTLE	313	REDOLENT	363	VINDICTIVE
214	AVERSE	264	JOCULAR	314	CATHARTIC	364	SCRUPULOUS
215	DIFFIDENCE	265	DECORUM	315	ENTHRALL	365	ECSTASY
216	JUXTAPOSE	266	DISGRUNTLED	316	MODICUM	366	SHREWD
217	VENERATE	267	REPUDIATE	317	PERTINENT	367	STAGNANT
218	GENIAL	268	OPAQUE	318	IMPERIOUS	368	ADVERSITY
219	CIRCUMSPECT	269	CAJOLE	319	FELICITY	369	PLIABLE
220	ASCERTAIN	270	IMPASSIONED	320	INSTIGATE	370	PROPAGATE
221	BANAL	271	ENTICE	321	VINDICATE	371	ELUCIDATE
222	DISCREET	272	THWART	322	HEDONISTIC	372	TREACHERY
223	CONDONE	273	DEMEAN	323	INGRATIATING	373	HERETICAL
224	STOIC	274	COMPEL	324	ONEROUS	374	GARISH
225	DAUNT	275	COMPLICITY	325	CONVIVIAL	375	CHRONIC
226	ORNATE	276	ARCHAIC	326	PERNICIOUS	376	NURTURE
227	EXUBERANT	277	OBTUSE	327	INSINUATE	377	VEILED
228	PERSEVERE	278	LANGUID	328	SQUANDER	378	AUDACITY
229	RUDIMENTARY	279	CONCUR	329	DOGMATIC	379	COPIOUS
230	INDIGENOUS	280	SUPERFLUOUS	330	LACONIC	380	DELETERIOUS
231	EUPHEMISM	281	SANGUINE	331	DIVISIVE	381	HARANGUE
232	ESTEEM	282	POIGNANT	332	GALVANIZE	382	INSIPID
233	OMINOUS	283	BELLIGERENT	333	VAPID	383	INCONTROVERTIBLE
234	KEEN	284	MOROSE	334	CORDIAL	384	PERSPICACITY
235	CARNIVOROUS	285	TACT	335	SPURIOUS	385	DIVULGE
236	IRATE	286	COHESIVE	336	PRUDENT	386	CURTAIL
237	DISPARITY	287	EPHEMERAL	337	OBSTINATE	387	MERCURIAL
238	INNOCUOUS	288	DISCREPANCY	338	DISPEL	388	TEDIOUS
239	DOCILE	289	ARID	339	ERUDITE	389	OBSTREPEROUS
240	ITINERANT	290	ESTRANGE	340	NEBULOUS	390	BOISTEROUS
241	LUCID	291	CONSTITUENT	341	VOLATILE	391	PREDILECTION
242	EFFUSIVE	292	WARRANT	342	VICARIOUS	392	INUNDATE
243	TERSE	293	ALLEVIATE	343	WAVER	393	SAGACIOUS
244	FLAMBOYANT	294	CIRCUMSCRIBE	344	DETER	394	PROPENSITY
245	EXTOL	295	CLANDESTINE	345	HACKNEYED	395	NEGLIGIBLE
246	STRIDENT	296	TACIT	346	OPULENT	396	DILATORY
247	ABSTRUSE	297	HAMPER	347	IMPECCABLE	397	FRUGAL
248	TRACTABLE	298	IMPUGN	348	POLARIZE	398	VIGILANT
249	ILLICIT	299	ABATE	349	DISSENT	399	ADULATION
250	FERVENT	300	OBSEQUIOUS	350	TUMULTUOUS	400	ENERVATE

401 IMPARTIAL	426 CLAIRVOYANCE	451 INTELLIGIBLE	476 EQUANIMITY
402 EXALT	427 URBANE	452 POMPOUS	477 AMENABLE
403 ABHOR	428 PROPRIETY	453 BRUSQUE	478 VOLUBLE
404 GREGARIOUS	429 CAUSTIC	454 COMPOSED	479 AVARICE
405 CEREBRAL	430 DISCRETE	455 ATROPHY	480 INCISIVE
406 MERCENARY	431 EXEMPLAR	456 LUXURIOUS	481 MIRTH
407 TRANSITORY	432 COGENT	457 REBUKE	482 SUBVERT
408 INTRANSIGENT	433 UNASSUMING	458 DOGGED	483 PUGNACIOUS
409 INVIGORATE	434 DELINEATE	459 ESPOUSE	484 OFFICIOUS
410 RANCOR	435 CONTRITE	460 TRITE	485 VILIFY
411 CIRCUMVENT	436 EFFACE	461 VACILLATE	486 BERATE
412 VERBOSE	437 SCOFF	462 EFFICACIOUS	487 OBTRUSIVE
413 REPREHENSIBLE	438 AUSPICIOUS	463 HAUGHTY	488 INSULAR
414 GRATUITOUS	439 EXACTING	464 ENCROACH	489 ASSIDUOUS
415 PRECIPITOUS	440 DEPRECATE	465 OBDURATE	490 FACILITATE
416 ABSTINENCE	441 SCATHING	466 FRENETIC	491 CIRCUITOUS
417 FORTHRIGHT	442 ELATED	467 ACRIMONY	492 PENITENT
418 IMPEDE	443 DESPONDENT	468 BURGEON	493 VOLUMINOUS
419 INDICT	444 NEGLIGENT	469 GARRULOUS	494 SPECIOUS
420 USURP	445 CONSOLIDATE	470 TORPOR	495 BUTTRESS
421 AMICABLE	446 FEASIBLE	471 EXORBITANT	496 RECIPROCATE
422 ASPIRE	447 SPORADIC	472 AMELIORATE	497 SPURN
423 GRATE	448 CURSORY	473 BANE	498 TRANSIENT
424 MEAGER	449 BUOYANT	474 INCORRIGIBLE	499 DISCORD
425 REFUGE	450 BRAZEN	475 FLORID	500 LATENT

APPENDIX E: SUMMARIES

MATH SUMMARY

MATH TECHNIQUES

General Strategies

- Before you do anything else, **circle the question** you're being asked.
- **Show your work** for every question. Don't do math in your head.
- If you need a figure that isn't given, **draw one**.

Common Mistakes

- **RTFQ**: make sure you answer the question you're being asked!
- **Fool's Gold**: if a choice seems too easy for a hard question, it's probably wrong.

Target Numbers

- Don't do all the questions! **Skip the last ones**.
- If you take **more time per question**, you'll cut down on carelessness and are more likely to get them right.
- It's not that those questions are too hard for you. It's about doing **fewer questions**, but doing them **more accurately**.

Plug In

- **Pick a number** for the variable.
- Do the problem with that number and get a number for an answer.
- Put the number you chose into the choices and see which gives you the same answer.
- Check all choices. If more than one works, pick a different number.
- Sometimes you have to plug in for more than one variable. Sometimes plugging in for one gives you the value of another.
- Sometimes there are implicit variables—there are no variables with letters, but there is an unnamed value you don't know.
- If a question asks about a **relationship**, try Plug In. That often means **variables in the answer choices**.

Backsolve

- **Start with choice (C)**. Assume that's the answer.
- That's the answer to the question. Put that number through the information given to see if it all matches.
- If it matches, that's your answer. If it doesn't, pick another one.
- If (C) fails, often you can tell whether you want a higher or lower number. If you can't, just pick one.
- If a question is asking for a **value**, try Backsolve. That usually means there are **numbers in the answer choices**.

Guesstimate

- As a rule, all figures are **drawn to scale** unless the question specifically says they aren't.
- Look at the picture. Compare the value you want with the values you know. Get a **rough guess** of what the value should be based on the picture.
- Eliminate choices that are obviously too big or too small. Then you can refine your guess with precise measurement.

MATH FUNDAMENTALS

Arithmetic

- Know some basic **definitions** of numbers: integer, factor, multiple, prime number, remainder, positive/negative, even/odd, prime factor.
- Know how to add, subtract, multiply, and divide **fractions**.
- Solve **ratios** by cross multiplying. Make sure units match across the equals sign.
- A **percent** is a ratio out of 100. Know how to manipulate percents and percent change.
- Know the rules of combining exponents:
  - To multiply exponentials, **add** exponents.
  - To divide exponentials, **subtract** exponents.
  - To raise an exponent to another exponent, **multiply** the exponents.
- Know how to compute **averages**. In a list of terms:
  - *Mean* is the sum over the number of terms.
  - *Median* is the number in the middle when written in order.
  - *Mode* is the most frequent number.
  - Average problems can often be solved via the **sum** instead of the terms. The average times the number of terms equals the sum.

Algebra

- Solve an algebraic equation by getting the **variable by itself**. Move terms around by doing the opposite of any function (e.g. $x + 7 = 12$ means $x = 12 - 7$).
- To multiply binomials, use **FOIL**: Multiply the First terms, the Outside terms, the Inside terms, and the Last terms.
- If a question asks for an **expression** instead of a variable, try to solve for that expression **directly**.
- Know the binomial **identities**:
  - $(x + y)(x - y) = x^2 - y^2$
  - $(x + y)^2 = x^2 + 2xy + y^2$
- **Inequalities** can be manipulated just like equations. Remember to flip the inequality sign if you multiply or divide by a negative.

GEOMETRY

General strategies

- Use **Guesstimate** whenever possible. Try it on *every question with a figure*.
- Need a formula? **Look it up!** There's a bunch of them given at the beginning of the section.
- Not sure what to do? Just start writing down **what you know** about the figure.

Angles

- A **straight line** equals 180°.
- A **triangle** equals 180°.
- An **isosceles triangle** has two equal sides and two equal angles.
- **Vertical angles** are equal.
- **Parallel lines** with a transversal produces two kinds of angles: big ones and little ones.
    - All the big ones are equal.
    - All the little ones are equal.
    - Any big plus any little make 180°.

Triangles

- In a right triangle, **the Pythagorean theorem** says $a^2 + b^2 = c^2$, where a and b are legs and c is the hypotenuse.
- A **45-45-90** triangle has dimensions $x, x, x\sqrt{2}$.
- A **30-60-90** triangle has dimensions $x, x\sqrt{3}, 2x$.
- Any two triangles with the same three angles are **similar**. The lengths of their corresponding sides are in the same ratio with each other.
- The **third side of a triangle** must be smaller than the sum and bigger than the difference of the other two sides.

Perimeter, Area, Volume

- The **perimeter** of a figure is the sum of the lengths of the sides.
- Know some formulas for **area**: triangle = $(1/2)bh$; rectangle = ℓw; square = s^2
- **Shaded area** problems can best be done by subtraction: find the area of the whole figure and subtract the part you don't need.
- **Surface area** is the sum of the areas of the faces of an object.
- Know some formulas for **volume**: box = $\ell w h$; cube = s^3; cylinder = $\pi r^2 h$

Circles

- A circle's center has **360°**.
- The **diameter** goes from end to end of a circle, passing through the center.
- The **radius** goes from the center to the end. The radius is half a diameter.
- The **area** of a circle is πr^2.
- The **circumference** of a circle is $2\pi r$.
- A **slice** of a circle is a fraction of the circle. Everything about that slice is the same fraction: angle, area, and arc length.

FUNCTIONS

Funny Symbols

- If a problem uses a funny symbol, **follow the directions**: the symbol is defined in the question.

F(x) notation

- The notation "$f(x)$" works the same way: **follow the directions**. The value **inside the parentheses** tells you the value of x.
- **Plug that value in** for x. If $f(x) = 2x + 5$, then $f(4) = 2(4) + 5$

Graphing

- Know how to read a **coordinate plane**. The x-axis is horizontal, and the y-axis is vertical.
- A **graph of a function** is a picture of its solutions. Saying "$f(3) = 4$" means that the point $(3, 4)$ appears on the graph of $f(x)$.
- The **slope** of a line is the change in y over the change in x.
- The **equation of a line** can be written $y = mx + b$, where m is the slope and b is the y-intercept.
- A **parabola** can be written with the equation $y = ax^2 + bx + c$, where c is the y-intercept.

MISCELLANY

Combinatorics

- When combining two **separate groups**, multiply the two numbers.
- When arranging things into slots, where **order matters**, multiply the number of possible items for each slot. Once you put something in a slot, you can't use it again.
- If **order doesn't matter**, do the same thing but divide by two, or just write out all possible groups.

Probability

- Probability is the number of **winning events** divided by the **total possible events**.
- The probabilities of all events associated with a problem must **add up to 1**.

Sequences

- If a sequence only has a few terms, treat it like a function: **follow directions** and continue the sequence.
- If a sequence question asks for a really big term, **look for the pattern**.

Absolute Value

- The absolute value of a term is its value without its sign—that is, **make it positive**.

WRITING SUMMARY

ERROR IDENTIFICATION 1

Don't pick (E) too much!

- Choice (E) occurs about as often as any other choice—**about 20% of the time**.
- Use your ear to inform your decision, but don't rely on it—**actively check for structural errors**.

Verb Agreement

- When a verb is underlined, **find its subject** to see if they agree in number, singular or plural.
- Ask yourself: who is **performing** the action of verb?
- Find the **core sentence**. Cross out:
  - phrases separated by commas
  - prepositional phrases
- The subject might come **after the verb**. Look out for **"there is"**.
- **"Neither"** gives you a singular subject.

Pronoun Agreement

- When a pronoun is underlined, **find its antecedent** to see if they agree in number, singular or plural.
- Ask yourself: **what does the pronoun refer to?**
- Watch out for singular words that **seem plural**.
- There may be **vague pronouns** that have more than one option for the antecedent.
- There may be **mystery pronouns** that have no option for the antecedent.
- Watch out for **pronoun shifts**: be consistent with generic pronouns like "one" or "you".

Parallelism

- Use **parallel structures** for **parallel ideas**. If two or more similar ideas are equated, compared, or related, they should be in the same form.
- All elements of a **list** must be in the same form.
- Remember that **special pairs**
  - must appear as the correct pair
  - must be followed by parallel structures.
- When making a **comparison**, you must compare similar *concepts*, not just similar forms.

ERROR IDENTIFICATION 2

Verb Tense

- The **tense** of a verb tells us what *time* the action occurs. To check the tense, look at:
  - explicit time words, e.g. "yesterday"
  - the tense of other verbs in the sentence
- The **present perfect** (e.g. "I *have loved*") refers to events that start in the past and extend to the present.
- The **past perfect** (e.g. "I *had loved*") refers to past events that occurred before another past event.

Pronoun Case

- The **case** of a pronoun tells us what role the pronoun plays in the sentence, e.g. "I" versus "me".
- If a question has a pronoun together with another person or thing (e.g. "Roger and I"), check the pronoun by:
  - **deleting** the other person or thing
  - **combining** both into a plural pronoun

Diction

- Some questions cannot be solved structurally—you have to know **rules about particular words**.
- **Idiomatic** rules dictate what words *follow* a particular word, such as
  - words that must be followed by particular **prepositions**—"listen to", not "listen at"
  - the preposition may also affect a **verb** that follows, e.g. "to touch" vs. "of touching".
- **Word choice** questions may present a word that does not mean what it appears to mean.

Miscellaneous rules

- **Adjectives** modify nouns, while **adverbs** modify verbs, adjectives, or other adverbs.
- **Noun agreement**: nouns sometimes must agree in number just like pronouns (e.g. Scott and Bob want to be an astronaut).
- **Who** can only be used for people; **which** is used for non-people.
- The **comparative** form ("larger") is used for two things, and the **superlative** ("largest") is used for more than two.
- Some verbs have **irregular** participles in their perfect forms (e.g. "wrote" vs. "had written").

SENTENCE IMPROVEMENT

Introduction

- All the rules from Error Identification still apply.
- An **independent clause** can stand by itself as a sentence. It must have a subject and main verb.
- A **dependent clause** cannot stand by itself as a sentence.
- A **modifier** is a phrase with no main verb that modifies something in the sentence.

Fragments

- Every sentence must have **at least one independent clause** with a subject and verb.
- Find independent clauses by finding the core sentence. Cross out **dependent clauses** and **modifiers**.

Run-Ons

- Don't connect **two independent clauses** with a comma alone; that's a **run-on**.
- You *may* connect independent clauses with:
    - a comma and a **conjunction** (and, but, because, although…)
    - a **semicolon** alone.
- You may also correct a run-on by **changing one of the independent clauses** to a dependent clause or modifier.

Dangling Modifiers

- If a sentence starts with a **modifier**, the thing that it describes must be the subject of the main clause, **directly after the comma**.

Big Sentences

- Don't put up with **BS**. Keep your sentences **short and direct**.
    - Check **the shortest choice**. If it doesn't violate any rules, pick it.
    - Eliminate **redundant** phrases that repeat information already given.
    - **Active** sentences are often more concise than **passive** sentences.

Miscellaneous topics

- Watch out for **double subjects**, when an unnecessary pronoun repeats the subject.
- Make sure the **connector** conveys the appropriate meaning (contrast, causation, etc.)

ESSAY

Scoring

- Essay will get two scores, each 1 to 6. Scores cannot differ by more than 1 point.
- Essay is graded in 5 categories: *Development, Organization, Language, Sentences,* and *Grammar*.
- It's generally easier to improve your development and organization skills than your language, sentence structure, or grammar.

Development

- The topic will ask a generic question that has two sides. **Choose a specific side**: it doesn't have to be the side you actually believe.
- Pick **two concrete examples** to support your point. These can be things from school, personal stories, or pop cultural references like movies or TV shows.
- Before you take the test, **choose 5 all-purpose examples** that can be applied to a variety of topics.
    - Choose examples from **different areas**: history, literature, science/technology.
    - Choose examples that you **know something about** so you can give details.
- **Facts don't matter**: you will not be penalized for factual errors. But don't actively try to make stuff up—it's really hard.
- Pick a side to argue that **best fits your examples**. Don't force your examples into an argument where they don't fit.

Organization

- Make an **outline** of your essay:
    - Introduction
    - Example 1
    - Example 2
    - Conclusion
- For each example you write about, you should include two things:
    - **Background** of the example (who, what, when, where)
    - **Relevance** to the topic (why, how)

Language

- Include **vocabulary** you learned for the Critical Reading section.
- Make sure you use **concrete language** whenever possible.
- Use **complex sentences** with a varied structure.
- Watch out for **grammatical mistakes** (like those we discussed in the other chapters).

READING SUMMARY

SENTENCE COMPLETION SUMMARY

LEARN VOCABULARY!

Anticipate

- **Ignore the answer choices.** Focus on the sentence alone.
- Read the sentence to figure out the **meaning** of the word in the blank.
- **Clue words** that tell you what the sentence is about. **Connectors** that tell you about the relationship between parts of the sentence.
- If you can't come up with a specific anticipation, figure out if the blank is a **good word** or a **bad word**.

Eliminate

- Now ignore the sentence. Find a choice that **means the same thing** as the word you anticipated.
    - Put a check (✓) by it if it matches.
    - Put an ✗ by it if it doesn't.
    - Put a question mark (?) by it if you **don't know what it means**.
- **Don't eliminate mystery choices.** If you don't know what it means, leave it and come back later.
- If you're not sure whether a choice works, don't eliminate it. Start by eliminating the choices that **definitely don't match** your anticipation, then come back to what's left.

Guessing

- If you get down to two or three mystery choices and can't decide, **guess one.** Don't leave it blank.
- See if you can guess the meaning of the words based on their **roots.** See if they look similar to any words you do know.
- When in doubt, **guess the hardest word.** Hard words are more likely to be right than easy words.

Two-blank Questions

- Sometimes two-blank questions are just like two one-blank questions stuck together. **Anticipate separately** for each blank.
- **Divide and conquer**: sometimes one blank is really hard to anticipate for, but the other one is really easy. **Anticipate for the easy blank** and eliminate what doesn't work.
- For **relationship questions**, you can't anticipate for the blanks directly, but you can figure out the relationship between the blanks.

READING PASSAGE SUMMARY

The Passage

- Read quickly and get the **Main Ideas** of the passage, paragraph by paragraph.
- To find the main idea, ask: **what's it about**?
- If you can't find the main idea, read the **first and last sentences** of the paragraph.
- Don't spend too much time. Don't overanalyze. If you're not sure, **move on**.

The Question

- Read the question, **ignore the choices**.
- When there's a line reference, **go back to the passage** and read the line.
- **Read the whole sentence**, not just the line referred to.
- If that line is unclear, read the **sentence before** or the **sentence after**.
- Try to answer the question with what you just learned. That's your **anticipation**.
- If you can't anticipate, go to the choices to **eliminate**.

The Choices

- If you find a choice that matches your anticipation, pick it.
- If you don't find a match or if you don't have an anticipation, **look for wrong choices**. You can eliminate even if you don't understand the passage or question.
- **Work quickly.** If you're not sure about a choice, skip it and come back later.
- Eliminate choices that are **random, false,** or **irrelevant**.
- As you eliminate, **cross out** words that make a choice wrong.
- If you get down to two or three choices and can't decide, **guess one**.

Other types

- For **vocab-in-context questions**, treat the word in question as a blank and anticipate its meaning. Use the context of the sentence and the meaning of the word itself as clues.
- **Tone questions** often come down to *positive, negative,* or *neutral.*
- For **double passages**, do the passages separately. Read the passage 1 and do the questions about passage 2. Then read passage 2 and do the questions about passage 2. Then do the questions about both of them.

© A-List Services LLC

– 313 –

PERFORMANCE LOGS

MATHEMATICS

Techniques

Plug In Drill _____

Backsolve Drill _____

Guesstimate Drill _____

Big Technique Exercise _____

_____

Fundamentals

Number Concepts & Definitions _____

Fractions _____

Ratios _____

Percents _____

Exponents _____

Averages _____

Basic Manipulation _____

FOIL _____

Solve Directly for Expressions _____

Big Arithmetic & Algebra Exercise _____

_____

Geometry

Angle Drill _____

Triangle Drill _____

Perimeter, Area, Volume Drill _____

Circle Drill _____

Big Geometry Exercise _____

_____

Functions

Funny Symbols Drill _____

F(x) Drill _____

Graphing Functions _____

Lines _____

Graphing Drill _____

Big Function Exercise _____

_____

Miscellany

Combinatorics Drill _____

Sequences Drill _____

Absolute Value Drill _____

Appendix A

Plug In Drill _____

Backsolve Drill _____

Fraction Drill _____

Ratio Drill _____

Percent Drill _____

Exponent Drill _____

Average Drill _____

One-variable Algebra Drill _____

Multi-variable Algebra Drill _____

Solve Directly for Expressions _____

Angle Drill _____

Triangle Drill _____

Perimeter, Area, Volume Drill _____

Circle Drill _____

F(x) Drill _____

Graphing Drill _____

WRITING

Error Identification 1

Verb Agreement Drill _____

Pronoun Agreement Drill _____

Parallelism Drill _____

EID Big Exercise 1 _____

_____

Error Identification 2

EID Big Exercise 2 _____

_____

Sentence Improvement

Introductory Drill _____

Fragment Drill _____

Run-On Drill _____

Dangling Modifier Drill _____

Avoiding BS _____

SI Big Exercise _____

_____

Paragraph Improvement

PI Big Exercise: _____

_____

Appendix B

Verb Agreement Drill _____

Pronoun Agreement Drill _____

Parallelism Drill _____

Verb Tense Drill _____

Fragment Drill _____

Run-On Drill _____

CRITICAL READING

Sentence Completions

Anticipation Drill _____

Elimination Drill _____

Easy Exercise _____

Medium Exercise _____

Hard Exercise _____

Reading Passages

Main Idea Drill _____

Anticipation Drill _____

Elimination Drill _____

Double Passage Drill _____

Reading Passage Exercise _____

_____

Appendix C

Sentence Completions

Easy Drill _____

Medium Drill _____

Hard Drill _____

Reading Passages

Explicit Questions _____

Vocab-in-context Questions _____

Inferential Questions _____

Main Idea Questions _____

Strategy Questions _____

Tone Questions _____

NOTES

NOTES

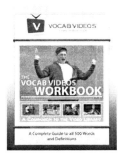

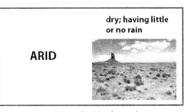

CPSIA information can be obtained at www.ICGtesting.com
Printed in the USA
BVOW04s1610230814

363673BV00001B/1/P